THE STORY... ...L
FOR BRA... ...R FANS

"Tim McCarver is one of the most intelligent men in America. I only wish more politicians and educators were in his class. To support my claim, I refer all readers to this simple volume, the most intelligent book ever written about our secular national religion."
—PETE HAMILL

"A discourse that all players could study profitably from, from Little Leaguers to major league regulars. . . . McCarver and Peary have joined forces to produce one of the most significant baseball books in years."
—*Publishers Weekly*

"This is the *Gray's Anatomy* of baseball. The game's preeminent broadcast analyst, along with sportswriter Danny Peary, identifies, isolates, and then fuses the ganglia of this remarkably complicated activity. They show how this simple playground game has nuances and imagery extending far beyond that of any other sport."
—*Business Week*

"This is perhaps the best book I've ever encountered to understand how a pitcher decides what to throw; what goes through a hitter's mind as he steps into the batter's box with the game on the line; how an infielder positions himself; or how a speedy runner uses his savvy to know when *not* to steal a base. Readers will be nodding their heads and saying, 'Ahhh. So *that's* how (and why) they do that.' "
—*Bookpage*

"Full of the sort of inside stuff active players are obliged to lie about. . . . I started McCarver's book because I was sure he would teach me something. I finished it as Casey Stengel."
—*The Cincinnati Enquirer*

"For anyone who wants to know what's really going on down there on the field, this is an indispensable tool."
—*The San Diego Union-Tribune*

"Read any chapter and you'll never watch baseball again in quite the same way."
—*The Arizona Republic*

"Offers a fascinatingly quick-paced, easy-to-read explanation of what goes on during a game."
        —*Library Journal*

"Moves along much in the manner of a McCarver broadcast—voluble, detailed, and fact-filled."
        —*St. Louis Post-Dispatch*

"McCarver is a marvel at discussing strategy."
        —Newark *Star-Ledger*

"Baseball is the most nuanced of our sports, and Tim McCarver is the most cerebral of its announcers. . . . Don't let the 'brain surgeons' stuff scare you, though. While McCarver does get into the game-within-a-game-within-a-game, the writing is clear. . . . The book can serve as a primer for youngsters learning how to play the game."
        —*The Philadelphia Inquirer*

"McCarver takes you as painlessly and entertainingly through the game's intricacies on the printed page as he has done for so long on the air as a highly respected TV analyst. . . . He goes inside the game while making it understandable to outsiders, and it's a treat to hear him on the players and the game he knows so well."
        —*Newsday*

"I will recommend this book to many people. I will keep this book on my shelves and will refer to it, in the next ten years, hundreds of times. I will recommend it to young people who need to know all kinds of detailed stuff to write about baseball or broadcast it."
        —*The New York Times Book Review*

"A steady stream of baseball thoughts from an articulate sportscaster who can't get enough baseball theory."
        —*USA Today*

"McCarver and Peary answer virtually every strategic question about how the sport is played."
        —*Baseball Weekly*

TIM McCARVER'S BASEBALL FOR BRAIN SURGEONS AND OTHER FANS

Also by Tim McCarver

Oh, Baby, I Love It!

Also by Danny Peary

Cult Baseball Players
We Played the Game: 65 Players Remember Baseball's Greatest Era, 1947–1964
Super Bowl: The Game of Their Lives

Tim McCarver
WITH DANNY PEARY

TIM McCARVER'S BASEBALL FOR BRAIN SURGEONS AND OTHER FANS

Understanding and Interpreting the Game
So You Can Watch It Like a Pro

VILLARD

NEW YORK

Villard Books is a registered trademark of Random House, Inc.

This work was originally published in hardcover by Villard Books,
a division of Random House, Inc., in 1998.

Library of Congress Cataloging-in-Publication Data
McCarver, Tim.
Tim McCarver's baseball for brain surgeons and other fans: understanding
and interpreting the game so you can watch it like a pro / Tim McCarver
with Danny Peary.
p.   cm.
Includes index.
ISBN 0-375-75340-0
1. Baseball fans.   2. Baseball–Defense.   3. Baseball–Offense.
I.   Peary, Danny.   II. Title.
GV867.3.M37   1998
796.357–dc21   97-49301

Interior design by Robert Bull Design

Random House website address: www.atrandom.com

Printed in the United States of America

4 6 8 9 7 5 3

For the teachers who spent countless hours with me, especially George Kissell, Eddie Stanky, and Joe Schultz. They taught me how to play the game, how to think it, and, ultimately, how to talk it.

And also to teachers everywhere.

ACKNOWLEDGMENTS

Danny Peary and I would like to express our gratitude to the people whose inestimable support made this long-planned book come to fruition. Foremost, we thank our longtime agents and close friends, Robert L. Rosen and Chris Tomasino, for bringing us together for the first of several collaborations back in 1986 and for reuniting us for this project more than ten years later. We are equally indebted to our new friend, our stalwart editor, Ian Jackman, the rare person with a British accent who can speak fluently about baseball.

We thank Jonathan Diamond, Gary Rosen, Maria Hettinga, Craig Foster, Maury Gostfrand, Gail V. Lockhart, Barbara Hadzicosmas, Laura Schiffman, and everyone else at RLR Associates, Ltd., for their behind-the-scenes work and hospitality during our many all-day writing sessions.

At Villard, we are grateful to Adam Rothberg, Amy Edelman, Beth Thomas, Brian McLendon, Bob Bull, Melissa Milsten, Dan Rembert, the late Jeff Smith, James Lambert, Carole Lowenstein, and Joanne Barracca. In particular, we acknowledge former Villard publisher David Rosenthal, who signed up our book, and his successor, Brian DeFiore.

Special thanks to my broadcast partners, Joe Buck and Bob Brenly at FOX and Ralph Kiner and Gary Thorne at WWOR-TV.

At FOX, we'd also like to acknowledge David Hill, the president of FOX Sports; Ed Goren, the executive producer of FOX Sports; senior coordinating producer of baseball John Filippelli; director Bill Webb; Vince Wladika, the senior vice-president of media relations; Lou D'Ermilio, the vice-president of media relations; publicist Dan Bell; associate director Cathie Hunt; and broadcast associate Barry Landis.

At WWOR, we also gratefully acknowledge director-producer Jeff Mitchell, executive producer Rick Miner, statistician Arthur Friedman, assistant director-producer Steve Oelbaum, high-home cameraman Jack Williams, stage manager Vinny Sinopoli, and production assistant Amy Faas for graciously answering numerous questions about the technical aspects of a baseball broadcast. In addition, we thank John Calabrese, Matthew K. Ryan, Artie Gress, Larry Mandt, Greg Curry, Ed Berman, Jeff Rubin, Keith Desantis, Vinny Scaffidi, Gene Genovese, Curt Singer, Howard Spaulding, Jean Martin, and Ron Aruda.

At Shea Stadium, we received welcome assistance from everybody's pal, Jay Horwitz, the New York Mets' director of media relations, and his able assistants, Stella Fiore, Shannon Dalton, and Chris Leible. Thanks to Bob Murphy. And to "Murph" and Joe at the Diamond Club entrance and "Boss" at the clubhouse door.

We also are most grateful to Chip Caray, Steve "Psycho" Lyons, Steve Hirdt and the Elias Sports Bureau, Steve Horn, Larry Shenk, and Billy Sample.

And last but not least, we thank our wives, Anne McCarver and Suzanne Rafer.

–TIM MCCARVER

CONTENTS

INTRODUCTION

I was signed, I was traded, I was waived, I was released. I played it and plied it. I was angered by it, disappointed in myself because of it, gladdened and heartened by it. I was cheered in parades, I was booed off the field, I was treated with silent indifference. I was on world champions and cellar dwellers. I was a hero, and I failed miserably. I felt on top of the world and like I wanted to crawl under a rock. I spiked and was spiked, took out hard and was taken out hard. I was hit by "that little white rat" more times than I could count. I hit it hard, I hit it weakly. I lifted it, grounded it, popped it, and lined it. I hit it foul and fair while realizing there was nothing fair about it. Baseball. I've been thrilled about it and wearied by it, but more than anything else I've lived it—and always loved it. I've been talking about it for many years. Now I am writing about it.

* * *

During the Philadelphia Phillies' successful run for the 1980 National League pennant, some of the fans at Veterans Stadium might have done a double take when they saw someone in a Phillies uniform conducting postgame interviews down on the field. I was the guy with the microphone. Having played for the Phillies from mid-1975 through the 1979 season, I had been activated in September so that I could become a rare four-decade major leaguer. Although I wasn't on their World Series roster, I was part of the team and dressed for each game. I still had on my Phillies cap but was "wearing" my new hat, that of a Phillies broadcaster.

I had officially retired the previous October, and, as had been agreed on two years before, I became the fifth announcer in the Phillies' four-man booth, joining the much-missed Richie Ashburn, Harry Kalas, Andy Musser, and Chris Wheeler, who'd be my partner on cable games. I had no training in the booth, so in preparation I spent three months with Chris honing my skills at an empty studio at Channel 17, WPHL, in Philadelphia. The first time we sat there, Chris put on a videotaped game minus the sound and waited for me to start describing the action as if I were broadcasting to people in their homes. Cowed by the silence, I looked at the television and looked at Chris. Finally, Chris said, "Go ahead." I stammered, "Go ahead and *what*???" It was terrifying. In my broadcasting career, I guess you could say that was when I first started to find my voice, both figuratively and literally.

I worked for the Phillies through 1982 and in 1983 went to New York to broadcast Mets games for WWOR-TV and, for a time, SportsChannel. Ralph Kiner, who has been broadcasting Mets games since their inception in 1962, introduced me as Tim MacArthur, although I had arrived, not returned. I have been with the Mets ever since, doing play-by-play and color.

In 1984, I also started working with ABC. My first postseason experience as a broadcaster came that year, when I was a roving reporter in the stands during the Chicago Cubs–San Diego Padres National League Championship Series. I was on a per-game basis and was tickled to death that it went the full five games because I needed the money. In 1985, Howard Cosell came out with his controversial book and ABC fired him ten days before the World Series and assigned me to do my first Series. I stayed at ABC through 1989, then was with CBS from 1990 through 1993, including my Winter Olympics assignment. In 1994, I went back to work at ABC, where I was reunited with Al Michaels and Jim Palmer. We did five games, and then the strike hit, which blew us out for the postseason. In 1994, The Baseball Network, which was a joint venture of ABC and NBC, came into fruition. We split postseason play in '95 with NBC.

In 1996, I found a home at FOX and began my partnership with Joe Buck, working strictly as an analyst. So today I divide my time between FOX for the *Game of the Week,* the All-Star Game, and postseason play and WWOR for Mets games, working with Ralph and the ubiquitous Gary Thorne. In my business they say, "Long season, small booth," which means you have to hope for a good partner. I know I'm fortunate because I've heard of nightmare situations involving mismatched twosomes. One story that makes the rounds is of a broadcaster who couldn't find his nineteen-cent Bic pen five minutes before the game started, and just as his partner was settling in, he boomed accusingly, "You know, it's tough to work with thieves in the booth!" So I'll joke with Gary sometimes: "Where's my pen? It's tough to work with thieves . . ." Fortunately, Gary and I have similar senses of humor.

To succeed as a major leaguer, you must be able to adjust and adapt continually, and that's what I've tried to do as a broadcaster. As I earlier indicated, finding a voice was my first aspiration, because in sports broadcasting that's the equivalent of learning how to walk. Every step of the way in my second career, I've discovered that to find his voice, the good broadcaster must, oddly enough, learn when *not* to talk. At the very beginning, Richie Ashburn, the minimalist among sports broadcasters, said to me, "Tim, somebody told me years ago—I forget who it was—that if you don't have anything to say, don't say it." A simple but wise statement. Former Phillies television producer Gene Kirby also gave me valuable "advice" when he told me, "Don't talk through the goddamn pitch."

I learned from experience not to start a long story (or ask a guest in the booth a complicated question) with two outs in an inning. And though I continued my eternal quest for the right adjectives, I learned, with prompting from Al Michaels, to eliminate the verb when doing play-by-play on television. On radio, a broadcaster will say, "There's a ground ball to the left side. Vizquel plants his foot and throws to Thome. It's in time." On television, as Al would point out, you say, "Ground ball to Vizquel . . . over to Thome . . . one out." If it's a spectacular play, you can convey that with the excitement in your voice, and after your call you can go over it in more detail, perhaps with a video replay.

Television is a visual medium, and not talking at the right moment and allowing pictures to take over can be golden. On a FOX telecast, Cleveland's Manny Ramirez belted a grand slam that broke open a game against New York and the home crowd went wild. I said nothing during the replays, although I had made comments every time we had gone to videotape before. I let it play for about twenty-five seconds—the only sound was the cheers of the crowd. In Game 4 of the 1997 American League Championship Series, Joe Buck, Bob Brenly, and I all gave way to the boisterous Indians crowd during replays of Sandy Alomar's dramatic ninth-inning hit that beat Baltimore. Sometimes words add nothing and are distracting. It's not dead air just because you're not talking—it's air that's alive. If I'm channel surfing and pass a channel where a crowd is going bonkers, I'm going to stop. That's human nature. Viewers don't need to be told to listen to the crowd.

Richie Ashburn's counsel not to talk unless I had something to say has stuck with me through the years. I think for some time it made me self-conscious because, knowing Ashburn, I believed he was insinuating that no one ever has anything so important to say that they must go into detail about it. But I decided to take his words at face value and came to the conclusion that whenever I had a point to bring up *and* the time was right, it was my responsibility to say it. As a broadcaster who had spent twenty-one years in the major leagues, I had been hired to talk about what I learned as a player, not to keep quiet.

And I had expertise. I had been schooled in the Cardinals' system by such remarkable teachers as Eddie Stanky and George Kissell, and I played for such philosophical big-league managers as Gene Mauch. I had caught Hall of Famers Bob Gibson and Steve Carlton and a lot of other pitchers who used their wiles rather than dominant pitches to get out batters. I had batted against the likes of Sandy Koufax, Don Drysdale, Juan Marichal, and Tom Seaver. I had watched my Cardinals teammate Stan Musial battle pitchers, and I caught behind all-time greats like Willie Mays and Hank Aaron. Catching allows for observation denied to players in other positions. I had learned a great deal from playing the game—watching, asking questions, and from having been around some of the craftiest players, managers, and coaches the game has ever known. The strong opinions I found myself voicing in the booth were formulated during those many years I had spent down on the field. I had an eye for the game. I was cut out to think about baseball and I was cut out to talk about it.

But the one thing I didn't take enough into consideration in the early years of my broadcast career was that my new audience was different from the players, managers, and coaches to whom I'd been talking baseball all those years. It dawned on me that finding a voice wasn't sufficient; I had to find the *right* voice to be able to communicate all my knowledge of the game and genuine passion for it to the fans. My problem was that I would say things about the game matter-of-factly, as if everybody listening at home knew it as well as I did. It's a trap many ex-ballplayers fall into. It took a while to realize that nobody outside the game knows it in the same way as people who are in it. What is routine to the player is not necessarily routine to the viewer. So you have to tell viewers at times what is and is not significant. It's not hyperbole or anything; it's knowing how to accentuate the points that you really think viewers should pay attention to. The hope is that the next time the same situation arises on the field, they will be able to think along with me, or be one step ahead—and maybe even disagree. That, in fact, is the premise of this book.

I had always loved baseball, but I gained a whole new appreciation of it once I began watching it as a broadcaster, high above the field. As a player you know it's fun and exciting, but you're so focused on executing that you never take into account how the fan sees the game. As a broadcaster, you look at it differently. You don't want to forget how you saw it as a player, but you also start to see it the same way fans do. If you put those two viewpoints together, then you can have a good package for viewers. You are thinking like the fans, and the real challenge is to get them to start thinking like you.

Looking back, I see that it was a stroke of luck for me that my arrival in New York in 1983 coincided with the Mets starting their rise that would make them world champions in 1986. Also, the Mets' roster in my first years there would include a lot of interesting and popular players like Keith Hernandez, Rusty Staub, Gary Carter, Darryl Strawberry, Len Dykstra, Ray Knight, Mookie Wilson, Jesse Orosco, Ron Darling, and Dwight Gooden. People who hadn't paid much attention to baseball suddenly were tuning in and wanted to know more about the players—broadcasters should never forget about the human side!—and about the game they played. I wasn't the first to talk strategy—announcers like Tony Kubek had been doing that for years—but it seemed like so many new and returning baseball fans, including adults, suddenly wanted to *think* baseball instead of just watching it. Now people wanted to know what options the manager was considering in certain situations, what the individual players were doing at different points in a game, what everybody's responsibilities were on a given play.

I could give those Mets fans only *my* opinion and my philosophy, as I do in this book. When any announcer broadcasts a game, he is both reporting the game and giving his personal view of it. And that in a sense becomes the theme of the telecast. As viewers get to know an announcer—which they do better in baseball than in any other sport—they will decide if what he says has merit. If viewers are stimulated into forming opinions when I broadcast a game, then I don't care if they agree with me. Disagreement means people are listening and paying attention. I don't mind being wrong, and I'll admit it on the air in a second when I am. It's impossible to be right all the time when you're giving opinions on a sport that has no absolutes. In fact, I am sometimes guilty of giving a reason why a player did something only to discover when I talk to him after the game that he has no idea why he did it. That's particularly true with an inexperienced player. No matter: Whether he was thinking of it or not, I want to tell the viewers what he should have been thinking.

I'd estimate that 25 percent of the mail I get expresses dissenting views, and that's fine. I will say that they don't often disagree with my criticism of a team's strategy, but they'll come to the defense of any player I mention even when I'm not critical of him. Women in particular will get angry with me: "Well, *I* like Butch Huskey." One of the major problems all broadcasters have is that a player's wife or family member or friend will hear what you said about him and by the time it gets back to him, he thinks you came just short of emasculating him.

As a broadcaster, I try to be informative, interesting—giving novel opinions as well as original takes on things that have been discussed in baseball for a hundred years—as prescient as possible and, aspiring to be honest rather than controversial, provocative. With such a style, I expect to be accused of talking too much on occasion. It does happen, although not nearly as much as it did early in my career. In fact, when I was on Don Imus's morning radio show before 1997's All-Star Game, he predicted that my partners in the booth wouldn't get a word in edgewise. Imus was joking . . . I think.

I also have been accused of psychobabble. In 1997, as a camera panned the dugout of the Cubs as they suffered their National League–record-breaking fourteenth straight loss opening the season, I quoted a line from Shakespeare's *Love's Labour's Lost* about how "mirth cannot move a soul in agony." I was attacked in one New Jersey paper for trying to wax eloquent during a baseball game. Not long after that, however, I received a touching letter from a man who said those words I quoted really hit home with him and his wife. It turned out that he headed an organization for people who have lost children to violence, and he read those words I had called to his attention at a gathering of the group. More than giving me vindication, that letter affirmed my belief that the words some people find empty touch a responsive chord in others.

Baseball doesn't exist in a vacuum, and its fans are more than baseball fans. When they turn on their sets, they bring with them a wealth of experience and knowledge, just as announcers do when they enter the booth. That's why I think that if you don't go entirely off track or become tasteless, you can bring outside references to a broadcast without turning off viewers. To me, the biggest gift you can bring to a game is to go beyond the obvious. Just like my singing idol Frank Sinatra interprets the same song in many different ways according to how he's feeling at the time, your way of presenting a game can change. You have the responsibility to be imaginative, without getting away from or interfering with the game. You don't detract but add to the game by finding different ways to say things. To me, it makes the tradition of the game richer. What you're doing is communicating. In trying to explain the game to the novice, you want to use examples and outside references that will make things clearer to them. That's what I always try to do.

While I do get serious at times, especially when I present a human interest story involving a player going through rough times, I never forget the place of humor in broadcasting. I'm very serious about my business, but the times I get in trouble now are when I take myself too seriously or when I take the game too seriously. So I'll quote Steven Wright or I'll bring in George Carlin's observation "If the Reds were baseball's first team, who did they play?" You can make funny remarks about a team when you're doing a national game, but when you're doing the local broadcast—"The Mets have stranded more men than Elizabeth Taylor"— you'd better make sure it hasn't lost seven or eight games in a row or the fans won't be in the mood for you to be flippant. On a network game, even if you offend one side, at least you'll amuse the other. But you don't want to go too far.

During a baseball game, the action ebbs and flows, so there is time for whimsical thought, serious thought, playful thought, analytical thought. It takes a skillful announcer to know the proper time for each. When the game is on the line, the only thing you talk about is the game. When there are two outs in the ninth inning and the tying run is on base, you don't want to be joking with your partner or fitting in a story you meant to tell in the third inning. The words have to fit the picture and the action, and they have to be concise. Succinctness in a close game becomes more imperative the later it gets. The picture should be telling the story.

What rankles me more than anything is when I'm told that people who watch baseball games are only half listening. They are trying to tell their broadcasters something. And those guys should pay attention. It's not all the listener's fault. If a speaker is dull at a dinner, you can't blame the audience. A broadcaster has a responsibility to say things that are worth listening to and to be stimulating.

What makes baseball hard to broadcast is that the game can look so much easier than it is (especially on television) and sound so much harder than it is. Great players like Ken Griffey, Jr., make hitting and defense look so effortless that the average fan can't fathom how difficult it is to play successfully. It's hard for them to appreciate that the game's stars play it so "easily" only after they have found ways to simplify its many intricacies by spending a great deal of time in preparation. Only on the field do they let their instincts take over. Baseball is as much mental preparation as it is physical action, and that's why it isn't so easy to grasp for casual fans *or* some players.

There is no denying that on one level baseball is cerebral, yet you don't have to be a genius to be a savvy fan or to have success as a manager or player. My onetime manager Danny Ozark proved both these points when he exclaimed: "Half of this game is ninety percent mental." Albert

Einstein failed in his attempt to learn baseball from catcher Moe Berg, but, as I've often said, you don't have to be an Einstein to comprehend how the game is played. Einstein couldn't watch the game on television. You can.

The beauty of baseball is that it can be enjoyed at all levels. But I think the more you learn about it and the more exposed you are to its many subtleties, the more you will be able to think along with the players, managers, and broadcasters and the more fascinating it will become to you. Television can improve a fan's knowledge dramatically with visuals and the play-by-play, the judicious use of replays from various camera angles, and sharp commentary. Elucidation leads to anticipation, and when what you think might happen does, it's as much fun for you the fan as for the broadcaster.

For the television viewer, I try to elucidate and illuminate—and simplify when needed—so that he or she can understand all aspects of baseball (batting, pitching, catching, fielding, running, managing) and get into the heads of all the game's participants. That is also the purpose of this book. Intended for fans who want to learn more about baseball, it is a mix of perception and philosophy, a few stories and a lot of strategies. It is, quite simply, my view of how baseball is played and how it should be played. Directed at fans at home as well as at the park, it is also a look at baseball from up in the booth and through the lens of the camera.

Be advised that when I contend that a particular strategy should be employed in a given situation, I am speaking of the typical situation, not the extreme case. There are so many variables that must be factored into the equation before a solid strategy can be devised. You should remember that when you watch a game, any strategy, whether conceived by an announcer or by you, depends on the answers to such questions as: Who is pitching and how is his stuff today? Who is the batter and is he hot or cold? Who's on deck? Who's on base? What's the defensive alignment? What's the count? What's the score? Which relievers are available? I hope this book will stimulate you to ask the appropriate questions in a given situation and to use the answers to decide for yourself what the best strategy should be.

This book is an explanation of baseball to some degree, but I like to think of it more as an interpretation—just as I see a baseball broadcast as the interpretation, in words and pictures, by the play-by-play man, analyst, and the producer and director and their crew, of the game on your set. While I stand by all the theories I advance here, including all those with which managers and other announcers may disagree, my hope is not that they automatically be taken as gospel by those of you who are trying to better learn the game. I would prefer that you put my ideas to the test whenever you watch baseball on television or at the park. Use them as a starting point, but go further on your own. If soon you begin to think along with a broadcaster, whether it's me or anyone else, and you find yourself either agreeing with his "version" of the game or interpreting things a bit differently, then I will have achieved my goal. At that point, you will have learned how to watch baseball like a pro.

PART I

In and Out of the Booth

1

THE PREGAME ROUTINE

Viewers often ask me what I do prior to a telecast. It surprises them to learn that the broadcast itself amounts to only half of the work I put in on the day of a game. In fact, I usually arrive at the ballpark three or four hours before the start of the game, whether I'm announcing a national game for FOX or a Mets game for WWOR-TV in the New York metropolitan area. In the postseason, I might get to the park at three o'clock for an 8 P.M. game to familiarize myself with the extra graphics and statistics. I also will need extra time if I'm scheduled to tape interviews or special segments.

At Shea Stadium, my first stop is the control room, which is located downstairs next to the clubhouses. One of the few self-contained control rooms in a major-league stadium, it has monitors for each of the cameras around the field, replay equipment, and computers that call up statistics and place graphics over images on the screen. Amid all the pregame bustle, I'll have brief, informal production meetings with coordinating producer-director Jeff Mitchell, executive producer Rick Miner, and associate producer-director Steve Oelbaum. We'll run ideas by each other. For instance, I might tell Jeff that I'd like a particular visual during the game, such as a "low-first" shot (so called because of the camera position) of a pitcher with a good pickoff move, and he might let me know about some particular graphics that have been prepared for the game. Also present is

Arthur Friedman, who has been the Mets' statistician for thirty years. During the game, he will be feeding Gary, Ralph, and me stats, but here he'll just update me on anything that has happened in baseball that I might have missed and give me some random thoughts about the upcoming game.

When the Mets are on the road, only Jeff and Steve are on hand, working with a local crew and sitting in an equipment truck outside the stadium. FOX always works out of a truck, so I'll go out there to have pregame meetings with director Bill Webb and coordinating producer John Filippelli. Ed Goren, executive producer of FOX Sports, is usually back in the studio in Los Angeles.

* * *

Next, I'll venture into the two clubhouses and dugouts and stand by the batting cage conversing with the managers, coaches, and some of the players. Often, we'll just renew old acquaintances; other times, I'll try to get some information that will help me with my broadcast. For instance, if I haven't seen a rookie pitcher, I might ask his manager or his catcher what to look for. Oddly, while I was standing by the cage before the first Mets-Yankee game at Yankee Stadium in 1997, outfielder Paul O'Neill asked *me* who the Mets' relievers were and what they threw. I had to laugh. I kiddingly told Paul that George Steinbrenner hadn't hired me to be an advance scout. While Paul and I are friends, I don't necessarily want to be friends with players. But I do try to be friendly.

BATTING PRACTICE

I like to watch batting practice because I think it's very enlightening. Some players take the wrong approach, and it becomes a home run derby. It shouldn't be just for show. You can definitely tell the smart hitters by how seriously they take batting practice. The best way to approach b.p. is to hit from line to line because it helps establish muscle-memory for the front shoulder to be locked in. Willie Mays hit to all fields in batting practice instead of just hitting five-hundred-foot homers. Dick Allen, when he took batting practice, always worked from the opposite side to the pull side. He'd hit ground balls the other way and then explode on the last couple of pitches—and he was ready. The remarkable Tony Gwynn, the hardest-working hitter in the game today, thinks it's vital to swing at one hundred balls a day in order to build and retain muscle-memory. Watching him take batting practice is an education on good hitting.

During batting practice, players often reveal what they will do during a game. One day, I saw Mets pitcher Rick Reed practicing squeeze bunts, which was highly unusual. When he came up in the game, I told the viewers to be ready for him to lay it down. I wasn't trying to be prescient; I was just using common sense. Sure enough, Reed squeezed his second time up. Before a game against the Phillies, I saw the left-handed-hitting John Olerud practicing going the other way so I wasn't surprised when he blasted a two-run homer to left off Curt Schilling in his first at-bat. When I see Mets catcher Todd Hundley going the opposite way during batting practice while batting from the left side, I might not predict an opposite-field hit during the upcoming game but I'm aware that his front shoulder is locked in and that he may hit homers to right on balls that he'd ordinarily pull fifty feet foul. You see, most good hitters use batting practice to prepare for the game. Perhaps b.p. should stand for *batting preparation*.

EVALUATING STATISTICS

About ninety minutes before a Mets game, I am handed detailed statistical sheets on the two teams. I use these in conjunction with the stats passed on to me before the game by Arthur Friedman. Arthur's computerized database is supplemented by the amazing Elias Sports Bureau. We have numbers for things like what a guy is hitting with runners in scoring position in late innings and how a pitcher does with men in scoring position. On FOX games, Steve Horn is our information man, and one of his many jobs is to sit in the booth next to Joe Buck and supply us with stats and pertinent facts. The people in the FOX truck receive a stat printout from Elias and, like Arthur Friedman, are constantly on the phone with Elias for verification of certain numbers.

I don't like to inundate viewers with numbers, especially toward the end of the game, so I only want to be given stats that are both interesting to viewers and important to the managers and players. Steve Hirdt of Elias, who is the source for much that goes on the air, tells me that almost every manager and general manager subscribes to their pitcher-versus-batter reports and most want general stats on pinch hitters and relievers. These are both significant stats and historical references interesting to viewers. (What else they want, Steve says, is confidential because managers don't want the opposition to know what they're asking for.)

Because baseball is a game of *firsts,* I'm interested in firsts, so Steve gives me data on them. For example, the team that scores first wins two thirds of the games. (I think this stat is particularly pertinent if Brady Anderson leads off the game you're watching with a home run.) Moreover, if the first batter in an inning gets on base, his team will score about 51 percent of the time, but if he makes an out, his team will get a run in that inning only 16 percent of the time.

What other stats do I consider valid? A batter's average and production numbers with two strikes. The strikeouts-to-walks ratio of both pitchers and batters. How many sacrifice bunts the number two hitter in a lineup has. How many pickoffs the pitcher has and how many runners his catcher has thrown out stealing. How often the batter has grounded into double plays, especially if the pitcher he is facing is a sinkerballer. How many inherited runners have scored and how many have been stranded by a particular reliever. The earned run average of a starting pitcher. On many other stats something has to be dramatically different from the norm to be of consequence. Two examples: A batter hits one hundred points higher in the daytime; a pitcher is 8-0 at home and 0-8 on the road. It's up to the announcer to bring the stats to life. Simply rattling off numbers doesn't get the job done.

It's easy to misuse stats. One April, I was watching a game where one team had the bases loaded with two outs and there was a 2-2 count on a

I've learned that All-Star Games are the most difficult to broadcast because strategy goes out of the window. You prepare differently to include more about the personalities involved and how they do what they do. Statistics become magnified. Numbers become nuggets. And stories are pure gold. For instance, when ABC broadcast the 1986 game, I related a story I had heard from Yankees publicist Harvey Greene about American League All-Star Don Mattingly. I said that before Mattingly traveled to the game, he had graciously agreed to use the bat of his teammate Mike Fischlin, an obscure utility man on the Yankees who wanted his bat to make an All-Star appearance because he knew he'd never get to the game himself. I ended by telling Al Michaels, who was doing play-by-play, "This is probably the only time Fischlin will ever be mentioned at an All-Star Game." Without missing a beat, Al asked rhetorically, "What do you mean *probably*?"

right-handed batter. After a foul back, the announcer said, "Keep this in mind: He hit .352 last September, so the pitcher's not out of the woods yet." What does what he hit in the last month of last season have to do with anything? It doesn't prove he's a hot hitter. There have been *only* five or six months since he was hitting well.

In 1997, I got a stat sheet from the Pirates which said that in Jon Lieber's first seven starts the team scored a total of twenty-one runs but only ten with him in the game. They had mustered a total of only six runs during his five-game losing streak, and in his fourteen starts had scored a total of only twenty-three runs while he was on the mound, an average of 1.6 per appearance. With these numbers they were implying that Lieber was a hard-luck pitcher who deserved to be better than 3-8. What they didn't stress is that with his 4.52 ERA, he hadn't held up his end of the bargain. His record was warranted. It's to be expected that teams' publicity departments do a little spin-doctoring and enhance their players' performances by using numbers that appear to be impressive, so it's up to the commentators to determine if those stats have validity or are meant to obfuscate poor performances.

So when you see stats on your screen, you have to decide whether they are an accurate measure of a player's performance. Often you have to follow a guy on a day-to-day basis to know how much better or worse he is from the statistics that are presented. When we were teammates on the Cardinals in the sixties, Curt Flood, who would later sacrifice his own career to start the fight against the reserve clause, used to give himself up on productive outs about twenty times a year to move runners to second or third. He'd still bat over .300, but it could have been much higher—and people who didn't follow the Cardinals didn't realize this. What he did was the kind of thing that legitimized the line "You won't see that in the box score tomorrow."

Steve Hirdt correctly points out that statistics are no longer the domain of drooling eggheads, but are increasingly integral to the baseball-viewing experience. He muses, "People accept TV ratings that are determined by a tiny sampling, but a baseball fan needs to know exactly how many putouts Edgardo Alfonzo has at third base or what Tony Gwynn's batting average is to the third decimal point."

Steve Hirdt's stats mean something. Al Michaels says, "He piques your curiosity so that it brings out other stuff that usually is as important as the original point. The questions that one of his stats may spawn may lead us to say 'I didn't know that' four or five times." Stats should be catalysts for thoughts.

UPSTAIRS

About forty-five minutes before the first pitch, I will settle into my chair in the still empty broadcast booth and do my final work for the game. I'll fill out the lineup cards and jot down any pertinent information, stats, or stories I have on the individual players, including anything I picked up since I arrived at the park. People often ask me how I prepare for a game. The answer is total immersion—I prepare for anything and everything because, as Douglas MacArthur said, "Chance favors the prepared man." I try to cover all the angles, and the temptation is to try to get it all in. But as esteemed broadcaster Dick Enberg estimates, "You only use ten percent of your preparation." If you try to get in all your research, viewers may stay tuned in, but they'll tune you out. If you've done your work, that 10 percent will add to, not detract from, a viewer's enjoyment.

2

THE BROADCAST

During the game, you'll find me amid the thick cigar smoke in the corner of a broadcast booth in the second tier of the stadium, above the plate. I'm easier to spot than my broadcast partner to my left because Joe Buck or Ralph Kiner or Gary Thorne is usually seated. Perhaps because our location reminds me of all the years I squatted behind the plate, I often stand through much of the game. To our left is the stage manager, who will hand us promotional tie-ins after the wrap-ups each inning and, via the control room, let us know if a reliever gets up, a pinch hitter grabs a bat, or anything else occurs we might not be aware of.

I can hear Jeff Mitchell on my earpiece throughout the game, as can my broadcast partner. When I want to speak to him during an inning, I push a "talk-back" button, which prevents our conversation from going on the air. I can ask for graphics, stats, a replay, the camera to pick up a particular player while I talk about him, or even a split screen to show several people at once. Or I can ask Jeff for a "sequence," a concept he pioneered about five years ago. I remember that during the 1996 season, we had a fascinating sequence that showed Bobby Jones get out three Dodgers in succession, all on defensive two-strike swings, proving how in control Jones was.

On three-man broadcasts on FOX, when Bob Brenly, another ex-catcher, joins Joe and me for the All-Star Game and postseason fare, the potential for congestion exists. However, I feel we do a good job of not stepping on each other, with either feet or words. The longer you work together, the more you learn each other's rhythm and the times you talk at the same time become infrequent. Bob and I will hand-signal each other when we want to say something, but even that's not really needed. There is a silent language that the three of us understand. That's how it was at ABC when Jim Palmer and I worked as coanalysts with Al Michaels doing play-by-play.

A monitor that shows exactly what you see at home is positioned in front of the play-by-play and color men, jutting out from the booth. Watching the monitor is something I had to become accustomed to. As a player I was taught to always watch the game. While you sat on the bench, you may have fooled around or gotten into a conversation, but you never missed a pitch. When I became a broadcaster, I had the dual responsibil-

When it's 5–0 in the third or fourth inning, you hope the game will sustain the interest of viewers. That's more likely to happen if the home team is ahead. On network television, we obviously don't care who wins, but we feel fortunate when the home team at least stays close because we want the crowd to be into the game. Noise creates interest. If the visiting team is way ahead, the crowd is quiet. So if you talk to network producers about ratings, they'll say, "Give me a home team that wins every time."

People always ask me how I deal with having to broadcast a blowout. It's no problem at all. What we may try to do is change our focus. For instance, the game may be over because of the lopsided score, but if Mark McGwire has two more at-bats, we will remind viewers of this. I don't refer to time, unless it is part of the story. A broadcaster should never complain about how a game is dragging. Baseball is one of the respites for those with Type A behavior, who want everything over with quickly, whether it is sex or baseball. That a game takes longer doesn't necessarily make it less interesting. A long, even poorly played game can be enjoyable. It's proper for the broadcaster to have the same enthusiasm and care that he would have in a close game. He owes it to new fans, all the other fans, the managers, his employers, the broadcasting profession, and all the players who are busting their butts on the

ity of watching the field to see the action and watching the monitor to know what part of the action the viewers were seeing. However, it's very dangerous to just work off the monitor if you are doing play-by-play because when the ball goes up in the air it flies off the screen and you don't know right away where it has been hit or how hard it has been hit. Even the best cameraman can't pick up the ball with his lens as fast as you can with your eyes if you are looking at the field. So it's up to the broadcaster to fill in the where-and-how-far information during the time the cameraman is trying to track the ball down.

Everybody gets into trouble watching only the monitor. One time, when I was doing play-by-play for a game in the Astrodome, I was watching the monitor and I saw the batter lift the ball to the left side. Also on the screen, I saw the shortstop run out into the outfield. I told the viewers that he was about to catch an easy pop-up. Then I looked out on the field and

field to not let down. I remember that Yul Brynner said he gave his all during every performance of *The King and I* because there were always people in the audience who had never seen the show before. As a broadcaster I feel the same way.

Strategy becomes moot during a blowout, so it's natural for us to go into the memory bank, as we do when there's a rain delay. During blowouts, it's natural to talk about comebacks. For instance, in 1964, when I was with the Cardinals, we were leading the Phillies 10–1 in the bottom of the ninth inning with one out and a man on. It was a laugher. Three relievers later, the game ended 10–9, when Alex Johnson was thrown out by Curt Flood, trying to stretch a single into a double. I can't tell you the anxiety that we felt.

I'll also recall a game in 1976, when I was a member of the Phillies. We were trailing 13–2 to the Cubs in Wrigley Field in the top of the sixth inning with one out and nobody on. We won 18–16, when Mike Schmidt belted his fourth homer of the game in the tenth inning off Paul Reuschel, his first having come off Reuschel's brother Rick. There are several parks in which you can be honest when you say during a blowout, "No lead is safe here." Wrigley when the wind is blowing out, Fenway Park, Coors, and the Kingdome have been the scenes of many improbable comebacks.

saw that the reason the shortstop was racing out was to point to where the long fly ball was going. As the viewers now saw on the screen, the left fielder was backpedaling toward the wall in order to make the catch. I had no choice but to tell the truth, that a rare indoor Texas gale had taken hold of the ball.

Ralph Kiner laughs about the time eight or nine years ago in Montreal, when he was looking at the monitor and lost the ball off the bat. Judging by the sound of the bat striking the ball and the crowd noise, he said, "Gone, gone, good-bye." And then he saw that it had been a grounder that the left fielder was chasing down in the outfield.

GRAPHICS

There is a second monitor in the box that shows upcoming graphics. The graphic on this monitor will soon be on the monitor in front of us and on your screen. (Similarly, in the control room what is on the preset monitor will shift to the program monitor.) We see graphics in advance so that we will be prepared to either comment on them or say nothing when they appear on your screen. Steve Oelbaum tells me that the typical Mets broadcast has about two hundred graphics, counting the adjusted stats for every time a batter comes up and the changing scores of out-of-town games. And that is only about 30 to 40 percent of what is prepared by Steve and Arthur Friedman. Some of the ideas are inspired by Arthur's immense knowledge of stats, as well as suggestions by us in the booth, and by notes supplied by Steve Hirdt. Everything is programmed three or four hours before a game, so Arthur knows exactly what is available if a particular situation arises on the field.

A lot of it is hunch. For instance, if a guy comes up with the bases loaded, Arthur will want to have a graphic ready that gives not only his career stats with the bases loaded but also the last time he hit a grand slam. As Arthur says, "Bringing it up two batters later is sloppy." In 1997, Mets reliever John Franco came in with a three-run lead, so Arthur quickly prepared a graphic for the last time Franco had given up three runs in an inning. Surprisingly, Franco was pounded for three runs, yet we were ready with the graphic. Similarly, when Giants reliever Rod Beck came in to face the Mets, a graphic was ready showing that he owned the two hitters due up back-to-back, Todd Hundley and Bernard Gilkey. It provided a new perspective on a crucial situation. Beck might not have relieved that game and the graphic wouldn't have been used, but it still would have been comforting to know that it was available if needed.

Steve Hirdt tries to anticipate how a graphic may give a situation more import. So if Rickey Henderson, for example, is playing in the World Series, Steve will try to impress both us and the viewer with a graphic. It might have to do with Henderson's remarkable on-base percentage during Series play. When you see his name listed with Babe Ruth and Lou Gehrig, you realize you are watching somebody who ranks with the all-time greats. And you wonder: Will he get on base now?

In terms of graphics, I think the golden moment is when you start talking about a player, say Andre Dawson, having done something rare—Dawson became one of only three guys to have three hundred homers and three hundred stolen bases—and the minute you start talking about it, the graphic appears on the screen. You haven't prepared anyone in the control room for what you're going to say at a precise moment, yet the producer hears you getting into something and, knowing what graphics he has on hand, quickly gets that graphic on screen. When you're on the same wavelength, you know you're really clicking.

THE TELESTRATOR

As John Madden continues to prove in football, the Telestrator can be a very powerful tool if used properly. If viewers are just half listening or are confused, a drawing will get their attention, and if you're playful enough you can get a point across and have fun, too. I'd had one for many years at CBS, but through the encouragement of FOX I've been able to use it to better effect, especially in postseason play. In the '97 divisional playoffs, for example, I outlined Sandy Alomar's chest protector to show the wide target—much bigger than the mitt—that is used for a young pitcher like Jaret Wright, who throws hard and has a lot of movement. It has become easier to make marks now that we can just touch a screen that is hooked onto the monitor with a finger instead of using a pencil.

MICROPHONES

Television announcers have learned well from radio announcers that sounds can mean a great deal to the viewer. At home, while you're watching the game, you're also listening to it. You can sense the atmosphere at the ballpark when announcers allow the sound to play, as opposed to talking nonstop. The crack of the bat, the sound of a fastball hitting a mitt, the roar of the crowd, and the umpire's loud calls all make you feel like you are there. The good producers will run a playback in real time so you'll hear the natural sound. In trying to bring the game into your living room, the various networks have placed microphones around the field. I think FOX has been the most innovative. We miked the bases, which I find very useful. On a play at first, you can hear the ball hitting the first baseman's mitt, the batter's foot coming down on the bag, and the umpire's call. Like you, the umpire is basing his call on sounds as well as on what he sees, so you can judge whether he is right or wrong even before the replay.

We've miked the foul pole, and the ball has hit it. For the 1997 ALCS, we had sixty mikes along the outfield fence and on a real-time replay you could hear Cleveland center fielder Marquis Grissom slam into the wall trying to make a catch. Ouch. We've miked managers and coaches, but only to play back on tape so profanities won't slip in. I think the use of microphones is a real asset if handled properly. Anything that can make the viewer feel more like he is at the park is very helpful to television and ultimately the game itself. You want viewers to feel that they are part of the action.

THE CAMERAS

Baseball is so much harder to televise than the other sports because it is a game of angles. It constantly amazes me how the good producers and directors like Bill Webb, John Filippelli, and Jeff Mitchell are able to cover everything that goes on during the course of the game, making viewers feel like they know every inch of the ballpark they are watching. These guys really know how to use cameras, not only to show action but also to bring out the emotion felt by the people they shoot. For the 1997 All-Star Game, FOX had sixteen cameras, including the new ten-ounce Catcher-Cam, on the receiver's hockeylike mask. This is about twice as many cameras as an independent station uses. On Mets games, Jeff has six or seven cameras at his disposal, for which there are five tape machines.

Camera-One, the low-third camera, is located next to the third-base dugout. Jeff uses it to shoot all left-handed batters, right-handed pitchers, the runner at first, and the trail runner. On fielding plays to the left side, the camera will stay on the shortstop or third baseman after the throw to get his reaction to whether the batter was called safe or out. That shot of him can be used in a replay. If a steal is a possibility, I might ask that the two dugout cameras shoot the second baseman and shortstop, so we can tell who's covering. The camera can sneak behind the gloves they use to cover their mouths. An open mouth means "you cover." (If there is a steal attempt, Jeff will have three or four cameras directed at second base.)

Jeff likes to use the low-third camera to cross-shoot into the opposite dugout. It's a better way to get the true emotions of the manager, coaches, and players than by using the camera right next to them, which makes them self-conscious. Moreover, if the other team has a camera in there with yours, they will often obstruct each other. So cross-shooting is usually preferable, particularly if everyone in the dugout is in a bad mood and doesn't want a lens in his face.

Camera-Two, the high-home camera, is located on the far left of the broadcast booth, opposite me. Turned into the booth, it is the camera that is used when we do our on-camera pregame intros and postgame wrap-ups. Facing forward, it can display the entire field or zoom in for a shot of the backs of the umpire and catcher, side of the batter, and front of the pitcher. Usually, the cameraman has the plate, mound, and second base centered in the frame, but with men on second and third, he might frame it so that second base is at the far right on your screen. He will zoom into a close-up of the pitcher on rare occasions.

As soon as the ball is hit fair, Jeff will switch from the center-field camera to the high-home camera. The cameraman won't look at the monitor or viewfinder to find the ball but at the field. He will zoom in as outfielders track down flies and grounders or as infielders or the catcher near home catches pop-ups. He will follow the ball through the play. On a grounder to short, Camera-Two will follow the ball as the shortstop picks it up, throws it across the diamond, and is caught by the first baseman. High-home is a reaction camera—the ball is hit, the cameraman follows; the play ends, the camera goes back to a wide-angle shot of the field. The other cameramen are thinking more about the specific players the announcers are talking about. In a situation with base runners, they're asking: who's got the batter, who's got the pitcher, who's got the lead runner . . . ?

Camera-Three, the high-first camera, is located on the second level of the stands behind the first-base dugout. It can get crowd shots, shoot into both bullpens, double-cover plays in the outfield, and pick up the catcher getting a pop-up if he comes back toward the screen and is lost by the high-home camera. It can be an important "shag" camera, which means it follows the ball wherever it is hit. Jeff is adamant that no camera should be used to get a meaningless shot of the ball against the high sky. He doesn't want "golf shots": He wants only shots where the ball and a fielder are seen together.

In some parks there is no high-third camera on the second level of the stands behind the third-base dugout. Shea hasn't had one in a few years. Jeff has the use of high-third cameras in some other parks and is considering getting one for the home field because he finds it useful in showing pickoff attempts at first base, as well as the positioning of defensive players and base runners, which is always desirable. It's also good for getting reaction shots in the first-base dugout if your low-third camera is blocked by a player or coach walking down the line.

Camera-Four, the low-first camera, is located by the first-base dugout, opposite the low-third camera. Jeff uses it to shoot all right-handed batters, left-handed pitchers, the lead runner, and individuals in the third-base dugout. It scores all runners. After the right-handed batter swings and it looks like it's going to be a single or double, the low-first camera will pick up the runner coming home. If a second runner is coming home, this camera will cover him, even while Jeff cuts away briefly to pick up a fielder making the throw home. If Jeff finishes with the high-home camera in order to show both the ball and player coming to the plate simultaneously, the low-first shot will be used in the replay.

On a squeeze bunt, Jeff will follow the runner across the plate with the low-first camera because he wants to see the eyes of the runner and his expression as he reaches home. The low-third camera would just show the back of his head and his name on his jersey.

The low-first camera is also used for pickoff attempts. However, it works better on network games where we can have a low camera further down the line. In that way, within the frame, you can see the pitcher looking right at the runner and first baseman, who have the umpire standing right behind them. When the ball is thrown over and the runner dives back, and the first baseman makes a swipe tag, and the umpire gives his signal, and it's all seen in close-up, it makes great television.

Camera-Five is the center-field camera. The home team, visiting team, and possibly a network covering the game have their own cameras out in center, with the home team getting the position with the least distortion. The shot over the pitcher's right shoulder as he looks in at the batter is probably on screen 65 percent of the time. It's the camera we use to identify pitches and to gauge whether they are balls or strikes and whether the umpire is calling them correctly. That shot is ideal for replays of individual pitches or sequences when I am trying to make points. The center-field camera can also give a good view of a runner on second taking a lead while the pitcher watches him over his shoulder. In replay, it is helpful on a close play at home.

If there is a swing and a miss, Jeff may cut to a low camera. Otherwise he will maintain the center-field shot of the pitcher looking toward home until there is contact. Then he will switch to high-home for the action, at which point this camera can shag, picking up the ball in flight or an out-fielder picking it up. It also can shoot anywhere in the stands, including behind home plate. In addition, the center-field camera gives us "hero shots" of players who have done something special going into the dugout and receiving high fives and praise from their teammates.

On the road, Jeff may have a second center-field camera available. This comes in handy when there is a hit with a couple of runners on base because it can stay on the batter and free the low-first camera to get on the lead runner even before there is contact.

Camera-Six, which is more likely to be used by a network than an independent station, is located behind the low stands on the third-base side of home plate. If you follow the first-base line past home and past the stands into the walkway, you'll find the camera. It shoots right up the first-base line, all the way to the foul pole. If there is a left-handed batter and a runner on first, the camera operator can have the pitcher, runner, and batter in a triangle within the frame.

Camera-Seven, which also is more likely to be used by a network, is located behind the low stands on the first-base side of home plate. It shoots right up the third-base line to the foul pole. If you have a right-handed batter and a runner on third, the cameraman can place the pitcher, runner, and batter in a triangle.

* * *

Jeff likes the **Overhead Camera** more than I do and will use it if it is offered to him on the road. I'd trust it more if it were directly overhead, not at an angle to the right or left. Jeff will use it to add another element for viewers at home, not because it can dispute the umpires' calls. Too often viewers assume that this camera is the judge and jury on a ball-and-strike call because we show its angle *after* the center-field-camera angle. Although we show it second, it may actually be a more distorted view. I think the overhead camera is better for close plays at home than for balls and strikes. The umpires complain about it, but what it does is confirm that they are right most of the time.

I do like the **Catcher-Cam,** which gives the catcher's point of view on pitches coming into home plate and lets us see what the catcher sees as he fields bunts and pop-ups and makes throws to various bases. It also shows the runner coming down the third-base line—as long as the catcher keeps his mask on. In the All-Star Game, we didn't have any live shots using this camera, just replays. This camera will probably be used more in time, but I doubt if it will be used on a consistent basis because pitchers and umps believe it reveals too much. I think it can be fun and enlightening and offer a unique perspective.

* * *

Jeff will use his cameras differently if a game lacks excitement. He'll find something off the ball, like the left fielder trying to stay interested during the third or fourth pitching change. If it's a blowout, he'll try to jazz things up, perhaps finding some unusual people in the stands. The emphasis changes late in a game. If it's a tight game, he stays with the action. Jeff and I both like to have tension shots, such as close-ups of eyes and jittery fingers on the bat. You can isolate on the pitcher in the dugout, maybe the starter watching the reliever. Dissolves were originally set up to show a transition in time, but they are effective in a nail-biting situation when you dissolve from one manager to the other manager to the pitcher to the batter, even to nervous fans. Emotion is exciting to watch.

Televised baseball works when the audio and pictures complement each other. The picture should support the words, and the words should support the picture. At its best, when you start talking, the producer doesn't wait for you to finish a thought but already has the visual that supports what you're saying. Or he has a visual and the announcers try to weave a story around it. I often think of the roles everyone has in a telecast. But Jeff is the one who expresses it best. He says, "I consider the announcers to be the authors of the television story, the players to be the actors, and myself and the crew to be the illustrators. They narrate the story and we put the pictures up there, and when we work well together, we have a hit show."

PART II

In the Clubhouse

3

THE MANAGER

When Jim Palmer and I did color for ABC, our partner, Al Michaels, used to accentuate that the best way for an announcer to find out the approach of the two opponents was to talk to the managers. I found this to be true. Managers know better than the players. They can't tell you everything, but whatever they tell you could help with your broadcast. As long as you don't misuse their information, managers will be honest with you.

A manager will tell you a number of options that he is considering. He may talk about how long he'll go with his starter, or how he'll use his relievers against the opposing team, or what player he'll send in for late-inning defense if he has a lead. If he has a great starter, he may say that he'll try to bunt early in the game to get ahead. Atlanta's Bobby Cox might say, "Yeah, we can do a lot of things with Mark Lemke batting second. He's not as strong a hitter from the left side, so I'd be more inclined to bunt him against a right-hander—which isn't to say that I will do that." Occasionally, a manager will guarantee that he'll do something, but it won't be a revelation. He's not going to put himself in that situation. He may start out with a plan and then go with his gut feeling. When I talk to viewers I concede that nothing the manager said to me is etched in stone.

Baseball used to be so strapped to custom that everybody knew what a manager would do in a given situation. I've never believed that he should be such a traditionalist that he would never do certain things (squeeze-bunt or hit-and-run, for example) under certain circumstances. I think about how Robert E. Lee was such a successful general on the battlefield because he knew the opposing generals wouldn't do anything that wasn't in the books they'd all read at West Point. Meanwhile, he used his imagination to make it a level battlefield. Nobody did what he did. Nobody else adhered to this theory: When you have an inferior force, attack. He said the rules are good to know, but common sense is often better. Lee would have been a hell of a manager, not only because he made so many decisions quickly, but also because he understood that when the odds are against you, a combination of unpredictability and aggressiveness is essential to victory. Pittsburgh's Gene Lamont, Milwaukee's Phil Garner, and other managers of overachieving teams surely think in these terms. Making use of their knowledge and experience and what has always been done in baseball, managers play hunches when they bunt in the first inning, hit-and-run, squeeze, and play the infield in or halfway or deep. A good manager takes advantage of the fact that baseball is a game of options, rather than a game where what is done is determined by what is written in "the book."

There are some clear-cut situations in baseball. There are times when you have to bunt and times when you can't. But when a manager has options, a major part of his strategy should be to make the opposing manager think he's going to do one thing and then do another. He's not relying so much on trickery as he is on just shrewd operating. The less potent his team is, the more unpredictable and creative a manager must be. We have seen that Tony La Russa, Jim Leyland, Joe Torre, and Lou Piniella rely less on their imaginations and more on their players when they have stronger teams.

The mistake some less successful managers make is that when their team hits a dry spell, they are more conservative. They should be more aggressive. Teams that revert to tentative play will lose, particularly in the postseason. In the playoffs and World Series, players especially need to take an assertive approach to turn pressure and fear into positives.

Gene Mauch, for whom I played in my brief stint with Montreal in 1972, was the best defensive manager I ever saw. All the moves he made defensively were smart and well motivated, but I think he went wrong when he applied his defensive mind-set to his offense. It was tough to have big innings because his offense was designed to score one run, particularly when he wanted to get ahead and would give up an out to move up a runner. He'd always have his runners go around the bases by the numbers instead of challenging outfielders' arms by taking extra bases. Mauch knew that the defensive part of baseball should be played tightly, but he didn't understand the abandon with which you should sometimes play the offensive game. The same principles that are successful when applied to the defense can inhibit offensive performances.

I can understand why Dodgers manager Bill Russell would have a more conservative approach than Florida manager Jim Leyland because the Dodgers have the better pitching staff, among the best in baseball. If he doesn't want to wait for Mike Piazza and his other big guns to turn on the power, Russell can play for an early lead, giving up outs for a quick run, and then go into a defensive mode because he figures his pitchers can hold any lead. (In his long managerial career, Mauch rarely had pitchers

Gene Mauch hated the terms "Let's peck away at those guys" and "Let's give them a finish." It meant his team was way behind. Those terms are said in the dugouts of trailing teams to keep players from lying down. Yogi Berra and the "fat lady" also will be mentioned. Equally sensible is that tried-and-true baseball motivator "Let's catch 'em in hits and then take our chances." If they have twelve hits, you try to pick up twelve hits. If you do and still trail, you think about trying to get the tying run to the plate. A manager can tell his men that if they can cut their deficit to less than five runs, they can bring the tying run to the plate. You may eventually lose by four runs, but you'll feel satisfied to have given yourself a shot by getting the bases loaded before the final out is made. Those base runners don't matter, just getting the potential tying run up is what counts.

The losing manager doesn't give up hope and at the very least wants to have something positive happen. When the Yankees came up trailing 6–0 in the top of the sixth in Game 4 of the 1996 World Series, manager Joe Torre said, "Let's cut the lead in half." They did that after getting runners on first and second with nobody out. Then, Torre says, he got greedy and wanted it tied. They were able to do that with three runs in the eighth inning on Jim Leyritz's shocking homer off Mark Wohlers. Then they won in the tenth inning, 8–6. Torre and his team didn't panic and came up with the blueprint for impossible comebacks.

who could do that.) Russell can be innovative when he manipulates his starters and strong bullpen, and his own aggressiveness is revealed more through his pitchers than his hitters because they aggressively shut down the other team. It's like in football when a coach elects to kick off because he has faith that his defense will stop the other team.

I'm as tired as you are of the baseball-is-like-life metaphors, but there's no denying that in managing, as in life, there are many formulas for success. A lot of today's managers believe that the early part of the game will be deliberately paced, with a lot of sparring, and that most of their team's offense will come when the opposing starter is replaced by the weak middle relievers and setup men who are found in abundance on current major-league rosters. They expect to be making the majority of their moves as the game winds down and for there to be a frenzied ending. It's a scenario that I think too many managers are comfortable with.

As I have said, baseball is a game of firsts. First pitch, first strike, first out, first base runner, first hit, first run. I understand why a manager would put emphasis on scoring the game's first run because the team that scores first wins the majority of games. But why stop there? If I had to do it over again, the one thing I would want to do differently as a player is to change the tempo of the game by attacking early (the best time being the first inning of a doubleheader because it can carry you through eighteen innings and two victories). An aggressive manager should have his offense speed up the pace of the game and move away from the passivity that characterizes hitting in the early innings in today's baseball. If you wait until later in the game to switch into an aggressive mode, you might be behind by four or five runs by then. I'm not suggesting that the manager should instruct everyone to swing at the first pitch—a batter always must show patience and a good eye—but he will want his players to make the game frenetic from the start. They can do that by getting on base—taking walks from a wild starter is a good way—stealing or threatening to steal, putting on the hit-and-run, and first-and-thirding the defense. First and third with nobody out really sets the stage for a big inning. Of course, many teams do score a lot of runs in the first inning, but it's inadvertent rather than part of the offensive philosophy. I like when it's done by design with, perhaps, groundbreaking leadoff men like Maury Wills, Lou Brock, Davey Lopes, Pete Rose, Rickey Henderson, and Brady Anderson igniting the fuse.

Minnesota's Tom Kelly had this burst-out-of-the-gate mentality at the 1992 All-Star Game in San Diego. We miked Kelly, and at one of the few pregame meetings that had purpose, he told the American League All-Stars, "We're going to win this game tonight in the first inning. We're going to go out and really pound Tom Glavine." It turned out that those batters had the ideal approach against Glavine. Many of them were power hitters, but they went the other way on Glavine's pitches on the outside corner. They scored four runs in the first inning and another in the second inning, when they knocked him out of the game. They went on to a big victory, 13–6. Jim Leyland got his Marlins batters to attack Glavine in the same way in Game 6 of the 1997 NLCS. They also hit the ball the other way and touched Glavine for four first-inning runs on the way to victory and the National League title.

What Kelly and Leyland said to their players was so intelligent. They got them to be aggressive in the first inning, which would have surprised any pitcher, and also got them to do it against a pitcher who is known for having first-inning problems. The better the pitcher, the earlier you have to get him. Once he gets loose and churns himself into a rhythm, hitting him will be more difficult, so you should make the most of the early opportunities. He can be like a car in the morning that won't run smoothly until it warms up.

I think baseball will catch up with the idea that if you are aggressive early you can be conservative late when you protect a lead. I have a lot of respect for the current crop of aggressive managers.

There used to be more of the buddy system in baseball, where general managers were joined at the hip to their manager friends and would take them along wherever they got a job. That's rarely true anymore. Due to the scrutiny of the press, I think most of the current managers were hired because of their reputations, not only for being excellent at making moves on the field but also for handling players off it.

When people ask me who is the best manager from a strategical standpoint, I honestly can't answer them because there is such a narrow margin between the best. Tactically, there are ten or fifteen managers who are very similar. Some managers are known for certain things: Tony La Russa likes to work his bullpen left and right to get the optimal matchups late in the game; Bobby Cox likes to squeeze and lives with his pitching; Phil Garner likes to work his running game; Joe Torre likes to employ in the American League the aggressive, through-the-base running style that he learned in the National League; Davey Johnson and Don Baylor like to play for big innings; Jim Leyland, perhaps more than anyone, likes to switch one player to make opposing managers use up two players; Bill Russell plays conservatively because of his pitching; and so on. But that doesn't mean other managers don't do the same things as often and as effectively or that these managers don't have other favorite bits of strategy.

If I say that Leyland uses his bench well, which he does, that doesn't mean Tony La Russa, Don Baylor, Terry Collins, Gene Lamont, and five or six others don't. In fact, in 1997 *nobody* was better than Bobby Valentine at using his bench. (By keeping everybody sharp enough to play every day, a manager sends a confidence-building message to all his players and reinforces the team concept.)

If you were to hook up managers to some device that measured their knowledge of strategy, probably three quarters of them in the National League would have the same reading. It's very difficult to determine who are the best managers, but I'd say that what makes a few stand out—and this is where readings would vary drastically—is their better understanding of human nature, *baseball* human nature.

Jim Leyland is an expert strategist, but I think what makes him a superior manager is his understanding of the temperament of major-league baseball players. He knows of the fears and the pressures they endure and is aware of their insecurities, sensitivity to criticism, and capacity for humor. Leyland has empathized and sympathized with players like Barry Bonds and Bobby Bonilla and others and yet has stood right in their faces and screamed at them when he needed to. Players appreciate openness, and Leyland is someone who tells them right away if they do something

During games, managers have different styles. For instance, Tommy Lasorda was a cheerleader. Some managers sit back and watch. Tony La Russa isn't one of them. He is always at work, giving signals and making moves. Bobby Valentine manages, he admits, with a touch of arrogance. The low camera that shoots into the dugout from the opposite side of the field is quite revealing. You might see La Russa or Jim Leyland standing in the shadows, giving signs or studying the lineups on the wall. You might see Leyland go off into the tunnel to try to relax. I think Tom Kelly handles his emotions the best, balancing what he reveals with what he keeps inside. Sitting on the bench, Joe Torre shows absolutely no emotion, but his stomach is churning. Sitting on the bench, Bobby Cox looks so aggravated on almost every pitch in a big game that you can't help but worry about his health. We once cut back from an antacid commercial to show the Braves' manager grimacing, and my quip was too easy: "The Battle of *My*lanta."

wrong rather than letting things pile up. He has had the same number of bad guys as Tony La Russa, but with Leyland you've never read anything about friction in the papers. I would be more like La Russa in dealing with difficult players. If I failed as a manager, it wouldn't be because of the strategic part of the job, but I'd lag far behind Leyland in the diplomacy department.

I think La Russa is a terrific manager, and you can't argue with success, but his autocratic style isn't one I'd prefer as a player. Perhaps he takes on too much of a load himself. Players often look for his strategy to win games rather than taking on a more active role. When the strategy doesn't work, they don't know what to do. I liked playing for managers who said: We're going to talk to you to help with your preparation, but once you are out on the field, it's up to you to react and make plays.

One manager I admire is Felipe Alou. I don't agree with many of the strategic moves he makes, but that's overshadowed by the intense loyalty that his players have for him. The Expos will leave their blood on the field for this guy. Tom Kelly, who would be talked of as a future Hall of Famer if he managed in New York, is another manager who is adored by his players. He has as much knowledge of personalities as he has of the game. One of his great traits is that he won't take bullshit from anybody. Even Leyland will absorb it on occasion. I don't think anyone commands more respect than Kelly.

Davey Johnson isn't a great tactical manager, but he has the ability to make his team think that it is the best. He has that proud arrogance about him, and he struts for his team. He sticks his chest out individually for them collectively. Bobby Valentine does the same thing on the Mets.

When Lou Piniella used to play the outfield for the Royals and Yankees, he'd yell at hecklers in the stands, "Go home and check your wife, we've got a ballplayer missing." As a manager, he has retained that feistiness, and that is what inspires his players. Most managers become more diplomatic with age, but not Lou. Nobody can change him. Neither George Steinbrenner nor Marge Schott bothered him when they owned the teams he managed. Try that tandem on anyone else.

Unlike Piniella, Dusty Baker and Don Baylor have made the transition from being tough, aggressive players to calm, patient, mature managers. They are among the premier leaders in managing. Baker's job in 1997, when he guided an undermanned Giants team to a divisional title, ranks among the most impressive of recent years. Any time a team is better in the standings than it is on paper, you know the manager is doing a good job.

Bruce Bochy is interesting because he gets a lot out of his team by not trying to extract too much out of the players. San Diego would resent a manager of the Piniella ilk. They need a manager to calm them down, while other teams need a manager to spur them on. What's good for one team may not be good for another team. Everyone said Dallas Green fit in well when he took over an undisciplined Mets team. So why has Bobby Valentine gotten better results with virtually the same players?

The relationship between a manager and his players is difficult because a manager can't make everyone happy. It sounds paradoxical, but he must have consummate regard for a player's feelings yet have a complete disregard for them. That's because he's the guy who decides who will and who will not be in the starting lineup and what changes will be made during the course of the game. He can't worry if players are unhappy with their playing time or are sensitive to being removed for a pinch hitter or defensive specialist. He doesn't want to bruise egos, but his first responsibility is to field his best lineup and then to use his bench to try to secure a win. You might think a player will be amenable to his manager's decision even if it means less playing time. But there has always been a lot of healthy selfishness in baseball. Don't believe the benched player who insists he is content "as long as my team wins." That dog won't hunt. As Gary Thorne says, "You can't make a living if you don't make a contribution to your team winning." His agent will remind him of that.

Sparky Anderson was the guy who really understood the role of the manager in handling players. He was their mentor, friend, and father figure, but when he had to make a move, he was willing to become their enemy. He was so quick at yanking pitchers that they called him "Captain Hook." He didn't take back talk from anybody.

In general, a manager will stay with a star pitcher longer because he respects him. He may try to nurse him through five innings so he can get a victory, especially if he hasn't won for a while (which doesn't explain why Toronto's Cito Gaston left ace Pat Hentgen in long enough to give up eleven runs in a 12–11 loss in 1997, the most runs ever allowed by the previous year's Cy Young winner). Or the protective manager might take him out with the potential winning run at the plate to make sure he doesn't get a loss after a good performance. The manager is thinking of future games. Similarly, a manager will try to show faith in a batter by letting him bat or pinch-hit although he's been hitting poorly. It may be a poor strategic move at the time, but it's a good psychological move for the future. Also, if two players are doing poorly, a manager will stick longer with the player who has produced in the past, especially if he's a better fielder.

It's important for a manager to pat the back of a player who is struggling. Don Baylor has been doing that since he was a player. Cardinals third baseman Ken Boyer, who became a very supportive manager, used to get annoyed when he was a player and our manager, Solly Hemus, would give about two hundred bucks for dinner to a player who had a big game rather than to a guy who was mired in a slump. He said that the guys who were doing well didn't need the same support. In some cases, the more poorly a player does, the further the manager gets away from using his first name. I would go from Timmy to Tim to Mac to McCarver the deeper I went into a slump. When McCarver finally came, I was so down I needed help!

Sometimes a manager will have to determine if a veteran player is through. It is often a difficult situation for everybody involved. (In 1979, Earl Weaver was agonizing over how he'd tell the aging Brooks Robinson that Doug DeCinces should be starting over him, but Brooks had such a marvelous attitude when they finally talked about it that making the change was easy.) It's another situation entirely when the player is only going through a bad period. In the mid-seventies, I fell into the trap of listening to those people who were convinced I was finished, which affected my confidence and competitive edge. I was released twice before the Phillies picked me up and I was able to prove that I could still play. There's nothing more enjoyable than proving your critics wrong and achieving something significant when nothing is expected of you. I am still grateful that the Phillies had faith in me. And I was heartened by Bobby Cox's loyalty toward his shortstop Jeff Blauser, who everyone else said should be discarded after a couple of bad years. With his injuries healed, Blauser paid back Cox by having a terrific season in 1997.

If managers sometimes lose patience with struggling veterans, it's no wonder some give up quickly on struggling young players. A manager must decide whether their mistakes are the result of youthful exuberance or if they're simply not as good as they were touted to be. (Some organizations will champion minor leaguers only until after they trade them.) Understandably, most rookies are a little lost as they try to adjust to the big leagues. I know that in my first game as a seventeen-year-old with the Cardinals in 1959, I cheered loudly from the dugout when my boyhood idol Henry Aaron strode to the plate for the Braves, before my teammates reminded me that it was inappropriate to root for players on the other team.

In my first at-bat, my knees shook. It wasn't until 1963 that I stuck in the majors.

A manager knows that even a rookie who gets off to a hot start may think the game is so easy that he gets lazy. He also knows that some "can't-miss" prospects miss. If a manager thinks he has a future gem, he might try to hasten his development by letting him play right away. Throwing him into the water and letting him swim may be a smart move, but the manager is taking a risk if he doesn't have job security. Often managers are fired before all their players develop fully. They are like farmers who plant the seeds for fine crops but must sell their farms before the harvest.

Fans blame the manager when things go wrong. Sometimes it is his fault, but more often than not it's the whole organization that is responsible for the team that is fielded. Tony Gwynn told me during a recent interview that he doesn't want to become a manager because he sees that today's teams aren't managed only by the manager but also by the general manager, the owner, the press, players' agents, and even the increasingly vocal fans. Particularly in the Northeast Corridor, press and fans put unrelenting and at times unreasonable pressure on managers and their players. Elsewhere it's a 162-game season, but in Boston, New York, and Philadelphia there are 162 one-game seasons, as panic often sets in after a loss.

A manager can teach a team how to win, telling young players they have to be consistent and stressing to everyone the necessity of having a vulture mentality. (It may have sounded cruel when Joe Schultz used to say, "Get 'em down and stomp the piss out of them!" but that's smart, vulture-mentality baseball.) A manager also can motivate his players to play hard through personal slumps and stay the course through the cold days of early spring, the dog days of late summer, and the September pennant run. And he can get his players to rise to the occasion in the postseason, when there is so much pressure, particularly in the playoffs, that water goes down in lumps and there is a constant fear of failure. His shrewd strategy can win games. There's no doubt about any of this. But while the manager is a factor in every game and is the guy who makes the moves, baseball is *never* a manager's game. No matter how clever he is, the players make the plays, and that's why baseball will always be a player's game.

MANAGERS AND ME

There are a number of managers whom I like a great deal. But in my role as an impartial broadcaster, I don't really care if I'm liked by managers, players, or umpires. I see it as being of secondary importance.

However, I don't want them to think I'm out to get them when I point out anything negative. When managers say they get mad at broadcasters for second-guessing them, that really touches a nerve. Any moron can sit in the booth and say, "He shouldn't have bunted there. He should have . . ." Shoulda, woulda, and coulda. After twenty-one years of playing in the majors, I'm not going to waste my experience telling people what should have happened. That's not my style. I'm interested in what might happen. If I talk about something that might happen and it does happen, then talking about it afterward isn't second-guessing. In fact, it's what I'm paid to do.

One reason that managers get angry with broadcasters is that they hear secondhand what was said in the booth. I remember Lou Piniella becoming furious with me after the fifth game of the 1990 NLCS between Cincinnati and Pittsburgh because of what people told him. In the top of the eighth inning, when the Reds cut the Pirates' lead to 3–2, Piniella sent up pinch hitters for both his starting catcher Joe Oliver, who was seventh in the order, and reliever Norm Charlton. After the inning, he brought in a new battery, Jeff Reed, the only other Reds catcher, and pitcher Scott Scudder. What I suggested was that instead of putting Reed in Oliver's spot, Piniella should have had Scudder bat seventh and Reed ninth because this was one of the odd double switches where it was more important to protect your catcher and keep him in the lineup than the pitcher. The Reds had many pitchers available but nobody to replace Reed if Piniella wanted to pinch-hit for him. I said, "This might not happen because the third-place hitter, Paul O'Neill, is up first in the top of the ninth, but if the seventh position should come up Piniella's not going to be able to bring in a right-handed-hitting pinch hitter for the left-handed-hitting Reed when Jim Leyland brings in a lefty reliever." As it turned out, Reed did come to bat and Leyland brought in lefty Bob Patterson. And Piniella had to let Reed hit for himself. Bobby Bonilla made a great play on Reed's ball, turned a double play, and the game was over. It was unbelievable. The next day I showed up at the ballpark and Piniella was fuming. In front of Jack Buck (my broadcast partner at CBS), Pat O'Brien, and Steve Hirdt, he aired me out, saying, "God, I've received phone calls all f——ing day that you went on and on and on about it." I said, "The reason I went on about it was that I had brought it up an inning before and then when it happened viewers were entitled to a detailed explanation. I'd do the same thing if I had to do it all over again." I offered to give him the tape, beginning in the eighth inning. I told him he could decide for himself if I had been fair. The Reds ended up beating the Pirates in the sixth game, and

Lou never said another thing about it. In the spring we had a clean slate. We've never discussed it since then, but I can't help thinking that he respected me for giving him the tape.

* * *

When Cito Gaston was given Manager of the Year honors by *The Sporting News* after Toronto won the 1993 World Series, he was coming down on the beat writers in Toronto when one writer mentioned broadcasters. Gaston said, "Yeah, I'm sick and tired of Tim McCarver coming down on the field and smiling before the game and getting information from me and then going up there and ripping me in the booth." That comment was absolutely unsubstantiated. As a matter of fact, two years before that I was blowing the horn for Gaston to get a contract extension. He thought I had been overly critical of him in the World Series. Actually, I had criticized him only twice. In Game 5, I criticized him for letting reliever Tony Castillo bat for himself in the seventh inning with the Blue Jays down by five runs. I thought he was conceding a game his team had a chance to win and, sure enough, it scored six runs in the eighth inning and won, 15–14, in one of the wildest games in Series history. Another time I explained why he had to send in a lefty reliever to pitch to Darren Daulton and not wait until the next left-handed batter, Jim Eisenreich, was due up because he would end up facing a right-handed pinch hitter. But he waited, and that scenario played out and the right-handed pinch hitter, Pete Incaviglia, knocked in the tying run. Those were the only two times that what I said could at all be mistaken for pointed criticisms. And again, I was offering an opinion *before* the plays took place.

I fired off a four-page letter to Gaston explaining that he had been wrong in thinking I had attacked his strategy throughout the Series. I even called the Blue Jays and told them to have Gaston call me back. I never heard from him, not one word. I kept asking Howard Starkman, the PR director of the Blue Jays, "Has Cito received that letter yet? The mail sure is slow; I mailed it five years ago." Gaston got fired near the end of 1997 having never responded to me. It still upsets me.

4

PREGAME MEETINGS

Pregame meetings are probably the least productive of the pregame rituals. Team meetings are usually held before the first game of a series and, particularly in the postseason, before some individual games. It wouldn't interest me to take the cameras into a clubhouse meeting because I attended enough of them as a player to know they are often a waste of time. They can be particularly frustrating for a catcher and the starting pitcher. Unfortunately, because baseball has always done it this way, catchers and pitchers don't go off by themselves before a game to formulate a game plan since meetings usually involve everyone.

With the entire team present and too many guys "contributing" (an outfielder will chime in, "I saw that batter in the Winter Leagues in '92, and he has trouble with the . . ."), these pregame meetings are usually numbingly long. The length of the meetings directly corresponds to the insecurity of the manager. If the manager is secure he's going to know what to do, but if he starts fumbling for suggestions it's going to take a lot longer. And after all of that, the only players who benefit are the outfielders, who will decide how to position themselves once it is decided how opposing batters will be worked. The starting pitcher is made to feel that the outfielders should position themselves on the other side of the fence because he'll have little chance against what sounds to be a lineup of Babe Ruths.

As Steve Carlton used to say, "What these meetings usually turn into are negative assessments of a pitcher's stuff. The only thing that anyone does is tell me what I can't do, not what I can do. I'd like to go to the meeting where the manager and pitching coach will say what I could do best to get a guy out—maybe by throwing the fastball away and then running the slider inside to him. That would be positive and emphasize my strengths. But all anybody does at most meetings is compliment the hitter. Why should I go into the game thinking the hitter has the edge?"

Unfortunately, except when Chuck Tanner, the Norman Vincent Peale of baseball managers, was conducting pregame meetings with the White Sox, Pirates, and A's, pregame meetings have always been founded on pessimistic concepts. No one has heeded the sound advice of Johnny Mercer and Harold Arlen, who told us in song to "Accentuate the positive; eliminate the negative." You may have heard Jim Palmer tell a funny story about a meeting prior to a World Series game in which he was pitching. Everyone was saying, "This guy's a high fastball hitter; the next guy's a high fastball hitter; the next guy's a high fastball hitter . . ." And Palmer heads out of the room. Ray Miller, who was then the pitching coach, calls out, "Where are you going?" Palmer replies, "I throw a high fastball." Miller was unable to soothe him by saying, "We're not talking about *your* high fastball."

Advance scouts don't appear at the meetings but send reports to the manager. While most scouts do a conscientious job, these reports too often contribute to the negativism by making opposing batters seem too dangerous to pitch to. I preferred it when scouts just gave a general overview of opposing batters and the pitcher and I could take that and then mix in our own assessment from having pitched to them before. If one scout's reports coincide with what you think, then you realize that he has a pretty good idea of the way to go after a batter. Repetition is the one thing you have to be wary of because every hitter can't be approached the same way. You definitely want to burn reports that tell you all nine batters should be pitched high-and-tight and low-and-away. My daughter could write that. In the 1968 World Series, we got scouting reports that contended Tigers slugger Willie Horton had a tough time with the breaking ball low-and-away. We all laughed because Saint Peter has a tough time with a breaking ball low-and-away.

Veteran Cardinals catcher Del Rice saw that I didn't agree with a lot that was said at a pregame meeting early in my career. He advised, "At these meetings, you will hear all the information and various opinions on how to get guys out. It's good that you listen, listen, listen . . . but then go out and call the game your own way." He was right. You make a judgment from listening and gathering all the facts, but more important from both your own experience and what you feel when the batter comes to the plate. You're the only person who can see enough to make the best determination.

Baseball is primitive in that it stresses what you might do wrong over what you already do right. This is not surprising because it is a game of people rather than numbers and, as you know, people tend to be negative. How many people do you run into who are upbeat and positive? Maybe 5 percent? People get up in the morning and are looking for a reason to be unhappy. Unfortunately, too many of these people run pregame meetings.

PART III

On the Mound (and Behind the Plate)

5

INTRODUCING
THE PITCHER

The players think it's ludicrous when we begin a telecast with side-by-side photos of each team's hitting star as a "hook." They think we're indicating that a game between the Atlanta Braves and Houston Astros boils down to a personal battle between Chipper Jones and Jeff Bagwell. Players laugh at that. If we use pictures of Greg Maddux and Shane Reynolds, it's a bit better, but the pitchers themselves will tell you that they're going against the other team and not the opposing pitcher. A guy will say, "I'm pitching against Toronto, not Roger Clemens." However, with that said, they'll look back over three starts in which they were 0-2 with one no decision, and they'll say, "Well, do you know who I faced? Clemens and Cone and . . ." So pitchers are weird in that regard.

When setting up the game for viewers, announcers will commonly mention the stadium and the weather conditions, but most of the time the emphasis will be on the starting pitchers. I maintain that pitchers are the biggest key to predicting how a game will go. They, more than anything or anyone, will dictate the pace of the game. It seems to me that they are much more consistent from game to game than batters, so it's right to assume that if they pitch as they have been of late, then the game promises to be either high- or low-scoring. There are, however, surprises. Star pitchers are knocked out early, and pitchers who seem overmatched by a powerful lineup go deep into the game. Before and during the Phillies-Atlanta playoff series in 1993, I prognosticated, "If this is a low-scoring series, the Braves will win because of their pitching." I was no Nostradamus. It *was* a low-scoring series, but the Phillies won, emerging victorious in all four low-scoring games.

Of the many stats supplied to us on the starting pitcher, the one that I think is the most significant is innings per start. If he's pitched a lot of innings, it stands to reason (particularly in the National League) that his other stats will be impressive: win/loss percentage when combined with earned run average, the ratio of strikeouts to walks, walks per nine innings, base runners per inning, and, if there is a significant difference, the batting average of left-handed and right-handed batters against him.

If a pitcher has a good lifetime record against a particular team, it isn't necessarily a salient point. It depends when that record was accumulated. If the pitcher did well against a certain team five years ago, but has been in the other league since then, his record means nothing. He's not facing the same team. It's important to know if he's facing the same lineup he beat or who beat him. Also, if he's 6-3, that sounds impressive until you find out he has lost his last three decisions.

The term "quality start" drives me nuts. I don't agree with the definition. Who came up with three runs for six innings being a quality start? That means the ERA would be 4.50. To me a pitcher has quality starts if he gives up fewer than three runs for every seven innings. When a starter hovers around 3.50 for his ERA, he's doing his job on a game-to-game basis.

A broadcaster should remember that stats obscure personality. To a viewer, how a pitcher pitches takes on new meaning if we have put a face on him. As Roone Arledge always said, "It's the human part of the game that people want to know about." Why present the game to human beings as if you were funneling numbers into computers? So, along with the baseball numbers, I will always try to comment on something like Yankee David Wells wearing an authentic Babe Ruth cap that he'd purchased for $35,000 in a game and the fact that he wears the same size hat as Ruth did, 7¾. (Wells wore it only in the first inning of his start against Cleveland before the umps asked him to remove it, and I don't think it was coincidence that it was his best inning of work.)

In the 1988 playoffs, Brian Holton, a right-handed pitcher for Los Angeles, made his first postseason appearance and was whistling to help him relax. Afterward, I asked him the tune. He began whistling, "You take the high road and I'll take the low road." He said at the time he was whistling "Loch Lomond" he had no idea what it was. He didn't remember hearing it before, so why would he pick it to calm himself down? He called his mother and whistled the tune to her in the hope she could solve the mystery, and she told Brian that was the song his father had whistled to him when he was a baby. He said he'd never heard that song since. I told that story on the air, and Al Michaels said it was more fitting for *Psychology Today* than *The Sporting News*. Certainly, it was a refreshingly long way from the standard stats-driven story. For me the Brian Holton story confirmed my belief that if I'm going to be giving people numbers I shouldn't overlook the human side.

6

THE PITCHES

It's easy to define a pitcher by his statistics, but what distinguishes one pitcher from another is how he, with his catcher, goes about getting batters out. The object of pitching is to have the hitter put the ball in play on the pitcher's terms, and some guys do it with power, some with deception, some with pinpoint control, and the best use a combination of the three. It's important for the viewer to know from the outset the approach of the pitcher he's watching. Of course, his approach depends on the pitches in his repertoire. During the game, the announcer will tell viewers what pitches are being thrown as a matter of course, but he also should take a moment to define the various pitches in terms of how they are held and thrown and describe the action on the ball as it both approaches and crosses the strike zone. Visual accompaniment–perhaps distinguishing the break of the slider from that of the curve or the movement of a tailing fastball to that of a fastball that sails–is always helpful when explaining pitches.

High in the booth, I'm rarely fooled on what pitch was thrown. I was behind the plate for twenty-eight years, so I can see a slider breaking from two stories up and don't need to look at the monitor. I saw so many pitches as a catcher that it's really routine to determine what the pitches are. To make things easier for you the next time you look for particular pitches on your TV screen, I offer this overview of pitches thrown by big-league pitchers, beginning with the various fastballs.

It's not the speed of a fastball that's crucial but the unmeasurable pop at the end of the pitch. That's why the radar gun isn't a good indicator. If you continually put the speed of fastballs on the screen, the implication is that the speed of the pitch is the most important factor in getting guys out. It's not always true. Movement and location plus deception are more important than velocity. Real good velocity can cover a multitude of sins, but only for so long. A short reliever may get away with just rearing back and throwing hard, but unless you're Randy Johnson and you've got the batter just thinking survival, the *controlled fastball* is preferable. If it is controlled, it is going where you want and moving like you want. You will hear the adage "Everything comes off the fastball"; this is the fastball that is being talked about.

The controlled fastball is the best pitch in the game. There isn't a more versatile pitch. You can use four seams for a ball that goes up or two seams for a ball that goes down, and you can use different grips and finger pressures to make the pitch tail or sail or dart. And you can make it seem like several pitches by varying speeds and using both sides of the plate. Or, if you have a Bob Gibson–type exploding fastball, you can do this simply by throwing into the strike zone and allowing it to move in unpredictable directions.

My first major-league manager, Solly Hemus, would complain that the young Gibson threw every fastball at the same speed. That's like saying an atomic bomb explodes with the same power every time so you can't use it. What Hemus failed to understand is that when Gibson threw the fastball it could have any of five different results, so it was like five different pitches, all strikes and all hard to catch up to. When their control is good, Robb Nen and Bobby Witt have exploding fastballs that are several unpredictable pitches in one, but I haven't seen anyone's more devastating than Gibson's.

Many pitchers vary the speeds of their fastballs to keep batters off balance. Tug McGraw used to have names for his three different-speed fastballs. His "John Jameson" fastball was named after an Irish whiskey—it was his straight hard one. The "Bo Derek" fastball was the one "with the nice little tail on it." He didn't really throw it—it was just good banquet material. He did throw a "Peggy Lee" fastball when he was behind in the count, and batters would vocalize, "Is That All There Is?"—the title of one of her classic songs. If a pitcher throws that batting-practice fastball on a

2-0 or 3-1 count, it will surprise hitters who are looking for something six or seven miles an hour faster. It's like an unintentional change-up.

Fastballs of all speeds can be useful, even just to set up another pitch. McGraw threw the fastball, but his trademark pitch was his screwball. Steve Carlton's fastball was *heavy* and hard to drive on September 15, 1969, when he struck out nineteen Mets to set a new major-league record, but almost every other time I caught him it was too light to be the out pitch his slider was. But since he could control it, his fastball was an ideal setup pitch for his slider. Throwing his fastball, he occasionally had a mechanical problem that is common to pitchers whose fastball is hit hard. He would drop his hand and push his fastball instead of throwing it. If you push a fastball, it flattens out and gets ripped. Phillies pitching coach Ray Rippelmeyer would have to tell him to keep his hand straight up and to keep two fingers on the inside of the ball to prevent his hand from dropping. This is good advice for other pitchers with that habit.

A hard thrower who uses his fastball as a strikeout pitch will usually throw a cross-seamer, or four-seamer. A four-seam fastball, on which the

Y ou will hear announcers refer to "light" and "heavy" fastballs. I'll tell you the difference between the two. The faster light fastball is a four-seamer that stays on one plane or has a bit of a hop as it comes into the hitting zone. Batters often swing and miss, but when they connect with the sweet part of the bat, there is a wonderful click and the ball can go a long way. The heavy fastball is a two-seamer that is either a tailing fastball or a sinker. When a batter hits this ball, there is usually a thud and occasionally the bat breaks. On the memorable night in 1969 when Steve Carlton set the major-league record by striking out nineteen New York Mets in Busch Stadium, he was able to throw a heavy fastball that stayed on the same plane. Pitchers aren't supposed to be able to throw such a pitch, and Carlton himself threw it few other times in his twenty-four-year career. About twenty years after that game, Carlton revealed to me that he knew something strange was going on when he warmed up in the bullpen because his ball was just exploding. Then as he was walking in to pitch, he found himself staring at his left hand and arm as if they were foreign to his body, his borrowed weapons for one miraculous night.

index and middle fingers cross all the seams, is truer and faster than all other pitches because the pitcher uses the seams for leverage and just throws it as hard as he can, the same way the eight position players throw. The rising fastball, *the rider,* seems to rise around the letters at the last moment, and batters swing under it. The fastballs of Tom Seaver and Nolan Ryan had hop at the end because they'd drive off the mound with the lower part of their bodies. Unlike what a pitcher is supposed to do, Seaver didn't get on top of his fastball to bring it down, and the good result was that it came toward the plate on one plane and then hopped to a higher one as the batter swung. To get on top of it, we batters felt like we needed a chair. John Smoltz and Roger Clemens are among those who currently throw the rider; the young Dwight Gooden dominated with it until batters laid off it and umpires made him bring the ball down to get a called strike.

The four-seamer is a swinging-strike pitch, unlike the two-seamer, which is a contact pitch. There's no inward movement to jam and unnerve the batter. When a pitcher goes from four seams to two seams, usually he sacrifices velocity for movement.

To keep batters from leaning over the plate, you need a *tailing fastball* that comes inside. A tailing fastball is a two-seamer that tails parallel to the ground, with a break that isn't as dramatic as the slider's. From a right-handed pitcher, a tailing fastball bores in on a right-handed batter and moves away from the left-handed batter; from a left-handed pitcher, it bores in on a left-handed batter and moves away from the right-handed batter. A pitcher can throw a tailing fastball inside to the opposite-side batter, but instead of darting into him that pitch is designed to start in off the plate and tail back over the corner.

A *sailer,* which has a little wrinkle on the end, is often a four-seamer. Thrown by a right-hander, it runs away from the right-handed batter and runs into a left-handed batter. A sailing fastball moves similarly to the *cut fastball* and slider, but in degrees of break, least to most, it would be a sailer, a cut fastball, a slider.

I define a cut fastball as a slider without slider spin. What pitchers do is put pressure on the middle finger, and that cuts through the ball. When peerless right-hander Greg Maddux applies pressure on the middle finger, he makes the ball sail away from a right-handed batter and in on a left-handed batter. The batter has a hard time picking up its spin for the simple reason that there is no spin, just action. He approaches it like a fastball but, poof, instead of its going to the fat part of the bat it bites a little in on the trademark. He is fooled by the little dart—the cut—at the end of the action.

Sailing fastballs and cut fastballs are primarily reserved for right-handed pitchers for some reason. They are more adept at throwing them than left-handers. Left-hander Andy Pettitte, however, has a vicious cut fastball that sails into a right-handed batter's wrists. Jerry Koosman, who won 222 games between 1967 and 1985, was another lefty who made right-handed batters feel uneasy with a late-moving cut fastball.

A *runner* and tailer are similar pitches. With some pitchers, like Tony Fossas or onetime Pirate John Candelaria, they are the same. It depends on how heavy the pitch is. Candelaria's fastballs weren't heavy, but they ran so much that it was very difficult making solid contact.

The *biter,* or biting fastball, is one that tails or sinks dramatically. Tailing fastballs are lighter than biters. All pitches that bite are heavy. If the pitch is effective, the batter makes contact just above the trademark rather than on the good part of the bat and hits a weak tapper. Even if the hitter makes good contact, he will often pull it foul.

A tailing fastball can have that heavy motion in on the hands that a *sinker* has, but it doesn't always sink. For example, sometimes the tailing fastball of Kevin Brown runs and sometimes it sinks. The heavier the pitch, the more it sinks. All tailers don't sink, but all sinkers tail. Very few sinkers go straight down.

The sinker is a sinking fastball. It is thrown with two seams and is usually a heavy pitch because of its dead spin. To throw it, your hand cuts through the ball and comes to the inside, though not in as pronounced a manner as when you throw a screwball. If a pitcher throws a four-seamer, he may also throw a two-seamer when he wants to come down in the strike zone, as Bob Gibson would. You still hear announcers describing Curt Schilling as a sinkerball pitcher and at the same time say he throws ninety-five mph. Nobody throws a ninety-five mph sinker because balls that are down have a speed-diminishing sinking action. Schilling has changed from being an occasional sinkerballer who would throw the slower two-seamer down in the strike zone after getting two strikes on the batter. Now he is a pitcher who almost always will stick with the high four-seam ninety-five mph fastball with two strikes. He didn't get 319 strikeouts in 1997 with sinkers.

Kevin Brown throws a hard, top-heavy sinker, but don't be as interested in the velocity of his pitches as in their movement. His sinker explodes in on the hands, the same as a tailer. He has the best natural sinker in the game today. The bottom falls out, and it resembles a splitter. It's very tough to hit the bottom part of the ball against him and get any lift on it. Ground balls don't go out of the ballpark. Brown, a righty, is especially tough on right-handed batters. Also, he has benefited from being in the National League because umpires are more likely to call the low strike.

Andy Benes can throw an overpowering sinker. Batters hate it because it is extremely heavy and is painful to hit. Ken Hill also throws a hard and heavy sinkerball that can sometimes make batters feel as if they are hitting an anvil. The bat almost reverberates in the hands. Darryl Kile has a similar sinker that tails into batters. The sinker on the hands that left-handers Claude Osteen, Tommy John, and Jim Kaat used to throw would bite. That was a little more radical. Left-handed hitters really detest that pitch.

As Ray Miller has taught Scott Erickson and others in Baltimore, the best sinkers are thrown from the eleven o'clock position so that they will have bite and go down. If the pitcher doesn't stay on top and drops to the ten o'clock position, the ball will flatten out. As hard as the good, downward-moving sinker is to lift, it is equally hard to read. Because the arm speed and speed of the sinkerball are consistent, a batter can pick it up easily but will have a tendency to hit the top half of the ball, which results in a lot of grounders. That is what the sinkerball pitcher wants. You can tell his sinker is working if batters are fouling the ball off their feet. It's going *down*. The pitcher who throws mostly sinkers isn't a strikeout pitcher—batters don't swing through (or pop up) low fastballs—but is instead a contact pitcher who tries to induce batters into hitting weak grounders rather than line drives. The chances of the batter hitting the top half of the ball and bouncing it to an infielder are greater if the ball is down and going down than when it is up and staying up. When it's up, as when it is thrown from the ten o'clock position, it ceases to be a sinker. As I've said on the air, catchers don't catch high sinkers. Batters hit them hard.

In most matchups the sinkerball pitcher has a great advantage over batters, especially those inclined to ground into a lot of double plays. Particularly in a homer haven like Coors Field, the sinkerballer can have success. But it's not always so easy. For instance, a right-handed sinkerballer can rarely come in to a left-handed batter because that pitch tends to flatten out. Also, a sidearmer must be finer with his sinker because it is easier to read than the sinker of an over-the-top pitcher. Interestingly, the sidearmer can make the ball go down only by throwing a two-seamer. A four-seamer thrown from down under won't sink but will flatten out—and flat fastballs are akin to hanging sliders. (Understandably, the sidearmer's breaking balls will never go down but will either stay on the same plane or go up.)

The only sinkerballer who consistently throws four-seamers is Mark Clark, a strange pitcher. He has to keep the ball down because he doesn't have overpowering stuff, but he's still not a ground-ball pitcher because his four-seam sinker is light and easy to lift. I'm surprised at how effective he is because if his erratic splitter isn't working, he doesn't really have an out pitch.

The *split-finger fastball* goes down, but it is a different pitch from the sinker. For one thing, it topples more. Also, with the splitter, the arm speed and the speed of the ball are not consistent. While the splitter is thrown with the exact motion of the fastball, it's not thrown off the fingertips but through split fingers, which slows the ball down. On a close-up from the center-field camera, you occasionally can see the middle and index fingers split apart prior to a splitter being thrown. There are different ways to hold the splitter, but usually the pitcher uses the bottom seam for leverage and the split fingers are on either side of the smaller seams. Pitchers who have longer and stronger fingers can better hold it down toward the tips of the fingers. The closer to the ends of the fingers the ball is held, the more of a toppling motion it will have and the more of a splitter it will be, as opposed to the forkball.

Because it isn't choked back in the fingers, the splitter is thrown harder than the forkball. The batter's reaction, however, will be the same on both split-fingered pitches: If he's expecting the straight fastball, he'll swing awkwardly and without power as the slower pitch tumbles down sharply, usually out of the strike zone. A home-plate umpire has a hard time telling if the splitter is a strike because it changes planes once it reaches the hitting area. The later the break, the more effective it is and the harder it is for the batter and umpire. The first-base and third-base umpires will come into play because there are a lot of checked swings. The batter will commit himself and bring the bat back too late. The Dodgers' Hideo Nomo has two splitters: One he throws for called strikes, and the better one he throws for swinging strikes out of the zone.

The splitter usually goes straight down, but if the pitcher wants to move his in and out, he can do it without catching his finger on a seam. If you are a right-handed pitcher and just turn your hand a little bit, you can make the ball go away from a left-handed batter. It would be similar to how you throw a screwball, the pitch some lefties use instead of a splitter. (Only recently did I realize how few left-handers have thrown an effective splitter.)

A pitch that is hard to hit and hard for an umpire to read is also hard to catch. It takes courage on the part of a catcher to call for the splitter with an important run on third. In the 1993 All-Star Game, John Smoltz came in, and his catcher was Darren Daulton, who had already had eight knee operations. I said Smoltz and Daulton were a bad combination because Smoltz had led the National League in wild pitches three years in a row and Daulton couldn't get down very well. Sure enough, the next pitch was a wild pitch on a splitter. If the pitcher is consistently wild with the splitter, he's asking his catcher to be a goaltender.

To my knowledge, the first pitcher to throw the splitter with any frequency was Cubs reliever Bruce Sutter in 1977. It became the rage in the mid-eighties, when Jack Morris and Dan Petry helped the Tigers win a world championship and Houston's long-fingered Mike Scott won the Cy Young Award. The splitter is now in the arsenal of numerous pitchers. Many relievers, including Rod Beck, Roberto Hernandez, Rick Aguilera, and Mark Wohlers, have devastating splitters as their specialty pitches. I remember that when Aguilera was learning the pitch, the low-dugout camera would show him stretching his fingers with a softball. In addition to Nomo, other starters who have great splitters are David Cone, Roger Clemens, and Jeff Fassero. The one left-hander in this group, Fassero throws a splitter that disappears in a hurry. The worst thing for a batter is not to pick up a pitch, to be unable to see the ball well.

Choked more than the splitter, the *forkball* also is held between the index and middle finger and slides through the two fingers. On the fastball, you have your fingers behind the ball, giving it force, but to throw the forkball, a pitcher with long fingers will wrap two fingers around the ball to slow it down, making the arm speed and ball speed different. He doesn't get the rotation he gets on a fastball. It breaks down with a tumbling motion, making it very hard to catch or hit. It gives the illusion of a strike but rarely is. Usually it sinks, but forkball pioneer Joe Page would have one of his fingers get a little pull on a seam to break it in or break it out. ElRoy Face, who went 18-1 as the Pirates' ace reliever in 1959, threw his formidable forkball the same way every time, but sometimes it moved in and out rather than going down.

* * *

The *slider,* which became popular in the early fifties and hastened Joe DiMaggio's retirement, is a breaking ball, similar to the cut fastball but with a harder break. I disagree with announcers who call it an off-speed pitch because most pitchers throw it only one to three mph slower than their fastballs. It is hard stuff. To help viewers distinguish between the slider and curve, two breaking balls that go the same way as the arm, every few games I ask Mets director Jeff Mitchell to run videos that show the distinct breaks. With a view from the center-field camera, you can see that the slider's break is horizontal to the ground while the curve's break is vertical to the ground. In fact, the slider slides, hence its name.

The hard slider is usually thrown with two seams, but it depends on the pitcher. When Dick Ruthven asked Steve Carlton how to throw the slider, he replied, "You hold it like this and throw the shit out of it." Dick said sarcastically, "Thanks a lot, Steve." On the slider, the hand stays outside the ball. On any pitch it is dangerous to drop the hand under the ball, but this is particularly true of the slider. If you drop the arm to the ten o'clock position, you will get under the slider and the spin will become fat. One pitcher who was hurt from getting under the ball was Anthony Young, who dropped at least eight games in his major-league-record twenty-seven-game losing streak because his slider lost its bite and flattened out instead of going down. Not only do you court damage to your ERA when you throw from under the ball, but you risk injuring your elbow. That's why the Dodgers' organization teaches the curve instead of the slider in the minor leagues. Even guys who throw good sliders and don't employ the twist that hurts the elbow still experience a vicious strain because of the pitch's torque. Bob Gibson was extremely strong, but his right arm is crooked now from throwing the slider. When he is measured for a sports jacket, the tailor keeps pulling his hand down through the sleeve, saying, "Straighten your arm." Bob insists, "It *is* straight, and don't do that again."

Carlton was correct in thinking that if he could become very strong from his fingertips to his elbow, he could throw the slider effectively by just cutting through the ball and never hurt his elbow. Because he didn't use the damaging twisting motion of his hand, he rarely made a mistake with the slider. From plunging his left hand and forearm into huge tubs of rice and squeezing steel balls, he became so strong that without turning his hand he could put the same spin, only better, on his slider that other pitchers get throwing the cut fastball. Lefty, whom I caught in both St. Louis and Philadelphia, had the best slider I've ever seen because he gripped the ball so tightly in his hand that it would spin like a gyroscope and go down into right-handed batters. Because he held the ball so tightly its seams had, from the perspective of the catcher and batter, a "dime" spin. The dime spin is a tighter spin than the "quarter" or "half-dollar" spin, and that means it moves faster and goes down with more bite. That doesn't necessarily mean the pitch will be better, but the tighter the spin, the more controlled the pitch can be, and Carlton could put it right where he wanted it. He ate up both right-handed and left-handed batters.

The spin of a quarter slider has the unpredictability of a tornado. However, since the spin is loose it often can be dangerous to throw. A batter can recognize this pitch two thirds of the way to the plate and have a much easier time adjusting to it than the late-breaking dime slider. And because it has a tendency to hang, it can be hit a long way. Sometimes the quarter slider can back up and be a funky pitch, but, generally speaking, a pitcher would rather throw a dime. When Joe Becker was the pitching coach for the Chicago Cubs, he thought the dime slider was so effective that he wouldn't let any of his starting pitchers leave practice until they had thrown five in a row on the outside corner.

A left-hander's slider runs inside on a right-handed batter and runs away from a left-handed batter. (If a lefty wants to come in on the left-handed batter, he would forgo the slider for a fastball that tails or runs inside.) Throwing to a right-handed batter, the lefty wants the slider to run inside on the hands. Or it can be of the sweeping variety that Randy Johnson throws, which doesn't necessarily have to come in on the hands. Johnson throws a terrific sweeping slider with a very big spin. To coin a phrase, it has a "thirty-five-cent" spin, in between that of the quarter and half dollar. The sweeping slider Johnson throws is not a backup slider—it appears to start breaking when it is released from the hand. It is the antithesis of a late-breaking slider in that a batter can pick it up easily, but he can't react

The day before Steve Carlton's induction into the Hall of Fame, there was a banquet at the Otesaga Hotel in Cooperstown. In front of numerous Hall of Famers and their guests, I was nudged into making a little speech about Carlton because I was his catcher and good friend. Humbled, I said, "If Carl Hubbell will be known as having the best screwball in the history of the game and Sandy Koufax the best curveball, Steve Carlton will go down as having the best slider in the history of the game." Lefty and I hugged, and it was all really emotional. That was the end of the dinner, and everybody started mingling. I stood up, trying to compose myself, and I saw this figure weaving through everybody. It was Bob Gibson, with this scowl on his face. And I could tell he was coming over to me. He finally got to me and said, "The best *left-handed* slider in the game!" And then he left. That was it; that's all he said. He had that evil little laugh: Hee, hee, hee. Gibson at his sarcastic best.

to it. Johnson gets a lot of called strikes on the outside corner to right-handed hitters because they can't believe it will sweep over the outside of the plate after being so far outside. It's like a chinook—it blows in from nowhere. Left-handers have much more of a tendency to throw this pitch, though not many do. Bob Gibson was one of the few right-handers to throw it. He didn't have a tight-spin, dime slider.

When a right-hander throws a slider to a right-handed batter, it breaks down and away. If he throws that exact pitch to a left-handed batter, it goes down and in. So instead he tries to throw a slider on the hands, although this can also be a dangerous pitch if it flattens out and hangs. (Another thing to keep in mind is that sliders from right-handers are more predictable in their movement than sliders from left-handers.) Righties usually have a tight dime spin without the big break. Gibson's sweeping slider with the big break was an anomaly. In 1968, as the Tigers' slugger Willie Horton took a called third strike to become Gibson's World Series–record seventeenth strikeout victim, I heard him let out a frightened gasp because he thought that ball was going to hit him. It must have broken eighteen inches in order to cross the plate.

The *backup slider* is the hardest pitch to hit in the game. It appears to the hitter to be going two ways, although this might be an illusion. I don't really know what the physics are to this pitch. When a guy releases it, either because of the grip or hand motion, he causes the ball to have a fat eye, the quarter spin. The batter gets under it and it's a fly to left field or a pop-up. His only chance is to stay on top of that pitch, but that's not easy.

I've heard a few pitchers talk about throwing a backup slider, but I've never seen anyone throw it intentionally. Before a game in Milwaukee, Bob Purkey, who had come to St. Louis from Cincinnati in December of 1964, said he wanted to throw Hank Aaron backup sliders because he claimed to have had success doing that with the Reds. He said he would intentionally come under the ball and have the slider back up to Aaron and cross the inside of the plate. Ken Boyer interrupted, "Not with me playing third you won't. I have a family."

* * *

The *curveball,* whether thrown over-the-top or three-quarters, breaks perpendicular to the ground, the more downward the better. Its break is different from the parallel-to-the-ground break of the slider. Unlike the slider, it is an off-speed pitch because it is wrapped by the fingers to slow it down. The degree of its break is determined by finger pressure and the twist or snap of the hand and wrist. On the curve it is imperative that the pitcher stay on top of the ball and follow through to make the ball move properly. Picture someone pulling a window shade that is all the way up all the way down.

The best and rarest curve can go directly downward, as if falling off a table, but normally when thrown by a right-handed pitcher, the curve goes from right to left, and when thrown by a left-hander, the curve goes from left to right. Always. That's why a right-hander can get in trouble if he throws the same curve to a left-handed batter that he throws to a right-handed batter. For instance, the effective down-and-away to the right-handed Gary Sheffield is a dangerous down-and-*in* to the left-handed Barry Bonds. So an adjustment must be made to Bonds.

Just because the batter knows the direction of the curve from both righties and lefties doesn't make it a predictable pitch. In fact, the curve is a marvelous deception pitch because it can vary in movement and vary in speed. A pitcher can throw the curve one hundred times and there might be twenty-five different movements on it. That's enough to keep the batter honest. The same curve can vary in speed six to eight mph from pitch to pitch. That speed variation is caused by a tightening or loosening of the grip that the pitcher may or, more likely, may not be doing intentionally. The looser the grip, the faster the curve; the tighter the grip, the slower the curve.

Generally, it is not appropriate to say the pitcher "took something off the breaking ball" when all he did was grip it tighter, using more tension with the thumb and the first two fingers. More precisely, he's "putting something on"—more pressure on the ball. You'll even hear young hitters coming back to the bench griping, "Boy, he took a little off that curve." Nah. The pitcher didn't "take something off." It's a made-up expression that is very misleading. Ask any pitcher and he'll tell you that he's trying to throw the same curve every time (unless it's a right-hander throwing a back-door breaking ball to a left-handed batter). It's his changing grip that's changing the speed, not that he's deliberately taking anything off anything.

It can usually be said that pitches easy for the receiver to catch are the easiest for the batter to hit. However, curves are easy to catch, but some aren't easy to hit. The hard curves of Sandy Koufax, Camilo Pascual, and Burt Blyleven and other great curveball pitchers from the past sure weren't easy to hit. In fact, Koufax's curve was nearly impossible to make clean contact with because in addition to velocity it had tremendous downward movement and precise location in its favor. Koufax threw the nastiest curve imaginable, using his long fingers to make the ball go down, down, down. There are very few 12-to-6 (on a clock) downers anymore. Darryl Kile comes the closest today, throwing the tightest-wrapped, hardest-to-hit curveball in the National League. It's hard to imagine anyone throwing a curve as good as Koufax's, but Kile's overhanded curves are also of the straight-down variety, what we called "drops" as kids. Most of the other curveballers must settle for 11:50-to-5:20 downers.

The *slurve* is usually thrown harder than a curve but not as hard as a slider. You're trying to throw a curveball, not a slider, but you don't get on top of it enough and it has a break from side to side more than from 12 to 6. It's not a slider break, but it's more parallel to the ground than perpendicular. The slurve is an in-betweener, and most 'tweeners aren't as effective as either of the two pitches. It can, however, be a good pitch. David Cone throws a great slurve. It's a late breaker that sometimes sweeps. Jesse Orosco's tightly wrapped curve is actually a slurve.

* * *

After a pitcher establishes the arm motion and speed of his fastball and has something to change from, the *change-up* becomes a valuable weapon. But every pitcher who has a fastball doesn't have a good change-up because it's a technique that must be worked on. It is thrown with the same arm motion as the fastball, but instead of being thrown off the fingertips it is held back in the hand so it won't have the same speed. When batters see the arm motion, they think fastball and speed up their bat heads, opening their front shoulders and bringing their hands forward too soon for the slower pitch that is coming toward the plate. They swing at arm movement, not the ball, and can't make contact with powerful extension in front of the plate.

Usually, the change-up cannot be thrown with the tips of the fingers because that would make the arm movement and speed of the ball consistent. It has to be choked, and the ring finger usually is involved. The change-up is the only pitch other than the palmball that utilizes the ring finger. Even the little finger is used at times. John Franco, Jimmy Key, and Greg Maddux, who throw effective straight changes, choke the ball with the forefinger, middle finger, and ring finger. The circle change, which is being thrown more often today, can be held with three or four fingers. Brooklyn Dodgers left-hander Johnny Podres threw the most effective circle change, and it still serves as the prototype. He gripped the ball with only his last three fingers while his thumb and index finger formed a circle halfway up on the ball. It was a change-up that he could throw on any count.

One mistake young pitchers make when trying to fool the hitter on the change is to speed up their bodies. Batters pick up on that immediately, and I got a ton of hits off young pitchers who didn't know that the only speed that should be changed is the speed of the ball. Body movement, like arm movement, must be the same as on the fastball. That doesn't mean you can't jerk your head like Stu Miller used to do. The one-time Orioles and Giants closer threw a seventy-five mph fastball and his change-up was only a little bit slower, so he needed extra deception. So he'd jerk his head before throwing it and sluggers like Harmon Killebrew would have their timing so discombobulated that they looked like they were swinging at a feather.

The most dangerous area to throw a change-up is, not surprisingly, down-and-in. Left-handed batters seem particularly adept at handling that change-up, but their right-handed counterparts also hit it well. Although down-and-in is to be avoided at all costs, the low, *away* change-up is a good pitch even to a low-ball power hitter—it gets the power hitter to go forward, and when he brings his hands forward with his body, he spends his power and leaves only his arms with which to hit.

A change-up on fastball counts is often a good idea if you can get the ball over. Not too many hitters will crush a 2-0 change-up because they will be expecting a fastball. They may freeze. The reason a change-up is unusual on a hitter's count is because batters who are fooled are more apt to just take this pitch rather than to swing at it. So if there will probably be no swing on a 2-0 or 3-1 change-up, the pitcher had better get the ball over the plate to get the needed strike call from the umpire. It's not necessarily an easy pitch to throw for a strike. Greg Maddux is such an artist that he can get it over the plate on any count.

A change-up is definitely more effective the first couple of times you face a batter. Familiarity robs it of its deceptive quality. For instance, John Smiley has a very good circle change, but I believe he gets into trouble with it because he throws it too often. There should be an element of surprise involved. A pitcher can use it to try to get the strikeout after several fastballs—batters have more trouble adjusting to a straight change than the curve—or it can be injected into a fastball sequence to break up the pattern and make the next fastball look faster. A fastball helps the change-up, and the change-up helps the fastball.

The *palmball* is a change-up-type pitch that really is thrown with the palm. The ring finger and pinkie are usually involved to choke the ball and keep it back in the grip. The derivations of the pitch depend on the size of the hand and what kind of action the particular pitcher can get. As on the change-up, batters swing at the arm motion, thinking it's a fastball, and commit themselves too soon. Not as many pitchers throw the palm-ball today, as the change-up and splitter are the pitches usually chosen to fool batters looking for the fastball.

* * *

The *knuckleball*, a slow technique pitch, isn't thrown with the knuckles but with the fingertips. But calling it a "fingertip ball" wouldn't be too cool. At least, "knuckle" describes the movement of the ball. It has no spin if thrown correctly. No one knows how it will move, so it's hard to hit and very hard to catch unless you're a practicing lepidopterist. A knuckleball is one pitch, but it could be fifteen pitches wrapped into one because its movement is unforeseeable.

When you throw a knuckleball, you're pulling down, as you do with a curveball. Think again of pulling down a window shade. Hoyt Wilhelm, who knuckled his way to the Hall of Fame, held his famous pitch by the tips of his fingers and hooked his fingers behind the seams, where he could pull with his thumb. It makes sense. When you use the seam, it makes the ball dance. The worst thing that a knuckleball can do is roll or topple—batters won't miss it because it's so slow. In order to keep it from toppling, the pitcher should use the seam and push the ball rather than throw it. Sometimes the ring finger is involved. Barney Schultz threw the best knuckleball I ever caught, and when a batter saw there was no spin on it, he knew he was in trouble. As Charlie Lau said, "There are two theories on hitting the knuckler. Unfortunately, neither of them works."

Other knuckleball pitchers who come to mind are Eddie Fisher, Wilbur Wood, Charlie Hough, Phil Niekro, Joe Niekro, Tim Wakefield, Tom Candiotti, and Dennis Springer. It's a fun pitch to throw because of its weird movement, and position players often fool around with it on the sidelines. Tony Kubek claims Mickey Mantle had the best knuckler in the American League when they played together in the late fifties and early sixties. Duke Snider told me that first baseman and former catcher Gil Hodges had the best knuckler in the National League. Snider learned from catching Hodges on the sidelines that the best way to both hit and catch the knuckler is with relaxed arms. Catcher Bob Uecker, my former teammate in St. Louis, had some funny theories on the best ways to re-trieve the knuckler as it rolled to the screen, but he understood that the key to catching a knuckleball pitcher like Schultz was to keep the ball in front of him. And you can't do that unless your arms are relaxed.

In the 1986 All-Star Game, Charlie Hough was pitching in the eighth inning with the winning run on third. Rich Gedman was the catcher, and though he hadn't experience catching a knuckler with regularity, he felt obliged to call for Hough's dominant pitch. It took courage. I saw that Gedman was opening his right hand next to the glove on each pitch. It was actually farther ahead than his glove. That's what often happens—you want to stab at the ball before it bites you. That is a sign that the catcher's arms aren't relaxed, and it's hard to have the gloved left hand relaxed when the right hand is stiff. Understandably, Gedman didn't realize that the arms have to be back close to the body and loose to catch a knuckler, so he was just inviting a wild pitch. The viewers were alerted and, not surprisingly, two pitches later the run scored on a wild pitch and the National League won, 4–3.

The *knuckle curve* has been thrown by only a few guys in the last thirty years. Burt Hooton used to throw it in the eighties, and Mike Mussina is about the only guy since then associated with the pitch. It's a heavier-than-normal curve with a dead spin and a favorable rotation that takes it down. Mussina, who has thrown it since he was eight, holds the ball with the index and middle fingers as if he were going to throw a knuckler, only with this pitch the ring finger is never involved. He actually flips the ball out of his hand. It's amazing. He holds it with his fingertips, and in order to keep it from rolling, he uses the seam, and actually flicks or flips the ball toward the plate. It's beyond me how he gets that type of rotation on a flicker. You have to have awfully strong fingers to do that.

* * *

On a *screwball* you come all the way around with your hand. Yankees broadcaster Jim Kaat says the viewer should picture opening a door with the right hand and turning the knob to the left or opening it with the left hand and turning the knob to the right. Because of the unusual turn, the screwball is the only pitch to go the opposite way, with the possible exception of a backup slider. The screwball has inverse spin to a slider and curveball. From a left-handed pitcher, the ball that goes from right to left is a screwball; from a right-handed pitcher, the ball that goes from left to right is a screwball. Or it will just spin down. I would swear that some of the screwballs right-hander Mike Marshall threw just skewered straight down.

I had a fight with Marshall in 1972 and never liked him, but I admit he threw the best screwball I've ever seen. He was a kinesiologist and built up the triceps in his right arm, which was much bigger than his left arm. The triceps, which runs on the outside of the arm from the elbow to the shoulder, is the most important muscle when you throw. When you twist the hand outward to throw a screwball, it puts a strain on the triceps. Pitching isn't a natural motion to begin with, and this really isn't natural. (Old screwball pitchers have arms that are hanging and crooked.) By building his right triceps, Marshall protected his elbow from damage. He was able to relieve in a record 106 games in 1974, an astounding total that won him the Cy Young Award. He pitched a lot of innings for many years, and his ball always had snap. So did his arm, but it never got hurt. Marshall remains one of the few right-handers who has ever thrown a good screwball. The other screwball specialists I can think of have all been left-handed: Carl Hubbell, Johnny Antonelli, Warren Spahn, Tug McGraw, and Fernando Valenzuela. More right-handers don't toy with it because they don't want to go through what Marshall did to have success.

* * *

What about *illegal pitches*? There's no doubt that a lot of pitchers doctor the ball in some way to get an advantage. Scuffing the ball has always been popular. Guys cut the ball with a belt buckle, a nail—no, not the nail on their fingers—or a tack—yes, it is tacky. If you throw the ball using only the smooth surface, you get no leverage. But by putting an indentation on the surface, you create an unusual seam to give you leverage and you can do different things with the ball. Some guys use it to sink the ball dramatically; others may use it to keep the ball on the same plane.

When a pitcher throws a spitter, he doesn't put his fingers on any seam. He uses the slick part of the ball. The application of saliva, grease, slippery elm, Vaseline, or some other foreign substance gives the ball a dead downward spin. The pitch is heavy like a sinker but breaks down more sharply, making it easy to identify but difficult to hit. It's tough to throw for strikes and tough to catch. Some pitchers put clear pine tar on their hands or uniforms before every inning. We used to say about guys like Bob Moose that if you shook hands with them you'd have to take them home and you couldn't get rid of them till November.

Because of video-replay cameras, the spitter, or greaseball, is less in fashion today than when Lew Burdette and Gaylord Perry raised suspicions with every strange-moving pitch. The cut ball, however, is still in wide use. These pitches don't necessarily intimidate batters because illegal pitches aren't always effective. Not everybody can throw illegal pitches effectively or more guys would do it. I once homered off an 0-2 spitter thrown by Don Drysdale that just kind of stayed there for me. The next time up, his catcher Johnny Roseboro, known to his teammates as Gabby because he rarely spoke, made me laugh when he told me, "You hit a spitter, but you hit it on the dry side."

COMBINING PITCHES

Some fans mistakenly think a pitcher can throw strikes anytime he wants and that he has a full arsenal of pitches from which to choose. They wonder why he doesn't throw a curve now and follow that with a slider and a knuckleball and a change-up and so on. Standard equipment for a pitcher is only the fastball (in all its incarnations), the curve, and the slider, but in the major leagues few pitchers throw all three effectively. The typical starter has two real good pitches and along the way adds a third pitch that he can get away with. Many pitchers with good fastballs don't necessarily have good change-ups; few pitchers throw both curveballs and sliders; only a few lefties throw a screwball; unless a pitcher has long fingers—Greg Maddux is the extreme exception—he probably won't have effective curves or splitters.

A major-league pitcher must work with what he has, combining two or three pitches that work well with ones that don't to create patterns for getting batters out. Joey Hamilton, for example, has a fastball and slider as his two excellent pitches, but he will occasionally slip in his mediocre curveball to throw off batters when he is behind in the count. It doesn't have to be a good curveball, just a spinner that goes for a strike. When you're behind in the count, you don't have to throw a good-quality breaking ball if the batter is looking for the hard stuff. Often, the batter will freeze even if it's a strike because the spin will surprise him.

Pedro Martinez's two best pitches are his fastball and the best change in baseball. He'll use the first pitch to make batters go backward and the other to make them go forward. He has the same arm motion for both, and batters can't protect both the front and back of the plate. Those pitches are great for getting guys out, but to get a surprise called strike he'll throw the breaking ball—his third-best pitch—when behind in the count.

It is common for many hard throwers to add the split-fingered fastball to their repertoires to give them a deceptive out pitch and to make their fastballs more effective. They don't have to vary their arm motions to throw the splitter, just their grips. Rick Aguilera's fastball is light and in the strike zone, and batters teed off on it when it was his only pitch. He became a great reliever when he added the splitter to the fastball. Roger Clemens also learned the splitter, which made a great third pitch to go along with his rider and slider. It's a good thing that Mark Wohlers throws the splitter because his slower slider alone isn't a good complement to his high fastball. Wohlers highlights his heater over his splitter. Hideo Nomo also throws those two pitches—he came to the majors already throwing a nasty splitter—but takes the opposite approach, highlighting the splitter.

A pitcher can mix different types of fastballs effectively or make the same fastball seem like many pitches by locating it well. Or he can feature the fastball and the curve as Koufax did and many pitchers do today, including young Justin Thompson, who, remarkably, struck out Ken Griffey, Jr., six times in succession with his fastball and sweeping curve. In the absence of a great fastball, many pitchers emphasize the curve. For instance, left-handed Shawn Estes has one curve that goes in to the right-handed batter—he tries for a strike but it often ends up low—and a sweeping curve that starts out off the plate and comes in over the outside part of the plate. Hitters give up on his sweeper.

Pitchers who rely on movement to get out batters often throw the sinker and slider as their primary pitches. They can go inside and outside with those two hard pitches and every once in a while also throw a running fastball to keep guys off of the plate. These guys throw low pitches and tempt batters to swing at balls out of the strike zone, getting a lot of ground-ball outs that way.

Usually, if a pitcher throws a sinker, he has a slider to go with it, rather than the curveball. So you'll hear broadcasters talk about sinker-slider pitchers but seldom hear them mention sinker-curveball pitchers, though there are rare pitchers like Darryl Kile who showcase those two pitches.

Interestingly, Greg Maddux almost always follows a curve with a slider. Maddux figured it out: A hitter sees a curve, an off-speed breaking ball, and the seed is planted for another slow breaking ball. On the second pitch, the hitter will see the spin and know it's the faster slider but won't have time to adjust before the ball is on top of him. Even if the batter puts it in play, it will likely be hit weakly to the other side.

Not many other pitchers throw both a curve and slider because they usually detract from each other. That's one reason Sandy Koufax decided not to learn the slider and remain a two-pitch pitcher. (Of course, he could overpower batters with his ninety-five mph fastball and incredible curve.) Generally speaking, if you have a good curve, don't try a slider, but if you have a good slider, try the curve. The curveball will not adversely affect your slider as much as the slider will harm your curveball. What the addition of a slider to your repertoire does to the curve is affect its spin. If you are one of the few guys who have a toppling spin on the curve, you may lose that. For instance, Dave Mlicki has an excellent curve, but I think that his throwing the slider has taken away from it to the point where it is a slurve, an in-betweener. If you have a real good curveball, don't mess with it. This underlines the fact that, in pitching, not every combination works and often less is more.

7

DELIVERIES AND STYLES THAT TROUBLE HITTERS

Lefties generally get by with less. Because there are fewer lefties, batters don't bat against them often enough to feel comfortable. Moreover, while right-handers have to do something to the ball to make it move, lefties have a natural tail. Consequently, they don't have to throw as hard or have as good stuff as right-handers to be in the big leagues. Pete Rose used to hate it when Randy Jones or other slow-throwing lefties got him out and he'd heckle from the dugout, "If you were a right-hander you wouldn't even have been signed." It's very difficult for left-handers to throw a ball that doesn't move. I once told Chris Short to hold the ball across the seams and throw the ball straight. He couldn't do it. (Chris Short had the odd mind-set most lefties have. He tossed me a ball once and said, "Check this ball. There's a cut in the upper left-hand corner." Think about it.)

Right-handed batters hit lefties well, but in general they don't hit them as well as left-handed batters hit righties. And they hit righties better than left-handed batters hit lefties. Hard-throwing left-handers can terrify left-handed batters. Rusty Staub and I agree that Pirates reliever Ramon Hernandez was the toughest left-hander we faced in our careers. I'd have nightmares about him because I must have faced him twenty times and I didn't come close to hitting him. He would ride the fastball up and in and then throw the sweeping curveball. We left-handed batters thought Pirates starter John Candelaria was the devil in disguise. He was 6′7″, threw with a strange arm angle, and was a bear to pick up. At times his high fastball tailed up and in to left-handed batters. That was no fun.

Big Bob Veale, who pitched for an earlier Pirates team, would open my eyes wide before he even threw his fastball—by wiping off his glasses with his bandanna. Still another Pirates left-hander, Joe Gibbon, was even more intimidating. On his delivery, he'd drop his arm to first and our rear ends would follow—it was impossible to stay in against him. I said, "I'm going to stand away from the plate, and I'll take anything inside." But when I moved off the plate, he'd cleverly follow me with his sinker. I still couldn't extend my arms. I'd lose all sense of where I was in the box.

I'm glad that I didn't have to face Randy Johnson. His velocity makes hitters too leery to take a toehold. Now that Don Mattingly has retired, all left-handed batters bail out on Johnson. As Greg Maddux, his All-Star Game opponent in 1997, noted, he gets guys out before the game. He's that intimidating, like a left-handed version of Bob Gibson, just as mean but in an eight-inch bigger frame. Larry Walker stayed out of a game in 1997 against his good friend, then turned around and batted right-handed for one pitch in the All-Star Game after Johnson threw the ball over his head. I know how hard it would be not to bail out on Johnson. If Larry Walker gets nervous standing in against him, you know he is one of the most terrifying pitchers ever.

Less imposing but equally impressive is Tom Glavine, the cagey Braves left-hander whose balls go in to left-handed batters. I'd estimate that 75 percent of his money comes in that one area of the plate. (Some left-handed relievers use that area 85 percent of the time because they primarily face left-handed batters.) Tom throws low-and-away to right-handed batters and on the hands to left-handed batters. He raises the pitch—a running fastball—six inches to lefty swingers because the same pitch would be down-and-in to them, which is where they like it. That six-inch slot is where Glavine is most effective.

* * *

When a left-handed pitcher drops down, many left-handed batters open up early. Although Glavine throws three-quarters, he can make a left-handed batter bail out. That's my definition of a left-handed sidearm pitcher: a guy who can make that hitter's right side leave before he wants it to.

The more common right-handed sidearm pitchers throw from a lower angle—"the Australian fastball"—and their balls move on every pitch. The ball has to sink or tail; it can't go straight. No hop, just a tail. A right-handed batter can feel very intimidated facing a right-handed sidearmer and have difficulty not bailing out. Back in the late 1940s when right-handed sidearmer Ewell Blackwell threw a ninety-nine mph fastball that tailed in to right-handers, even Ralph Kiner's legs would wobble. It was a very heavy fastball.

But what is menacing to a right-handed batter is often in that happy zone of a left-handed batter because he sees the ball a lot better when the guy drops down with his arm. When a right-handed sidearmer comes inside, the ball flattens out against a left-handed batter. There is no tail, so it is not difficult to hit. However, if the pitcher is always painting the outside corner, like Kent Tekulve used to do, the left-handed batter may see it well but still not be able to put it into play on his terms.

* * *

Hitters mention pitchers with *extension* when discussing pitchers they don't like to face. Guys like Andy Ashby. Batters talk about wanting to "get the head out," but extension messes up a batter's timing and pushes the bat back so he has to fight off pitches. To have the best extension, the pitcher is usually tall, which is intimidating to begin with, and when his long arm extends toward the plate it's almost like the ball is released in front of the hitter's face. The batter wants to be 90′6″ away rather than 60′6″ because it's hard to recognize pitches before they're on top of him. The batter gets the impression that he doesn't have time to get the barrel of the bat out in front of the plate.

With big men like Randy Johnson, Bob Gibson, and Steve Carlton, extension not only helps their sliders but helps their overall pitching. Extension helps everything, which is why it is unfortunate that many pitchers release the ball without it. That's because they don't fully understand how it affects a batter. Hitters are reluctant to divulge weaknesses even to pitchers on their own team because they might end up on opposing teams, so they don't tell them about the difficulty they have when they can't get the bat head out. And pitchers take a look at the success of Greg Maddux, who isn't tall, hasn't long arms, and doesn't have extension, and don't recognize that Maddux is the exception to the rule.

* * *

Johnny Sain, who became one of the great pitching teachers, was an unorthodox, deceptive pitcher in the forties and early fifties who kept batters off stride with a variety of breaking balls, by changing speeds and using different deliveries. The batters who gave him the most trouble were those who could wait, but his motion was so quick it was hard to do that. As a pitcher and coach, he was a major proponent of changing release points to keep batters guessing. He theorized that if a pitcher has a predictable release point, the batter becomes too comfortable. John Smoltz, whose pitching coach at Atlanta is Sain disciple Leo Mazzone, varies his release points to great effect. Tommy Glavine and Greg Maddux rarely do this as part of their deception routine, but it's usually a trait of power pitchers. If a pitcher varies his release point for a reason, I think it can be a good idea, but if he's doing it unconsciously, it's a sign that he can't find the release point he wants. At least this holds true for pitchers who were trained in America to come over the top with their deliveries. (Those pitchers who have the same delivery and release point on every pitch must thwart batters with a large pitch selection and excellent control.) It's different with the free-throwing Latino pitchers, who have grown up pitching from various angles, with different arm motions—even slinging the ball on occasion—and numerous release points.

* * *

Pitchers who move left or right on the rubber change the angles of their pitches. The Mets' Bob Apodaca makes his pitchers more conscious of that than most pitching coaches. When left-handed John Franco moved toward third on the rubber, that meant he could come inside more to right-handed batters. He no longer had to throw across his body to get there. It helped him have an excellent season in 1997.

* * *

Pitchers without dominating stuff find ways to throw off a batter's timing. They might do this by changing release points, but some pitchers instead try to enhance their pitches with some odd body and head movements that catch the batter's eye when he should be looking only for the ball leaving the hand. The herky-jerky guys around today are following the tradition of Curt Simmons and Stu Miller. A hard thrower when he was young, Simmons came up with a herky-jerky motion after severing half of his left big toe in a lawn-mower accident, and he ended up having his hip replaced at an unusually young age. His weird motion made him tough, particularly on left-handed batters. Likewise, Miller's dramatic head jerk fooled batters and made them commit too early on his change-up. Pitchers refer to such pitchers as "funky." Batters say, "He doesn't throw hard, but I can't pick him up."

Luis Tiant and later pitchers Fernando Valenzuela and Valenzuela clone Dennis Reyes turn away from batters and look up and about to throw off timing. Slow windups followed by fast pitches throw off timing. Sid Fernandez also fooled batters with a strangely timed delivery. When a pitcher's foot hits the ground and is planted, the batter expects the pitcher's arm at the same time, but Fernandez's arm came around a moment later so the batter was usually behind his pitches.

* * *

In addition to throwing off a batter's timing with his odd delivery, Sid Fernandez hid the ball so well that his pitches were hard to pick up until they were on top of a batter. So Fernandez got a lot more strikeouts than pitchers who had better stuff. The quicker the batter can see the ball released, the better chance he has of catching up to the pitch, regardless of how good or hard the pitch is. That's why Bob Apodaca is among those who believe a pitcher's success is determined by how late a read he gives a hitter, particularly if he doesn't have overpowering stuff. If a pitcher gives the batter a late read, the batter is less able to determine what the pitch is, how fast it is, where it's going to go, and all the other things that are essential to getting the fat part of the bat on the ball. About ten to fifteen feet from the batter is where you can tell the effectiveness of breaking balls by their speeds and spins. Consequently, those pitchers who throw their curves and sliders with late breaks are the most effective.

* * *

As confirmed by what happened to both Simmons and Fernandez, a pitcher whose delivery includes odd, out-of-sync movements of the arm and body is susceptible to injury. Hard throwers with questionable mechanics are particularly vulnerable. Former Reds reliever Rob Dibble struck out more than a batter per inning, but his delivery put tremendous strain on his shoulder. He threw hard and opened up, and his arm dragged behind his body. I could see the career-curtailing injury to his rotator cuff coming. Often what will make a pitcher so hard to hit is the reason he breaks down. Force can cause injury.

Rick Sutcliffe comes to mind as a hooker. The Cubs' right-hander would take the ball out of his glove and then bring his right hand back. He had to develop arm problems throwing like that. He could have reduced the chance for arm strain by instead bringing the glove back to the hand and then throwing the ball. By bringing the glove back, he could have closed his front shoulder naturally, putting it into the proper position for throwing. A pitcher must keep his shoulder down so throws will go down instead of upward. He should drive the front shoulder toward the plate, just as a mechanically sound hitter drives his front shoulder toward the mound.

Tom Seaver had the best mechanics imaginable. He had huge thighs and would use them to drive his body forward, taking the pressure off his arm (but requiring him to wear a pad over a right knee that would scrape the ground on most pitches). A pitcher needs drive from the back leg in order to bend his back—you don't want the body upright in pitching—and Seaver's leg drive was justifiably famous. Seaver influenced the deliveries of other young Mets like Jerry Koosman and Nolan Ryan. Nolan couldn't have had such a long career throwing so hard if he hadn't learned the importance of using the lower part of the body to increase velocity. Today, you should watch Roger Clemens to see a pitcher who really knows how to use the lower part of his body. He has outstanding mechanics.

8

THE CATCHER'S SIGNS

One advantage television viewers have over fans in the stands is that the center-field camera lets them be privy to the catcher's signs to the pitchers. If there is no runner on second trying to steal signs, it is easy for the viewer to figure out what all those flashing fingers signify. One finger is a fastball, two is a curve, three is a slider, a wiggle is a change. It's that simple, although for guys like David Cone and Armando Reynoso, who have huge repertoires, a catcher may as well take off his shoes and use his toes as well.

The catcher has signals for inside and outside, high and low. When the catcher uses the pinkie, it's to indicate to the pitcher the desired location for a fastball. For a right-handed pitcher, the pinkie pointing to the inside of the right thigh means to keep it away from a right-handed batter and in on a left-handed batter; the index finger pointing to the inside of the left thigh means to keep it in to the right-handed batter and away from the left-handed batter. I would also point with my right forefinger, as if I were admonishing a child, when I wanted to tell my pitcher to really think about what he was doing, usually on an 0-2 or 1-2 pitch. If, after I pointed with my forefinger, I then pointed the pinkie to my thigh to get an inside pitch, it was to remind my pitcher to throw it way inside, off the plate. If I then put my palm up between my legs, he would know it would have to be a high fastball out of the strike zone. Also, there are different signals for fastballs with different movements. If, for instance, a right-handed pitcher throws both a fastball that sinks and a fastball that sails away from right-handed batters and in to left-handed batters, the forefinger is for the regular fastball and the pinkie is for the sailing fastball. When I caught Larry Jackson, I'd need different signals for his riding and sinking fastballs, so I'd use the pinkie for the rider.

On pitches other than the fastball, location is implied, so the catcher doesn't have to point in either direction. For instance, if the right-handed pitcher throws a breaking ball to a right-handed hitter, there's no point signaling direction because every time it is designed to go away from him. The lone exception is the back-door breaking ball that is thrown on rare occasions. (When a right-handed pitcher is facing a left-handed batter and maybe the count is 1-2, the catcher may give a sign for a slider and point to the inside of his left thigh, signifying away—incidentally, the back-door breaking ball actually comes back over the plate through the side door, not from behind the catcher.)

With pitchers who have unpredictable, exploding breaking balls—like Bob Gibson or Jaret Wright—you don't necessarily signal location because neither you nor your pitcher knows where it is going. You just put your mitt down the middle of the plate and let the movement take care of getting the batter out.

It is imperative that pitch location be kept secret from a batter because it often implies the type of pitch as well. So you'll see catchers try to decoy batters by pounding their mitts on one side of the plate, only to move to the other side of the plate to catch the ball. Because batters peek—this was a specialty of Keith Hernandez's—and because the runner on second will signal the batter the direction where the catcher moves, catchers have taken to setting up late in the last three or four years. They wait until the delivery begins to move into position because that is when the batter must be locked in on the pitch. In 1997, during a Mets-Reds game at Cinergy Field, a Reds fan would wait until Todd Hundley set up before each pitch and then shout out its location to the batter. Hundley had to figure out how to cross up the fan, and his manager, Bobby Valentine, had to resort to shouting gibberish to drown him out. That's how important location is.

A catcher can prevent the third-base coach and a runner on third from seeing his signs by blocking their views with his mitt. He can't block the view of the runner on second, so he and the pitcher will use a more sophisticated set of signs to keep him confused. The catcher might give several signals and use the first, second, or last sign that he puts down. Or the sign he uses can change in three-inning increments: He can use the first sign in the first, fourth, and seventh innings; the second sign in the second, fifth, and eighth innings; and the third sign in the third, sixth, and ninth innings. Not much more complicated, but perhaps too fast to figure out on television, is a signal system where you put down one to three fingers and then add pumps to determine the pitch. Rolling over after three numbers (for three pitches), a fastball now would be 1 and 4, a curve would be 2 and 5, and a slider would be 3 and 6. Two fingers–curve–plus 1 pump becomes 3, a slider. Two fingers plus 2 pumps = 4, a fastball, and 2 + 3 = 5, a curve. Sometimes a catcher will cross himself up. He can put down so many fingers that he forgets what he called. Then he has to start all over.

A wild pitch or passed ball may occur when the catcher is crossed up. He can adjust to a slower pitch than he's expecting but not to a faster pitch. It's frightening for the catcher when he's looking for the local and gets the express. A viewer can't usually tell if a catcher has been crossed up unless the catcher is sitting with his mitt down and there is a high fastball and he doesn't move. It takes a trained eye, and sometimes we can't tell. One telltale sign is a catcher going out to the pitcher after a ball has gotten by him with a runner on second base. That's when they are using a more sophisticated set of signs.

The catcher will signal a pitcher to try a pickoff, usually after getting a sign from the bench. This sign varies, but most of the time it's the thumb toward first. Unless there is a man on second, the fist is the catcher's sign for a pitchout. There's a much-told story about Tom Seaver and catcher Junior Ortiz. About twelve years ago, Junior, who is a funny, dear man, was trying to learn English and Tom was trying to help him with a crossword puzzle. The puzzle asked for a four-letter word for "clinched hand." Tom clinched his hand into a fist and said, "Junior, think about this." And Junior piped up, "Oh–pitchout!" So that shows how universal a fist is for a pitchout.

Joe Becker, the Dodgers' pitching coach when Maury Wills stole a record 104 bases in 1962, told me that Wills could be on first base and still steal every sign from the catcher. I said, "Bullshit. Catchers are trained to put their right knee in front of their left knee to prevent the guy on first from getting the signs." I didn't ignore what Becker said, but I didn't want to put too much stock in it because I thought if I became paranoid about it, it would influence how I called the game. I don't know if Wills got the signs, but he ran on an awful lot of breaking balls and never fell victim to the pickoff or pitchout. He never ran when I signaled for a pitchout.

Another signal that uses the thumb is the one for a knock-down pitch. The catcher just flips his thumb as if he were flipping a marble. Because of the center-field camera and increased use of replay machines, fewer knock-down signs are given because the league office will have video proof.

Of course, a pitcher doesn't always go along with a catcher's pitch selection. He'll either stare off or shake off the sign. When he stares off a sign, he won't go into his windup until the catcher puts down the sign he wants. For some reason, when the pitcher wants a different sign, he usually prefers to throw something other than the fastball. Batters know this. So if a pitcher shakes off for a change-up, the change-up will not be effective because the batter will be looking for an off-speed pitch. But a catcher is smart enough to know that a batter will gear up for something other than the fastball when he sees a pitcher shake him off, so he will try to set a trap. If the pitcher throws three fastballs in a row, the batter will undoubtedly be sitting on a fourth fastball—unless he sees the pitcher shake off the catcher. So in order for his pitcher to throw a fourth fastball, the catcher will shake his head *no* in order to get the pitcher to shake his head no. Watch at home: If a catcher shakes his head and then the pitcher does the same, there may be no change of pitch at all. Seeing the shake-off, the batter assumes the pitcher has shaken off the fourth straight fastball, but that's just what the pitcher will throw. The catcher got the pitcher to shake his head as a ploy.

Head movement can get pitchers in trouble. When Bob Gibson didn't agree with my signal for the location of his fastball, he wouldn't shake his head because he didn't want me to go through the signs again. A rapid-fire warrior, he'd try to save time by angling his head in the direction he

There can even be a sign for the spitter. I'm reminded of Lew Burdette, the star Braves pitcher who came to the Cardinals in 1963. I was twenty-one and he was much older than dirt and we became tight friends. When I wanted him to throw his famous spitter, I would tug on the bottom of the chest protector and whatever signs I gave after that were decoys. In 1984, we were playing golf together in a tournament in St. Petersburg and I reminded him that his spitter went down as much as any spitter I ever caught. And Lew said, "I didn't throw a spitter." I said, "What? Don't you remember that we even had a sign for it?" He said, "I never threw a spitter." He never admitted it the whole day.

wanted to throw the ball. I'd say, "Bob, don't do that because it gives away location. And when you give away location, they know you're throwing a fastball."

Often a pitcher will give away that he's throwing a fastball when he shakes his head at the catcher, yes, no, yes, because he's saying, "Yes, I'll throw that pitch. No, I don't want it there. Yes, I want it there." So the hitter doesn't know where it's going to be but knows it's a fastball because location is being signaled. (The first pitcher who understood the implications of head shaking was Don Sutton, who was really ahead of his time in figuring it out.) So catchers have got to tell pitchers that they are giving away pitches, which too many do. Instead of shaking off a location for a fastball, he should just wait for the catcher to go through his signals until he gives the location he wants. If a pitcher is going to give away the pitch, why should the catcher bother giving signals at all?

9

THE CATCHER-
PITCHER TANDEM

At the twentieth anniversary of Veterans Stadium, Jim Bunning was going to throw out the first pitch. I told Larry Shenk, the Phillies' longtime publicity director, "I'll catch it, but don't expect me to squat. I might never get up."

When I think of the many things you have to do as a catcher, I am shocked that I did that for a career, especially for over twenty years. I'm not trying to throw bouquets my way, but it is an extraordinarily difficult position from a physical and mental standpoint. The squatting takes its toll on your quads; your legs wear down from running to first to back up plays and from chasing and sliding after balls that go to the backstop; your hands and body take a beating from moving fastballs, foul tips, pitches in the dirt, throws that skid, and hard-sliding runners; your right arm and shoulder suffer from hurried attempts to gun down base stealers; your mind is in overdrive because from a defensive standpoint you must be alert to every possible occurrence in every situation; and through it all you must strategically call the game for the pitcher and work the umpire to make sure he isn't shortchanging him. The most revealing shots of the Catcher-Cam are on pitches with men on base when the batter misses a bunt or swings through the pitch: Nothing has happened, but the camera's movements from side to side as the catcher surveys the entire infield give fans a pretty good idea of all the responsibilities he has on every play. It is such a grueling job. But it's also fascinating because on every play you initiate the action and the results can be very satisfying.

The typical fan focuses on the pitcher-batter confrontation and tends to lump the catcher with the umpire and pay attention to neither. Because the job requires that he spend the entire game facing the opposite direction of his eight teammates, squat between the crouching batter and umpire, and wear a mask and other protective paraphernalia, the catcher seems to court anonymity. So it's not surprising that few fans really pay enough attention to the catcher to appreciate his contribution. I am not exaggerating when I say that the man who dons the "tools of intelligence" might very well be the most indispensable player on a winning team. The role of the catcher in the pitching game cannot be overestimated.

With apologies to John Stockton and Karl Malone, there is no stronger bond between two players in any sport than the one between the pitcher and catcher. When they're working well together, it's almost as if there is a string running from one to the other so that one's motion pulls the other along. The thinking comes before the game to allow for instinct, activity, and animation during the game. More than any other combination in sports, this one relies on a rhythm and cadence to be successful. It's a feel, it's dancing. The two are on the same wavelength, communicating without talking.

I've heard some announcers say that all a catcher does is *suggest* a pitch and the pitcher is the one who makes the final decision. It's much more than a suggestion. Bill Dickey, the Hall of Fame Yankee catcher, was the first person to impress upon me that the catcher must be the one to select the pitches because the pitcher's primary concern is his own technique when throwing the ball. In the pitcher-catcher tandem, the catcher is not only the receiver but the quarterback as well, making all the calls. Smart pitch selection by the catcher makes the best use of a pitcher's good stuff. It also can overcome the lack of stuff by a marginal pitcher or a good pitcher who is having an off day.

A catcher's "handling" of a pitcher isn't talked about as much as it should be, so it's something you should zero in on yourself. What a catcher tries to do is build the pitcher's confidence both in himself and in his receiver, so the right pitch will be thrown. On television or at the park it's possible to determine if the catcher has the pitcher's confidence by watching the duo when signs are given before pitches. If the pitcher is shaking off pitches or there is an air of indecision on his part, then it's clear that the pitcher doesn't trust his catcher. The catcher may be making the smart pitch selection, but perhaps the way he's doing it doesn't instill confidence in the pitcher.

Indecision is an awful curse for a pitcher, but it's worse for a catcher because he can take the pitcher down that uncertain path with him. The pitcher responds with assurance to a catcher who is decisive with his signs and with skepticism to a catcher who seems unsure of what to put down. The catcher mustn't let him throw with doubt because, for example, if he calls inside when the pitcher wants outside the pitch might go down the middle. When some pitchers are hit hard, they place the blame squarely on the catcher for making a bad call, but the catcher should stand by his decisions. A catcher can't constantly second-guess himself because the pitcher will often follow suit. Anyway, who knows what the right pitch would have been? Most of the time you do everything right and a Mark McGwire, Tino Martinez, or Barry Bonds will still pop it. After an early home run, you want the pitcher to just chalk it up to good hitting instead of poor pitch selection. If the batter homered off a particular pitch, maybe the pitcher's best pitch or a good fastball, he can't *not* throw it for the rest of the game. The catcher needs to keep the pitcher's confidence up so that he won't hesitate to come in with the same pitch in the same situation later in the game.

The catcher also has to maintain his own confidence. I remember when my Phillies battery mate Steve Carlton threw a pretty good curveball that Keith Hernandez still hit to right to put the Cardinals ahead of us late in a game. That was the key hit that cost us the win. I was beating up on myself, thinking I'd gone to that particular well once too often. Our pitching coach Ray Rippelmeyer said, "You can't fault yourself for throwing the right pitch. Sometimes you just tip your hat to the hitter." He was right. Catchers will sometimes be too tough on themselves.

A veteran catcher has the advantage over a young catcher in winning the confidence of a veteran pitcher, but if any catcher makes pitch-selection calls with conviction, he will win over the pitcher. The appropriate thing for a smart, conscientious catcher to do is make rapid decisions. Although he was expressing annoyance with me rather than intending to disseminate wisdom, Bob Gibson made perfect sense when he said, "The first sign you think of, put it down." The catcher *should* fire down the first thing he thinks of. It's like a multiple-choice quiz in school, where your first, reasoned guess is usually the right choice. If you go back and rehash all the possibilities, you'll get confused and talk yourself into the wrong answer. You might make mistakes with quick choices, but over the long haul, it's the right approach. If you put down tentative signs you're going to get tentative pitches. That's always been my contention.

The catcher needn't adhere to any pitching theories or rules of thumb in order to defend his calls to his pitcher. He must know what the conventional ways of doing things are, but that isn't enough. Then he should use common sense—maybe it should be called *un*common sense, because if it were common more players would have it—and be innovative and sell his pitch choice to his pitcher. He has to have complete faith in his own experience, knowledge, intelligence, and instincts and be willing to take responsibility for everything, from telling the pitcher to throw a certain pitch to telling an outfielder to move in or back for a particular hitter. He is paid to be a manager on the field.

The catcher will have a game plan of some kind. Naturally, he's going to deviate from it, but there is always the sense that "we're going to do this, and we're going to do that." When in doubt, he should go back to the pitcher's strength. Standardize rather than play hunches. Catchers don't play hunches but act on what they *feel*.

As a catcher, early in the game, you are simultaneously trying to work a lineup with your pitcher, work the umpire for your pitcher, and determine what kind of stuff your pitcher has. You work with what a pitcher has that particular day. The catcher must emphasize what a pitcher can do and deemphasize what he can't do. He must keep a pitcher aware of his own limitations, yet at the same time give him enough confidence to throw in a crucial situation a pitch that he himself may underrate. The catcher must be honest with his pitcher.

If a pitcher has four effective pitches, he won't necessarily throw them all early in the game. The catcher may want to use the early innings to bring one or two pitches around and will keep the rest in reserve in case the other stuff never jells or becomes less effective in later innings. It usually doesn't take long for a catcher to determine a pitcher's strength in a game, especially on those pitches he throws from the outset. You can warm up some guys before the first inning and know if they've got a live arm, and after the first inning you will have a pretty good idea about what kind of stuff they've got. This is usually the way it is with wiry guys, but with some pitchers with muscular builds it will take longer. Randy Johnson, at 6'10", probably hits the ground running.

If a guy doesn't start off with real good stuff, often the catcher can't take him deep enough into the game so his stuff can come around. (That's where you get the old saying "He just doesn't have it today.") But that's not to say your pitcher isn't going to get stronger as the game goes along.

(That's where you get another old saying, "You gotta get him early.") Some starters who are pitching with an extra day off because of a rain-out may have trouble finding their rhythm early in the game. Others, like Curt Schilling and Tom Glavine, who have been known to get hit early on, may be confident enough to stroll into a game rather than treating it as if it were World War III. It may take them seven or eight minutes more than the usual fifteen-minute warm-up time to get loose. As a catcher, you know the pitcher's history and just try to ride out the part of the game when some of his best pitches aren't doing much.

A fan may wonder why a catcher keeps calling for a pitch that the pitcher can't control or is being hit hard. The reason is that most pitchers don't have a whole array of pitches to switch to. Four-pitch pitchers like David Cone are rare. So if a key pitch in a pitcher's arsenal isn't working early, you can't give up on it entirely. Instead, you should try to work it in at times it won't hurt him and hope it will start working. A curveball is often slow to be effective. Early on, it may be sloppy, flat, without bite, out of the zone. It could take up to four innings to get this curve working, especially if men get on base and the pitcher has to go to the stretch instead of the windup or if he has trouble loosening up because of cold weather or lower back problems. But the curve will never work if the pitcher doesn't have the chance to throw it, so the catcher might call for it whenever less risky situations arise. The ideal time is with two outs and nobody on, even against marvelous off-speed hitters like Barry Bonds or, in my day, the Cubs' Billy Williams. The downside to showing a hitter his "strength pitch" is that he may pop one. You chance getting hit hard at certain times if it will help the overall game. My philosophy is: You try to bring around a curveball by throwing it at times the batter may be looking for it. By doing this you will get him to think, mistakenly, that you will throw it to him again later in a much more crucial situation.

A pitcher also can have a bad fastball early in the game. If a sinkerball pitcher is giving up a lot of fly balls, the catcher will come back to the sinker as an out pitch when the pitcher's arm is more tired and his ball will go down. If his fastball's velocity is low and there is little action, the catcher will look for ways that the pitcher can loosen his arm so he'll be able to air it out later. If the trouble is wildness, more radical methods may be needed to keep the pitcher in the game. Say a right-handed pitcher keeps throwing up and away to a left-handed batter although the catcher's mitt is in the middle of the plate. Onetime Cardinals pitching coach Howie Pollet suggested that the catcher should move his mitt down and toward the batter and tell the pitcher to forget about velocity and arm angle and just throw to the target. The catcher might sit inside and have him throw the curve because the motion, which, remember, is like pulling down on a window blind, will force him to follow through and come all the way down.

If the pitcher can't get the ball over the plate no matter where the mitt is, the catcher should change his target from the small mitt to the four corners of his body: the knees and the shoulders. It's usually pointed out that Sandy Koufax became a great pitcher once catcher Norm Sherry convinced him he could get batters out just as easily by throwing ninety-five mph as one hundred mph, but I think the young Koufax's wildness was cured mostly because he relaxed once Sherry advised him, "Don't pick up my mitt, pick up my body." With a wider target, Koufax no longer tried to be a dart thrower, which, as Sherry knew, was impossible for someone who threw so hard. This works for a lot of pitchers.

Often it is difficult to get stubborn pitchers to throw pitches they have no confidence in. In 1971, Rick Wise would never throw his curve when he was behind in the count. Never. He was hardheaded. I said, "Rick, you don't realize how good your curveball is." "No," he argued. "I was taught not to get beat on anything other than my fastball." I countered, "That's a fine philosophy at a certain point in the game, but if you employ it on every pitch, you're saying that all 120 of your pitches can cost you the game. That's a hell of a burden to carry to the mound. Think about that." Rick was an intelligent guy, but it was like pounding granite. One night in Pittsburgh, I said, "The Pirate batters are used to seeing you throw fastball after fastball. Regardless of how good the fastball is, major-league hitters will catch up to it if they know it's coming. I guarantee that if you throw the breaking ball, even to breaking-ball hitters, on a 2-0 count, the quality of your breaking ball doesn't have to be that good to fool them." So we get to a 2-0 count on Willie Stargell, who can handle breaking balls. I signal Rick to throw the curve. He does, and Stargell hits it so hard and so deep, way into the shadows. Rick was so livid at my pitch selection that he would have choked me if it were legal. I said, "Remember, we talked about how there will be bad results sometimes. It doesn't work all the time, but you have to have faith in your stuff." We had argument after argument, and finally Rick came around. He realized that he was putting together an excellent season (he won seventeen games) and it got to the point where all he wanted to do was throw the curveball. I said, "Wait a minute. Wipe that thought out." Rick thinks that was a pivotal point in his long career. As a matter of fact, that season, in what was one of baseball's greatest feats, Rick pitched a no-hitter and belted two two-run homers in a

5–0 victory over Cincinnati. After the season, he was traded straight up for Steve Carlton. He would continue to throw the curve with success.

Sometimes a pitcher is getting hit hard because he's throwing his setup pitch as his major pitch and not enough of his best pitch, the one that is supposed to be set up. Such was the case with Steve Carlton. When I came back to the Phillies in 1975, Lefty had gone through two subpar years. At a meeting where we discussed Steve's situation with Phillies owner Ruly Carpenter, manager Danny Ozark and catchers Bob Boone and Johnny Oates all said, "Steve's just not throwing the fastball well." It was my turn, and I was in a weak position because I was the third-string catcher. But I said, "I have had a chance to play against him, and his problem is not his fastball but that he's not throwing his slider." Actually, I had told Carlton the same thing after he'd been knocked out of the box when the Phillies came to play us in St. Louis. I hesitate to admit that we had met under the stands so we wouldn't be accused of fraternizing. His confidence was shattered, and he asked me why he wasn't having the same success he'd had pitching in St. Louis from 1965 through 1969 and in Philadelphia at the beginning of his remarkable twenty-seven-win season in 1972. I said,

No one knows pitchers better than their catchers. Curt Flood and I were really close friends, but I got really upset with him once in 1966. Larry Jaster had pitched for the Cards against the Braves and gave up five or six runs in six innings and we had lost the game. Afterward, Curt and I were shaving and Curt said to me, "You know, one fastball after another . . ." I turned beet red. First of all I hate when people talk to me when I'm shaving because when I talk I cut myself, and, second of all, he was really second-guessing how I called the game. I had called for curveballs but not enough to suit Curt. I asked, "Have you ever seen the rotation on Jaster's breaking ball? The only thing you can do with his breaking ball is to try to work it in as much as you can during a game without his getting hurt. He's a one-pitch pitcher." Curt said, "I know that, but how are you ever going to find out if the curveball works if you don't call for it?" I said, "Curt, you're so far out of line." That was the only time Curt and I ever raised our voices to each other, and by the time we finished talking I'd cut myself in about thirteen places and was bleeding everywhere.

"Steve, you can listen to the people who say you aren't throwing the good fastball, but your fastball is as good as it has ever been. Which means you have good control over it, but it is too light and feathery to try to use it to overpower guys. On the other hand, your slider sinks and slides—it has movement that other pitchers' sliders don't have. That's the pitch that gives you an advantage over batters. That's the pitch you should be throwing." When I became Carlton's catcher on Philadelphia, I had him throw sliders and more sliders. And I had him use his fastball, which could be caught with those cellophane gloves workers use in trendy food emporiums, to set up the slider. His slider returned him to greatness.

If a pitcher is getting hit on a particular pitch, an announcer might say: "The pitching coach will make a note that he doesn't have that pitch today." Nonsense. The catcher is the guy. The pitching coach may say he has a bad fastball, but he has nothing to do with whether it will be called for. The catcher knows the pitcher, he knows his arsenal, he knows what is working and not working that day. Catchers are experts on the results of pitches, far more than the manager or pitching coach in the dugout. They can tell location but not what kind of action was on that pitch. Late action is vital. And the catcher is right there. He called the pitch, and he knows his pitcher.

Sometimes the problem isn't that the pitcher's good stuff isn't working well, but that it is working too well. When Mike Torrez was a young Cardinals pitcher, he was tougher to catch than Bob Gibson. I caught his first outing in 1969, and the Cubs were laughing at me. I was struck on the inside of the wrist on one pitch without the ball even touching the mitt. That's how much his ball was moving. It was heavy and exploding. It's frightening not to be able to catch the ball firmly because you have to keep calling for the same pitch because it's so effective. When a ball moves that much, you get the pitcher to throw it down the middle of the plate. If you can't catch it, the batter won't be able to put the good part of the bat on the ball. You just hope beyond hope that the batter will put the ball in play.

As a game progresses, a catcher can tell if a pitcher is losing his stuff. There are indicators that will tell him—as well as fans watching television—that the pitcher is getting tired. For instance, batters are hitting the ball hard, or are right on a power pitcher but are, for now, fouling fastballs straight back. It's common for baseball people to assume that a pitcher is tired just because his ball is up. This isn't a good indicator that the pitcher is tired except, perhaps, on breaking balls. When a power pitcher is strong, he throws high fastballs by guys; when a sinkerballer is too strong, he's up. If a guy is way up, it may be an indication that his legs are tired, but not necessarily his arm. Tired legs will result in the breaking ball being up.

A pitcher usually throws 110 to 130 pitches in a complete game. If he has thrown that many by the seventh inning, he may not be able to throw much longer. Or he may. Pitch count is a nebulous thing. It's always driven me wacky. Pitchers will tell you that there are times when they feel stronger than others. It's preposterous to think you can always gauge a pitcher's effectiveness from the pitch count. But some people hang their coats up on it. Coach Ray Rippelmeyer would say, "The hitters will tell you when they're through." You don't need a pitch count. It's overrated. If a pitcher has thrown eighty-seven pitches in just four innings, that's not necessarily bad. The game plan doesn't necessarily change. It depends on the pitcher. Roger Clemens and John Smoltz can throw forever. If you turn on your television, you couldn't tell if you were watching them in the first inning or ninth inning. The catcher won't have the pitcher economize to save his arm. He can rest in November.

What about your ace pitcher coming back after only three days' rest? Then should you monitor his pitch count? There's no reason he can't come back strong on three days' rest in a crucial series or in the postseason and pitch a complete game. I don't understand the controversy. Until twenty years ago every team had a four-man rotation and pitchers had long, productive, injury-free careers with three-day rests. And remember how Lew Burdette, Bob Gibson, and Mickey Lolich won three times in a seven-game World Series? Nobody babied their arms. Steve Carlton made start after start with three days' rest. His arm didn't tire: He struck out sixteen Cubs in 1982 using exactly the same stuff he used to strike out nineteen Mets in 1969. His durability matched his consistency. When I caught him, I never bothered counting his pitches.

You can combine the catcher's knowledge of the hitting game with the pitcher's knowledge of the pitching game and get a pretty good idea on how to confront a hitter. Unless he is a Mike Piazza, Todd Hundley, Sandy Alomar, or Ivan Rodriguez, the catcher shouldn't take his offense nearly as seriously as his handling of the pitcher or his own mechanics behind the plate. However, since he takes four turns at bat each game, he should introduce the pitcher to the offensive part of the game that he may not be familiar with, especially in the American League.

That's not to say that a catcher should rely solely on what he himself can't handle as a batter. If a catcher can't hit sliders, for instance, that doesn't mean he should call for many sliders from a pitcher who has a mediocre slider. Gary Carter and Johnny Bench were very predictable catchers in their early years. They would call for too many fastballs when they were behind in the count. Until later in their careers, they didn't apply their knowledge as extraordinary hitters to how they called the game. I was fortunate that in the Cardinals' system, Eddie Stanky and George Kissell taught catchers the importance of being unpredictable.

Today, the young pitcher's trait is to throw a fastball on the first pitch and then throw too many breaking balls. Particularly in the American League, pitchers are reluctant to throw fastballs, especially when they are behind in the count. Like batters who don't realize how fast their hands are, young pitchers often don't realize how fast their fastballs are. They fall in love with the breaking ball and won't challenge hitters, the assumption being that every hitter can hit the fastball and nobody can hit the breaking ball. That's ridiculous. They don't understand that everything should go off the fastball. It's the easiest pitch to locate, the best for power. Establishing that they will throw the fastball on any count should be a primary objective for most pitchers.

A catcher will tell his pitcher such things, but not in the dugout during the game. Almost everything that has to be said is said before the game. In fact, you probably won't see a catcher sitting with his pitcher between innings. I didn't. In the dugout, the catcher becomes one of the hitters. Anyway, it's hard to approach the pitcher on the day he's pitching. Pitchers are usually the loneliest of characters. Nobody wants to talk to them, and they don't want to talk to anybody. It's also not a good idea to hang out with a starting pitcher during the week because you're playing on days he's off and he may be upset about the last game or preoccupied with his next start. You have your own job to concentrate on. Most pitchers by their very nature are eccentric. They are individualists. If you take a pitcher out of his milieu, which is pitching, he is bored with the game. The only pitchers I have ever seen who were really into a game between their starts and legitimately rooted for their teammates are Jim Lonborg, Boston's Cy Young winner in 1967, Jim Kaat, and Orel Hershiser.

Managers who were catchers like Joe Torre, Gene Lamont, Jim Leyland, and Bruce Bochy understand more than anybody why a catcher should call his own game. Torre went out and got Joe Girardi to be the Yankees' catcher in 1996 because he knew how much his pitchers would respect the way Girardi called a game with intelligence and great instincts. Their catchers are blessed because they won't be second-guessed by a former catcher who hated being second-guessed by a manager who had been a position player. They train catchers to think for themselves without feeling paranoid. It takes a lot of courage for a manager to give a young catcher-pitcher tandem freedom to make mistakes because during their learning period, he might lose his job. The next manager is the one who benefits.

The learning process for pitchers and catchers is painful. They can't learn from observing; they must get their brains beaten out and their fingers burned. Which reminds me of my beer story, which took place in Homestead, Florida, during spring training of the AAA Miami Marlins (who would temporarily become the Puerto Rico Marlins). Willard Schmidt and Bob Tiefenauer, who were an ancient thirty, younger pitchers Bob Sadowski, Frank Funk, and Bobby Duliba, and one young catcher, *moi,* bought a case of beer. We were sitting around sipping it out of cans when Schmidt said that his beer tasted weird, in an awful way. So we all had to try it. Why would anyone be so stupid or curious to taste something that someone else gagged on? No woman would do that. But we young men all insisted on tasting it, one after another. None of us expected to like the beer—in fact, we wanted to find out just how bad it was. When we sliced open the can and found that a dead mouse was responsible for the ghastly taste, we thought about suing. But we probably deserved it. A fact of life and baseball: Left to their own devices, young men—and in this instance a group of young battery mates who would be allowed to call their own games—will do exactly what other men do before them, even if a bad outcome is guaranteed. The moral for managers to consider: Young pitchers and catchers will learn only from their own mistakes.

10

WORKING A LINEUP

As you watch a game, it's very important to understand that the pitcher and catcher aren't simply trying to retire one batter at a time, but are continually "manipulating" the opposing lineup so that the best hitters will come to the plate as few times as possible and when they can do the least damage. When they are "working a lineup," they are executing a constantly changing game plan that puts emphasis on keeping leadoff hitters off base each inning, splintering sluggers who bat back-to-back, and vigorously going after the eighth-place hitter with two outs so that the pitcher or, in the American League, the weak-hitting ninth batter, will lead off the next inning instead of the first batter in the lineup.

When you work a lineup, there are no insignificant batters and no insignificant at-bats. Pay attention when a seventh-place hitter bats with nobody on and two outs in the second or fifth. Keep in mind that if the pitcher allows him to get on base it will mean that one more batter in the lineup—perhaps an extremely productive cleanup man—will get an extra at-bat late in the game. It's understandable that most fans pay strict attention only when there is action, but you should take into account that what seems to be an innocuous moment in an early inning can have major impact on the outcome of the game.

When attacking a lineup, you think: first hitter, first pitch, first out. No matter who leads off an inning, you try to "get the leading lady," as former pitching coach Joe Becker would remind his pitchers before they took the mound. Pitchers are aware of one stat that has real meaning: Over 50 percent of the leadoff men who reach base eventually score. And it's perhaps substantially more than that if that batter has walked. So get the first batter out every inning, especially when it's the other team's leadoff hitter because he's the guy who can create havoc on the basepaths, disrupt a pitcher, and ignite a big rally. The best way to limit the leadoff batter's offensive arsenal is to keep him from leading off after the first inning. You particularly don't want him leading off in later innings, which is a major reason you bear down on the eighth-place hitter with two outs. It makes sense to force leadoff hitters to be the RBI men and RBI men to be leadoff hitters.

Most managers like to have two terrific power hitters batting back-to-back, usually in the third and fourth spots in the order. There have been such frightening tandems as Babe Ruth and Lou Gehrig, Mickey Mantle and Yogi Berra, Roger Maris and Mantle in 1961, Hank Aaron and Eddie Mathews, Barry Bonds and Matt Williams, Jose Canseco and Mark McGwire in the late eighties, and, today, Ken Griffey, Jr., and Edgar Martinez. If a pitcher must face two standout hitters who bat consecutively, he will try to split them apart. The ideal situation would be to have the first batter make the final out in one inning so the second batter will lead off the next inning when no one is on base. Of course, some teams like the Baltimore Orioles, Seattle Mariners, Colorado Rockies, and New York

When Jim Riggleman first became a major-league manager with the San Diego Padres, he was at the winter meetings when he was called over by Sparky Anderson, whom he had revered for a long time. He was excited because he thought Sparky wanted to talk to him at great length about the psychology involved when a manager deals with players. But all Sparky said was "Jim, always walk the eighth-place hitter. Always." And that was it. He left Jim standing there. What Sparky meant was with a man on second and the pitcher on deck you should always walk the eighth-place hitter. Jim said, "Well, Sparky Anderson said that, so . . ." But he thought it over and said, "I don't agree with that. But I can't tell Sparky that." He still doesn't agree with that. Neither do I. It all boils down to: There is no *always* in baseball.

Yankees have several big guys. What can you do? The best you can. You can only try to limit the at-bats of dangerous hitters by getting out the other guys. Again: It is essential to get out the weaker hitters early so the big guns won't have opportunities to hurt you later.

Sandy Koufax, who could *really* work a lineup, understood how getting out a batter in one part of the game makes things easier for the pitcher later on. So it's not surprising that he was fanatical about chewing up the eighth-place hitter with two men out. Bob Gibson also would try to knock the bat out of the eighth-place hitter's hands. This meant that the weaker-hitting opposing pitcher would lead off the next inning and when the lead-off batter did come up there would likely be one man out already. I doubt if the great Koufax of the 1960s ever walked the eighth-place hitter with men in scoring position and first base open if there were two outs. He was the first guy who said, "He's hitting eighth for a reason."

But let me say that if men are on second and third in a pivotal situation and the eighth-place hitter is not your typical eighth-place hitter but someone productive like Jeff Blauser, then you might put him on and face a poor-hitting pitcher if it can get you out of the inning. It's often the manager's decision to do this.

As you work a lineup, you will come up against certain batters and say that it is essential to get them out. This is almost always the case with the opposing pitcher. His getting a hit, either with men on base or leading off an inning, throws the pitcher's game plan off kilter. So rather than taking for granted that the opposing pitcher will make an out, the pitcher will really bear down against him. What do you throw to a pitcher? Some baseball pundits say you should always throw curveballs and just leave it at that. It doesn't even matter if the pitcher on the mound has a curveball. Obviously, a pitcher at the plate has much more trouble adjusting to a major-league breaking ball than does an everyday player, but that doesn't mean you can throw him one curveball after another. The point is this: You mix your pitches less and challenge more.

If your pitcher the previous day had success against the opposing lineup, you don't necessarily attack it the same way. Two different starting pitchers are going to pitch one team's lineup differently. Especially a left-hander and a right-hander: Sandy Koufax and Don Drysdale, Chris Short and Jim Bunning, Curt Simmons and Robin Roberts, Andy Pettitte and David Cone. So the first time through the lineup, the catcher begins to find out what kind of stuff his pitcher has that day. The greatest gauge on a pitcher's effectiveness on any pitch, be it a fastball, slider, change, curve, anything, is the hitter's reaction. As the catcher watches, he is thinking: "We'll see what develops. Things change, and we've got to be able to adapt. We've got to be innovative, resourceful, and imaginative, but at the same time lay a foundation."

Going through the lineup the first time, Randy Johnson will probably let his fastball rip seven of nine times, but if you're Randy Anybody Else, you've got to mix it up. While establishing his own rhythm, the pitcher will try to show that he can throw any pitch at any time. He is trying to impress this fact upon not only the batter but also the guys who are coming up later. The only pitch I don't think is smart to throw the first time you face a batter is the change-up because you aren't changing from anything. However, the second time you face the batter a change can be an effective first pitch. For example, if in his first at-bat you throw him four fastballs and a slider—five hard pitches—you will face him with five pitches in your bank that you're changing from. The hitter may be thinking he has to turn it up a notch based on the first at-bat and, whoa, he is out in front of the change-up.

From the outset, the pitcher should follow the simple credo of Ray Miller, the Baltimore Orioles' manager and former pitching coach: Work quickly, throw strikes, change speeds. Add to this: Mix breaking balls with fastballs and throw to both sides of the plate, going out and in, out and in. You will see sinker-slider pitchers doing this. A successful starter gets ahead in the count, doesn't walk anybody, and scatters hits. Total base runners per nine innings is a relatively important stat for a pitcher; if he limits the other team to an average of about one and a half base runners per inning, he's doing very well. (Of course, he could give up five solo homers and still not have any base runners.)

Working quickly shouldn't be underestimated. By doing so, the pitcher shows the other team (and his own manager) that he is confident, determines the pace of the game, and keeps the defense on its toes. The faster he works, the more alert his fielders will be to make plays. He doesn't want to be slow because his infielders will lose their concentration and get back on their heels. I think of amusing images of ten-year-olds when their pitcher is taking forever and they're looking up in the sky with gloves under their chins or on top of their heads. There are few successful starting pitchers today who don't pitch fast. Greg Maddux is the prime example of a fast worker. His games usually last just over two hours. Maddux is the type of guy who would have told Lincoln to hurry up his Gettysburg Address or told Chopin to shorten his "Minute Waltz."

* * *

No matter how well you work a lineup, there probably will be at least one time the other team's biggest threat comes to the plate with runners in scoring position. If first base is open, what do you do? It depends on the inning. In the early innings, you're not inclined to put the guy on, especially by walking him intentionally or by pitching around him. Pitching around a batter implies that you throw fastballs off the outside part of the plate—out of the batter's hitting zone but *not* in the dirt where the ball can get away from the catcher. (The thinking, in later innings, is that if the pitcher makes a mistake away, the batter may only single, but if he makes a mistake inside, it's a long ball.)

The likely result of pitching around a batter will be a walk, and walks lead to big innings. If you allow a big inning early, you may be knocked out of the game before it really starts. But if a Mark McGwire or Ken Griffey, Jr., is on a homer binge and his team's pitcher doesn't give up many runs, you might want to walk him even if it's early in the game. Also, if you have a sinkerballer on the mound, walking a batter may be a sensible option even if a power hitter is on deck, because the stat sheet may say that the power hitter grounds into a lot of double plays. The thing to remember about early innings is that the more base runners you allow, the bigger chance there is for a big inning that will knock out the pitcher and put the game out of reach. So you try not to allow anybody to get on who doesn't earn it with his bat. You challenge more. Unfortunately, you'll see a lot of pitchers pitching around batters early in the game. A pitcher will come to the majors and instead of being told to challenge batters, particularly early on, he'll be brainwashed: "First base is open, don't give this guy anything good to hit." If you don't give a guy anything good to hit, you will give the other team another base runner and a better chance to have a big inning against you.

I blame our business for both pitchers and fans thinking it's the smart thing to pitch around batters in early innings. For instance, early last season a team had men on second and third with one out in the first inning and the cleanup man at the plate. The play-by-play guy says, "You know first base is open, so the pitcher isn't going to want to give him anything good to hit." HOW MANY TIMES HAVE YOU HEARD THAT! I'm going, "What? It's the first inning!" It's fashionable among baseball people: Regardless of the inning, if first base is open, walk him. That's nonsense.

Now in the middle innings, you will be a little more cautious about pitching to dangerous hitters with men in scoring position. You will be

more likely to pitch around them. If it's late innings, it's a totally different deal. You don't want the other team's best hitter to beat you, so if
runners are in scoring position and first base is open you will be inclined
to pitch around him or intentionally walk him even if he represents the
go-ahead run.

Baseball tradition says never intentionally walk the potential winning
run, but I don't agree. I would never do it with nobody on base, but there
are other times when it seems like smart strategy. It depends on the situation, the batter, the pitcher, and often the man on deck. For instance, if
you are ahead by two runs and there is a low-ball pitcher facing a devastating low-ball hitter like Todd Hundley, he should walk him with the
tying runs on second and third and two men out in a late inning. You intentionally put the go-ahead run on base to pitch to the less effective low-
ball hitter. You're taking a chance on losing by walking a better first hitter
and pitching to the on-deck batter with the bases loaded, but you should
do it if you think the risk would be even greater if you let the first batter
hit with only the tying runs on base.

* * *

The first time through the lineup you have a pretty good idea how to work
a team. But like a football offense that throws two interceptions during its
first fifteen plays, a catcher and pitcher might deviate from the script when
things go differently than expected. You may run into problems—say Jay
Buhner is up with the bases loaded and one out in the first inning—and you
are going to have to pitch to a batter like you had planned on pitching him
his third time up. You may have intended to work him in and out and
throw him different-speed pitches his first two times up, but you no longer
have that luxury. If he's vulnerable inside, now is the time to exploit that
weakness rather than waiting for a crucial time later in the game. You go
right to his weakness and keep pounding it.

There are a few times when a pitcher so dominates a particular batter
that he can just pound him inside or away every at-bat, game after game,
and the batter won't ever figure out how to hit him. But most big-league
hitters aren't so vulnerable. Most think and learn. That's why a starter
should refrain from going to a hitter's weakness the first two times he faces
him. Nor should he reveal his own strength the first couple of times
through the order. A catcher knows the strengths and weaknesses of both
the pitcher and the batter and might be tempted to repeatedly go with the
pitcher's best against the batter's worst. But he realizes that this would sab-

otage one of the principal things he is trying to accomplish as he and his pitcher work a lineup, which is to keep a batter's weaknesses weak and a pitcher's strengths strong until later in the game.

Everybody says, "All you have to do is throw the breaking ball, or keep it down, or pound the guy inside," but if that's all you do, batters will look for it and adjust to it, and it will become less effective. If the guy's an off-speed hitter, you can't throw him all fastballs. That's courting disaster. The guy will become a good fastball hitter, too. More accurately, he'll become a good hitter against *your* fastball. You will see that the more familiar the batter becomes with a pitcher's best pitch, the more adept he will become at hitting it. For a good analogy, think of how a virus will build up resistance to even the strongest medicine if the treatments are too frequent. So the first couple of at-bats, the catcher doesn't want to establish a pattern for when he will have his pitcher go with his strength. The pattern is *no pattern*. No comment is a comment.

Remember, to keep a batter's weaknesses weak early in the game, the pitcher might have to funnel pitches into the batter's strength. You can throw any pitch to any hitter, and that means sometimes you have to go into his strength. You may look for a noncritical situation and then throw the fastball hitter a fastball or a notorious off-speed hitter an off-speed pitch. If you're hit hard it's at a time when the least damage can be done. What the catcher and pitcher want is for the batter to think they know little about his strengths and weaknesses and may naively throw him his favorite pitch for a second time in a crucial situation later in the game. In fact, they have no intention of doing so. They are just reserving the pitcher's strength for a key situation late in the game. Longtime baseball fans remember how with a big lead, Hall of Famer Robin Roberts didn't mind risking a solo homer on a straight fastball down the middle, but if the score was close the same hitter would get Roberts's lethal fastball with some pop on it, and instead of it being on the fat part of the plate, it would graze the corner.

Unless the pitcher has superior stuff and is unhittable for nine innings, no matter what he throws, there is usually a difference in how a pitcher goes through the lineup the third time. You are coming closer to the end of the game, and by this time the catcher is using the pitcher's strengths and going at a batter's weaknesses, having kept them weak throughout the game. He has a vulture mentality and is going for the jugular. He wants no pitch held back. If he goes through a lineup for the fourth time, it is often the most difficult. By now, batters pretty much know his approach against them, which is why starters are often removed after going through a lineup three times.

But a pinch hitter will know how he's working only through observation. If the manager chooses to leave the starter in with the bases loaded and someone as good as John Vander Wal or Keith Lockhart pinch-hits, the catcher will go right to the pitcher's strengths and at the batter's weaknesses. He will face him only once, so his thinking is pretty much: "Here it is—hit it." The catcher is aware if the pinch hitter has gone five for his last seven, but asks, "Who did he get those hits off?" A pinch hitter's recent stats are less important to the catcher than whether he's the type who will come up swinging, like a Manny Mota. Because then your first pitch should be the one you would otherwise reserve for the 0-2 or 1-2 count since getting that deep in the count is unlikely. You may retire a very aggressive pinch hitter with a ball just out of the strike zone.

I don't want to contribute to the prevalent misconception that a hitter's weakness is the most important thing you consider when working against him. It enters your thinking if a batter has trouble with a particular pitch or struggles in a certain zone, but what the catcher focuses on far more are the pitcher's strengths. The pitcher's strengths—his arsenal of pitches and deception—are always the most important factors when facing any hitter. This makes sense, especially since a few guys like Tony Gwynn and Edgar Martinez have no discernible weaknesses. Occasionally a batter will do well against the pitcher's best pitch, particularly if he's expecting it, but more often he won't hit it with the sweet part of the bat. If a major-league pitcher makes his pitch—at the best time in the count, with the proper movement, and to the intended location—he has a decided advantage over any hitter. That's a point a catcher will try to impress upon his pitcher if they run into problems while working a lineup.

PITCHERS VERSUS BATTERS

When you see a pitcher and batter face each other for the first time, as often happens in All-Star Games, interleague play, and the World Series, you should know that the pitcher has the edge. In addition to the natural advantage pitchers have over batters anyway, he profits from the unpredictability that comes with unfamiliarity. It's more important for a pitcher to be unpredictable than a hitter; in fact, you only use the word "unpredictable" in regard to pitchers.

When a batter comes up for the first time in a game, the catcher and pitcher pay almost no attention to scouting reports unless they've never faced him before. Even then, they rely more on what they see than on what they read. For instance, if they see a batter standing on top of the plate, it probably means he likes the ball inside. And most batters who stand far away from the plate like the ball away from them. Batters like Paul O'Neill stand far from the plate, luring pitchers into throwing away. Bob Gibson often argued, "The guy away from the plate can't hit that outside pitch." I'd counter, "Bob, if he can't handle the pitch away he wouldn't have reached the majors."

Every pitcher is his own scout on how to go against every batter because the generic scouting report on how to pitch that batter may work for other pitchers but not for him. Right-hander Greg Maddux pitches the same batter totally differently from the way his left-handed staff mate

Tommy Glavine does. So if he gets a scouting report on how to pitch a batter, he has to whittle it down until it applies only to how he would pitch him, not how Glavine or anyone else would pitch him.

The only worthwhile thing a scout can say about a batter you have seen before is that there has been a significant change in his skills since the teams last met. But even if the report says, for instance, that the batter now drives the inside pitch that used to knock the bat out of his hands, it doesn't mean that the catcher will no longer call for inside pitches, only that he might want to choose his spots a little better. Otherwise, he forgets about reports and relies on his knowledge of the batter's style and prowess through past experiences. I never took notes about batters' weaknesses. But I always remembered. That's part of the job. Players who keep notebooks are considered smart, but I think it's the opposite. You can't refer to a notebook before you put down a finger. Everybody should know.

Just as Mets-game director Jeff Mitchell uses close-ups of batters in crucial situations to try to get into their minds through their emotions, a catcher will try to determine the batter's mind-set with a quick study of his feet, hands, eyes, and singular body language. Catchers will look at a batter's feet as he moves up or moves back. That's because—and this may sound strange—they can sometimes hear the brain working by the position of the feet, just as we can see into Greg Maddux's mind by watching his fingers explore the ball before a pitch. The body is a conduit from the mind to the feet, and the feet will tell the hands what to do in some instances. Some hitters don't even realize that they're moving up on the plate or moving back.

Scouts can't see what a catcher can see, and they can't see what he can feel. There's such an instinctive feel behind the plate. You're two feet away from the batter and you can see his eyes and his muscles twitching. A catcher has a very, very subjective view of the batter that gives him insight into what he is feeling and what pitch he is looking for. He searches for

It's funny some of the things that stick in your mind. Catching behind Willie Mays when I was very young (twenty-one), I noticed two things. One was the size of his fingers—you could see their strength. And I couldn't get over the fact that he had manicured fingernails. I was from Memphis and I had never seen manicured nails before. In fact, they were buffed.

fear in the eyes or tension in the hands or confusion, and if it is there instead of confidence he will try to take advantage of it. But I'll again stress that it's more important to know the pitcher's strengths on a particular day than to recognize vulnerability in a hitter.

* * *

If the pitcher is throwing really well, a catcher might put down any finger and not think about what had happened in earlier matchups. In most instances, however, what happened when the batter came up for the first time becomes a major factor in how you pitch the batter his second time up. And naturally, the first two times up become a major factor in how you pitch the batter the third time. Starters have to be flexible enough to adjust after having faced a batter in the recent past, and the most recent past is the batter's last time up.

The catcher should remember everything through the course of a game. As soon as the batter comes to the plate, he flashes back to the pitch sequences from his earlier at-bats. The graphic may say that the hitter is 0 for 2, and the announcer may remind you that he popped one up and struck out, but the catcher also remembers that he fouled off five balls before being called out on strikes. Moreover, he'll remember how they were fouled off. If a dangerous batter was right on several pitches but just missed them, the smart catcher will call for something different before coming back to how the pitcher got him out earlier. Catchers don't want to use the identical sequence on the same hitter two or three times in a row. If the pitcher diverges by even one pitch from the pitch sequence of the first two at-bats, then his risk of being hit hard is lessened.

Good hitters think with the catcher more than the pitcher, so the pressure is mostly on the catcher to not get into a pattern against a particular batter. Not long before he retired, Ron Santo, who was a terrific, hard-hitting third baseman for the Cubs, told me, "Goddammit, I've always had the toughest time figuring out what you are going to call. You're not the same, even with the same guy!" That was one of the supreme compliments. And it confirms that a catcher should vary his calls because batters are just waiting for the pitcher to become predictable.

It's rare that a pitcher records more than a handful of first-pitch outs during the course of a game, so it is usually a combination of several pitches, the patterns or sequences, that disposes of batters. The catcher and pitcher know how they want to approach a particular batter, using one or two pitches to set up another pitch, but it's vital that the pitcher concentrate only on the pitch that he's throwing or batters will take liberties. A sequence should develop one pitch at a time, with the catcher and pitcher factoring in the pitches that have been thrown earlier in the count before deciding on the next pitch.

First they *establish* that the pitcher will use a particular pitch to get a batter out by throwing that pitch more than once. When the batter then moves in the box so that he can better hit that pitch, it is, temporarily, no longer an out pitch. To *reestablish* it as an effective pitch, the pitcher must now throw another type of pitch that will keep the batter from keying on the first pitch for the rest of the count.

For example, if you throw two fastballs away to begin the count, you establish that you think you can get the batter out with balls on the outside corner. But the pitcher can't throw every pitch out there because a batter like Albert Belle will just lean over with the fat part of his bat and take that outside corner away from the pitcher. The outside corner is now the middle of the plate as far as Belle is concerned. To reestablish the outside part of the plate as his own, the smart pitcher will drive Belle back from the plate with one or two inside pitches. Belle will stop leaning. Bob Gibson

ODDITIES

There are frustrating times when the pitcher does his job, the hitter doesn't, yet the hitter is successful and the pitcher is not. Say the infield is in with men on second and third in a one-run game in the eighth inning. The pitcher wants the batter to hit the ball hard enough on the ground so that an infielder has a shot at the runner at the plate. However, if his pitch is so good that it jams the batter or fools him so much that he just tops the ball, there will be no shot at the runner.

A double-play situation is similar. A pitcher wants to entice the batter to hit the ball hard so that the infielders will have time to make the required throws to get two outs. Most other times, he doesn't want the batter to hit it sharply, so he is going against his instincts. Here, too, he doesn't necessarily want to break the bat with a ball on the fists or totally fool the batter because he might then dribble the ball toward third and then there will be time only to get one out at first base. The batter may even be safe on a weak grounder. It's another odd case where the pitcher can do a good job, the batter can fail, yet the batter will win the battle.

said, "The *outside* two inches are mine. If you're going to take it, you have to pay the price. The price you pay is you are going to get knocked on your ass by an inside pitch. If you think you can hang out there and take my bread and butter, you've got another think coming." Don Drysdale's thinking was similar.

Gibson also claimed the *inside* two inches of the plate. A pitcher can also establish inside. Say you want to get inside on a batter and jam him because he loves to extend his arms, as most batters do. (Low-ball hitters are the easiest to jam because they have slower bats.) You go inside twice, establishing the inside as where you believe you can get this batter out. If he adjusts to hit the inside pitch, making it ineffective to you as an out pitch, you then should go outside to tease him. By doing this you reestablish the inside part of the plate as your own. The batter will lean over the plate and look for a second outside pitch, especially if he is behind in the count, and then you come back inside. This in-and-out type of pitching is very effective.

The pitcher can establish a particular pitch, not just a pitch in a certain location. For instance, if he throws his fastball on the first two pitches, he could be establishing it as his out pitch. Unless both are balls. If he falls behind 2-0, his fastball will no longer be established as his out pitch because this is a count on which the batter will gear up for an expected fastball. However, if the pitcher then gets the count to 3-2 by throwing only breaking balls, his fastball will be reestablished because the batter is more inclined to look for breaking balls. It doesn't even matter if it's a slower-than-normal fastball because the batter now is understandably anticipating a slower pitch. The batter will move his body forward and you pop an eighty-nine mph fastball by him and it looks like it is going ninety-seven mph. Often pitchers who don't throw hard will get batters looking on two-strike fastballs if they are expecting slower pitches.

Here's another example. Two change-ups for strikes establish that pitch. Now, with the count 0-2 and the batter looking for another change-up, it's a great time to break the pattern with a "show-me" fastball outside the strike zone. That fastball may be off the plate, but it is dramatically faster than the change-up the batter could be expecting. It will get the batter's attention and influence him to look for a fastball on the 1-2 pitch. So the change-up has been reestablished as a good out pitch.

While a pitcher often throws an unhittable nonstrike for the express purpose of setting up the next pitch, at other times he will entice the batter with a pitch good enough to swing at. He is secure in knowing that if the batter doesn't put it into play—he either doesn't swing or fouls it off—that pitch will still serve to set up the next pitch, as the sequence continues.

A two-strike pitch over the inside corner to a leaning batter may be fouled off the handle and have no effect on the count, but it still fulfills the purpose of keeping a cautious batter from leaning outside, even if he thinks the next pitch may be out there.

* * *

Establishing and reestablishing pitches through a series of pitches is a sensible way to go after batters, but simpler, two- and three-pitch sequences often do the trick. When we show sequence replays after a batter has made an out, watch how one pitch sets up another pitch. A curveball on a 1-1 pitch slows the bat down; then a fastball thrown on 1-2 may cause the batter to be late on the swing. As I mentioned earlier, Greg Maddux usually follows a curve, which gets the batter to look for another slow pitch, with a hard slider so the batter is late with the swing. A ninety-two mph fastball can set up an eighty mph change-up; a change-up can make the next fastball seem like ninety-seven mph—follow a change with an inside fastball and the batter will feel very uncomfortable being crowded. As the White Sox's announcer in the seventies, the legendary Harry Caray would moan, "Here comes Jim Kaat—soft-throwing left-hander. When your change-up and fastball are the same speed, you're in trouble." (Kitty fooled everyone but himself by reviving his career and twice winning twenty games for the Sox throwing effective fastballs, noticeably slower change-ups, and other pitches for manager Chuck Tanner and pitching coach Johnny Sain. Harry became a huge Jim Kaat fan.)

Pitchers like Greg Maddux who like to economize on pitches and not go deep into counts usually try to go the shorter, two- or three-pitch route. (Maddux may use the last pitch from the batter's previous at-bat as the first pitch in a sequence with the batter in his present at-bat.) Again, if the batter doesn't swing at a pitch, at least he's being set up for a subsequent pitch (and he may be in the hole, 0-1). Common short sequences we will replay include:

- Slider or curve outside, same pitch outside—the batter leans outside—fastball inside.
- Change outside, curve outside—the batter waits for another slow pitch—gas. Most pitchers use off-speed pitches to set up fastballs rather than the reverse, but it's best to throw a change-up *after* something hard, so a pitcher shouldn't lead with it in the hitter's first at-bat.

- Fastball, fastball, slider. If a batter is looking for a fastball, he'll have a fastball swing and be fooled by the slightly slower, hard-breaking pitch that darts away. (However, if he can't catch up to the fastball it might not be a good idea to throw him the slower slider, unless it has tremendous downward action.)
- Slider inside, slider inside—batter backs up—go outside. (This applies only to pitchers against opposite-side batters.)
- Heater, heater, heater.

Three straight fastballs? Solly Hemus would tell Bob Gibson, "You can't throw three pitches in a row that are alike." Which is nonsense. It's a valid sequence. The most likely succession of similar pitches is three fastballs (moved in and out), but you can throw three consecutive curveballs, three screwballs, whatever—I wouldn't recommend three straight change-ups—as long as you make each pitch better than the previous one.

One common way hard throwers make their similar fastballs a bit different from one another is to "go up the ladder." Up the ladder is usually from the middle of the plate in, but the rungs of the ladder are more important than whether the pitch is inside or outside. You usually go middle, high, higher, not low, middle, and high because if you start at the knees rather than the waist, you may never get to the second rung. A sinkerball pitcher like Scott Erickson wouldn't go up the ladder because he wouldn't reach the top. You can go up the ladder against Todd Hundley and other low-ball hitters only if you throw hard enough. There aren't many pitchers who throw hard enough to do it.

To finish off a sequence with two pitches, it could be that you pitch inside in order to get the batter out outside, a formula that is pretty basic to good pitching. Ideally, against any hitter, pitchers will go to the time-honored "Pitch him high-and-tight and low-and-away." That was an approach Brooklyn Dodgers ace Don Newcombe claimed "would give even God trouble," although Newk admitted Willie Mays was a different story. Inside first—outside second is definitely a sound method for getting out batters, but there are times when the inside pitch will be enough, particularly on a two-strike count. If you have the control of Greg Maddux or Kevin Brown, you can get a called third strike on the inside corner. In fact, there's no strikeout I like watching more than when a right-hander like Maddux throws a tailing fastball to a left-handed batter who, thinking the ball is inside, freezes and lifts his arms, only to have the ball tail back under them and across the plate. (Incidentally, if your arms go up on an *outside* pitch, you don't belong in the big leagues.)

* * *

Broadcasters will tell viewers: "Pitchers have to throw strikes to stay ahead in the count." It's more accurate that they have to stay ahead in the count by getting strikes. Indeed, sometimes a catcher can tell the pitcher he can get ahead on a batter by *not* throwing him a strike. If you can compel umpires to call strikes on pitches just off the plate, there is no need to throw pitches over the plate. Or, if you're facing a free-swinging batter who will chase balls, why throw strikes? If a slumping batter will swing at a pitch you roll to the plate, why help him out by bringing it up? When a pitcher sees on the stat sheet that a batter has three times as many strikeouts as walks, he realizes he won't have to throw the ball in the strike zone to get him out. Against an overly aggressive, unintelligent hitter, you don't need perfect pitch selection–just go with stuff. There's no use trying to out-think a nonthinking batter because all you will do is out-dumb each other.

An excellent theory on how to get batters out has been advanced by Jim Palmer: "If you get ahead in the count, you expand the strike zone." This means that a pitcher who is facing a batter with reasonable knowledge of the strike zone should use the fatter part of the plate to get ahead and the edge of the plate and off the edge to get him out. In other words: Get ahead by throwing strikes early in the count and get batters out by throwing balls late in the count. I would estimate that as many as 80 percent of swinging strikeouts are on balls–check the replays to see if that's true–so Palmer's formula makes sense. Batters with two strikes on them will swing at pitches that they mistake for strikes–the "illusion of a strike"– or think are too close to take. Johnny Sain contended that "pitching is the art of fooling the hitter," and in many instances he is right. John Franco, for one, makes a living by getting batters to chase a change-up that is not only off the corner but drops below the strike zone. Two other left-handers, Jimmy Key and Tom Glavine, also get batters to swing at outside pitches, but they have an advantage over Franco in that their pitches stay up and even if the batter doesn't bite they are often called strikes by those umpires with a wide strike zone.

Expanding the strike zone is not the same as *nibbling,* although in both cases the pitcher throws off the outside corner. You do the first as a strategy only after you are ahead in the count; you do the second throughout the count because you fear catching too much of the plate and challenging a batter. You nibble mostly with off-speed stuff, trying to entice swings from frustrated hitters who haven't been getting anything to hit over the plate. Larry Bowa used to yell at opposing pitchers, "Challenge somebody, you nibbling prick!" That's one of those lines you can't use on the air.

The nibblers are starters who aren't confident in their stuff, so they think they have to be too fine with every pitch. I think this approach is dead wrong. A pitcher's priority should be to get ahead and stay ahead so that he doesn't have to throw his hittable fastball at a time the batter expects it. If on a particular day the pitcher doesn't have the stuff to challenge hitters, then it's even more imperative that he not fall behind.

Too many young pitchers are taught to be nibblers. As soon as they hit the majors, they hear, "Watch the first pitch. Don't give this guy anything good to hit." They don't think they can throw the guy a strike. A pitcher will have a ball one–ball two mentality, and that leads to ball three and ball four. Then he says to himself, "Goddammit, I just walked the leadoff hitter. Now I've got to make sure not to walk the next guy, too." Therefore, instead of nibbling with the next batter, he'll go toward the middle of the plate and he'll be hit hard.

* * *

Steve Carlton used to say that pitching should be a sophisticated game of catch between the catcher and pitcher. He'd tell me, "Let's go play some pitch and catch," and he'd act as if the hitter didn't exist or was just a spectator who had wandered onto the field with his bat. (He was in the crossfire between the pitcher who stood on the mound—the only elevated, warlike position in sports—and the catcher behind the plate.) Carlton concentrated on business, put all bad things out of his mind, and was absolutely fearless. He put cotton balls in his ears to block out crowd noise. If you ignore the hitter and throw to the target, you are doing something fundamental to proper pitching: A pitcher must throw through to the catcher, not to the batter. Throw to the catcher and there will be late action in the hitting area. If you throw to the hitter, the action on the pitch will stop when it reaches the plate. That's really what a hanger is, a pitch in which the action has stopped. A hanger can be high, low, outside, inside—it can be a breaking ball, change-up, fastball, or anything else—and when it hovers over the plate the hitter will send it hard the other way. That's a danger that can be avoided if you eliminate the hitter from your thinking as Steve Carlton and Tom Seaver once did and Greg Maddux and Andy Pettitte do today. I remembered working with Carlton when I saw this New York *Daily News* headline after Maddux pitched an easy victory throwing to his frequent catcher Eduardo Perez: BRAVES' PEREZ PLAYS

CATCH WITH MADDUX. And Lefty would have appreciated what lefty Pettitte said after a recent victory of his own: "I was seeing the mitt, seeing the signal, and throwing the ball. I learned that if I see the mitt and not the batter then I can get guys out."

* * *

When I'm asked what will work in given situations to get batters out, I can only suggest what I think has the best odds of working, because you're talking about a myriad number of combinations of pitches with a myriad number of velocities and pitchers whose stuff varies from game to game. Pitchers are different from one another: Some pitchers get out batters with power, others with deception, and some have both power and deception in their arsenal, available on every count. And pitchers are not always themselves: Sometimes everything works and you can put down any sign and get a good result; in other games everything is smoked. You're dealing with different elements every time a pitcher takes the mound. As a catcher you're dealing with human beings.

ODDITIES

With the winning run on second and two outs in the bottom of the ninth, a young pitcher who is trying to impress his manager faces a young batter who is trying to impress his manager. The pitcher makes a great pitch, and the batter hits it weakly. But the ball falls in behind the shortstop and the winning run scores. Maybe the pitcher was the only one to make a good impression, but the only guy who is going to be congratulated is the batter.

Outfielder Bob Skinner, who ended his fine career with the Cardinals, would come over to me after a flare that drove in a big run and say, "That will keep the pitcher up all night." Talk about frustrating from a catcher's standpoint. The pitcher does exactly what he wants to do, and the overmatched batter still cues a dying quail somewhere. If the batter had hit the ball on the good part of the bat on that pitch, it might have been lined to an infielder or outfielder—and even if it dropped in front of the outfielder it would have gotten to him so quickly that the runner would have had to stop at third. It seems unfair. That's when your most profane utterance escapes.

So if things get overly complicated when trying to get out batters, often it's best for the catcher to just go back to the basics, to what works more often than not. Here are things to consider:

- Throwing the fastball is essential. A pitcher shouldn't worry if he doesn't have tremendous velocity because, as Greg Maddux and Tom Glavine confirm, a controlled fastball is still the best pitch in the game. It's the easiest pitch to control, and a pitcher can vary its location. There is usually deception when the pitcher throws a curve and change-up if a fastball was thrown previously because the batter needs to see a dramatic change in speeds to have his timing thrown off. Anything off the fastball is still the best way to go after a hitter.

- Getting dangerous hitters to foul off pitches just out of the strike zone is a shrewd way to get ahead in the count. For instance, an overeager Todd Hundley often falls behind fouling off hard stuff inside. When Mike Piazza is trying to do too much, he'll fall behind by swinging at balls in the dirt.

- Changing speeds and using deception are ways to get out a lot of batters who stand on top of the plate and limit where you can throw the ball. Pitchers can rarely overpower them because they have the quickness to handle the fastball inside, so they can't only throw fastballs.

- Challenging a dangerous hitter can be done in areas other than the fat part of the plate, sometimes just off the plate. As Bob Brenly says, if a guy's a good low-ball hitter, throw it lower than low; if he's a good high-ball hitter, throw it higher than high. If a pitcher doesn't want to give a batter anything good to hit, he will make him go out of the comfortable zone where the fat part of his bat hits the ball. Watch how most pitchers approach guys like Gary Sheffield, Barry Bonds, and Jeff Bagwell, players who have complained they get nothing good to hit. A batter won't have to make an adjustment for a high or low pitch, so pitchers would do better to work it outside to a point where the batter can't reach the ball. You've heard of the unreachable star. Well, that's the unreachable pitch.

- Going for a strikeout is the wise thing to do in a close game when there is a runner on third with less than two outs and a free swinger is at the plate. A strikeout pitch is definitely a useful tool, especially in situations where any ball that is hit could bring in a run. Still, even strikeout pitchers like David Cone and Roger Clemens eventually learn that it's smart to go for strikeouts only when needed and to use their fielders at other times. You may pick up strikeouts when you're trying to let opposing batters hit the ball. Randy Johnson says that when he struck out nineteen Oakland A's in 1997, he didn't try to fan anybody until the eighth inning.

- Keeping batters from pulling the ball in hitter-friendly parks is essential. While you must pitch inside, even in Coors Field and Fenway Park, you do it for effect, to keep the batter from leaning, not to throw strikes. In Yankee Stadium, Tiger Stadium, and other parks where there's a lot of room in center and right-center, it's best to stay away from power hitters. In Fenway, where the Green Monster looms in left only 315 feet from home plate, for a left-hander to be successful—Mel Parnell, Bill Lee, and Bob Ojeda are among the few who have been—throwing fastballs that run away from right-handed hitters is the correct formula. When the right-handed hitter sees a fastball coming toward the middle of the plate, he thinks of the wall and swings, not expecting the late tail. Instead of the ball hitting the fat part of the bat, it hits toward the end. There's a big difference.

- Throwing a fastball that tails is the best way for left-handed pitchers to get out left-handed batters. Left-handed batters must keep their front shoulders in for a moment longer against left-handed pitchers, so the tailing fastball on the hands is a way for the pitchers to exploit this.

- Establishing that you have more than one out-pitch makes things very difficult for batters—even if your two out-pitches are two fastballs in different locations. If batters are trained to look for the fastball and adjust to a curve, it's hard to adjust when you have more than one fastball to look for.

- Returning to a pitch that was hit hard isn't always the most comfortable proposition for a pitcher, but his catcher must convince him to do so. If you eliminate every pitch that is hit hard, you won't have anything left to throw. That makes no sense. It takes guts to come back with the same pitch after the batter hits it five hundred feet foul. But after Tino Martinez missed a homer on an inside pitch by only six inches in the 1997 All-Star Game, Greg Maddux came back with another inside pitch and it got him out. Also, in the first interleague game between the Mets and Yankees, Dave Mlicki had a pitch that was up in the zone swatted four hundred feet foul by Cecil Fielder for strike two and then froze Fielder for strike three by coming back with the same pitch. A hitter thinks that if he hits a pitcher hard he can eliminate that pitch from the pitcher's arsenal for at least one pitch. If he hits a fastball out of the park foul, he thinks that if he gets another fastball it will be in a different location. The credit goes to the smart catcher for calling for that repeat pitch and to the gutsy pitcher for throwing it. Because if that pitch is hit, many people will ask critically, "What were they thinking by throwing the same pitch he almost hit out of the park the first time?"

- Being predictable is acceptable if you have a big lead. The only sin is to walk batters. Bases on balls are worse than home runs because they are more likely to start a rally. Pay attention during a multirun inning and see if a walk isn't sandwiched in there somewhere. From a psychological standpoint—and this really holds true when he walks the first guy in an inning—a pitcher becomes mad at himself and upset. What that anger does is redirect him to the middle of the plate, and that's when he really gets burned. So the pitcher should throw strikes. Predictability overrides finesse. If you refuse to challenge when you have a big lead, then you're going to be lost in a close game.

In 1968, when Bob Gibson was going toward his historic 1.12 ERA, he refused to be predictable even when he had a big lead. He didn't want anybody to score at any time, regardless of the score. One game we had a five- or six-run lead in St. Louis in the seventh or eighth inning and somebody, perhaps Jim Ray Hart, had a leadoff triple. In such a situation, the catcher always reminds the pitcher to throw to first on a ball hit back to the box because the out is what matters, not the run. I reminded Bob, and he said, "Nope, I'm coming to you." I exclaimed, "That's insane! You can't do that!" He shot back, "Don't tell me I can't do that. I'm doing that, so just be ready." We started arguing. He still kids me about that. No ball was hit back to him, but the run didn't score. He got a strikeout and pop-up and the third out was made and the runner was stranded. That's how a pitcher throws thirteen shutouts in a season. Bob gave up thirty-seven earned runs in over three hundred innings. That was one of the most remarkable athletic feats of our time.

- Reverting to a good ole country hardball may be the simplest approach to pitching, and at times it's the best. Forget all the cerebral stuff because this is a time when the pitcher is just trying to blow it by the batter. It's the Dizzy Dean approach: "Here's my fastball and if you can hit it, baby, you're the better man—but I don't think you are."
- Coming inside is absolutely necessary to be successful.

PITCHING INSIDE

Pitching inside, especially with two strikes, is fundamental to effective pitching, so it absolutely drives me crazy that so few pitchers do it. Everybody talks about the reasons for so many home runs being hit, but I think the biggest reason is that so few pitchers come inside, particularly with two strikes. Even if you don't have the good hard stuff to pound inside, you have to pitch everybody inside to some degree if just to give a leaning batter another pitch to think about. You can't live solely on the outside part of the plate or leaning batters will, in effect, bring it toward them.

When big men like Albert Belle, Frank Thomas, and Fred McGriff lean over the plate they can reach the pitch on the outside corner or just off it and go the other way with power. They like to extend their arms more than little guys. As a pitcher you can't let them do that. A hard thrower must pound inside to get them to back away so he can reestablish the outside part of the plate as his own. Pounding implies movement and velocity, so it is done with sinking or sailing fastballs or sliders. A tailing fastball or two into a batter's weak area in a crucial situation puts him on the defensive. Remember that big men have more to move and a lot more to do. Generally, the thicker the build, the more you pitch inside. When the batter is behind in the count and looking outside, it is the best time to pound inside and try to tie him up. Pounding is with hard stuff only. You don't pound with a change-up. That's like pounding with a velvet hammer.

A finesse pitcher can't pound inside, but he can *surprise* inside with a decent-enough fastball and then do his finessing on the outside. Left-hander Tom Glavine surprises inside to right-handed batters two or three times in the early innings, and that is enough to keep all the other right-handed batters in the lineup looking for that pitch for the rest of the game. A right-handed power hitter will see a left-handed sinkerballer on the mound and will, as Bob Brenly says, sing "Dixie": Look away, look away, look away. But the pitcher can't just go away, away, away, or this batter will lean, lean, lean. You stop the leaning by jamming. If you can't pound, surprise.

You use the inside part of the plate differently for different hitters. A good rule for pitchers to follow is: The bigger the stroke, the more you can tie up a batter; the shorter the stroke, the less you can come inside. Big, strong guys are scary, but if you can get in, on, or underneath their hands they have trouble. Also, when you see a batter with low hands, you recognize that he is a good off-speed low-ball hitter, so you should pound him above the hands because he has too much to do to hit a ninety mph fastball that is up and in. Pitchers also should go inside to batters whose natural stroke is the other way. For example, against a guy like McGriff, who has the arm strength to go the other way and loves to do it on balls that are waist-high right out over the plate, you try to impress inside and then go away. A left-hander going against a left-handed batter like McGriff has to throw a tailing fastball inside to set up the breaking ball away.

Pitchers don't seem to understand the effect of inside pitches on batters. This is particularly true in the American League, where there is the designated hitter, but it is also evident in the National League. In fact, the Cubs' innovative manager, Jim Riggleman, had his pitching coach, Ferguson Jenkins, throw inside to all the team's pitchers in batting practice so they could sense how intimidating they would be as pitchers if they threw inside fastballs to opposing hitters.

When you watch a game being played in one of the very hitter-friendly parks, see how few pitchers are willing to come inside. Pitchers arrive at small Coors Field and say, "I can't come inside here." But these small parks are where you most have to come inside. You may get the batter to swing at and miss a hard pitch on or just off the inside corner or you may get a called strike, but what I'm really talking about is impressing batters inside so you can lay claim to the outside corner. Remember—some pitches are thrown for effect, not to get the batter out. At Coors, where the ball travels 12 percent farther in the rarefied air—songwriter Randy Newman suggested that we lower Denver to make it fairer to pitchers—and in Boston's Fenway Park, where the left-field wall is so inviting, and other parks suited for power, right-handed batters expect pitchers to guard against the easy home run by pitching low-and-away. So they move up on the plate to be able to pull that pitch. The smart pitcher will respond with running fastballs up-and-in. The batter is pushed back off the plate, and now the pitcher can go back outside without fear of being pulled. You can *pitch* inside and try to get a strike on the corner. Or you can *throw* inside and make sure everything is way off the plate.

It isn't only shallow fences that keep pitchers from coming inside. Like onetime Phillies "Whiz Kids" Robin Roberts and Curt Simmons, some young pitchers worry about hitting batters and giving the other side base runners. More young pitchers, however, are intimidated by imposing batters, who in the last few years have taken to glaring at them or even charging the mound if they are hit by a pitch or simply think the pitch was too close. To show how ridiculous this trend is, a few years ago, Reggie Sanders charged Pedro Martinez after he was hit by a pitch, although the Montreal ace was pitching a perfect game and if he wanted to keep it going, he couldn't put anyone on base.

Martinez has remained one of baseball's best pitchers because he refused to let Sanders or any of the other batters who have threatened him with retaliation stop him from pitching inside. But some other pitchers have become more timid, and power hitters have feasted on a steady diet of outside pitches. They're afraid of hitting somebody, but it isn't necessary to actually hit a guy, only to make him think you are willing to do it by knocking him down. If a batter knows a pitcher will throw inside, he will be reluctant to dig in, and that's the edge the pitcher hoped he'd get. I think it was Stan Williams who told batters, "When you're through digging, I'll bury you." You keep them leery. As Hall of Fame pitcher Jim Bunning said, "Never let batters get too comfortable."

Bunning would knock you down in a heartbeat. So would Don Drysdale, Juan Marichal, and Turk Farrell. Early in his career, Bob Gibson would drill batters if they merely ran across the mound after making an out their last time up. He never had to hit batters his last eight years because his mean reputation kept batters from leaning over the plate. All you try to do is plant some element of fear in the batter. Upsetting his comfort level is the edge you're seeking, and you can't achieve that if you keep going away.

Sending messages to batters is a time-honored practice, but there is a major distinction between knocking down a batter and hitting him. It's really bush to hit the guy who bats after a homer is hit, as it is to throw at the legs of a fast runner. Worst of all is when a pitcher throws a pitch about nine inches behind the batter's head. That's extremely dangerous because a batter's reflexes take him away from the plate. It's unacceptable to throw the ball there.

The two scariest guys to pitch inside are Barry Bonds and Gary Sheffield because they have the hand speed and unusual mechanics to be able to hit the inside fastball into fair territory. Bonds is the better hitter of the two, but Sheffield is harder for pitchers to deal with because he stands on top of the plate and almost anything other than a strike will hit him. In the American League, Frank Thomas and Albert Belle are the two guys who come to mind who stand close to the plate and get angry if any ball is thrown in tight. They complain, and because of their prowess their complaints are respected. As a result, umpires become more sensitive and pitchers more timid. I think this is intelligent gamesmanship on their parts because, by constantly calling the umpire's attention to their being pitched "too close," they can, in effect, eliminate the inside pitch from the pitcher's arsenal. Then they can look in one area—away.

12

THE COUNT

A pitcher who has the admirable habit of staying ahead of batters doesn't have to have great stuff to be successful. Even if his stuff is in the bottom 25 percent of the entire league, he can have a winning record if he consistently stays ahead in the count, as the Mets' Rick Reed proved in 1997. At the same time, even the most talented pitcher won't be successful if he constantly falls behind in the count. I've never heard anyone say this, but I believe the ability or inability of the opposing pitchers to run counts in their favor determines the fate of a game more than anything else. Furthermore, I believe that counts—and who has the edge—determine the outcome of most pitcher-batter matchups.

There are twelve possible ball-strike counts: 0-0, 0-1, 0-2, 1-0, 1-1, 1-2, 2-0, 2-1, 2-2, 3-0, 3-1, and 3-2.

Everyone agrees that 0-1, 0-2, and 1-2 are decidedly pitcher's counts and 2-0, 3-1, and, though some batters won't swing, 3-0 greatly favor the hitter. However, it should be noted that pitchers with both great control and great stuff like Greg Maddux and Kevin Brown are not in as critical a situation at 2-0 and 3-1 as the typical pitcher.

It's my opinion that 1-0 and 2-1 also favor the hitter. They are good counts on which to put runners in motion and to hit-and-run. Some people think 2-1 is a neutral count because the pitcher is two balls away from a walk and two strikes away from a strikeout, but the real neutral counts are 0-0 and 1-1. Some people see 0-0 as being in favor of the pitcher because he gets to throw four balls before walking a batter and needs only three strikes to fan him. But this fails to take into account that the batter may foul off an indefinite number of two-strike pitches. (It should be pointed out that it drives catchers and pitchers crazy when a batter is able to repeatedly foul back high-caliber two-strike pitches.)

The other even count, 2-2, is a neutral count if the pitcher started out 0-2. Otherwise, I think it slightly favors the pitcher because if the pitch is a ball the batter is still at the plate and if it's a strike it's see-you-later.

A count of 3-2 also can go either way, depending on how it was arrived at. For example, if it was 0-2, the hitter has the advantage because the pitcher is trying to find the strike zone, but if it was 3-0, the count favors the pitcher because he has found it and come back from being in the hole.

It's important to note that every count change results in a shift of strategy by the pitcher and catcher. But in general, if a pitcher is ahead in the count, it's a good time to pitch inside because the batter will be protecting outside and is vulnerable inside. If the pitcher is behind in the count, the catcher will sit outside because the batter is looking for something inside to drive and is vulnerable outside. That's a sound philosophy, and, when in doubt, a pitcher and catcher should adhere to it. However, since smart batters know what pitchers tend to do on certain counts, pitchers must vary their approach. They can't pitch the same way to every batter or even the same batter every time up. At times, they must mix up pitches, locations, and speeds. That's what pitching is all about.

The first pitch is the most important pitch to every batter because it often determines the outcome of an individual at-bat. The two counts that can result from an 0-0 pitch, 0-1 and 1-0, are drastically different. When Sandy Koufax's first pitch was strike one, you might as well have returned to the dugout; if his first pitch was ball one, you had a chance. The same is true with Randy Johnson. A first-pitch strike is the pitcher's best asset because it will help him stay ahead in the count so he can have the freedom to work the corners and throw off-speed pitches as well as fastballs in and out of the strike zone. A pitcher strives for counts when he can be unpredictable, but a first-pitch ball will likely force the pitcher with average control to go to his fastball on his second pitch because he needs a strike or he'll fall behind 2-0. A ninety mph fastball is a great pitch, but any batter in the majors, including most pitchers, can put good wood on it if he knows it's coming into the strike zone. The farther behind a pitcher with average control goes in the count, the less unpredictable he can be with his pitch selection and the less effective he will be. The farther behind he goes, the more likely it is that he will have to chance throwing fastballs down the middle of the plate in an attempt to get strikes. *The less stuff a pitcher has, the more essential it is for him to jump ahead in the count.* A first-pitch strike gives the pitcher a good scenario: He will never be faced with a 2-0 or 3-0 count and have the batter be waiting for a run-of-the-mill fastball down the middle. Moreover, a strike on either of his following two pitches will really put the batter in the hole at 1-2 and he'll have two strikes on him for the rest of the at-bat. That old cliché "He's got two strikes against him" really applies here.

Pitchers understand why getting that first pitch over is so important, but what if the pitching coach tells the pitcher to get ahead and at the same time reminds him that the batter is a first-ball hitter? The easiest pitch for most pitchers to throw for a strike is a fastball, but if the batter is a first-ball fastball hitter, how does the pitcher get ahead of him? Therein lies the struggle.

Does he still throw a fastball? Don't rule it out. As a matter of fact, don't rule out any pitch, on any count. Does he throw a first-pitch curve and try to surprise the batter? Sometimes. Bob Gibson tells a funny story about how Jim Davenport was leading off one night for the Giants and at the pregame meeting, Johnny Keane, in his raspy voice, said, "If you throw a goddamn curveball on the first pitch I'll eat my hat if Davenport hits it hard. I might eat it if he even swings at it." With that in mind, Gibson opened the game with a curve to Davenport, and he smacked a double down the left-field line. Bob looked over to Keane, who was at the water fountain rather than looking at Gibson. So there is no surefire formula for that first pitch.

During the course of a game, the pitcher will get first-pitch strikes on batters. A count of 0-1 allows the pitcher to start expanding the strike zone, moving in and out, up and down. Factoring in the 0-0 pitch, he begins to develop an effective sequence for getting the batter out.

A count of 0-2 is one on which the pitcher can afford to waste a pitch and toy with the hitter because he's deep in the hole. But there should be an idea behind it, like setting up the next pitch. For instance, he may throw way inside in order to throw outside on the next pitch. I'm fanatical about 0-2 pitches, and it's deplorable how many you'll see that go right down the pipe. You can't thoughtlessly throw 0-2 pitches as if they were 2-0 pitches.

At 1-2, you most want to finish off the batter because never again in the count will he be in such a defensive posture. But that doesn't mean you foolishly challenge him with a fastball on the fat part of the plate or necessarily throw a strike.

On the other hand, 2-2 is the count where you most want to throw a strike because you don't want to run the count to 3-2. So catchers are trained to call for the pitch that the pitcher can get over the best. It could be one of two pitches or, rarely, one of three pitches.

When some major-league pitchers were Little Leaguers, they threw curveballs with the count 0-2 or 1-2. The reason was that if they missed with them, they would neither walk the batter nor fall behind in the count. So they grew up thinking that with two strikes on a hitter, it's the best time to throw a curveball. In the major leagues, it's usually the worst time to throw the curveball. This is a sophisticated point: When a batter is protecting away, as he must do at 0-2 and 1-2, his bat is actually slower on an inside pitch. If his bat is slower, then he has more of a chance to put the good part of the bat on the slower breaking ball than on the inside fastball. Former Little Leaguers have to flip-flop what they did as kids. Two strikes is usually the best time to bust inside on a hitter. Even if he makes contact, often he'll be jammed because he's protecting outside.

But let me qualify what I've just said. In general, a two-strike count—0-2, 1-2, 2-2, and 3-2—is the best time to throw the fastball *if* you've gotten there with something other than fastballs. If a good, thinking hitter like Chipper Jones has missed the first two fastballs but has fouled back two or three others, he probably has the heater timed. So if the catcher calls for another fastball on a 3-2 count, there should be a flashing yellow light in his mitt. Caution. Depending on the pitcher's control of his other pitches, this would be a great time for him to throw something other than a fastball. Because the pitcher has gotten there with hard stuff, a good breaking ball on a fastball count can buckle the batter's knees.

This illustrates a truly significant point: *The ability to get the breaking ball over on fastball counts and to get the fastball exactly where you want it on breaking-ball counts is what makes a successful major-league pitcher.* As I mentioned earlier, Johnny Bench and Gary Carter didn't become good game-callers until they applied their hitting knowledge to pitch selection and stopped always calling for fastballs when their pitchers fell behind.

As I've stated, it's smart to throw fastballs, preferably inside fastballs, on two-strike counts. But on which counts does a pitcher almost always have to challenge batters with fastballs? The fastball counts—when the pitcher can't afford to throw a ball—are 2-0, 3-0, and 3-1 and, if the pitcher doesn't have good control, 1-0 and 2-1. However, a veteran pitcher who has great control never has to be limited to throwing a fastball. When I played, I was shocked that Juan Marichal threw screwballs on 2-2 counts with the bases loaded. Bob Veale had enough confidence in his breaking ball to throw it on the 3-0 count. Today, guys like David Cone and Kevin Appier have such command over several pitches that they might throw any of them in crucial situations when they are behind in the count. You might see Greg Maddux shake off a catcher asking for the fastball with a 3-2 count and the bases loaded. If a pitcher gets a pitch other than a fastball over for a strike on a 3-1 count, he won't hesitate to throw it again on 3-2.

Earlier, I claimed that pitchers, particularly in the American League, are reluctant to challenge batters with fastballs when they are behind in the count. There are many contradictions in baseball, and now I would like to point out that there will be some odd times when those same pitchers will do completely the opposite and throw only fastballs—with equally bad results. Unfortunately, young pitchers are inclined to go almost exclusively to the fastball at those times when a batter is looking for one, as on 2-0 and 3-1 counts, and sometimes 3-2 counts. Of course, at 3-1, even more than at 2-0, a catcher will call for the pitch that has the best chance of being a strike. The young pitcher doesn't want to chance walking anyone with an inconsistent breaking ball, so he'll challenge with a fastball, not finesse the batter. The level of success a young pitcher can have if he has the ability to get all of his pitches over on any count can be summed up in two words: Pedro Martinez.

A count of 3-2 is an obvious fastball count if the bases are loaded, especially if the pitcher has been unable to finish off the batter after having had him in the hole 0-2 or 1-2. On a 3-2 count, however, there are veteran pitchers who get batters out swinging at balls out of the strike zone. If there is an impatient hitter up, pitches that look like strikes but aren't—the "illusions of strikes"—will serve a pitcher well.

At times with first base open, it's okay if a good hitter lays off your pitch off the plate. But there are other times the pitcher and catcher find themselves boxed in from not having stayed ahead, and they've got to say, "Here it is—hit it." If the bases are loaded and it's a tied game in the eighth inning and you're a young pitcher, what are you going to do? You can't pitch around everybody. You can't walk everybody. You aren't going to risk throwing a curve on a 3-2 count with the runners going. Your odds are better if you let the batter hit the ball and you use the guys behind you.

Oddly, 3-0 is not as frightening a count for the pitcher as 3-1 because most green-lighted batters don't really understand what they should swing at, which is a pitch in their zone and nothing else. On a 3-0 count, a pitcher can often throw a strike, not necessarily a ball right down the middle, and he will get a guy to pop it up. The batter does the pitcher a favor. If the pitcher is frightened of a dangerous hitter swinging at a 3-0 fastball, he might try an unexpected slider.

Because he doesn't want to get into such situations, I believe a pitcher must be aggressive early in the count. Bases loaded, close game, a real good hitter? It's better to challenge early than late because *late* may be too late. This is baseball's version of the "preemptive strike." With Randy Johnson, the catcher is thinking, "It doesn't matter if I fall behind this guy because he can come back and get strikes. So we'll just throw the ball. Or we'll try to tease the guy on the first couple of pitches because if he falls behind 1-0 or 2-0, it doesn't matter because he can still blow him away." You're not catching Randy Johnson every day, so the advice to follow is: The weaker the pitcher's stuff, the more important it is to attack early in the count. Also: The more formidable the force you are facing, the more you have to attack. That was Robert E. Lee's thinking for battle, and it is my thinking for baseball.

So the pitcher should challenge power hitters like Albert Belle and Mark McGwire by pounding them inside right away. They will become less jammable if the pitcher falls behind 1-0, 2-1, 2-0, 3-0, and 3-1 because then they will look for an inside pitch to pummel. That's why a pitcher should go outside on those counts. However, if his team is up by more than one run, 2-1 is a count on which to challenge a batter. When you face good contact hitters with power, like Barry Larkin and Mark Grace, the approach is a little different than with power hitters because these guys are more difficult. If it's 1-0 you keep it away, but the deeper in the count the batter takes you, the more inclined you should be to come inside. Against a nonhomer hitter, perhaps the leadoff man, if the count is 3-0, 3-1, or 3-2, the pitcher will likely challenge with fastballs, particularly if he's facing a fast runner or if there's a productive batter on deck. You don't want to give the gift of a walk.

In summary: The pitcher should challenge early and if he has good control, finesse on fastball counts. The effective area of the plate becomes like an accordion for the pitcher, opening wide as he moves farther ahead in the count and closing as he falls behind. However, he never forgets that the counts have different meaning with different hitters. He should know the batter he's dealing with: know his intelligence and his talent. Then he'll know what to do every time the count changes.

13

CONTROL

One of the most remarkable achievements in baseball was Ferguson Jenkins winning twenty games six times while pitching in Wrigley Field. He was hard to read and had a strong arm, but, more important, he had pinpoint control and never got the ball over the fat part of the plate. The difference between major-league and minor-league pitchers isn't velocity but control. The best big leaguers can hit the corners with a variety of pitches and have the confidence to do it when behind in the count. A pitcher doesn't have to have overpowering stuff to be successful because if he has the control and the smarts to work both sides of the plate, he will keep the ball off the sweet part of the bat. On successive pitches, two batters may cue a pitch on the outside corner and be jammed by a pitch on the inside corner.

You hear, "All he has to do is keep the ball down." That's rubbish. Working both sides of the plate, whether you're up or down, is still the best way of getting batters out. Moving in and out and using both lanes of the plate are the hallmarks of a good pitcher. Tom Glavine, Greg Maddux, and Jimmy Key are successful pitchers who have wonderful windage vision—side to side—and are remarkable at using the lanes of the plate. Young pitchers like the Pirates' Francisco Cordova, who pitched nine innings of a combined no-hitter in '97, also emphasize going in and out. Continuing the tradition of Bob Gibson, these control pitchers stake claim to the inside two inches and the outside two inches of the plate and give the batters the thirteen inches in between that they rarely throw into.

Gibson told Steve Carlton about the division of the plate when Lefty was a young Cardinals pitcher. I used to think Lefty was sleeping in the training room before games we worked together, and it wasn't until about eight years after I had retired that he told me that he had been in trances of sorts while visualizing both lanes of the plate. Apparently, if he thought about the lanes enough, he was able to eliminate the middle of the plate. So when he went out to the mound, there was only the inside and outside. (Carlton was doing visualization years before it became common among athletes.)

That's how Tom Glavine thinks. The Braves' left-hander uses the lane on the inside and the lane on the outside and rarely strays into the middle of the plate. He works the outside to right-handed batters better than to left-handed batters and better than anyone else in baseball. Because he pitches off the third-base side of the rubber, his tailing fastball can cut over the front part of the plate and be caught by the catcher outside the strike zone.

You want to throw strikes, but you can throw strikes on edges just like you can throw them down the middle of the plate. Or you can use the fat part of the plate on early strikes and then expand the strike zone. Then there will be an "illusion of strikes." Good control means not only throwing strikes but throwing balls that look like strikes. In fact, Bret Saberhagen, who always had uncanny control, usually got himself into trouble by throwing too many strikes rather than balls just out of the strike zone, like Tom Glavine and Jimmy Key do.

If the umpire was giving him the strike call, Hall of Famer Catfish Hunter, who had staggering control and movement, could throw the ball right "on the black," which is a half-inch strip bordering the plate. He then would move it a little more outside, make it unhittable, and still get the strike call. He was the master at that. Likewise, Glavine is so consistent that he can throw two inches off the plate and get strike calls. When hitters move toward the plate to be able to reach those pitches that are being called strikes, he comes inside enough to keep them honest. In the absence of velocity, Glavine relies on a controlled fastball and, for deception, a circle change. He's like a golfer who never gets much distance on his drives but is always in the fairway.

Like Glavine, Jimmy Key can lift the ball on the outside part of the plate to right-handed batters. He, too, can put it at kneecap level on the outside part of the plate and get strike calls. On the other hand, John

Franco, the other lefty who lives outside the strike zone, throws from the bottom of the knees to the shoelaces and must get swinging strikes.

Sinkerballer Kevin Brown benefits from being in the National League because he gets a lot of strike calls on low pitches as well as balls off the corners. When he tossed his no-hitter in 1997, he threw ninety-nine pitches and only fourteen were called balls. That was staggering, as was Greg Maddux pitching consecutive complete-game victories in which only forty-one balls were called in 177 pitches. That doesn't even average to two and a half balls per inning! How can you do that to big-league batters?

Both Brown and Maddux throw mostly first-pitch strikes, as do almost all control pitchers. They know that if there is no walk in an inning baseball's offenses will score only about 22 percent of the time, and only about 8 percent of the time will they score more than one run. Throwing balls is contagious. The momentum for not throwing a strike increases with each ball and balls lead to a walk and one walk leads to another or to a pitcher making too good a pitch. Many pitchers have a world of talent but are un-

A lot of people get the impression that all pitchers throw the ball exactly where they want to all of the time and that the pitch has the speed, spin, and late action that was intended. It's just not true. There are an awful lot of pitches that turn out differently from how the pitcher and catcher planned them. Yet someone recapping a game in which the pitcher gave up a homer or RBI double but won 5–1 will lament, "He made only one mistake or he'd have had a shutout." That oft-said "only one mistake or . . ." makes my skin crawl because it is so misleading. Even a pitcher will fall into that trap and tell reporters that he made only the mistake that cost him the run. The truth is he might have made fifteen mistakes that batters didn't take advantage of—maybe they didn't swing, or took a bad swing, or just missed and fouled the ball directly back. And maybe the best pitch he made the whole game was the one that a hitter put good wood on to beat him. If you looked at a replay of the game, you could find the mistakes that he got away with: high slider popped up, high fastball grounded out, etc. And see the good pitches that were hit, such as a low-and-away fastball that was smoked. Just know when you hear that "one-mistake" garbage that one-mistake pitching performances are nonexistent.

done by wildness and walks. Check out the starting pitchers with the lowest number of walks per nine innings and you'll find that they are the same guys with the lowest earned run averages. Maddux, whose ERA is almost a full run lower than any other pitcher's in the 1990s, is eerily efficient.

Maddux is an extremely interesting case study. He will rarely overpower anybody and he hasn't any extension, yet he gets a lot of strikeouts. How is he able to do that? He gets into the mind of a batter and can stay one step ahead of him, and he also has extraordinary control over all his pitches. Every time he throws the ball, he affirms that velocity is less important than movement and location plus deception. His control comes through the use of finger pressure, which is something batters can't see. The center-field camera on Greg Maddux's pitching hand can be very telling. You can actually watch how he thinks with his fingers on the ball in the glove as he studies the batter. He'll get a sign for one pitch, but then his fingers might walk to another pitch. He'll go into a stretch, and you'll see the fingers working. All his fastballs, sliders, and curveballs are thrown with the forefinger, middle finger, and the thumb. Whenever the ring finger becomes involved, then it's definitely a choked fastball or a change-up. He will use the middle finger to make the ball go right, the index finger to make it go left. Depending on the pressure, his ball will go one way or the other, almost always for a strike.

Maddux can get batters out in more ways than any other pitcher. During one Maddux outing on television, I drew a picture of the plate to illustrate how many different ways his balls go. He makes X's on both sides of the plate to left-handed batters. He'll throw the tailing fastball away and then drop the breaking ball on the outside part of the plate where the batter will give up on it because he wrongly assumes it is a ball. That's the X on the outside part of the plate. To the same left-handed batter, he may run the slider or cut fastball in on the hands and then get the strikeout by throwing an inside fastball that the batter assumes will be a ball but tails back across the plate under the frozen batter's lifted arms. That's the other X. Remarkable.

14

UMPIRES AND THE PITCHING GAME

If you think umpires can be influenced by a hitter's prowess, a lot of pitchers agree with you. You will often see them call balls if players of stature take marginal pitches. It stands to reason that an umpire will be more reluctant to call Cal Ripken, Jr., or Tony Gwynn out on strikes than less respected players. But batters don't influence umpires to the degree catchers do. They're up at the plate only four or five times a game, not there on every pitch like the catcher is.

WORKING THE UMPIRE

A catcher should, for the pitcher's sake, use every opportunity to influence the umpire. It's essential to establish a strike zone with the umpire. If an umpire is unfamiliar with a pitcher, the catcher will talk to him between batters. You want him to know you're not trying to get anything you don't deserve, but you want to make him aware of how your pitcher usually works to get strikes. For instance, you'll tell him your pitcher has been consistent with the slider on the outside corner, or that his breaking ball has the tendency to back up occasionally, so an umpire shouldn't give up on that pitch too early. The umpire doesn't know what's coming, so he can be fooled just like a hitter can.

A good catcher will try to get strike calls on balls, especially for pitchers who throw mostly off the corners. He takes the umpire into his pitcher's zone. If, for instance, the catcher sits outside, he can get a called strike by framing a pitch. The umpire assumes he wouldn't set his target outside the plate. Joe Girardi was a master at sitting off the plate when he worked with Jimmy Key in 1996. It's better than framing a pitch. You're preframing it with the movement of your body. You don't necessarily have to bring it back into the strike zone because the umpire moves with you. If the pitch hits the mitt, the umpire is inclined to give you the pitch. If the umpire doesn't call a strike the first time, that doesn't mean you won't do this again. You can't change your pattern because this is how the pitcher has made his living. You can't have a pitcher like Key suddenly trying to overpower batters.

As a catcher, you will take anything you can get. The lower you are to give the umpire a better view and the more smoothly you catch the ball, the better off you usually are. The best way to get a strike just off the plate (or a legitimate strike) is to catch with relaxed arms. If by pulling a ball back into the strike zone you'll be more inclined to get a strike, go ahead and do it. But you must do it smoothly, because if you're constantly stabbing at the ball, you won't get strike calls on borderline pitches. Say you want a strike called on an outside breaking ball from a right-hander to a right-handed batter. If the pitch backs up, the umpire probably won't call it a strike, even if it crosses a good chunk of the plate, because you must reach from the outside part of the plate to the inside part of the plate in order to catch the ball. It's understandable that you don't get that call.

In the National League, sinkerball and splitter pitchers want the low strike, and they often get it. When I played, Kent Tekulve wouldn't throw a ball above the knees if his mother were hitting. He would throw from the middle of the shin to the bottom of the knee. You didn't want to hit the ball on his terms, but if the umpire was giving him the low strike, you were in deep stew because he'd go even lower, taking advantage of the umpire. There was a gradual lowering of the strike zone, and to a lesser degree that's what batters face in the National League today.

As a catcher, you work on the umpire early in the game when he calls a ball on a borderline pitch. You may say, "If he's got to be that fine to get a strike from you, he'll be forced to throw the ball over the fat part of the plate and get beat." If you complain about a call, you do it looking straight ahead at the field. When you turn around it alerts everybody that you think the umpire missed a call and umpires don't like to be shown up any more than the rest of us do. An umpire has every reason to get into the catcher's face if he turns around to complain on a regular basis.

If the catcher and pitcher think an umpire is calling a bad game, there's not a lot they can do about it. You can't throw the ball over the middle of the plate instead of working the corners. Of course, an umpire's questionable calls will sometimes affect a pitcher that way. You'll hear a pitcher complain, "The umpire was squeezing me"—in effect some umpires squeeze the plate and make the strike zone smaller. The pitcher feels they are making him throw over the middle of the plate. You have to know the fairness level of an umpire. Some umpires never admit they are wrong. Some will say, "I blew that pitch," and that's all you can ask of a guy.

To make pitches easier for the umpire to call, it's very important for a catcher not to be too far behind home plate. For him to get favorable calls on breaking balls he has to be as close to the batter as he can. He'll have trouble getting calls if he's back too far and catching something with a hump in it, a curveball, for instance. Umpires will never admit this, but they assume that the ball is lower than it really is if the catcher is back and catching the ball low to the ground. If he were up six inches, he would be catching it higher and make it simpler for the umpire to see that it is a strike. The reason some catchers won't move up to assure better calls is that they fear touching the bat with the mitt and getting called for interference.

Even if the catcher is frustrated by an umpire's definition of a strike, he still will expect him to make quick calls when there are three balls on the batter and a man on base. He can tolerate an umpire who gives slow signals but not one who is slow with a verbal call. If the runner is stealing with less than two outs, a delay of a ball-four call means the catcher will have to throw the ball to second and risk an error.

PITCHER UMPIRES AND BATTER UMPIRES

In the 1967 Series, before the first pitch, home-plate umpire Ed Runge told me: "I don't know if you have heard about me or not, but if you can reach the ball, swing at it because I'll call a strike." Sure enough, he did and was like that for both sides. Today, there are similar umpires. The width of home plate measures seventeen inches, but some umpires have twenty-inch plates and others have fourteen-inch plates. It depends on the umpire rather than the league. If an umpire has a wide plate, he is considered a pitcher's umpire. Those who squeeze the plate are batter's umpires. Shrewd hitters like Rickey Henderson and Frank Thomas can coerce or intimidate an umpire into shrinking the strike zone. (I've seen Rickey get umpires to become his "partner" in getting ahead in the count—he'll verbally pat an umpire on the back for making a ball call on a strike.)

Batters as a whole have benefited over the last ten years from the umpires' unwillingness to call strikes on pitches from the batter's navel to his armpits. But that doesn't mean some of these umpires don't still favor the pitcher. Pitchers don't care as much if the umpire is calling strikes on high and low pitches because batters can adjust and reach those pitches with their bats. What pitchers hope for are umpires who are liberal with the outside strike. The umpire who is most unfair to batters is the one who calls strikes on pitches that are two inches off the outside corner. A hitter will position himself in the batter's box so that when he strides he can cover the outside part of the plate, but except when he has two strikes on him, he'll almost never position himself to be able to hit a pitch two inches off the plate. Why would he? That pitch is supposed to be a ball.

It's not that umpires can't tell the pitch is outside. Even though they work in the slot on the inside of the plate, the outside pitch is usually the easiest for them to determine whether it's a ball or strike; there's no hitter there to obscure their vision, as there will be on an inside pitch. As stated, it's very difficult to make correct calls on breaking balls that have backed up because catchers have to move their gloves from the outside part of the plate to the inside. An umpire probably has the hardest time on a good splitter, which is level until it reaches the hitting area and tumbles into the dirt. Even if that ball isn't a strike, it often causes a checked swing. Most home-plate umpires are willing to let the first- or third-base umpires make calls because they have a better view.

When interleague play was first discussed, everybody seemed overly concerned about how it would work when an umpiring crew from one league would call a game with teams from both leagues. I'm thinking, "Who cares?" You're always hearing about the difference in the strike zones in the two leagues, but I would say that the strike zone is more standardized than it was twenty years ago. Back then, American League umpires wore balloon protectors and couldn't see the low strike because they had to look over the catcher's head. They would give high strikes, while the National League came to be known as a low-ball league. Today, National League pitchers still get more low pitches called strikes than their American League counterparts, but not to the extent that they used to.

If there is a difference I've seen, it's that American League umpires have a more difficult time punching guys out. Jim Kaat first called this to my attention. For whatever reason, they'll call the first and second strikes, but they're not as quick to call the third strike as umpires in the National League. Go figure.

15

AVOIDING PITFALLS

A pitcher can have a successful game if he avoids a number of pitfalls. In many cases, it's as simple as not doing something; at other times, it's doing one thing instead of another.

* * *

One night in Crosley Field, I was catching when Curt Simmons threw a change-up to Frank Robinson. He threw it low, but Robinson homered. I told Curt that Robinson had gotten hold of a good pitch. He said, "No, it wasn't." I said, "But it was down." He said, "Everything down is not a good pitch. Did you see how far that ball went? No ball that is hit that far is a good pitch." It was bad because it had too much of the plate. Robinson was fooled, but he was such a good hitter that he kept his hands back and was strong enough to lift it.

"Keep the ball down" is advice that pitchers hear as soon as they become professionals, but as Simmons pointed out, keeping the ball down isn't enough. Balls barely off the ground can hang just like the high pitches, and power hitters like Frank Robinson, Stan Musial, and, today, Mark McGwire can make a living off them. They might be low, but there is no bite on those pitches and they stay in the hitters' power zones.

While it's true that most pitchers without overpowering stuff must keep the ball down in the strike zone to be effective, down-and-*in* is the most dangerous area in which to pitch any batter. You particularly don't throw power-hitting left-handed hitters balls that are low—from the shin to the knee—and inside because that is in their happy zone. You work low-ball hitters in the attic, not the basement. Pitchers mistakenly think they can get batters out down-and-in. In fact, when I joined the Red Sox in September of 1974, both Luis Tiant and Juan Marichal flippantly told me that they "get lots of batters out down-and-in." "Who?" I asked. "Some right-handers . . . ," they hedged. "Which right-handers?" They couldn't answer. It's up to *catchers* not to call that pitch. Usually, when a ball is hit in the down-and-in area, it is a pitch that has drifted there by mistake. As far as I know, the only pitcher who threw down-and-in on a consistent basis was Steve Carlton with his slider to right-handed batters. Steve could throw his slider down-and-in because it both sank and slid, usually out of the strike zone.

* * *

If a pitcher gets ahead 0-2 on fastballs that overmatch the batter, he is usually doing the hitter a favor by speeding up his bat head by throwing a curveball. In fact, if it's a strike, it is the easiest pitch for him to hit in that situation. Interestingly, high curves around the letters aren't nearly as dangerous as curves six inches lower. Not that a pitcher intentionally throws them there, but high curves from a right-hander to a right-handed batter aren't as bad as they look. They can, in fact, jam the batter. The curves that get hammered are the flat ones from the mid-thigh to the belly button.

* * *

Because batters can be sneaky, a pitcher must get to know their mind-sets. Steve Stone says Willie Mays was the best he ever saw at intentionally looking bad on a pitcher's curve to make sure the pitcher threw him another one in a key situation. Roberto Clemente was like that, too. He'd take a first-pitch breaking ball and look as if he were shocked by the pitch. That was so he'd get a similar pitch from the pitcher during that at-bat. Former Cubs manager Jim Frey told me about ten years ago that on a first-pitch inside fastball, Ryne Sandberg would rock the top part of his body backward as if he were fooled—"Oh, my God, where did that pitch come from?" He was enticing the pitcher into his lair with an Oscar-caliber performance. If the pitcher fell for that, he'd come back with the same pitch and be hit hard. Young pitchers and catchers occasionally fall for such ploys but will eventually catch on.

* * *

Our low cameras will often catch a pitcher throwing his glove and having a tantrum in the dugout after a bad outing. That's part of the human side of the game that we've come to expect. But if a pitcher loses it on the mound, it's a different story. In one inning, an unfortunate pitcher can experience boos from the fans, heckles from the opposing dugout, bad calls from one umpire and balk calls from another, an assortment of cheap hits, and botched plays by himself or his teammates, but he still must keep his poise. Composure indicates confidence, and that is a very important weapon in a pitcher's arsenal. When I first watched Yankees import Hideki Irabu, I had to question whether he had the demeanor to be a winning pitcher. If an opposing player detects annoyance, anger, or fear in the pitcher, he says, "We've got you. Your actions have changed our approach. Now we're going for the throat." In any competition, from baseball to poker, you can't let them see you sweat, or you're finished. As the Vikings of yore (not of Minnesota) once conveyed, "Never let your face show what your mind is thinking."

Maybe Irabu should look at some old tapes of Catfish Hunter, who played with a batter's mind without trying to. At the tensest moments, he was so calm that he didn't appear to sweat—and that increased the batter's anxiety.

* * *

In 1997, Yankees ace left-hander Andy Pettitte was totally baffled about why he was being roughed up by left-handed batters. He said naively: "I've got a pretty good curveball, and lefties should be easy to get out." Andy didn't realize that a curveball from a left-handed pitcher to a left-handed hitter is the most dangerous pitch to anybody, with the possible exception of a change-up down-and-in to a left-handed batter. Left-handed batters can make a move on the curve and be fooled and still have time to make another move to adapt to the pitch. The break of the ball, which could be deceptive to a right-handed hitter—I'm not talking about a nasty pitch down-and-away—usually can be handled by left-handed batters. Depending on the location of the ball and the type of hitter, the batter can go either way with the pitch or up the middle.

Quite a few left-handed pitchers don't understand this. When we became teammates on the Phillies late in our careers, Tug McGraw, against whom I consistently hit lasers for base hits, asked me, "How in the hell could you hit my curveball the way you did?" I said, "Unless you have a tailing fastball that bites in on left-handed batters, you're not going to be effective against them because they will have no fear of leaning over the plate to go after the curve." I could say those exact words to Andy Pettitte. All thoughtful left-handed hitters would say the same thing. A good left-handed batter forces himself to keep his front shoulder in against left-handed pitchers, so it would make sense that he would be vulnerable to a fastball that tails in on his hands. So a quality left-hander like Pettitte should develop a tailing fastball and pound the left-handed batter inside until it is safe to throw the curve away. You can throw any pitch to any hitter, but it depends what you threw to get there. In this case, it depends on what, if anything, the hitter has seen before he gets that curveball. You want him to have seen a tailing fastball, a very threatening, territorial pitch.

* * *

Pitchers can't give away their pitches; it's a young pitcher's foible. Steve Karsay, for example, has an excellent curve, but he slows down his body every time he throws it. A lot of pitchers will speed up their body when they throw change-ups. They try to fool you with the body, but the body doesn't fool anybody. It's the arm motion. You have to have the same delivery for every pitch, but some young pitchers don't understand this. Hitters can pick up on any nuance and know what's coming.

With change-ups, it's particularly important to throw through to the catcher instead of the hitter. The deception comes in the arm motion, and if the arm motion stops, the alert batter will have a hanger to hit.

* * *

I believe in the philosophy "Don't let their best hitter beat you." But it depends on how many "best" hitters they have. Seattle, for instance, has Edgar Martinez batting behind Ken Griffey, Jr., so they have two. But on the Giants, even with Jeff Kent driving in over a hundred runs, Barry Bonds is far and away their best hitter and you shouldn't challenge him in a key situation. You would instead pitch around him or walk him intentionally. You take that theory into a game, but you may change your approach as the game is played out. From a pitcher's standpoint, a batter shouldn't be given too much credit. Some young pitchers believe they are facing a lineup of supermen. Success changes that kind of thinking.

* * *

Don't get beaten on your second-best pitch when the game is on the line. A reliever usually has one out-pitch, while starters often have at least two of almost equal quality. The later in the game, the more the best-pitch philosophy comes into play. You don't throw your second-best pitch as your out pitch unless the particular batter has had tremendous difficulty with it in previous at-bats. Future Hall of Famer Dennis Eckersley will always regret the inside slider he threw Kirk Gibson in the bottom of the ninth in Game 1 of the 1988 World Series. That wasn't Eckersley's number one pitch. When a fastball pitcher throws a slider, it speeds up the bat head for the hitter. That probably was the only pitch the hobbling Gibson could have hit out of the park, and he didn't even have to swing hard.

In the 1996 World Series, Atlanta's Mark Wohlers threw a slider, his *third*-best pitch, instead of his great fastball or devastating splitter, and Jim Leyritz tied Game 4 with a three-run homer, propelling the Yankees to a victory that led to an eventual championship. Wohlers throws a ninety-nine mph fastball but went with an eighty-six mph slider. Wohlers has never admitted he threw the wrong pitch, and neither has Leo Mazzone, the Braves' pitching coach. I love Leo, but when he told me that if that slider had been low-and-away he would have gotten Leyritz out, I didn't buy it. I said, "Leo, we're dealing with odds in situations like this." Leyritz later said, "You know, I fouled back some fastballs in that at-bat, too," implying that he might have caught up with Wohlers's fastball if he'd thrown it. But he fouled them off to the right instead of straight back, which means he wasn't getting around on the ball. If Leyritz wasn't getting around on the fastball, it would stand to reason that he would have a much better chance if Wohlers threw him a pitch thirteen mph slower. As Jim Palmer says, when you throw a pitch like that you do what the hitter can't do: you speed up his bat head. By your pitch selection, you allow him to do it. If I'm Mark Wohlers and throwing ninety-nine mph, I say here it is, hit it. I don't want to take any of the credit away from Leyritz because he still had to hit the ball, but if there is one thing to remember about pitching, it is: *When the disparity in speed is great between one pitch and another, you have got to go with the better pitch in a game situation.*

* * *

A catcher takes his turns with the bat, so he should know that a pitch that is tough to catch is also hard to hit. That's why it's surprising that most catchers call for too many sliders, a pitch that is easy to catch. If a fast runner is on first base, see how often the catcher will call for a slider. I'm not talking about the wicked sliders of Steve Carlton, Bob Gibson, Sparky Lyle, or John Smoltz, but the less-than-great slider can be the most dangerous pitch to throw because more than any pitch, it flattens out. Unless the slider has sharp downward movement, it speeds up the bat head and allows a hitter who would have hit the fastball over the plate without power to hit the slightly slower pitch in front of the plate with power. The last thing a pitcher wants is for a strong guy to hit his pitch out in front of the plate and be able to keep it fair. If a pitcher is looking for deception— and isn't focusing on the base runner—he will be better off if he has an effective curveball or change-up than a slider because their speeds are much different from that of fastballs. With those pitches, the deception causes the bat head to speed up too much.

* * *

In 1997, the Mets' Bobby Jones reduced the number of curveballs he threw from the stretch, and that was one of the big reasons he was more effective with men on base, at least in the first half of the season. A curve isn't an easy pitch to throw from the stretch (which is why few relievers feature it). To throw a good curve, the hips, thighs, and rear end really come into play and there is a high leg kick. The pitcher loses some leg kick when he works from the stretch. If a pitcher throws both a slider and a curve, he often is better off going with the slider if pitching from the stretch. He still must use the lower part of the body, but the slider doesn't require the leg action that you need for a curve. As I've said, a slider can be an unsafe pitch, but from the stretch, a curve is more likely to hang in the strike zone.

* * *

Pitching is like a recipe. Too much of one thing will ruin the dish. You must vary pitches: If there's no variation in velocity, then vary the location.

16

MOUND MEETINGS

During a game, expect to see several meetings on the mound. The reason can be something simple like the catcher making sure the pitcher understands the signs with a runner on second, or something standard like the catcher wanting the pitcher to catch his breath after he has run on the bases or backed up a play, or something strategic like setting the infielders in a bunt situation.

Or it might be that the pitcher is showing chinks in his armor. In that case, mound meetings initiated by the catcher or some bold infielder, or by the manager or his emissary, the pitching coach, can be more problematic. You'd hope that a meeting on the mound is a meeting of the minds, but it's usually far from it. If you think pregame team meetings are negative, then you should eavesdrop on these powwows. I don't know why managers, pitching coaches, and even most catchers don't just say, "Get him out," instead of some drivel like "Throw strikes, but don't give him anything good to hit," "Don't walk this guy, but don't give him anything he can put good wood on," or "Be careful." These lines are worse than useless because they make the pitcher too timid to do anything. There is such a big difference between "This is what you should do" and "Be careful with this guy." If you plant uncertainty in a pitcher's mind, he'll try to think the ball to the plate instead of throwing it.

Often pitchers feel that their concentration is broken and rhythm thrown off when there is a visit to the mound. So if a catcher—or infielder—pays him a visit, he had better have something salient to say. If, after a base hit, he goes to the mound only to ask, "How do you feel?" the young pitcher will say, "Fine," and the older pitcher will chase him away. As Jim Kaat says, "Every time the batter swings and misses, the batting coach doesn't pull him out of the batter's box to ask, 'How do you feel?'" I've often spoken on the air about how Bob Gibson would verbally abuse me if he saw me heading to the mound—"The only thing you know about pitching is that it's hard to hit"—but the worst way for a pitcher to greet a catcher coming to the mound is with his back. It's humiliating because everybody in the stands and people at home watching close-ups from the dugout cameras can see how annoyed the pitcher is with you. But then again, why should the catcher insist on talking to the pitcher just because he bounced one pitch in the dirt or gave up a hit?

After a pitcher has given up a big hit or home run is not a good time to go to the mound. Everybody is watching you out there, so in essence you are calling more attention to his failure, adding insult to injury. Anyway, you're too late. It would have been wiser to have come out before the big hit. Then you might have prevented it.

I'm not saying there's no time to go out. But go out with something to say or don't go out at all. Remember Richie Ashburn's advice about announcing: "If you don't have something to say, say nothing." It's really that simple. Young catchers who have an annoying tendency to visit the mound at any sign of trouble should take note that the only reason Steve Carlton listened to me on the mound was because my visits were infrequent and I would discuss only one thing each time, usually the pitch that was working best. If you go out there all the time, he'll be less inclined to listen to you because you're prattling.

So talk about one thing, and be positive. For instance, you wouldn't say, "Let's get back into a rhythm," because the pitcher wouldn't have been thinking about being out of rhythm. You should say instead: "Here's what you're going to do against this batter. Throw fastballs off the plate away. It's okay if you walk him because we've got first base open. If he reaches the ball he's going to foul it off, and then we'll have him so conscious of the ball outside that we'll take one shot at jamming him or getting his arms to go up with an inside pitch. Once you get the arms to go up, you've got him. If the pitch is a strike, he's dead." It's almost like going into the hitter's mind. That's the leadership a catcher must show: knowing what you're talking about and then putting it into effect in a positive fashion. If a pitcher says, "Nope, I don't want to do that," that's fine because he's the guy who will make the decision and throw the ball. But he should have positive reinforcement.

When a manager or pitching coach goes to the mound during a jam to talk to a pitcher, you don't want them asking, "Well, what do you think?" A young pitcher in particular wants specific instructions. There is, however, the danger that he might come to rely on visits from his veteran catcher, pitching coach, or manager if he runs into any difficulty. That kind of dependency isn't beneficial. The pitcher should want to get out of trouble on his own and not try to do it by committee. He should want to pitch, not talk.

Most often, a pitching coach will come to the mound to discuss pitch selection to attack the batter. But the content of conversations will vary. On occasion, he might tell the pitcher, "You're dropping down, so try to stay on top a bit more," although he won't really discuss a pitcher's mechanics unless there has been a total breakdown. The time to work with a pitcher on mechanics is between starts. But it is appropriate to remind the pitcher about tempo and balance to make sure he's not drifting. A pitcher drifts when he rushes and the lower part of his body goes forward and the arm drags behind instead of being in sync. What a trip to the mound should be for a coach is a checkup from the neck up. He should work on the pitcher's brain, not his arm—they're not that far apart.

As a catcher, you feel like you have the best grasp of a situation, yet someone else—the pitching coach or manager—will make the decision to remove the pitcher. The most frequently asked, and worst, question from a manager or pitching coach to a catcher on the mound is "How's he throwing?" You've been trying all year to build up a line of communication with this pitcher and that can be torn down if you answer that one question. What are you supposed to say, "Aw, he's terrible, get him out of here"?

When a manager or pitching coach asks the pitcher the ever-popular "How do you feel?" the pitcher is thinking, "Just leave me in or take me out. Don't ask me how I feel." They shouldn't ask the pitcher or catcher but should make up their own minds about leaving a pitcher in or taking him out. Everybody tries to shift the focus to somebody else. If a coach asks the pitcher if he's tired and the pitcher says that he's feeling super and the next guy hits a three-run homer, the coach, to the press or himself, will say, "He told me he was feeling great," and accept none of the blame. Sometimes nobody wants to make a decision and take on responsibility.

What should be stressed is what the pitcher can do to retire the batter rather than what damage the batter might do. I remember when Cardinals manager Johnny Keane came out to the mound to talk to Ray Sadecki and me in the ninth inning of a one-run game with Jim Lemon hitting and a runner on first with one out. Keane said, "This guy's a good fastball hitter, and what we want to do is throw him the breaking ball." So far so good. Then Keane, whom I liked because he gave me my break, added, "But keep it up so McCarver can handle it." In other words, don't throw Lemon the good curve because if goes in the dirt, it will get by *me*. He added so many negative thoughts that something had to go wrong.

A lot of managers think it is important to go to the mound if men get on base. A pitcher goes into the seventh inning having given up only four hits, and then the first two guys get on with an infield hit and broken-bat single. It's now first-and-third with nobody out, and the manager rushes to the mound. What is he going to tell the pitcher? "Don't give up any infield hits" or "Don't jam a guy and make the ball fall in front of the outfielder"? The pitcher is throwing just as well as he had been, but now you've got the manager on the mound and the bullpen going. It's almost farcical.

I'll tell you how negative thoughts result in negative results. There was a game in 1963 when the Cardinals were in Chicago. It was the ninth inning and the tying run was on second when Ken Aspromonte came up to pinch-hit against Ron Taylor. Ron was a nervous, manically fast worker, like a tiger in a cage, so he wasn't happy to see our manager, Johnny Keane, come to the mound. Johnny said, "I wouldn't be out here if it weren't for the fact that this son of a bitch has beaten us with broken-bat hits too many goddamn times." So Ron asked, "So what do you want us to do?" Johnny answered, "Well, goddammit, I don't know what to do, but just don't put it where he can get a broken-bat hit." I asked jokingly, "Do you want us to pitch him out over the plate so he can hit the ball hard?" "Well, goddammit, I don't know . . ." Sure enough, on a 1-0 pitch, Aspromonte breaks his bat and bloops the game-tying single into center. And he wins it in the eleventh on an identical broken-bat hit, 5–4. I went into the clubhouse, saying, "You talk about the power of suggestion." I know that had Keane not come out there Aspromonte might still have gotten those broken-bat hits. But if you plant a negative thought, a negative result has a better chance of happening. I really believe this is true in baseball.

Barney Schultz was the Cardinals' pitching coach in 1973. By that time, Bob Gibson was so venerable that trips to the mound had to be done with extreme sensitivity, which isn't uncommon when you're dealing with star pitchers in their receding years. Whenever Barney came to the mound, Bob would ask him, only half in jest, "What can you tell me about pitching? You threw a knuckleball, but I don't throw one. If you threw a fastball you could tell me something. But right now we have nothing to talk about." It got so bad that when our manager, Red Schoendienst, would send him to the mound to talk to Bob, Barney would be reluctant to go. Red didn't want to go out himself, so he'd send Barney. One night, Bob gave up about seven or eight earned runs in 1⅔ innings. Red finally sent Barney out, and it was such a trek for him. He was just plodding out there, and all the players felt sorry for him. After the interminable walk to the mound, Barney arrives, expecting the worst. And Bob says, "Barney, where have you been?" That was one of the great lines ever. Then Bob added another one, "I've been getting my ass lit up, and you've been sitting in the dugout." Everybody around the mound roared.

17

RELIEF PITCHING

In the middle of an inning, my partner and I will often be alerted by a director that a reliever is warming up. Then, as we inform viewers about him, the high-first camera will focus on him in one of the two bullpens or warm-up areas on the opposite sidelines. (At Jacobs Field in Cleveland, there is a high-third camera that can shoot either bullpen.) On the monitor or with binoculars, it's hard to gauge whether a pitcher is up simply to get work in or is preparing to see action, but we know that today's managers are quick to go to the pen. Complete games are almost a thing of the past, and there's nothing a manager likes better than a reliever who says, "Gimme the ball."

The low-first or low-third camera will shoot across into the dugout so you can see the pitching coach phoning the bullpen to find out if the reliever is ready to come in. A short reliever can usually get ready at the drop of a hat, while a middle reliever, like a starter, usually takes longer. The danger of having relievers get up several times is that they might go from being loose to being tired, especially in hot weather. You don't want to leave it in the rehearsal hall. A reliever is like a broadcaster in that regard. The rule of thumb is: Prepare yourself so that you are at your apex coming in. If it's hot you may want to calm down and "soft toss." The chances are you won't be in for another couple of hitters and you'll have enough time to get ready.

If the reliever in the pen needs to get in his standard number of warm-up pitches, watch how easily a delay can be orchestrated. The catcher talks to the pitcher, infielders join the conversation, everyone talks with the umpire who comes out to rush things along. Finally, the manager emerges and you'll see him waving for the reliever as soon as he hits the top step of the dugout, as if he wanted to hurry the reliever into the game. In any case, two visits in one inning from the dugout to the mound will automatically remove a pitcher from the game, accompanied by, in visiting ballparks, Ray Charles's mocking "Hit the Road, Jack."

Broadcasters will give you statistics on an entering reliever, but you should know the numbers sometimes fail to disclose whether he has been effective or ineffective. For instance, a closer's high ratio of saves to blown saves may sound impressive, but this stat doesn't tell you what percentage of his saves came after he entered games with two- or three-run leads and how many saves and blown saves came when he was sent in to protect a one-run lead. The number of wins and losses relievers have means little. If a middle reliever has a lot of decisions, you don't know if that means he blew leads in "hold" situations; if a closer has a lot of decisions, you do know that he has blown a lot of saves.

Earned run average is not a good indicator because when a reliever allows inherited runs to score they don't show up on his own record, and when the reliever who follows him allows the men he put on base to score, the first reliever's ERA, not the second guy's, is affected. Perhaps the most revealing and interesting stat is one that is beginning to get more attention from broadcasters: the percentage of inherited runners who score. It gives you a pretty good idea of what a reliever does when it counts. But this is a more revealing stat for a middle man than a closer because a closer will allow meaningless runs to score in exchange for outs.

A reliever may come into a game when the outcome has already been determined, and he'll just try to get some work in to stay sharp. Or he may come in after a manager has lifted a favored starter before he has the chance to get a loss. But often there is much on the line. A reliever can come in with a one-run lead with men on second and third and nobody out. Perhaps the manager left the starter or previous reliever in too long, and now he wants the new reliever to fix the problem. There's not much you can tell the guy. He could pitch beautifully and get three straight outs, yet allow two runs to score on a ground-out and sacrifice fly. For the most part, the percentage of inherited runners who score off a reliever is a valid, telling statistic, but in this case he couldn't pitch better and still did not "do the job." He will feel terrible because allowing inherited runners to score is much like spending someone else's money. Your ERA doesn't go up, but the previous pitcher's ERA will rise, and you won't be looked at by anybody on the field or bench with gratitude. See if anyone on his team greets him when he enters the dugout. It's a bit unfair, but the reliever is a professional who understands the nature of his occupation.

When a reliever is called into a game, the catcher already has a good idea about his stuff, so it is unlikely that they'll discuss pitch selection. When relievers come into a game with runners on base, they are very anxious and want talk kept to the bare minimum. They're like a horse before a race, primed to perform.

When a middle reliever comes into a jam, the catcher may have him go to his strength immediately, the same as if he were the closer. Setup men who come in to face one batter will obviously use their best stuff, as will a left-handed specialist facing a good left-handed batter: Jim Poole against Larry Walker, Mark Guthrie against John Olerud, Tony Fossas against Barry Bonds, Paul Assenmacher against Paul O'Neill, Mike Stanton against Ken Griffey, Jr. There's no reason to save it. A reliever will have a different mind-set if he's expected to pitch for a few innings.

The long reliever may very well be the opposite of the starter. The opposing team may have five or six left-handed batters in its lineup to go against a right-hander, so if the manager replaces that starter with a left-hander in the fourth or fifth inning he may put the clamps on the left-handed-dominated lineup and give his team the opportunity to get back in the game or forge ahead.

A fan may not understand why a manager will not remove the long reliever for a pinch hitter early in the game although men are on base and his team is far behind. Jim Leyland says it properly: "Sometimes you have to sacrifice a game to save your bullpen for future games." If the bullpen has been overworked, a manager may leave the pitcher in to hit for himself even if his making an out may kill his team's best opportunity to rally. You keep the good hitter on the bench and sacrifice that pitcher and the game for the sake of the bullpen. To paraphrase Churchill, "Never have so few given so much to so many."

Later in a game, National League managers may take out a tiring starter or long reliever and still protect the bullpen by *double-switching*. In a double switch, a reliever replaces a pitcher and a bench player replaces a position player; the reliever goes into the position player's spot in the batting order and the good-hitting bench player goes into the pitcher's ninth spot, which may be due up next inning. If it's a smart double switch, that removed player wasn't due up for seven or eight batters, so the pitcher who takes his spot in the order probably won't have to be taken out for a pinch hitter for two or three innings and another reliever won't have to be used until then, if at all. Of course, in the American League, pitchers don't bat, so managers don't have to worry. The new reliever can stay in indefinitely.

A good middle reliever coming into a game is like Wyatt Earp coming into town to restore order. The importance of having a good pitcher in middle relief was never more evident than in Game 7 of the 1986 World Series when Sid Fernandez held the Red Sox scoreless from the fourth inning with two outs through the seventh inning, while the Mets came back from a 3–0 deficit. A contending team needs strong middle-inning relief and good late-inning setup men, including one of those left-handed specialists like Dennis Cook or Mark Guthrie.

One of the most ridiculous things in baseball is that a setup man comes in and pitches great for the seventh and eighth innings and is taken out for the closer in the ninth inning. Also because the stopper is the last pitcher, he gets a save and the first guy who pitched longer gets nothing other than a courtesy pop. Managers will say about their stopper, "That's what he gets paid for." What does the other guy get paid for? If he pitches twice as many innings and is twice as effective and gets no credit, what does he get paid for? The guy who kills a rally in the seventh or eighth inning gets credit for a "hold," but holds don't count in contract negotiations like saves do. Maybe it's because a guy who can throw a double-play ball or get a big strikeout to get his team out of the seventh or eighth inning isn't as noticeable as the guy who does it in the more dramatic ninth inning to get his team out of the game. But he may have done it when the game was really on the line.

A good setup man holds a lead and in many instances is more important to the victory than the guy who gets the last out. Mariano Rivera was the setup man for John Wetteland on the Yankees in 1996, and people were talking about a middle reliever who should have been on the All-Star team and who was a legitimate MVP candidate. It was unheard of. Because of Rivera, the Yankees revolutionized baseball because they played six-inning games: If they were ahead after six innings and Rivera came in for two innings and Wetteland for one inning, they won. It showed everybody that you can "shorten" games—you can win if you grab an early lead—if you have strong middle relief.

In today's game, middle relief is so important, yet only a few teams today have quality middle relievers. That's because if a quality setup man like Rivera breaks onto the scene, he will want to switch to the more glamorous and better-paid closer role the year after his lowly paid setup success. So his manager must revert back to putting the most important part of the game—the sixth, seventh, and eighth innings—in the hands of the weakest, lowest-paid part of the staff. These guys don't come in as mop-up men but enter one-run and tie games and give up key runs. If you watch your team enough on television, you will see that it will play competitively until late in games only to lose repeatedly because of its shaky middle relief. This makes no sense to me. Middle relief is so bad that today's manager should have his starter go longer—a good idea anyway—and then go directly to the closer, bypassing middle relievers entirely. In fact, Larry Dierker, a pitcher-turned-broadcaster-turned-manager, says his starters on Houston are their own setup men.

The better solution is to make middle relief strong by upgrading "hold" to a major stat almost on the level of "save" and increasing middle relievers' salaries. In this way, the Yankees could have kept Rivera happy as a seventh- and eighth-inning pitcher and retained Wetteland as the finisher instead of letting him go to Texas. All teams could bolster their middle-relief corps with grade-A relievers and shorten games. However, until management decides to pay middle relievers a salary commensurate with their responsibilities, middle relief pitching will remain poor.

Currently, when the weak middle men start to get battered around, few managers are bold enough to bring in their star closers because agents are insistent that their clients pitch only an inning or an inning and a third each appearance. If you think a manager should bring in his closer to snuff out a rally in the seventh or eighth inning, you're correct. That could be the game's pivotal point. There's no reason to save him for the end of the game because if the team falls behind he won't come in anyway. In game situations, the best reliever should be in there. At times managers do get so fed up with their leaky bullpens that they will go against the grain and send in the closer early to protect a lead or, rarer, keep his team tied or from falling further behind. That's how it was done in the old days when there was a team concept of relief pitching, but, of course, today's agents aren't going to allow their closer clients to be used frequently in nonsave situations.

* * *

Curt Simmons used to say, "You've gotta have a closer." He was right. Pennant contenders certainly need solid closers. And so do young teams, particularly expansion teams, because managers don't want their promising pitchers to be discouraged by blown saves. But finding an effective closer isn't simple. Lots of guys have great stuff, but the major-league closer must also have ice water in his veins, a single-minded devotion to the task at hand, and total concentration. A major-league closer is the one occupation in which you can't afford to have any incapacitating fears. In fact, many people are surprised that Mariano Rivera moved so easily to being a closer because they thought he would need a different mind-set. But being a setup man for George Steinbrenner's Yankees in a pennant race was preparation enough.

A short reliever comes into a jam. The television director cuts back and forth between him, the batter—perhaps a pinch hitter—the base runners, and at times the managers, using close-ups and dissolves to heighten tension. What will you see the catcher do with him? The closer will likely go at a batter with his best stuff from the beginning because he will not face him again. It's strength against strength and strength against weakness. Most short relievers are the complete opposite of guys who nibble at corners. They chalk up strikeouts or put batters on the defensive so they put the ball in play on the pitcher's terms. The quintessential closer is Dennis Eckersley, who once walked only seven batters in 131 innings over two years while accumulating 128 strikeouts. He'd say, "Here's a strike, I'm going to stay ahead." ElRoy Face, the Pirates' great forkballer from the late fifties to early seventies, was like that. He'd challenge anybody. Most closers have that mentality. Robb Nen, Rob Dibble, Goose Gossage, Dick Radatz, Billy Wagner, and Mariano Rivera in the late innings? "It's you and me, baby. I'm not going to try anything cute. You're just going to have to catch up to my fastball." (Randy Myers was like that but has added a change-up.) Usually, these guys are in one-run ball games, and they challenge hitters because, unlike starters, they can't afford the luxury of walking anyone. Managers have no patience for relievers who walk batters. That doesn't mean they have to be like Eckersley and throw only strikes but that they have to induce batters to swing. Few batters were disciplined enough to lay off Bruce Sutter's splitter in the late seventies and eighties as it dropped out of the strike zone; today, you can watch how young right-handed batters swing helplessly at John Franco's change-up off the plate.

The closer will attack batters with a smaller repertoire of pitches than the starter or long reliever. You rarely find a pitcher with standard equipment—a fastball, curveball, slider, and change-up—as the stopper. John Wetteland has a wicked curve, but you will see few other closers throw the curve as anything but a "show-me" pitch. A curve is best thrown with a full windup, and most closers pitch from the stretch because there are almost always men on base. In place of a curve, most right-handed relievers throw the splitter because it isn't affected as much when it is thrown from the stretch. (The screwball has been the specialty pitch of left-handed relievers like Tug McGraw.) Rod Beck probably has one of the best splitters of today's closers, and he uses it in conjunction with his conveniently demonic look to get batters out. Other relievers feature a splitter and fastball–Rick Aguilera's splitter is so good he gets away with a so-so fastball, and some like Mike Jackson and Mark Wohlers also throw sliders.

John Franco is different in that instead of hard stuff he throws an unusual three-finger change that acts like a splitter when it's on. As did Bruce Sutter, he dares throw his medium-speed fastball only when he falls behind. A few closers throw sinkers. Robb Nen throws a heavy fastball that has sinking action. The closer who is the antithesis of all the hard throwers is Doug Jones, who year after year gets batters out with fastballs that couldn't break a pane of glass. He doesn't throw them but "conjugates" them: slow, slower, and slowest.

I think today's closers are the best there have been at any one time. Some of the guys I've mentioned certainly will leave their mark on baseball history as did Hoyt Wilhelm, ElRoy Face, Rollie Fingers, Goose Gossage, Bruce Sutter, and Dennis Eckersley, the pioneers who altered the closer position. They truly impress me, so much, in fact, that I'd like to see more of them. I just wish short relievers weren't so obsessed with saves and would be satisfied with performances leading to wins because whenever the game is on the line, these are the guys I want to see on the mound.

PART IV

In the Batter's Box

18

THE LINEUP

Before each team bats in the first inning, we always present a graphic of the batting order. Unfortunately, we don't have time before the first pitch to go into detail about why a particular batter is leading off or batting fourth or hitting seventh or eighth or what the different requirements are for those spots. We try to be helpful to viewers during the game when we explain, for instance, why a particular player is an ideal leadoff man or second-place hitter, but perhaps we are guilty of presuming that viewers already know the logistics involved when a manager puts together his entire lineup. In truth, probably a great segment of the audience doesn't really know what he is thinking.

A manager will take into consideration power, bat control, and running ability when penciling players' names into certain spots in the lineup. The general idea is that a guy who can get on base and run makes a good leadoff hitter; a guy with good bat control, who can bunt and hit-and-run, is a desirable second-place hitter; the RBI men bat third, fourth, and fifth, and even sixth on power-laden teams like the Rockies, Yankees, Orioles, and Mariners; and the weaker batters fill out the order. There are a few catchers like Mike Piazza, Todd Hundley, Ivan Rodriguez, and Sandy Alomar and middle infielders like Jeff Kent, Alex Rodriguez, and Barry Larkin with enough pop to cause the manager to devise an atypical lineup, but usually you'll see fleet-footed outfielders or good-hitting shortstops leading off; the first baseman, third baseman, outfielders with power, and designated hitter vying for the three RBI slots; and good defensive, weak-hitting catchers and shortstops deep in the order.

But there are no hard-and-fast rules for matching players to particular spots in the order, especially since few managers have nine players whose talents are identical to the nine job descriptions. There has to be improvisation because players don't come to spring training with labels on their uniforms saying they are suited for only one spot in the order. When they compete to be a starter, hitting, of course, is a major factor, but it's to secure a position in the field and not to see who becomes the third or sixth hitter in the order, with the loser going to the bench. Usually, you don't say, "This guy can only lead off," you say, "He can hit first or second or sixth to ninth."

In theory, a player can bat anywhere in the lineup. A manager could confidently put Pete Rose in any spot, including fourth because he had occasional pop. Alex Rodriguez and Roberto Alomar can hit second or third with equal effectiveness, although those positions in the order are vastly different. I hit in all nine spots, including ninth in the American League. When I broke in, they started me out eighth and then moved me up to seventh and sixth, although against left-handers they moved me back and forth. Because I could hit with two strikes and didn't strike out a lot, they would at times insert me into the second spot, where I batted behind Lou Brock while he was on his stolen-base sprees in the 1960s. Although I was a catcher, I even led off about forty times in my career because I could run. Cardinals shortstop Royce Clayton pointed out to me that it is very difficult for a good base runner in the National League to be shifted back and forth between first and eighth in the lineup, as Tony La Russa did with Clayton in 1996 and 1997, because batting first allows you to run and batting eighth in front of a pitcher shuts down your running game.

When setting a lineup, the manager tries to insulate power and not divide speed. It makes sense for a manager to stack the batting order with left-handed batters against a right-handed pitcher or right-handed batters against a lefty because the rotation of the ball is more conducive to a batter who hits from the opposite side. It's not a good idea, however, to put several right-handed or left-handed batters back-to-back. If you have the personnel, you would like to sandwich a left-handed hitter between two right-handed hitters, or a strong right-handed hitter between two left-handed hitters, because if you have three in a row, it's easier for the opposing manager to make pitching changes late in the game. If instead of the three batters hitting left, left, left, they hit left, right, left, then the manager has to handle his bullpen differently. He may have to use up two left-handers to counter the two left-handed batters, and not too many bullpens are deep with good left-handers. If a team has only one effective left-hander, he may be held back until the second left-handed batter comes up, meaning the first left-handed batter will face a righty, or, if the manager wants to take out the pitcher immediately, the lefty reliever will have to face all three batters, including the right-handed batter in the middle. An offensive manager really would like to have a couple of switch-hitters in key spots in his lineup. One only has to recall the Cardinals of the mid-eighties, when they could put six switch-hitters in their lineup, to know what problems guys who can bat from both sides of the plate can cause pitching staffs.

Managers juggle their lineups from game to game. It may be because of the opposing pitcher, but often the manager just wants to give one guy a rest or a bench player a chance to start and get some at-bats. The lineup may include a backup catcher, especially in a day game following a night game, or a platoon player who has a good record against the opposing starter. It may not include a player with a nagging injury or a player in a slump. Or the manager may move a slumping player toward the front of the order to give him more at-bats, make him feel involved, and give him protection by having a more formidable hitter behind him. Or he may take the opportunity to insert a young player into the lineup rather than have him waste away on the bench. As a rookie, I was helped because there were so many good veteran hitters in the Cards' lineup taking the pressure off me, and I batted back in the order. A manager won't try to hide a bad hitter among better hitters because he will get better offensive production when players can bunch their hits. For example, if the first four men in the lineup all get two hits in a game, there's a good chance runs will score. Replace one of them with a batter who takes the collar, and maybe no runs will score.

Every team has high-salaried stars, but other players on the team may be equally indispensable. They may not have eye-popping stats, but they make key hits and are reliable defensively, which is the primary reason some shortstops and catchers are in the lineup. They are always there when they are needed. They possess the intriguing combination of "talent mixed with sheer will," which is how sports commentator Diana Nyad, the former long-distance swimmer, once described Pete Rose and Chris Evert, two athletes who refused to lose. They are winners who are needed in the lineup, even if that means sitting down players with better overall talent.

I can't stand when a player who has had a deplorable two weeks is asked by a beat writer why he's not playing that day and, taking the bait, broods, "The manager makes out the lineup." He never adds, "The manager has every right to keep me out because I've been awful," or "The other guy's better." While managing the Cubs, Don Zimmer once had a player come in to complain about not being in the lineup. Zimmer had the player change places with him and sit behind the manager's desk. And Zimmer took the role of the player and said, "How can you not start me although the two guys ahead of me are playing better?" Then Zimmer asked the player to respond as if he were Don Zimmer. The guy walked out with no argument.

Just as it's important to have different types of pitchers in the rotation, it's good to have diversity in the lineup. Some teams have all the same types of hitters, and they all play the same style of ball. Perhaps the stadium they play in has to do with a uniformly dull demeanor. As a viewer you will think they are too predictable. It is the unpredictable team that is usually successful. It has an edge. On offense, a manager wants a lineup that doesn't have too much salt or too much pepper—but he should want the proper dose of seasoning. The various players he sends up to the plate should display the variety that goes with their spots in the order.

THE TABLE SETTERS

When Roger Maris came to the Cardinals in 1967, he surprised me when he said that with all the power hitters the Yankees had during their championship years in the early sixties, Bobby Richardson and Tony Kubek, batting 1-2 and consistently getting on base in front of them, were just as vital a part of the offense. If you look back at all winning teams, you'll see that their first two guys were getting on base, serving as the catalysts for big innings. In baseball there's a feeling-out period at the beginning of games, as there is in boxing when they spar for the first three rounds. But if you get explosive guys on like Bert Campaneris and Billy North of the 1970s A's, Pete Rose and Joe Morgan of the Big Red Machine, or Lenny Dykstra and Wally Backman of the 1986 Mets, you can have a Mike Tyson–knockout approach to the first inning.

The leadoff hitter and second batter work in conjunction, always with the bat and sometimes with their feet. The plan is for the leadoff man to get on base and for the second batter to either take pitches so he can steal or move him along with a sacrifice bunt, productive out, or hit-and-run. By reaching base and threatening to steal, the leadoff man guarantees the second-place batter good pitches to hit. If the second batter has similar speed and bat control, he can take on the responsibilities of a leadoff man if he should lead off an inning himself or bat with nobody on base. It's interesting to note that Richardson and Kubek and Campaneris and North would switch their two spots in the order.

*　*　*

Don't miss the beginning of the game because that's when you see the leadoff hitter leading off an inning for perhaps the only time in the game. This is when the good ones shine. And I'm not talking about Rickey Henderson or Brady Anderson opening up a game with a home run, as they've been known to do, but Henderson, Anderson, and some of the real stolen-base threats "working the pitcher," in the batter's box and then on the basepaths. In the opening frame, the leadoff hitter will often take a couple of pitches, waiting until the pitcher gets a strike call. He will want to go deep in the count, not only because he may get a base on balls but also because he wants the pitcher to throw as many pitches as possible. I don't believe a high number of pitches in the first inning will necessarily contribute to the pitcher tiring early in the game, although some people will tell you this is the leadoff hitter's objective, but I do think a high pitch count is significant because it means the other batters in the lineup will get a look at most of the pitcher's repertoire before their first at-bats. They will also benefit if the leadoff hitter ends up walking and takes a big lead off

Because of their competitive nature, most injured baseball players always want to get back into the lineup before they are fully healed. Managers will have to decide whether their players are ready to return or need a few more days off. Rather than take unnecessary chances, it's usually wisest to keep recovering players on the bench or disabled list until you are positive they are healthy, especially early in the season when it's easiest to make lineup adjustments. Sometimes an injury to a star player will make a team come together and there can be positive results—at least that's what managers hope will happen. Besides, if you rush a player back too soon, he may develop a flaw in his swing that will remain even after his physical problems have disappeared.

first, as the pitcher will likely throw fastballs early in the count in anticipation of a stolen-base attempt and will throw to the fat part of the plate rather than risk a second walk. A leadoff batter can set the tone for the team.

The first inning will show you that Richie Ashburn, the best leadoff man of his era, was correct when he proudly asserted, "A good leadoff hitter is a pain in the ass to pitchers." The leadoff hitter's job, whether he is leading off an inning or not, is to get on base as often as he can by using any or all of his weapons and then to create havoc, doing everything in his power to manufacture a run. I say "weapons," yet I include passive traits, like having the patience, the good eye, and, as in the cases of Henderson and his crouching disciple Tony Phillips, the small strike zone that are necessary to work the pitcher for walks. Another weapon is the bat control that will allow the batter to foul off the pitcher's best pitches to keep his at-bat alive—Ashburn was a specialist at this—and to make solid contact with two strikes when he gets his pitch. And he should have speed to help him beat out bunts and infield grounders. By bringing the infielders in, he can shoot grounders past them for hits. If he also has power, infield hits will be easier because the men on the corners will be reluctant to creep in.

Traditionally, leadoff hitters have been batters who hit for average, have high on-base percentages, steal bases and score runs, and have little power to speak of. Ashburn, who batted leadoff with the Phillies from 1948 to 1959, and the recently retired Brett Butler were like that. Pete Rose lacked speed but was a great leadoff man because he had all the other attributes I've mentioned plus an intimidating aggressiveness on the basepaths and extra-base power. (The gritty Chuck Knoblauch steals more bases than Rose but otherwise seems to pattern his leadoff style after him.) Managers tend to put players with power in the middle of the lineup, but those few leadoff batters who can knock the ball out of the park as well as being able to run the bases have had an extraordinary impact on their teams. Henderson, who broke Bobby Bonds's career record for homers leading off games, Anderson, who broke Henderson's single-season record, Craig Biggio, Nomar Garciaparra, and some other current leadoff men put pitchers in a bad predicament every time they stride to the plate. Pitchers don't want to walk them and turn them loose on the basepaths, yet they are afraid to challenge them as they would less powerful leadoff hitters when they fall behind in the count 2-0 or 3-1.

Biggio, Houston's All-Star second baseman, is surprisingly productive from the leadoff spot considering that he bats behind the pitcher. I think American League leadoff men have an easier time because they bat behind a ninth-place *hitter* instead. That's one reason why Anderson and Garciaparra accumulate so many RBIs. Also, if the ninth-place hitter has speed, the two of them make an effective tandem on the bases.

It's a misconception that leadoff men are only dangerous when they're leading off. That doesn't make sense because leadoff men are guaranteed to lead off only once a game. They do, however, come to the plate at least as much as anyone else in the lineup during the game and far more times over the course of the season. Because the leadoff man has the most opportunities of anyone in the lineup, the manager wants someone in that spot who can score runners or move them into scoring position, or be able to manufacture a run even if he comes to bat with no one on and either one or two outs. Getting on base is critical. Henderson always has managed to fight his way on base when the game is on the line; Lenny Dykstra, with the Mets and Phillies, may have been even better. A home run could give a real lift to the team, but as a punch-and-run leadoff man like Tony Womack proves, speed on the basepaths is scarier to a pitcher than power. It can lead to bigger rallies than a solo homer.

Good leadoff hitters know only part of their job is done when they get on base, even if they aren't leading off that inning. They want to constantly pressure a pitcher by stealing a base or just threatening to steal; they may work a bunt play or hit-and-run with the second-place hitter. Getting to third with one out or second with two outs is their initial goal, and scoring is their ultimate goal. It's interesting to note that Henderson, baseball's stolen-base king, defines himself as a run scorer rather than a stealer. He realizes that the stolen base only matters if he comes around to score. That's the kind of mind-set you would expect from the best leadoff man in baseball history.

* * *

I thought it was great to bat second behind a base stealer, as I'm sure the switch-hitting Jim Gilliam did when he followed Maury Wills on the Dodgers in the early sixties. Those forty or fifty times when I hit behind Lou Brock I couldn't believe the pitches I saw. Fastballs down the middle. The pitchers were too concerned with Lou to pay full attention to me. There have been a lot of excellent right-handed second-place hitters like Alvin Dark, Dick Groat, Ted Sizemore, and, currently, Edgardo Alfonzo, but I think that a left-handed-hitting second batter behind a base stealer is preferable, as this setup is mutually beneficial. Because I batted left-handed, Lou knew that the catcher couldn't get a clear throw to second base on a steal attempt, and I was able to take advantage of the wide gap on the right side of the infield because the first baseman had to hold the runner. The one thing that can cause difficulty is if you are told to take pitches to give the stealer a chance to run and you end up falling behind in the count. Because after he steals second, there you are with a count of 0-2, 1-2, or 2-2, and it's tougher to pull the ball with two strikes. You don't want to take yourself into a hole—if you're going to go into a hole, you'd rather swing yourself there.

The second batter must be the team's best defensive hitter because he often finds himself in the hole after taking pitches. Without a doubt, more than any other player, he has to be unafraid to hit with two strikes on him. Of course, to hit with two strikes and be productive, he must be an excellent contact hitter with enough bat control to hit to all fields, bunt, and hit-and-run.

While the second spot in the order is unheralded, it is very, very important. It is the number two hitter who often determines whether the manager plays conservatively or not. What he is capable of doing with the leadoff man on first in the first inning might very well influence the manager to either try for one run or go for a big inning. Can he bunt, hit-and-run, go deep in the count? If he has stolen-base speed, wouldn't it make more sense for him to try to get on base than to intentionally give himself up with a bunt? The Mets' Edgardo Alfonzo and Florida's Edgar Renteria give their managers a lot of options. Alex Rodriguez, when he bats second for Seattle, and Roberto Alomar on Baltimore give their managers even more options because they can steal bases and hit home runs. Alomar is an extraordinary second-place hitter because he can do so many things necessary to get his team either one run or two runs or keep an inning going. He can start a rally or add to a rally. He's probably the most pivotal guy I have ever seen in the early part of a game. He adapts to every situation and gives his team exactly what it needs, including the long ball on occasion. He can move runners into scoring position for the power hitters, or he can be the power hitter. He can dictate how his manager approaches the game.

The second-place hitter is probably the team's most unpredictable batter. He must never let the pitcher know his mind-set. He keeps the pitcher guessing because his approach changes from game to game. Anytime the pitcher doesn't know how to go after a hitter, the hitter has the edge. If in the past he has taken a lot of fastballs from a particular pitcher with a base stealer on first, he may surprise him by swinging at a first-pitch fastball. So instead of having a man on second and being behind in the count 0-1, there are men on first and third with nobody out and the meat of the order coming up. Once the table is set, the power guys can go to work.

THE HEART OF THE ORDER

The third, fourth, and fifth batters are expected to drive in runs. Of the three, the third hitter has the most demanding role because he is also expected to score an equivalent number of runs. This means that in addition to extra-base power he must hit for a high average and, ideally, have speed and nerve on the basepaths. With runners on base, especially with two outs, his thinking is to both drive them in and, if he doesn't homer, get into scoring position. If he has speed, he will be expected to stretch singles into doubles and steal bases; as a base runner he will challenge the arms of outfielders. The RBI total of the fifth-place hitter in particular can be increased by the third-place hitter's base-running skills. If he goes from first to third on a single with less than two outs a cheap RBI could result, for instance. If the third-place hitter is on first, he'll usually try to score with two outs on a double.

Over the years, more good hitters have batted third than any spot in the order, including Babe Ruth, Hank Aaron, Willie Mays, Mickey Mantle (when Yogi Berra batted fourth), Roger Maris in 1961 (when Mantle occupied the fourth spot), Reggie Jackson and Jose Canseco in their MVP seasons, and currently Tony Gwynn, Larry Walker, Ken Griffey, Jr., Jeff Bagwell, and Barry Bonds. In most cases, your best offensive player bats third. A manager wants a skilled third hitter to take advantage of a pitcher who will throw good pitches to hit rather than chancing a walk with the fourth-place hitter on deck. Although he's protected by the cleanup man, just as he protects the second-place hitter, the third hitter must be disciplined enough to wait for balls he can drive. If he has patience, he will get better pitches to hit.

* * *

If the third-place hitter gets a lot of RBIs and homers, it is almost always because he is protected by an intimidating cleanup hitter. Ruth had Lou Gehrig behind him, Aaron had Eddie Mathews, Mays had Willie McCovey or Orlando Cepeda, and Griffey, Jr., has Edgar Martinez. These cleanup men are so consistent at driving in base runners that the pitcher can't pitch around dangerous third hitters and risk walking them.

Typically, the cleanup hitters who hit a lot of home runs are fearsome pull hitters ahead in the count, but the guys with strong arms like Frank Thomas, Albert Belle, Mike Piazza, Fred McGriff, and Mark McGwire also will go to center and the other way with power. Speed or base-running talent isn't necessary for fourth-place hitters because they are expected to drive in runs, not score them. In fact, a lack of mobility makes some players prime designated-hitter candidates. The doubles they get are rarely the result of stretching singles. They smack the ball off the wall and lumber into second instead of streaking into the base. Strikeouts are condoned more than with other hitters because they are swinging just as hard with two strikes. However, I would personally rather see a guy strike out 70 times and hit 25 home runs than strike out 135 times and hit 35 home runs.

I think many fourth-place hitters could be even more productive if they showed more patience. You'll notice that when Mark McGwire is launching homers almost every game, he's also walking a lot. When he's in a homer drought, you'll see that there are no bases on balls in his line in the box score. Mike Piazza is also much more effective when he has the patience to walk. On the other hand, American League batting champion Frank Thomas may be a little too selective, taking walks on pitches he could pound. That was also the gripe against Ted Williams. I think the advantage of walking isn't necessarily getting on base but to show pitchers that you're selective. Then they will give you pitches to hit in future at-bats to avoid more walks.

The value of the cleanup man and the other two batters in the middle of the order is shown less by their number of walks than by the good counts they get because of their selective eyes. If they are swinging at everything, they won't walk because, quite simply, they won't get three-ball counts. Instead, they will fall behind 0-2 and 1-2. When selective, they will get a lot of 3-1 counts and then need to swing at only pitches they like, hitting the ball on their terms. If the patient batter doesn't chase two straight balls, and then hits a screaming line drive against or over the fence, that big hit is the direct result of his getting into a favorable situation where the pitcher had to throw something he could hit. Sometimes walking the fourth-place hitter is a lot better than the alternative.

* * *

For the fourth-place batter to have success, he must be insulated. It is essential that the man on deck also be a solid RBI man with homer and extra-base power. The presence of a strong fifth-place hitter will force the pitcher to challenge the cleanup man. At the plate, his job is to drive in base runners. You never hear anybody saying that the fifth-place hitter is the most important player in the lineup, but when a team is winning, you'll usually find that he's picking up the third and fourth hitters if they were unable to score the runners. When the team is losing, you can bet that the same fifth batter makes the third out.

When I think of the fifth-place hitter, the first thing that comes to my mind is that more than anyone else in the lineup, he's the batter who can't allow himself to be pitched around. That's because on most teams there's a more precipitous drop in talent from the fifth to the sixth hitter than between any other two slots in the lineup. With a man on second and one or two out, pitchers would much rather pitch to the sixth batter, so they'll either intentionally walk the fifth batter or see if he'll chase balls off the plate, conceding the walk if he doesn't bite. Because of this, he has to have good enough plate coverage and the reach to go out of the strike zone to hit.

He can't accept a walk in this situation unless the pitches are far off the plate. Ernie Banks, who often batted fifth behind Billy Williams and Ron Santo on the Cubs, used to say, "If that run is in scoring position, I'm not going to save it for the next guy to pick up. That's my RBI, not his. Therefore I'm going to go out of my hitting zone. On a pitch just off the plate, which I'd take if I were leading off an inning, I'm going to swing if there is a man on second or third. My plate coverage is going to be greater than if no one is on." This thinking is valid with third and fourth hitters, but I think it applies even more to fifth-place hitters.

THE IN-BETWEEN MEN

I think that on most teams the sixth and seventh batters are the same entity, just as the first and second batters go together, and the three-four-five batters are the heart of the fillet, your leanest cut. It's common for them to be platoon players—right-handed batters who play against lefties and left-handed batters who play against righties.

On the rare teams without soft spots in their lineups, the sixth-place hitter may have a bigger role. In that case, he may be someone who has credentials similar to those of the fifth-place hitter and can be counted on to drive in between seventy and eighty runs a year. Moises Alou led the 1997 World Champion Florida Marlins with 115 RBIs batting sixth, so hitters can produce this far back in the order. Unlike the fifth hitter, he may be needed to hit for average rather than power, depending on the makeup of the lineup and the situation. His job is flexible, rather than defined. The same can be said of the seventh hitter, who is an everyday player. It's possible he is a player who can be dangerous at times and even deliver an occasional long ball but hasn't the consistency to be moved up into a slot that demands reliable clutch hitting. The seventh spot can be a good spot for a batter who is struggling with both his power and his average but is too valuable to the team to sit.

"Move the runner along" is a term you often hear in baseball. With no men out, some batters are expected to move the runner on second along to third, so the next batter can pick up an easy RBI. But if it's not late in the game, the sixth and seventh batters try to "move the runner *in*." It is their job to drive in the run and not leave it up to the weaker eighth and ninth batters. (With one out, the seventh batter must really bear down with a runner in scoring position.) However, their roles may change late in the game. Then, with no outs, the manager may tell them to sacrifice bunt or the batter may take it upon himself to move along the runner to third with a productive ground out to the right side. Late in the game, he is no longer leaving it up to the weak guys at the end of the order because the manager is ready to use his best pinch hitters.

THE BOTTOM OF THE ORDER

The deeper into the lineup you go, the more likely you are to find players who are in there for defense rather than offense. Because of their defensive skills, they will play the whole game with their team ahead while they will probably be removed for a pinch hitter if their team trails in late innings. In the National League, nonhitting shortstops and catchers are usually relegated to the seventh and eighth spots, in front of the pitcher, while in the American League they bat eighth and ninth.

In the National League, eighth is a very tough spot. It probably requires more patience than any spot in the lineup, and that's asking a lot from someone who doesn't get as many at-bats as the other guys. It's interesting to note that an eighth-place hitter often helps an offense not by hitting and scoring but by *clearing*. It is imperative for an eighth-place hitter to understand the value of clearing the pitcher so that the leadoff batter can open the next inning. His on-base percentage contributes to clearing the pitcher, not to run production. In 1996, Walt Weiss was a vital complement to a Colorado Rockies offensive juggernaut that was called "The Magnificent Seven" because of his ability to take care of two spots, eighth and ninth. In the National League, he was second to Barry Bonds in walks, and each time he received a free pass with two outs, he cleared the pitcher.

With two outs, the eighth-place hitter must figure out how to get on base so that the pitcher will bat—if the pitcher makes an out, it's preferable that it be the third out of the current inning rather than the first out of the next inning. For the same reason, the eighth-place hitter shouldn't try to stretch a single into a double with two outs unless the pitcher is coming out of the game for a pinch hitter. Nor should he attempt to steal second. Even with less than two outs, he is supposed to let the pitcher bunt him over. More than anyone else, he's expected to stay at first.

If the eighth batter is a better fielder than the sub on the bench, the manager will rarely pinch-hit for him if his team is ahead. Obviously, the better the hitter he is, the less often he'll be taken out for a pinch hitter if his team is trailing. If he's a good bunter, he won't be removed for a pinch hitter in a bunt situation—the good pinch hitter will be on deck to bat for the pitcher. The eighth-place batter will not sacrifice early in the game with the pitcher due up—if you see him do it, expect an early pinch hitter—but being able to bunt is an important tool for him in the late innings. Then he may be asked to sacrifice a runner to second or third with no outs in a one-run or tied game so that a pinch hitter can attempt to drive him in.

Another reason for the eighth-place hitter to get on base with two outs is to guarantee more at-bats for the big men in the lineup. If it's the eighth inning in a tie game, his reaching base will allow the number three hitter to bat in the ninth inning. If the third batter should homer to win the game, don't forget it was the eighth-place batter who made it possible an inning earlier.

The one good thing an eighth-place hitter can look forward to is being challenged when the count is in his favor. A pitcher will usually take his chances with an eighth-place hitter rather than walk him, especially with two outs. So what will happen if the manager decides to put a very good hitter in the eighth position? Braves manager Bobby Cox did that for a time in 1997 with Jeff Blauser, and the veteran shortstop responded by batting over .300 and driving in many key runs. If you can spare a guy like this at the top of the order to make the bottom part stronger, then it's worth a shot.

* * *

In the American League, a manager may put a fast runner in the ninth spot to provide back-to-back speed with the leadoff hitter. In this instance, he won't necessarily be the worst hitter in the lineup. Usually, however, the ninth-place hitter is the weakest of the nine players, either the pitcher or, in the American League, a standout defensive player or young player of indeterminate talents who is getting a rare start. It is mandatory for pitchers to learn how to bunt because with less than two outs they are often called on to sacrifice.

Curt Simmons used to say that it's not his batting average that a pitcher cares about, it's his at-bats. Curt meant that a pitcher will be happy with four at-bats in a game, even if he got no hits, because it means he has pitched well enough to remain in the game. But a pitcher should take his at-bats seriously, not bail and whale: Too many swing as hard as they can in case they hit it. Jim Kaat remembers that when he was with the Cardinals in 1982, Whitey Herzog got all the pitchers together in spring training and said, "I'm not here to talk about pitching today. I'm here to talk about hitting. We gave up too many at-bats last year."

It's been traditional in baseball for everybody to laugh about a pitcher's hitting. It's not a big joke. A pitcher who can help himself with the bat can pick up a lot of extra wins. While bunting is a most valuable hitting tool for a pitcher, he should have a modicum of skill at handling the bat. He can push the runner across and do a lot of other good things. The smart pitchers understand this and try to improve themselves. Pitchers love to hit, and if they can do it at the level of the Braves' John Smoltz, Tom Glavine, and Greg Maddux, they may get to stay in close games longer. A manager will probably pinch-hit for a trailing pitcher beginning in the seventh inning, or possibly the sixth inning if there is a rally brewing, but if his team trails by one run and there are two outs, a good-hitting pitcher might get to bat as late as the seventh inning.

THE DESIGNATED HITTER

I detest the DH. It changes the nature of the sport. Just because there are more runs scored in an American League game because the pitcher doesn't bat doesn't make the game more entertaining—and it certainly doesn't make it more interesting from a strategic standpoint. I don't see the appeal of two teams standing toe-to-toe and swinging mallets at each other. The game of baseball is built around strategy. Not only cerebral stuff but situations that initiate old-fashioned bleacher arguments, like: First bleacher bum: "You've gotta sacrifice in this situation!" Second bleacher bum: "Are you crazy? You can't bunt with this guy! He's gotta . . ." What we try to do in the booth is bring up all the options, and it's always true that the more possibilities there are, the more interesting a situation is. I think options are limited in the American League because of the DH, and that's why games are more engrossing in the National League.

Steve Hirdt points out that the most riveting games in the World Series in the nineties have been played in National League parks. Game 7 in 1997, in which Florida came from behind to beat Cleveland on Edgar Renteria's two-out single in the bottom of the eleventh inning, confirms what he says. Also memorable is Game 3 of the 1991 World Series, which was played in Atlanta. In that game, Minnesota Twins manager Tom Kelly kept insisting he'd have no problem managing in a National League game, where pitchers bat for themselves, but he immediately ran into a problem. He used up all his pinch hitters, so he had to let reliever Rick Aguilera bat for himself with the bases loaded in the top of the twelfth inning. He lined out and then gave up the losing run in the bottom half of the inning. I have the utmost respect for Kelly, but an American League manager in a National League park in the postseason could run into problems.

If there had been a designated hitter throughout baseball history in both leagues, many outstanding hitting pitchers would never have had the opportunity to pick up the bat. Steve says that if there had always been the DH in the American League, the hitting prowess of Babe Ruth might never have been recognized because he wouldn't have batted when he pitched early in his career with Boston. That's a hell of an argument against the DH right there.

One idea is that for all games in both leagues, the home team manager would be allowed to decide whether to use the DH. He can base his decision on how well his pitcher hits, how well the opposing pitcher hits in comparison, how well his top DH does against the opposing pitcher, and how the other team's DH does against his pitcher. The manager can save his DH; he may force the other manager to play his poor-fielding DH in the field. This idea would let good-hitting pitchers have at-bats and add some strategy. Do I endorse it? No, because the pitcher should bat in *every* game. Who wants to attend or watch on television those games that have less strategy?

There is another strong reason to eliminate the DH that has nothing to do with strategy. I don't know if anyone has ever pointed out that pitchers who bat for themselves have more expertise when they pitch. What they learn in the batter's box they take with them to the mound when they face batters. In the American League, pitchers don't have the opportunity to learn from their own hitting experiences. That's one of the reasons pitching in the junior circuit is often backward in regard to when to throw fastballs and when to throw breaking balls. If these pitchers haven't held a bat in their hands since high school, you can't expect them to get into the heads of the major-league batters they must face. Pitchers with good arms who understand hitting, and are good hitters themselves, have a decided advantage. They understand the hitting process in the major leagues.

THE PINCH HITTER

Almost all contending teams have at least one dependable pinch hitter who can bat for the pitcher or a weak hitter in a key situation. The pinch hitter may be someone who wouldn't flourish if he played every day, but for one at-bat against a particular pitcher in a certain situation, he may be a much better choice than the regular who is due up. With men on second and third late in a one-run game, a .300 left-handed batter coming off the bench to bat against a right-handed reliever is probably preferable to a right-handed regular who bats .240 overall and even less against right-handed pitching. A leadoff hitter given a day off is a good choice to pinch-hit for a player or pitcher at the bottom of the order who is scheduled to lead off the eighth or ninth inning in a one-run game. When his team trails by two runs and there is a man on base, a manager will likely want to send up a long-ball hitter to pinch-hit for a singles hitter.

But pinch hitting is very, very difficult. For proof: I had eighty-two pinch hits in my career, which places me in the all-time top twenty-five, yet I batted only about .220 coming in cold off the bench, more than fifty points below my career average. So, with failure so common, you have to accept that making an out isn't the end of the world. Habitually ineffective pinch hitters put undue pressure on themselves. It has always been that the most effective pinch hitters are veterans: Smoky Burgess, Jerry Lynch, Manny Mota, Greg Gross, Jose Morales, Gates Brown, Dave Philley, Denny Walling, Ed Kranepool, Rusty Staub. Matt Franco of the Mets and Keith Lockhart of Atlanta, two of 1997's top pinch hitters, may not have been in the majors for a long time, but they were older and more mature than the typical player trying to catch on in the majors. I think only a mature player has the mentality to be a good pinch hitter. He needs a mind-set that incorporates concentration and preparation, traits not always exhibited by young players.

If you make an out your first time up as a starter, you hope you have the opportunity to come through your second time up. As a pinch hitter it is more difficult because you have to cram everything you would consider in four at-bats into your one at-bat for the game. Since he has batted only five or six times in the previous eight or nine games and not at all during the game he's entering, it's very unlikely that he will be locked in, so he must really focus. He must decide what is needed from him, to get on base or hit the long ball. During the game he must mentally prepare for his one at-bat and be physically ready to bat from having hit off the tee. (A guy who pinch-hits only fifty times a year must also work at his job before the game begins.) He also should know a lot about the pitcher from having watched him go two or three times through the lineup. Through observation, he should know how the starter pitches to batters with similar traits. In most cases, however, he won't be facing the starting pitcher. If the opposing manager sends in a reliever to face him, he'll have to go into the memory bank and remember how this reliever pitched him the last few times out. Remember: The best pinch hitter will often face the other team's closer, making the situation doubly difficult.

Managers get involved in various cat-and-mouse scenarios. If the other team has a good left-handed pitcher on the mound, the manager of the offense might send up a right-handed pinch hitter just to induce the opposing manager to take him out of the game. When a right-handed reliever comes in, the offensive manager might then turn to a left-handed pinch hitter. Because of the rule that states a reliever must face at least one batter, the right-hander will have to pitch to this left-handed pinch hitter. This is a common scenario. The offensive manager has to figure out what the best move is. Does he prefer the final matchup to the original matchup? It depends on the identities of the pitcher, the original hitter, the guy coming up, the relief pitcher, and the second pinch hitter. It's like in chess when you trade pieces; there are fewer pieces on the board with which to play, but does that give either side an advantage? If you can get rid of a quality opposing pitcher who is still pitching well by bringing in a fair pinch hitter, it's probably a good move.

Pinch hitters love situations where they can drive in runs, like batting with the bases loaded and less than two outs. It's a chance to make some money. If you're the number one guy, you want to come into a game situation, even if it's the fifth or sixth inning. What you don't want is to be wasted. Last year, for example, Colorado manager Don Baylor sent up John Vander Wal, who holds the record for pinch hits in a season, to pinch-hit with two outs and nobody on in the seventh inning with his team trailing by two runs. I thought Vander Wal was wasted coming in that early because there were seven outs to go. If your other guys do their jobs, they will tie the game, and you will want your best pinch hitter to be available in the ninth inning. I would have understood Baylor making that move in the eighth inning because he might not have gotten another chance to use Vander Wal. On the other hand, you don't want to take your mulligan into the clubhouse, as they say in golf. You don't want the game to end without using your best pinch hitter.

A good pinch hitter won't be wasted if you send him up with two men out in the eighth inning and you're trailing by one run. If by getting one more base runner in the eighth, your best batter will be able to bat in the ninth, it makes sense to send up the batter who has the best chance of getting on base through a hit or walk. He might not score, but you're giving your team a better chance in the final inning. With two outs in the ninth, you can't ask for more than to have your best hitter come to the plate as the potential tying run.

It isn't always a good idea to send in a strong pinch hitter for a batter with less impressive stats. If the guy due up is a good fielder and your team leads, you must determine that the odds are good that you will be able to put the other team away. There are times when the weak-hitting shortstop is the better choice to bat than the better hitter coming off the bench. For instance, if you pinch-hit with a good left-handed hitter and the other team brings in a left-handed pitcher like Scott Radinsky or Billy Wagner, who neutralizes him, your odds would have been better with the shortstop batting against the original pitcher.

THE PINCH RUNNER

When you're ahead by one run in the eighth inning or top of the ninth and want insurance runs, you shouldn't pinch-run if it will hurt your defense. For instance, if you pinch-run for the catcher, you should have a good defensive catcher on the bench. If you send in a pinch runner for any good defensive player, you must be confident you will put the other team away.

If you are behind in the last inning, you pinch-run without regard for defense (unless, possibly, there is no other catcher on the bench). In the last inning, you always replace a slow runner who represents the tying run. A manager must decide whether to send in a pinch runner for a slow runner who represents the winning run because if he doesn't score there will have to be an adequate defensive replacement for the removed player. If you are behind by two runs in the last inning and have only one fast runner on the bench and two slow runners on the bases, what do you do? You pinch-run for the trail runner, the potential tying run, because he's the only run that counts.

A QUICK SUMMARY

If his team has a lead, the manager will go with defensive players the closer the game gets to the end. If his team is behind, the manager will stick with offense. A manager expects his lineup to work the pitcher so that his leadoff man leads off as many innings as possible, his cleanup man comes up with men on base, his sluggers bat back-to-back in the same inning, his best pinch hitter is available at the right time, and his best hitter comes to bat in the ninth inning if the team is down by a run. His batters must know that in working a pitcher, there is no insignificant at-bat by anyone in the lineup. As you are watching the game, remember: Early-inning hits by batters low in the order may not score runs, but they will allow the best hitters an extra time up late in the game. That is vital to winning close games.

19

BATTING MECHANICS
AND STYLE

When Hank Aaron reminisces about his hitting ability, he makes it sound so easy: "The pitcher only had a ball, I had a bat." What he fails to mention is that in addition to that long piece of lathed lumber that he used to hit a little round ball "squarely" to the tune of 755 homers, he had impeccable mechanics. He did everything correctly, from locking in his shoulder and keeping his hands back to—with a lift of his back heel and dramatic weight shift—hitting against the straight front side to generate power. (Aaron's timing with his left leg was as close to perfection as you could have.) As Aaron has known since he was a rookie, a batter can have an abundance of physical skills, but without proper hitting technique they will wither on the vine.

When a batter is going well, he can't really explain it. He'll resort to clichés like "I'm seeing the ball real well," but he won't say anything about his superb mechanics, probably because he is unaware of what he's doing right. If, however, I ask the same player why he has hit a dry spell, he'll start rattling off his defects:

1. I'm not keeping my shoulder locked in and my hands back.
2. I'm not positioned properly in the batter's box.
3. I'm not getting good bat extension.
4. I'm not recognizing the pitch before committing myself.

5. I'm not seeing the ball.
6. I'm not keeping my hands high (where are my hands, anyway?).
7. I'm lunging at the ball instead of staying down.
8. I'm hitting the ball over the plate instead of in front of it.
9. I'm opening up when I swing instead of driving my shoulder toward the pitcher.
10. I'm too slow with my hands.
11. I'm too quick with my hands.
12. I'm using my arms instead of my hands and lower body.

I assume another of his problems is "I'm thinking too much about my problems" because if he starts contemplating all the things he should be doing while he is at the plate he will confuse himself into making outs. There's something to "See ball, hit ball." A batter at the plate must limit himself to focusing on the one characteristic that is paramount to his hitting. For instance, Ken Griffey, Jr.'s dominant trait is the locked-in shoulder, and if he has been repeatedly fouling back the 3-1 pitch instead of driving it, the one thing he will do each at-bat is make sure his front shoulder is not opening up too soon. If a batter has one key in mind and does that correctly, everything else should fall into place because of muscle-memory.

There are many things you have to do at the plate, but I contend that the essence of good hitting mechanics is to keep the shoulder locked in and the hands back. To have any chance of becoming a good major-league hitter, you must practice these two interconnecting disciplines and also provide what I think are the two key elements to good major-league hitting: the virtue of patience and the physical attribute of quick hands.

* * *

As George Kissell used to preach, "Good hitting is like highway construction: closed shoulders." In order to hit the ball in front of the plate, all hitters, particularly left-handers against left-handers, must keep their front shoulders locked in. It's in vogue for hitters to say they want to "get the bat head out"—their thinking is that the more they use their body on the swing, the more out in front of the plate they will hit the ball and the more they will pull it. But one problem is that when a batter is too aggressive trying to get the bat head out to pull the ball, the front shoulder often flies open and instead of the batter connecting with authority in front of the plate, he hits the ball over the plate and is unable to pull it. The only time a batter can hit the ball effectively while his front shoulder is open is on a pitch down-and-in. The batter doesn't need extension in his swing to pull that pitch. He just drops the bat head. (Willie Mays was the only batter I ever saw who could hit with his shoulder out. He always was bailing out, but he was so talented and god-awful strong that it seemed he never got cheated when swinging.)

Pulling the front shoulder out is a more common trait of left-handed batters than right-handed batters. My broadcast partner Ralph Kiner has a good explanation for that. He says that left-handers are anxious to make the turn to get to first, while right-handers are already going in that direction. Ralph suggests that if third base were first base, right-handed batters would have the greater tendency to pull out the front shoulder because they would be the ones who have to turn before running. It's certainly food for thought.

In addition to causing the batter's head to go up, the shoulder opening up results in the hands coming forward too soon, leaving the batter with only his arms with which to hit. Unless he has extremely strong arms, like Albert Belle, Darryl Strawberry, Mike Piazza, Frank Thomas, and Fred McGriff, he will have no power left. He will have no chance against the outside pitch and little chance against anything else. With a view from the center-field camera, you can see that a batter cannot pull out his front shoulder without bringing his hands forward too early. However, if he keeps his shoulder locked in, he can be fooled on a pitch and start forward too early with his body yet still be able to keep his hands back and generate power. Stan Musial was the quintessential guy in this regard. You could fool Musial and his body would commit, but because his hands went inversely to his front foot, he had his hands back and, boom, he could still deliver his power. You don't see many films of Musial because we played in St. Louis, a small market, which is a shame because young hitters could study how he used his quick hands.

With regard to hand speed, here's a bad formula for hitting: in front of the breaking ball, behind the fastball. When you want to be quick with your swing against a hard thrower, you're often too quick with your hands. Particularly early in the season, after players have left hot, humid Florida and Arizona and hit the cold air, they're so strong that they have to fight being too quick and hitting the ball off the end of the bat. (I believe this is the cause of so many bats being broken in April and May.) Hitters don't give their hands enough credit for being quick and think they have to start their bodies in order to increase their bat-head speed. The reverse is true. A batter on a bad streak may tell himself to be aggressive, but in his eagerness to hit the ball hard, he might open up the shoulder and be unable to hold back the hands. Young players in particular must learn to be, as I define it, *patiently aggressive*. Waiting is crucial.

In fact, quick hands are tremendous assets only if you show patience on the pitch *before* turning them loose. Batters who commit too early have problems adjusting and are caught flat-footed. They must let the ball come to them. Those who wait the longest are much more effective because they are able to see the pitch develop fifteen to ten feet from the plate and then react with quick hands. Nobody is better at this than eight-time National League batting champion Tony Gwynn, whose hands are, remarkably, as quick as they were fifteen years ago. (One reason Hank Aaron kept his lightning-fast hands back is that he didn't want to commit early on what appeared to be a fastball and be way out in front if it turned out to be a change-up or curveball.)

Some pitches are difficult to hit even with quick hands. A lot of power hitters have trouble with the inside fastball because they like to extend their arms. It's tougher to determine whether the inside pitch will be a strike, so batters must be quicker than on the outside pitch. As I've mentioned, Barry Bonds, from the left side, and Gary Sheffield, from the right side, are the only two power hitters in the National League who can consistently turn on the inside fastball that is *just off the plate*. That pitch is too close to take. Florida manager Jim Leyland points out that they are so

Every batter constantly thinks about his mechanics, although not always in the same way. I'm reminded of Glenn Wilson, who was a hard-hitting outfielder for the Phillies and several other teams beginning in the early 1980s. When his career was winding down with the Houston Astros, he went into business, purchasing a service station in his hometown of Baytown, Texas. In 1990, he was in the midst of a frustrating season when he made an out in one game that was so foolish that a local sportswriter asked Wilson what he'd been thinking about during that plate appearance. Wilson shrugged. "My mechanics." "You mean . . . you weren't keeping your shoulder locked in?" ventured the timid reporter. "No . . . my mechanics," said Wilson. "My mechanics in my garage." Wilson knew it was time to get out of the game and retired after the season.

devastatingly quick that they can take a ball on the inside corner or even a little off the plate and hit it on the good part of the bat and keep it fair. If you hit that pitch with your hands in front of your body, you'll put the fat part of the bat on the ball but will pull it foul—Todd Hundley has the tendency to do that. So what Bonds and Sheffield do is move their hands forward a bit so that the bat head will move out farther in front of the plate. The ball will be pulled, but since there's no hook on it, it will stay fair. I think it's a natural talent rather than something a player can develop. Aaron was the best at it, but Bonds, Sheffield, and Ken Griffey, Jr., in the American League, are also remarkable.

* * *

Guys with big cuts have a tough time catching up to the fastball, inside or outside. The shorter your stroke, the longer you can wait and the fewer bad balls you will swing at. So it would be a good idea for some batters to spread their legs to cut down their strides, assuring their stroke will be more compact. You hear players talk about long swings. Remember: Short, quick, and strong is better than long and strong.

Edgar Martinez, a marvelous right-handed line-drive power hitter, has the ideal compact swing. He stands with his right foot close to the plate and left side slightly open, and looks for a ball to pull, although he also has success going the other way. Because of his short stroke, he is quick on the inside pitch and high strikes over the middle, and he is also very aggressive on the outside part of the plate. His hand quickness allows him to wait, and he gets great plate coverage, which I think makes him the toughest guy to pitch to in the American League. Most hitters adjust their swings because of the count or an intimidating pitcher, but not Martinez and the left-handed Tony Gwynn, the hardest out in the National League. They are fluid with all their swings.

Paul Molitor has a patented compact swing that works wonders for him but shouldn't be imitated by young right-handed batters. It would make more sense for them to pattern themselves on someone like Nomar Garciaparra, who exhibits no wasted motion, than on the rare batter who is virtually motionless at the plate. When the low-first camera focuses on Molitor, you will have a hard time understanding how he generates the power he displays because his hands don't go back to trigger his swing. He gets away with this because, like Joe DiMaggio, who was also motionless at the plate, Molitor has exceptional hand speed and weight transfer and uses the powerful muscles he has in his big pecs and forearms.

Almost all other batters need a trigger. You take the bat back and then forward and your hips move in unison. I had a problem in that I was comfortable starting my swing up front by my head, which meant I would have to pull my bat back pretty far to trigger my swing. Other left-handed batters didn't have to be as quick as I did because they started with their hands already back. I would run the risk of taking the bat back too far, and if you do that you make contact over the plate instead of in front. When I slumped, I'd hit the lazy fly the other way on pitches that were up and away . . . my nemesis.

* * *

If you can't wait on a pitch because you have to do too many things, then you're doing something that's not fundamental to good hitting. Ruben Sierra slumped himself out of the majors in 1997 with his high leg kick and moving head and hands. He did so many unnecessary things that trying to hit the ball seemed like an afterthought. Bret Boone, whose hitting woes resulted in his spending time in the minors in '97, hooks his bat around his neck, which means he must start his swing earlier to get the bat head into the hitting area. He can't stay back like you're supposed to. You'll see other guys wiggle their bats, another bad trait, even though it doesn't bother a few batters like Gary Sheffield. While they produce more power because they're coming from farther to hit the ball, very often the pitch is on top of them in a hurry and eats them up. They will rarely be quick enough to hit the ball in front of the plate and pull it.

If you curl the bat (so the bat head is angled toward center field), it means you have farther to go to get the bat into the hitting area. You've got to have young, lively hands to get the bat around. All left-handed batters fight a natural curl, but Darryl Strawberry is the quintessential bat curler, which explains why he has always been a streaky hitter. When you have as big an arc as the tall, long-armed Strawberry, you will generate more power but will have a difficult time getting out in front—you simply have too far to go in too short a time. Sluggers who swing from their hotel rooms can't pull a major-league fastball because they're coming from too far back and there's too much to do in order to hit the ball in front. Strawberry's pulled homers come only off change-ups or slow curves. If he is able to muster the long ball off hard stuff, it will be to the opposite field.

Despite the success of Eric Davis, his devotee Reggie Sanders, and others, I think batters who hold their bats low are doing themselves a disservice. They have to begin every swing by lifting their bats before they can get into hitting position. When switch-hitter Carl Everett bats from the left side, he holds the bat handle at waist level, and he really struggles when pitchers throw balls above his hands. That's the way pitchers should approach batters with low hands.

* * *

Ted Williams would say that when you grip the bat you have to be relaxed enough for someone to come along and take the bat out of your hands. That's how loose it should be. Don Mattingly and John Olerud are the guys I think of with soft, quiet hands on the bat. I also remember that Bob Horner, who teamed with Dale Murphy to give the Braves a fearsome 1-2 punch in the 1980s, stood right on the plate and his hands were so relaxed that he seemed to caress his bat. He was so calm waiting for the ball that he reminded me of a spider luring a fly into its web. He then struck with the quickest bat in the business. It's the opposite with Jeff Bagwell. If you tell a kid to emulate a stance, it wouldn't be Bagwell's because he never appears to be relaxed before the pitch. He squeezes the bat so much you hear the squeak of his batting gloves. Yet all his swings are frightening. There are no checked swings or cheap hacks, and he is never cheated. Unfortunately, the bone on his left hand has been broken three times by pitches, partly due to his crouched stance. He is so ready and locked in that often he can't get out of the way. That's scary for him because he's so productive that pitchers have to come inside on him occasionally.

* * *

A crouched stance in itself is not so bad. Remember that Stan Musial had the most exaggerated crouch imaginable, and he was a pretty fair hitter. I much prefer it to the open stance that is popular with a lot of young players today, although there are the extraordinary success stories of Andres Galarraga and other open-stance batters. Galarraga's stance is so ridiculously open that he's almost facing the pitcher. He can see the pitcher with both eyes, which he says is important, but, interestingly, by the time he hits the ball he'll be seeing it with only one eye anyway because the front shoulder has to be closed on contact. The open stance makes proper timing much more difficult to achieve because you have to bring your front side around before going forward with the swing.

I know about the open stance because I had to stop using it to be able to *hit* in the big leagues. In 1961, Hal Smith, who was a standout defensive catcher, was sidelined after a heart attack, so at nineteen, I spent June and July with the Cardinals. While I had some success, pitchers were consistently knocking the bat out of my hands. After I had been demoted, George Crowe, a terrific left-handed hitter before becoming the Cardinals' traveling batting instructor, got me to alter my batting style. At that time I had an open stance, with my right foot toward the first-base line. I learned that it was necessary to put my right foot in a good starting position so that I could reach the outside strike and hit it with authority. So George swung my right leg around and closed my stance, enabling me to hit against my front side. This adjustment saved my career.

* * *

I don't remember anyone ever describing my swing as "graceful," but that is a word usually reserved for left-handed batters, just as "crafty" is used for left-handed pitchers. If Billy Williams was the left-handed batter with the most graceful, purest swing of my day, then Barry Bonds has it today. Others with sweet swings from the left side include Ken Griffey, Jr., David Justice, Chipper Jones, Rafael Palmeiro, Wally Joyner, and Will Clark. While John Olerud has the quiet swing *beginning* that I love—you could balance a glass of water on his hands—Clark has the high *finish* that impresses. His power is in his finish. With Palmeiro, who searches for the perfect swing just as surfers search for the perfect wave, the power is in the contact. You aren't as impressed with Palmeiro's finish. Mo Vaughn, a prototypical home run hitter, has power in both his contact and his extension. Justice is among the few other left-handers with high finishes. As it is with Clark on the inside pitch, Justice's hips are so quick that he "bellybuttons" the ball. Hall of Famer Paul Waner used to use this term, which means you quickly throw your hips toward the pitcher. However, if you do everything right with the front shoulder, your hips will open with the proper timing. Clark and Justice do that so well.

The extraordinarily gifted Griffey and Bonds turn on balls with frightening hand-and-wrist speed. (When announcers say "turn on a ball," they are talking about a batter getting around on the inside fastball.) What you'll notice about Griffey is that he has an uppercut and that he's almost upright on every swing, whether the pitch is high or low. That's different from Tony Gwynn, who bends his knees; this explains why Griffey has more home run power than Gwynn. He has very long arms, which makes it easier for him to rake the low ball and hit it out. Some players who hit fifteen to twenty homers a year are as strong as the guys who hit thirty-five to forty homers, but they don't have the lift in their swings. To be a home run hitter, a batter must have strength plus lift, a rare combination.

* * *

When I look at Bonds, I see quickness inside and power the other way. Larry Walker, the National League's MVP in 1997, is similar because he has the same plate coverage, although he's not quite as quick inside. Bonds, Walker, Gwynn, Jim Thome, Tino Martinez, and most of the other left-handed hitters I have mentioned have the ability to hit well on both high and low pitches. Martinez is the rare left-handed power hitter who actually prefers the ball up. Mets catcher Todd Hundley is the left-handed slugger who is clearly identified with the low fastball. When you watch him from the center-field camera, you forget the balls from the mid-thigh up because, unless he's looking for a hanging change-up or hanging waist-high curve, he'll rarely hit that pitch out. But you can't throw the low fastball by him. (I'm reminded of Musial, the best low-ball hitter in the history of the game.) Hundley is a deadly low-ball hitter, but that's not to say a low-ball hitter can't sometimes turn on a high fastball. If it were that simple, pitchers would throw Hundley only high fastballs. And just because he is a low fastball hitter doesn't mean he'll always drive that ball. When he hits into double plays, usually he's hitting low fastballs.

Traditionally, right-handed batters differ from left-handed batters because they are high-ball hitters. Edgar Martinez, Paul Molitor, and Gary Sheffield fit into that mold. But there are currently a lot of low-ball-hitting right-handed power hitters in the majors, including Mark McGwire (an avid golfer), Joe Carter, Juan Gonzalez, Manny Ramirez, Cecil Fielder, and Matt Williams. For a high-ball hitter to hit the ball well, he has to have his hands high and the bat head out—he must have good extension. A low-ball hitter can hit the ball solidly without bringing the bat head all the way up. He gets the extension he needs for power because he can hit the slower low pitch farther back toward the plate. He usually has slower hands than a successful high-ball hitter. Good fastball hitters can handle the ball upstairs. It takes a quicker bat to handle the high fastball than the low fastball. To hit the high fastball hard and keep it in play, you have to hit it out in front of the plate; you can hit the low fastball over the plate. You're talking about a distance of two and a half feet or so in bat speed.

Then, would it stand to reason that most good low-ball hitters are good off-speed hitters? The answer is yes. The guy with the slower bat can usually handle the low-ball (mid-thigh to mid-shin) and off-speed pitches.

However, I do think right-handed hitters, especially those I've mentioned, have better bat speed on low fastballs than left-handed hitters. (Generally speaking, left-handed low-ball hitters have slower bats–even Todd Hundley doesn't have tremendous speed.) This is pure conjecture on my part, but this might have something to do with the right-hander's top hand on his bat being his right hand. The top hand in the swing generates bat speed, so you have an advantage if your dominant hand is on top. Batters who are right-handed throwers and bat from the right side have their right hand as their speed hand. But batters who are right-handed when they throw but bat from the left side have their weaker left hand on top, and that's why they don't have the same kind of bat speed. They're low-ball hitters because their dominant hand is their bottom hand.

* * *

Hitters say to one another, "Put the perfect move on the ball," meaning "hit it well," not "Make sure you follow through on the swing." If you put a good swing on the ball, a good finish will happen naturally, the result of

Larry Doby, who had been an outstanding left-handed hitter in his day, was the hitting instructor for me under Gene Mauch at Montreal. I asked him if it was worthwhile to have two hitting instructors, one for right-handed batters and one for left-handed batters. I was thinking how different they are. Left-handed batters—think of great hitters like Tony Gwynn and Wade Boggs—have a style that could never be emulated by a right-handed batter. (In fact, Tony told me that he doesn't know if he could teach hitting after he retires because what works for him might not work for anybody else, including other left-handed batters.) What really is different is the curl, the little loop in the swing that most of us right-throwing, left-handed batters have trouble correcting. The reason, I think, is that the dominant hand for a left-handed hitter is the bottom hand on the bat. I think Larry was offended at first by my insinuation that there should be separate batting coaches, then he warmed to that idea. But no one has talked about it since because it would mean adding another coach to the payroll.

what you did well in the hitting zone. You shouldn't be thinking that at a certain point in the swing—contact—you have to switch into a follow-through mode. I disagree with the influential theory advanced by the late Charlie Lau and former White Sox hitting coach Walt Hriniak that the top hand should leave the bat on contact. The batter seems more concerned with the follow-through than the swing. Hriniak, for whom I have tremendous respect because he was so dedicated to his job, says he and Lau were not emphasizing the hand leaving the bat, and he may be right, but that's what their pupils came away with because it is their dominant trait on the swing. There are many batters who hit homers releasing their top hands, but those who follow the Lau-Hriniak philosophy appear to be more concerned with the release upon hitting the ball than with hitting the ball and having the hand come off the bat. The left-handed Fred McGriff often releases his top hand in the strike zone, but I don't think he is a proponent of the Lau theory because there is an uppercut to his swing and an unusual, helicopter finish—it's almost a fencing move he does with his right hand. He's much different from Hriniak student Robin Ventura, who has a downward swing and a follow-through that begins on contact. Ventura was a good hitter coming out of college, and I think he would have progressed further if he had waited for the finish to happen naturally and hadn't had the need to start thinking of following through even before hitting the ball. I think young batters would be better off watching Tony Gwynn. The game's best hitter is concerned with the repetition in his swings, with the head on his shoulders following the head of his bat and making contact with the ball in that one little sweet area of his bat. He's not worrying about his follow-through.

STANDING IN THE BATTER'S BOX

There's no set number of inches you have to stand away from the plate. A hitter should position himself so he can cover the outside part of the plate but still be quick enough to handle the pitch on the inside corner. You'll see that as soon as a lot of guys get into the batter's box, they make sure their bats can reach the other side of the plate. That's what we were all taught to do when we first started playing baseball as kids.

As mentioned, if you see a batter standing far away from the plate, it usually means he likes the ball away from him and doesn't like the ball inside. He wants to extend his arms. If you see a batter standing on top of the plate, you can assume he prefers pitches on the inside of the plate (although he might overestimate his ability to handle them). He also may be standing very close in order to limit where a pitcher can throw the ball without hitting him.

A batter will move back and forth in the batter's box, even between pitches during the same at-bat, depending on how the pitcher is going after him. What he wants when you see him move away from the plate is to be able to extend his arms if the pitcher throws a strike from the middle of the plate in. He'll be able to swing the fat part of the bat through that area of the plate. If the pitcher is going away, away, away, like Tom Glavine or Jimmy Key might do, the batter may compensate by crowding the plate, which means the fat part of the bat will go over the outside corner. But by doing this, of course, he becomes more vulnerable to the inside pitch.

HITTING TO THE OPPOSITE FIELD

During the course of a game, if you see a batter hitting the ball hard to the fat part of the field (left-center to right-center) three or four times you know he's in a good-hitting mode. A batter who hits the ball through the middle is locked in with his shoulder and has the potential to hit the ball to all fields. A line-to-line hitter has great bat control and is the type of guy you want up in a game situation if you need a base hit in lieu of a home run. You will find that almost everybody who has a high average hits to all fields. You can go right down the list, beginning with Tony Gwynn and Wade Boggs, who share a ton of batting titles between them. Larry Walker's average went way up when he also started hitting to left. Former American League batting champion John Olerud's average climbed back up in 1997 because he was out of Toronto and was encouraged by his new manager, Bobby Valentine, to go the other way. When Sandy Alomar and Nomar Garciaparra had lengthy hitting streaks in '97, they were hitting balls to center and right as well as left. Two other skilled hitters who stand out at being able to go the opposite way are the right-handed Derek Jeter, who drags the bat through the strike zone, and Edgardo Alfonzo, whose natural stroke is to right. Most Latino hitters are free swingers and have the tendency to hit the ball up the middle and the other way as their strength.

You will rarely see a pull hitter have a long hitting streak. Just as it usually isn't practical to try to push an inside pitch to the opposite side, it's usually not a good idea to try to pull outside pitches. A pull hitter like Ron Gant will try to jerk everything, but it takes extraordinary plate coverage to take a pitch on the outside corner and bring it toward you. They always say of guys like Chipper Jones, "He takes what the pitcher gives him." In other words, he can't change the type of pitch or its location, but he'll do what is required to get on base, which means going the other way on the outside pitch. Paul O'Neill will become an opposite-field hitter with two strikes, sending outside pitches down the left-field line. When Tony Gwynn gets two strikes on him, he will usually either hit a line drive or hard grounder up the middle or just flick his wrist and drop the bat head on an outside pitch and stroke it to left field.

There are also players who have great power the other way, particularly Mike Piazza, Albert Belle, and Frank Thomas. The right-handed Alex Rodriguez likes to extend his arms, which is why he has such power the other way, especially to right-center. The left-handed Fred McGriff crushes the ball he likes from left-center to right-center. More than any other power hitter, McGriff, in his prime, used the fat part of the park. Some batters don't have home run power to the opposite field, but by being able to hit the other way, they will develop the habit of keeping their front shoulder in, and that will enable them to pull balls for home runs instead of fouling off those pitches. When Todd Hundley, batting left-handed, kept fouling off balls he should have been hitting to the left of the right-field foul pole, Tom McGraw, who was then the Mets' batting coach, got him to think about hitting balls to left-center. If you're conscious of the middle or opposite field, you can't pull the front shoulder out of there.

When a batter thinks opposite field, he hits the ball more over the plate, with the head on his shoulders following the head of his bat. Think about how logical that is. When the head and shoulders go in a different direction from the bat head, the batter pulls away from a pitch that is going away. So he is going to hit the ball off the end of the bat, the perfect double-play grounder or weak ground-out. But if the batter makes sure his head and shoulders follow the movement of the ball outside, then that's where the fat part of his bat will meet the ball. That's what Tony Gwynn does. I think you hit the outside pitch the same as an inside pitch. The difference is that your hands react quicker on the inside pitch.

Interestingly, the back-foot movement is different when pulling the ball and going the other way. When a batter pulls the ball, he will spin off the back foot, turn, and belly-button the pitcher. The pivot results in the hips opening. But when a batter tries to go to the opposite field—and this is more common with right-handed batters—the reach of the bat pulls the back foot off the ground. Gary Thorne called this to my attention during a broadcast late last year, and our director, Jeff Mitchell, put together a beautiful replay sequence that showed the lifting of the foot. I have been involved in professional baseball since 1959, and while I may have known that it happened, this was the first time I had seen it confirmed on television.

BATS

The great majority of bats are supplied to major-league batters by Rawlings, Louisville Slugger, Hoosier, and, in the case of Mark McGwire, the NASA Jet Propulsion Laboratory. All bats aren't created equal. Hitters look for a bat with a wide grain and, even better, one with a knot on the sweet part of the bat, indicating the wood is hardest there. (Think of knotty pine.) Thin-grained bats dry out too early and start peeling and chipping. Those are the bats sent to nonstar players and benchwarmers. The bat manufacturers deny any favoritism, but I don't believe them. The better you are as a hitter, the better the bats you will receive. In the early sixties, everybody on the Cardinals used to kid about how Stan Musial got all the good wood for his bats from the manufacturer. He'd get twelve dozen bats at spring training. They'd all be wide grained, and seven out of eight would have the knot right on the hitting surface.

The bats I used ranged from thirty-one to thirty-three ounces, not big but heavier than those used by Musial. Still, the Giants' Willie McCovey and Willie Mays mocked their size. With his slow baritone, McCovey would ask me, "How do you hit with that little toy?" Once I came out on the field at Candlestick Park and he was using my bat to pick his teeth. McCovey socked his tape-measure homers with a large bat, but the biggest one used in my playing days was Dick Allen's. It weighed over forty ounces, and he could have used all that lumber to panel his den.

Allen was extraordinarily strong and could jump on fastballs with his heavy bat. But possibly he could have been even better with a lighter bat. Batters can't have a short, quick stroke if they use a heavy bat. If waiting and then using your quick hands are the two elements of sound hitting, then why would you use a heavy bat? If you have a heavy bat, you have to start sooner. Lighter bats make it easier for you to speed up the bat head so you can wait longer—and by waiting longer you pick up the ball better and then use your quick hands. There are too many arguments against a heavy bat, especially as more hard throwers come into the big leagues. That's why Barry Bonds, who is the best fastball hitter in baseball, uses a thirty-one-ounce bat. A toy.

20

BUNTING MECHANICS

Cardinals manager Tony La Russa and Mets manager Bobby Valentine are smart to have bunting drills during the season for all their players, not just the pitchers. Everyone spends time bunting in spring training, but once the season starts the nonpitchers often concentrate solely on their hitting. They think bunting is routine until they are called on to do it when it counts. So it's a good idea to sharpen bunting skills through the year, especially on teams that bunt a lot, like the Cards and Mets. Bunting can be a key part of a player's or a team's offense. When a player wants to ignite a rally or needs a hit to break out of a slump, he can lay down a bunt single; when the hit-and-run or straight steal seems too much of a gamble, the sacrifice bunt is the safe alternative for moving up a runner; when getting the runner home from third seems problematic, the squeeze can be more prudent than swinging away.

BUNTING FOR A BASE HIT

When bunting for a base hit, all players have to take the same approach, which is to put the bat head on the ball while in full stride toward first. In executing a good drag bunt toward third, the right-handed batter must angle the bat down the first-base line and bunt the ball on the bat from the sweet part to the end. He will try to deaden the ball so the surprised third baseman has a long way to come in to field it. The bunt should go down the baseline, not between the third baseman and the pitcher. There are two reasons for this: The third baseman's throw to first will be longer and from a tougher angle, and if the bunt goes foul, the batter will get another shot with the bat.

Batters from both sides of the plate should lay bunts down the third-base line. But they use their hands differently. While the right-handed batter slides his top hand up the bat and coddles the barrel, the left-handed batter slides his left hand to just above the trademark and moves his right hand high on the handle to catch the ball on the bat more than the right-handed bunter does. It's difficult for left-handed batters to bunt directly down the first-base line, so they will try to find a seam between the pitcher and first baseman, just like passers and runners in football try to find seams through defenses. Sometimes you'll see the first baseman and pitcher converge at the ball a few feet from first as the batter races by them to the unguarded bag. But when the left-handed bunter takes the ball with him, he would like the second baseman to come in to field it.

When the right-handed batter wants to bunt for a hit to the right side, he tries to push the ball past the pitcher. Unlike the batter who lays down a sacrifice bunt, the push bunter remains mobile because he doesn't square around toward the mound. He is more square to first base as he tries to push the ball between the first baseman and the pitcher. He, too, wants the deeper second baseman to have to field the bunt because by the time he picks it up it will be too late to throw him out. So he neither deadens the ball nor hits it too hard, but relies on "feel" to bunt it in between those extremes. Right-handed batters don't push the ball to the left side. Left-handed batters are much more adept at doing that because the bat must be angled down the first-base line. Right-handed batters have that angle only when they drag bunt.

Is a push bunt a drag bunt? Not technically, but the two are combined in the drag-bunt category because in both cases the batter is on the run as he hits the ball in order to beat the throw. The term "drag bunt" covers all bunts where batters are trying to get base hits.

HOW TO SACRIFICE BUNT

When you sacrifice bunt you expect to be thrown out at first. You give yourself up, sacrificing your at-bat to move up one or two runners for the team. So, unlike on the drag bunt, you don't run until after the ball is bunted because your only concern is to put the ball down on the ground. But there is still the problem of putting the bat on the ball. You will see unskilled and timid bunters trying to sacrifice from their batting stances. They leave their back foot planted and turn, pretty much spinning on that foot. The real disadvantage of bunting from the stance is that you can't reach the outside pitch. The proper way to sacrifice is by squaring around. The batter turns his body and faces the pitcher, bringing his right foot around if he's a right-handed batter and his left foot around if he bats left-handed. He slides his top hand halfway up the barrel so that he has better control of the bat. With knees bent slightly and arms extended fully into fair territory, he puts the bat directly over the plate and hits the ball with the exposed area on the end of the barrel. The barrel must be above the hands. He doesn't jab, stab, punch, or push the ball, but lets the ball come to the bat. When a batter bunts, he lets the ball hit the bat, as op-

In a game in 1966, seven years before the DH, Chicago White Sox pitcher Jack Lamabe failed to lay down a bunt and ultimately struck out. The Sox won big, but it didn't matter to Sox manager Eddie Stanky, who believed in fundamentals over everything else. Winning was important, but it was just as important how you played because the good habits picked up in winning properly translated into future wins. Stanky, whom Lamabe loved as much as I did, went to his pitcher after the game and told him that he didn't get the bunt down because the bat wasn't in fair territory. Jack denied it, but Stanky told him, "I think you were afraid. You bunted that ball as if you were fearful of getting hit with the pitch. So be out tomorrow morning at nine A.M. and we'll go down to the cage and I'll throw different pitches to you . . . and *at* you. And we're going to get rid of that fear . . . Oh yeah, wear a helmet." If someone tells you to wear a helmet as one of the prerequisites to your doing something, and the words "at you" are used, you know he's serious. Lamabe showed up the next morning, wearing a helmet, and after having Stanky throw balls to him and at him, he became, as he would tell me, "less fearful as a bunter and a better bunter." I doubt if many players today would be willing to go through Stanky's interesting bunt-or-be-hit exercise, but those who are scared to square around must do something to rid themselves of their fears.

posed to when he swings away and tries to make the bat hit the ball. He simply "catches" the ball with the bat to deaden it. I describe it as "embracing the ball," as softly as you would if someone gently tossed a box of eggs into your arms.

The only disadvantage to squaring around to bunt is that a batter may experience fear. Fear of being hit by the pitch is why some batters bunt from the stance, although there is less likelihood of success. The batter faces the pitcher when he squares around so the pitcher seems closer and pitches seem on top of him in a hurry. He may be reluctant to put his bat, with exposed hands on that bat, into fair territory and to confront a ninety mph fastball. His apprehension isn't entirely unjustified—in 1986, David Cone had his right pinkie smashed while trying to bunt against Atlee Hammaker—but he has to work on getting rid of it because this is the effective way to bunt.

It won't surprise you that the slower the pitch, the easier it is to bunt. That's why you will see some pitchers come in with high heat when they expect the batter to square around. A bunter should take that pitch for a ball and make the pitcher bring the ball down. He must put the barrel of his bat on the top half of the ball in order to bunt it on the ground, and he would need a stepladder to do that on a high fastball. It's much easier to get on top of pitches that go down in the strike zone.

21

BATTERS VERSUS PITCHERS

Baseball is the most difficult sport to play well, and batting with consistency is the most difficult part of the sport. As sophisticated as television has become, it still doesn't convey how complicated it is to be a hitter. Like all athletes, the batter is taught to be aggressive, but he's also supposed to be patient, and, obviously, these two approaches can run counter to each other. A viewer at home may look at him and say, "How can he take that pitch?" or "Why didn't he lay off that pitch?" or "Why didn't he smash at least one pitch in that at-bat?" Even the Catcher-Cam can't fully reveal the difficulty a batter has facing an endless array of pitchers who have different deliveries and release points and throw, in various combinations, a wide assortment of pitches with all possible speeds, movements, and locations. What is it like to face a pitcher with extension and late movement? To really know, you would have to be in the batter's shoes, and TV can't put you there.

It's amazing that anyone ever gets a hit. The pitcher has all the advantages, including unpredictability. Even if the batter hits the ball, the pitcher still has seven guys behind him. If the pitcher allows you only three hits in ten at-bats, he has been unsuccessful because .300 is a very impressive average. In fact, the highest-average hitter in history, Ty Cobb, made hits only 367 out of every 1,000 at-bats. So most times the batter makes an out. But there are times when he can move the odds in his favor.

Stan Musial was one of many who believed that hitters get one good pitch to hit every at-bat. For the most part that's true. The difference is that a good hitter puts that ball in play and the average hitter—or a good hitter who is having a bad time—fouls it back much more often. Getting a good pitch and putting it in play on his terms instead of the pitcher's is, in essence, what a hitter tries to accomplish in the batter-pitcher confrontation. A good hitter can get hits off terrific pitches, but not as often. What he prefers is a predictable pitch because if a major leaguer knows what's coming, the chances are good that he will crush the ball. (This doesn't necessarily apply to dominating pitchers like Sandy Koufax, Randy Johnson, or Roger Clemens.) A good hitter is able to get a pitch that is predictable in velocity and/or location by working the count in his favor. Inferior hitters will get behind in the count by swinging at balls and leave themselves in a situation where they can't predict what's coming, and the result is that they will put the ball in play on a pitcher's pitch.

WORKING THE COUNT

The ability of the hitter to get ahead in the count will very often determine his success. It's like starting out with an ace or picture card in blackjack as opposed to a five or six. When a batter is hitting well, he's swinging at hittable 1-0, 2-0, 2-1, 3-0, or 3-1 pitches. He can afford to guess and look for a certain pitch. When he struggles, he's always hitting behind in the count, 0-1, 0-2, or 1-2, and is flailing defensively at pitches. He can't afford to guess. By working the count in his favor, he creates a situation where the pitcher must limit what he can throw to avoid a walk. This is a major consideration because if a batter knows what to expect, he has a great advantage.

If the batter is ahead in the count, he makes the pitcher throw strikes. That's where the old expression "Make him come to you" comes in. That means he has to throw a ball over the plate and you can look in that sweet area where you can drive the ball. Hitters are more inclined to go after balls when they are behind in the count, so then the pitcher will expand the strike zone and he'll have even more of an advantage.

Ralph Kiner explains it very well. In selecting where he is going to swing at the pitch, the hitter imagines a box in front of the plate. Its size changes according to the count. At 0-0, it's the size of the entire strike zone. It becomes larger at 0-2 and 1-2 because now the hitter is in a defensive mode and can no longer afford to take a borderline pitch. The more the count moves in favor of the hitter, the more offensive-minded he becomes and the imaginary box out of which he must hit becomes smaller and more manageable. Now, he needs to swing only if the pitch is in the small area of the strike zone that he likes best. He can lay off everything else. As I say elsewhere, think of the hitter's box as an accordion: It becomes fully extended when the pitcher gets ahead in the count because the defensive batter will swing at balls just off the plate, and it shrinks or nearly closes when the hitter gets ahead.

In an important situation, the batter wants to work the count in his favor in order to make the pitcher throw a pitch in the strike zone. I don't think the term "strike zone" has ever been broken down, but I believe it's where pitchers will get *strikes* and also where the fat part of the bat is going to *strike* the ball solidly. You position yourself in the batter's box to strike a ball in the strike zone with the fat part of the bat. You don't position yourself in the batter's box to hit a bad pitch because you won't hit it with the part of the bat that will do the most damage. It is understandable that dangerous hitters like Jeff Bagwell, Barry Bonds, and Gary Sheffield often position themselves so they can reach the outside pitch against a pitcher who throws only balls off the corners to them, but even they will swing only slightly out of their zones. If a batter goes dramatically out of his zone, he ends up cuing the ball or gets jammed or something else happens to take his natural stroke away. Reaching for the outside pitch puts him off balance.

It's frustrating when the pitches you get are out of the strike zone, but if you choose to leave your zone to hit the pitch off the corner, you have to make sure you will be in position to put good wood on the ball. There is little margin for success. The difference on the bat between a home run and a foul ball may be a quarter inch or even smaller. It's no coincidence that almost all the pitch-caused indentations on the bats of Stan Musial, Hank Aaron, and Tony Gwynn are on the prime hitting area that is only two widths of a ball. Poor hitters have marks all over their bats and break them much more often. An announcer will see a ball just clear the fence and say, "Oh, it's a game of inches." Well, the game of inches is really on the bat—that's what determines whether the ball is hit feebly or with authority. Also, if you hit it on one spot instead of another, it may cause it to go up in the air or on the ground. We're talking round ball, round bat, hit it square.

The way you work the count in your favor is by having patience enough to go deep in the count, and getting the pitcher in the hole by laying off balls just off the plate with which he got you out in the past. A batter in the hole at 0-2 or 1-2 can get the count to 3-2 by fouling off good two-strike pitches that he doesn't want to put into play on the pitcher's terms.

As a hitter, if you run counts, you count runs. This means that if you go deep into the count, you will get predictable pitches to hit and have a better chance of putting the good part of the bat on the ball. The deeper into the count you go, the more you can look for one particular pitch. Tony Gwynn, Barry Bonds, and Rickey Henderson are outstanding at working the count in their favor. Gwynn has the confidence to go deep in the count because he is such an amazing two-strike hitter that he never has to assume a defensive posture. (Over the last five years he has batted over .315 when behind in the count and over .320 with two strikes, including a staggering .439 with a full count; one year he batted .380 with two strikes on him because he always uses the same swing.) Bonds is willing to go deep in the count because he has two-strike power if the pitcher gives him a pitch to hit; he also will accept being walked on pitches off the plate.

Having played against Keith Hernandez and announced games in which he played for the Mets, I would say he was the best I ever saw at getting the pitcher into a situation where he'd have to come inside to his strength on 2-0 or 3-1. When he faced a young, wild pitcher he would take intentionally. Or, he claims, he'd guess on the first pitch and be right 70 percent of the time. Then, if he took that pitch and the count became 1-0, he would be right 90 percent of the time on the second pitch. If he took the 1-0 pitch for a ball, then he figured he'd be right 100 percent of the time on the 2-0 pitch. Rusty Staub, Joe Adcock, and Dick Groat were also great at that.

Even a batter who strikes out a lot can learn to work a pitcher. I'm thinking of batters who have a tough time making contact or power hitters

ODDITIES

From a hitter's standpoint, there are times when too much contact can be detrimental. I was a contact hitter, and if I swung at one hundred pitches, I'd miss only about seven times. You might say, "What a great trait." It's not to that degree. Often when a pitcher makes a good pitch to you early in the count, swinging through it is preferable to putting it into play. I could not handle the strike up-and-away, but instead of missing it or fouling it back I would hit a lazy fly ball the other way. I'd be out. Too much contact and putting the pitcher's pitch in play is a deadly combination.

who rarely change their approaches from one count to the next. Through patience, they can work the pitcher into a predictable situation where they will get the pitch they want, but the difference is that they will swing through the pitch more often than contact hitters do.

Many aggressive batters never come to understand how they can benefit if they lay off balls off the plate and get ahead in the count. Mariano Duncan would bite the head off a rattlesnake before he'd take a high fastball. Geronimo Berroa will swing at a shadow—even if it's outside. Many Latino players are free swingers and bad-ball hitters because, as Juan Samuel once said about playing in the Dominican Republic: "You don't *walk* off the island. You *hit*." They and a lot of young American players who enter the majors never learn the concept "If you take, you hit."

It's hard to convince a young hitter that he has to take in order to hit. It's a conundrum. He must be willing to go deep in the count and even take walks in order to get pitches to his liking. Because once pitchers see that he's selective enough to take walks, he'll start to get pitches to hit when he is ahead in the count. Frank Thomas, Barry Bonds, Jeff Bagwell, Edgar Martinez, and other very selective hitters put up big numbers because when they don't walk they get good pitches to hit. Batters who have walked enough to have a high on-base percentage—a meaningful statistic—also will be high up in other statistical categories.

The batter also will help his team if he works the pitcher for a walk. You've heard Little Leaguers say, "A walk is as good as a hit." That's certainly the case when your team is down by two runs in the ninth inning and the man on deck represents the potential tying run. Being down by two runs instead of one becomes major beginning in the seventh inning, and a walk in the seventh, eighth, or ninth inning is a good starting point for a comeback. If the batter leading off an inning walks, it's very likely he'll score and often ignite a rally, as the pitcher, afraid to walk anyone else, may give the next few batters good pitches to hit. Rarely will a multi-run inning not include a base on balls sandwiched in between hits. Walks = runs.

Batters don't go up to the plate thinking specifically that they want to walk. The mind-set is: "This pitcher is going to have to throw me a strike. He'll have to show me that he can get the ball over the plate before I'll swing." The batter doesn't stop being aggressive; he just waits until the count is more in his favor.

Unfortunately, there's a proliferation of young hitters who don't know the strike zone. It used to be that a good ratio for a young player coming up from the minors was two bases on balls for every strikeout. Today, a 1:1

walks-to-strikeouts ratio is good, not just acceptable. There are some keys on statistical sheets, and walks and strikeouts are important for when a pitcher looks at a hitter and a hitter looks at a pitcher. If a pitcher has sixty walks in eighty innings, it's likely that he'll have control problems. If you're a hitter and not looking at stats like that, then you're not preparing yourself properly for when you face him.

What about an intentional walk? Few hitters like getting one. It means it's up to the next guy to deliver the hit. You want to hit when you're in good position to drive in the runs. But the pitcher is taking the bat out of your hands. There's nothing you can do about it, so take it as a compliment.

The First Pitch

Most first-ball hitters are not smart hitters. Typically, they go after the first pitch because they are free swingers and not because they have deduced what the first pitch will be from having studied the pitcher. A first-ball hitter may be a productive hitter, but it's because of his talent rather than his thinking. Some batters almost always take the first pitch their first time up. Some will take the first pitch the first couple of times up so that the pitcher will assume they'll be taking their third time up. Wanting a quick strike, the pitcher will throw the first pitch into the batter's wheelhouse and be surprised that the batter is swinging. In my playing days, Orlando Cepeda was the best at setting up pitchers that way. Dick Groat, one of the smartest hitters I ever played with, took the first pitch almost every time. He reasoned, "What do you lose by taking that pitch?" Not a lot because if the count is 0-1, you should have enough confidence in your ability to still be in an offensive mode.

Of course, you have to pick your pitchers. You're not going to always take the first pitch from a pitcher who is always around the plate. You don't want to fall behind pitchers who will come at you. It makes the most sense to swing at the first pitch if the pitcher is someone like Greg Maddux, Bob Tewksbury, Kevin Brown, or Dennis Eckersley because they rarely walk anyone and try to get ahead in the count immediately. Also, you don't want to let a hittable strike go by from a pitcher who gives you all kinds of trouble. You need all the swings you can get against him.

There are times you know before you reach the plate that you will be taking the first pitch. You want to see the pitcher, particularly a guy you've never faced before. If he's a young pitcher, you'll be inclined to take a pitch or two so you can see the movement on his ball. If it's a guy you've

There's a saying in baseball that you "want long *ins* and short *outs.*" You want to spend a long time in the dugout and a short time on the field. In football, teams don't want the defense on the field for a long time. In baseball, it's not the whole defense that gets tired—it's the pitcher. If the offense goes down one-two-three on three first-pitch outs, your own pitcher doesn't get much of a breather, but what's worse is that the opposing pitcher has had too easy an inning. If the first guy makes an out on the first pitch, the number two guy shouldn't swing at the first pitch. But if he also makes an out on the first pitch, the third batter should choose a pitch he likes and whack away, even if it's also on the first pitch. If he makes an out, it's still the number two batter who is at fault for the inning being so brief. After the leadoff man has made an out on the first pitch, it's only okay for the second batter to swing at the first pitch if, through past at-bats in this situation, he has established in the mind of the pitcher that there is no way he will be swinging.

Dick Groat was the first player who talked to me about protecting the on-deck batter by taking pitches. By taking a first-pitch strike a batter leading off an inning allows the second hitter to swing at the first pitch. By swinging at the first pitch and making an out, he forces the second batter to take the first pitch to him. Let's say I was batting in front of Groat and leading off against Don Drysdale, a right-handed pitcher who was extremely tough on right-handed batters. He wasn't as much of a problem for me as for Groat because I batted left-handed and all Drysdale's sinkers came in to me. Because I wasn't afraid of falling behind Drysdale 0-1, I would be inclined to take the first pitch to allow Groat to swing at the first pitch to him. If I made an out on the first pitch, Groat would have been strapped into taking the first pitch even if it meant falling behind in the count against someone who gave him a lot of trouble. If I were the one who had trouble against a particular pitcher, I would want the freedom to swing at the first pitch. In that case, the next batter wouldn't worry as much as me about falling behind 0-1.

seen before but still have a tough time picking up, then you need the three strikes and won't be willing to give him a strike. The worst thing is to be caught in between: "I'll swing at it . . . no, I won't." That's the thinking of a batter in a slump. The mind interferes with the swing, and there's undue pressure. Because if you guess an inside pitch and swing through it, big deal. There will be times when you guess right and connect.

As a hitter who was also a catcher, I realized that the pitch the great majority of pitchers get over the most consistently is the fastball, but that didn't mean I'd always expect the fastball on the 0-0 count. And the pitcher couldn't depend on my taking the first pitch. A lot depended on my previous at-bats against him. If I was going to really, really battle a tough left-hander, I would be reluctant to take a strike. I needed three strikes, not two. I needed swings and timing. However, if the pitcher was a sidearming right-hander and I had no trouble picking up his pitches, I'd more or less play the cat-and-mouse game with him. Maybe I'd go deep into the count, or maybe I'd just make him think I'd take the first pitch and then swing away. You will see many batters stand casually at the plate, trying to bait a pitcher into throwing a strike they can swing at.

If the pitcher averages 4 or 4.5 walks per nine innings, then batters should take the first pitch. Even if they guess right that the wild pitcher will throw a first-pitch fastball, it might not be a strike. A batter also might take the first pitch from a pitcher who usually has good control but has walked a couple of hitters in the inning. Or he might jump on the first pitch if he reasons that the pitcher is so concerned with throwing strikes that he might be willing to put the ball over the fat part of the plate.

But when trailing by three runs or more, it's not good hitting when the first batter walks and the next two batters swing at the first pitch. If the pitcher hasn't shown he can get the ball over the plate, you become a much more passive hitter. Patience and common sense go together. If he gets a strike on you, then things go back to square one. But until that happens the momentum for not throwing a strike increases and the heat is really on the pitcher.

Ahead in the Count

Ahead in the count, a batter can be choosy. If the count is 1-0, 2-0, 2-1, 3-1, or, if he has the hit sign, 3-0, he can wait for a pitch to his strength, which he can drive. A low-ball hitter will want a mid-shin to mid-thigh inside pitch and the high-ball hitter will want the mid-thigh to waist-high inside pitch; for a batter who stands away from the plate, "inside" means on the inside corner, and for the batter who stands on top of the plate, "inside" is located more toward the middle of the plate. (A left-handed batter in particular will look for a ball down-and-in.) An announcer may say that the pitcher got away with a mistake when the batter didn't swing at a letter-high pitch, but even high-ball hitters prefer it lower, down at the belly button.

Ahead in the count, the batter shouldn't be jammed. He is selective if the count is at 1-0, more selective at 2-0, slightly more selective at 3-1, and the most selective at 3-0. Although 3-1 and 2-0 are almost the same, the batter should be more selective at 3-1 because if the pitch is out of the strike zone, it's ball four. The unselective hitter may swing at and miss a 3-1 pitch that is out of the strike zone, moving him one strike closer to being struck out. He would have more leeway to swing on the 2-0 pitch because if he misses, he still has the hammer at two balls and one strike. Going from 3-1 to 3-2 by swinging at a bad pitch is worse than going from 2-0 to 2-1, which is still a good hitter's count. In fact, 2-1 is the best hit-and-run count. (The counts 2-0, 3-0, and 3-1 are not conducive to the hit-and-run because the batter doesn't want to become defensive by having to swing at balls out of his zone to protect the runner.)

With the count in the batter's favor, he can guess that a pitcher who is struggling will go to his fastball, the easiest pitch to throw over the plate. So he can be aggressive. He should just pick a zone, and if it goes into that zone, he should swing from the heels. You try to get the pitcher into a 2-0 or 3-1 situation so you can crush his next pitch. A batter can't freeze on a 2-0 or 3-1 inside fastball because that's the pitch he wants to drive. Unfortunately, you will see tentative young players take pitches in their hitting zones on 2-0 and 3-1 counts. To develop into a good hitter, a player must learn that these are the pitches he must hit with authority. It's bad hitting if he picks up a strike on a checked swing. These are hitters' counts, and the batter should whale away. In cases where *your* bat can do the most damage, you don't want to take the pitch, even if you will walk on ball four. That's a huge, huge point in hitting.

A good time for an eighth-place hitter to become a power hitter is with nobody on, two outs, and a 3-1 count. The pitcher does not want to walk him because he wants the ninth-place hitter to lead off the next inning. The batter should look for a ball on the inside corner and turn on it. He has to be at his most aggressive on a pitch down-and-in. Even light-hitting Rafael Belliard homered off that pitch in 1997, breaking a ten-year homer drought. A walk, for the most part, is not what the batter is looking for. He wants to drive the ball and get an extra-base hit.

Let's say the team at bat trails by one run with two outs in the seventh inning. There's a man on second and a 3-0 count. Which batters should be allowed to swing away? Usually, the guy who gets the 3-0 green light is in the middle of the order and has home run power, but you could just as easily give the swing sign to a very good contact hitter. Do you need a hit or a home run? Obviously, a home run would be better, but a base hit would tie the game. You don't give a free swinger the go-ahead on 3-0 unless he is really locked in. You prefer a hitter with discipline because he has to consolidate all his hand-eye coordination into only one spot. A hot hitter wouldn't take the 3-0 pitch; a hot left-handed batter would lay off only the pitch that is down-and-outside. It's always important for the batter to consider the pitcher in these situations because if he is someone with shaky control, it doesn't make great sense for the hitter to swing at the 3-0 pitch unless he just doesn't want to walk.

A lot of green lights are given on the 3-0 pitch, perhaps so the batters won't feel insulted, but batting coaches should first impress upon these batters that they should swing at the pitches they hit best, not just strikes. If that's the case on 3-1, then it's more true on 3-0. You won't see that many homers coming on 3-0 pitches. I think most batters are overly anxious and swing at pitches that aren't really to their liking. They see the strike and want to jump on it instead of being patient for a strike in their zone. The point is this: For you to swing, the pitch has to be a strike in *your* zone, not necessarily in the strike zone. If you were going to hit a ball off a batting tee, you would have the ball be exactly where you could hit it the hardest, and that is where the 3-0 pitch should be for you to swing at it. If you're a low-ball hitter, that pitch would be down; if you're a high-ball hitter, it would be up. You should know your own strengths.

Behind in the Count

Down in the count 0-1, the batter must show restraint and not chase a ball way off the plate or he'll be deep in the hole at 0-2. But he can still be aggressive. If, however, he falls behind 0-2 or 1-2, he must be in a defensive mode. *Behind in the count, the batter protects the outside corner and adjusts to the inside pitch.* This is the opposite of when he is ahead in the count. In this case, it's understandable for the batter to be called out on a pitch on the inside corner, but not on the outside. Vulnerable inside, he also is susceptible to being jammed. He hopes to foul that ball off rather than put it in play.

With two strikes, the batter might spread his legs a bit, choke up a little on the bat (or, better, choke up in his mind), and concentrate on protecting the outside part of the plate and making good contact on anything in the strike zone. He'll hope to foul off anything he can't put the sweet part of the bat on, hoping the pitcher will eventually throw a ball or two and the count will no longer be in the pitcher's favor. It is definitely an offensive weapon to be able to foul off good pitches. If you protect away with two strikes, you can still foul off inside pitches, but if you were to look inside instead, you couldn't reach the strike away. If you're looking outside, you can still put the bat on the inside pitch, but if you're looking inside and the pitcher slices the corner outside, you can't pull the trigger. You look inside until you get two strikes, then protect outside and adjust to the inside pitch. The thinking is that you can't protect the whole plate. Interestingly, with two strikes, a batter who is not adept at going the other way and who isn't trying to go that way may get the opposite-field hit anyway just by protecting away.

Most batters don't have two-strike power. Barry Larkin and Mark Grace are two examples. They are good hitters with two strikes, but because they cut down on their swings and go the other way on outside pitches they don't hit as many long balls. But, on occasion, Larkin, who is much like Edgardo Alfonzo with power, can make the pitcher think he's going the other way with a certain pitch with two strikes and surprise him by turning on it.

If a power hitter protects the outside part of the plate with two strikes, he is already compromising his power. He doesn't have to tell himself that he must try for a single rather than a home run because he might get the single anyway because of his defensive approach. This doesn't mean he can't hit a home run, but a defensive hitter is less apt to do it on a 1-2 pitch than a 2-0 or 3-1 pitch. Barry Bonds, Gary Sheffield, and Ken Griffey, Jr., are among the few batters who are as dangerous with two strikes as they are with the count 2-0. These talented individuals can be defensive and still have the power to hit inside or outside pitches out of the park.

* * *

Although the batter is always in a defensive frame of mind with the count 0-2 and 1-2, it's not always the case with the other two-strike counts, 2-2 and 3-2. If the count began 0-2, the batter has the edge on the pitcher on both these counts. The opposite is true if the counts began 2-0 or 3-0. It all depends on the hitter. Some batters have trouble anytime they are one strike away from striking out. A Tony Gwynn can more than hold his own at 0-1 and 1-2 and is deadly with the count at 2-2 or 3-2.

LOOKING FOR A PITCH

A batter can have success on any count if he has figured out how to predict a pitch. If he doesn't want to rely solely on what he sees when the ball is about ten feet from home plate, a smart batter will learn the patterns of a pitcher to know what he throws in all situations. It helps to have a pitch in mind when the pitcher delivers the ball so that what he sees ten feet from home won't surprise him but will instead only confirm or contradict his guess. He'll take a pitch he wasn't looking for.

At the beginning of the FOX telecasts, we put up a graphic with a three- or four-line thumbnail scouting report on the starting pitcher. These notes are to help the fans, not the players. In fact, the players may disagree with our reports because the pitcher may have a completely different approach against them. A player has to be his own scout. He has to slice and dice the generic scouting report until it fits how the pitcher on the mound pitches against *him*. He does that with every pitcher. At-bats are different against each pitcher. That's why the batter takes into account how the particular pitcher he is facing has worked him before.

Baseball is the one sport where adjustments are made as individuals—a hitter to a pitcher, a pitcher to a hitter—rather than as a team. If a batter has had trouble with a pitcher, he will have to figure out a way to adjust. A good hitter spends his entire career adjusting to all the pitchers in the league. He knows the pitcher's tendencies in certain situations and on certain counts. Is he going to try to get you out with a certain pitch or a certain series of pitches? Have you hurt him on off-speed pitches so often that he won't throw them to you anymore? Or does this pitcher think he can throw breaking balls at any time, even when he's behind in the count? If that's his tendency, start looking for breaking balls. If his tendency is to try to overpower you, then gear up for the fastball and turn it up a notch—and if he throws a breaking ball, tip your cap to him.

You want to know the pitcher's out pitch, whether it's a riding fastball to strike you out or a sinker to make you hit a weak grounder. When a teammate who made an out would return to the dugout shaking his head, Ted Williams would ask, "How the hell do you not know what that pitch was? How can you ever not know what a pitch was?" He's right. A hitter can't come back to the dugout oblivious to what pitch got him out because that's perhaps the same out pitch he'll get the next time he faces the pitcher. Young players impress you when they have an "idea" of how to play the game. Last year, young Pirates outfielder Jermaine Allensworth didn't swing at a slider off the plate after it got him out the previous time up. He took the pitch, got ahead in the count, and came up with a single when the pitcher had to throw the ball over the plate. That was smart hitting.

There is a lot of brilliance to the admonition "Don't try to think too much." When asked if he held the batting label up or down, Yogi Berra, perhaps the best bad-ball hitter ever, would say, "I don't go up to the plate to read." And Willie Mays revealed no more about his hitting success than "He throws it and I hit it." But there is more to hitting than that. Willie did a lot of thinking and outthinking; he just didn't want you to know he was doing that. A batter has to have an idea about what the pitcher is trying to do against him. I know firsthand how important it is to figure out the patterns of the opposing pitcher-catcher tandem. As I gained experience behind the plate in the big leagues, I learned the thinking patterns of my own pitchers and put them to use as a hitter. I think my training as a catcher increased my batting average fifteen to eighteen points.

The first time a batter faces a pitcher in a game, he remembers past games to determine possible patterns. The second time up, he factors that in but really looks to his first time up. The predictable pitch he seeks may not happen until his third or fourth time up, based on how the pitcher and

Everyone wonders why Tony Gwynn has such an astronomical batting average against Greg Maddux, baseball's best pitcher, and the explanation might be that Gwynn knows Maddux's pattern against him. Gwynn studies film endlessly, and there's no more challenging a pitcher to study than Maddux, a pitcher so mysterious that, as I said during 1997's All-Star Game, he's as "hard to read as a Russian novel." Gwynn has done a lot of talking with Ted Williams, and it's interesting to note that Williams was often better against great pitchers than average pitchers because he studied their patterns much more and figured out how they would approach him.

catcher have worked him earlier in the game. It doesn't matter if a reliever is now pitching because the batter knows that the catcher remembers his earlier at-bats and will be taking them into account when working with his new pitcher. Remember: *A smart batter always hits off catchers more than off pitchers.* His team faces a starting pitcher about every fourth or fifth time they play an opponent, but the regular catcher might play in every game. So the batter remembers if the catcher has used a particular pattern against him in previous games, particularly when working with similar pitchers. If the catcher's pattern has been consistent, the batter will be able to anticipate with a high degree of accuracy what pitches will be thrown.

If you have batted twice against a pitcher in a game, it's quite possible that his pattern will be different the third time. You might be able to figure out what a pitcher may throw you by watching him from the dugout and on-deck circle. When I would watch a pitcher face my teammates, I would check his speed and tendency to throw strikes. More significant, I would concentrate on how the pitcher worked other left-handed batters because that might tell me how he would work me. Even those pitchers and catchers who make sure not to repeat themselves when they work individual batters will throw certain pitches to most left-handed batters and certain pitches to most right-handed batters.

The good major-league hitter looks for a certain pitch in a certain situation. He prepares for the fastball and adjusts to the breaking ball, which is something the soon-to-be-demoted player can't do. (Joe Torre told me Paul O'Neill is one of the few batters who can look for a breaking ball and still hit the fastball.) But there are a number of other things he may take into consideration, such as:

- If there is a base stealer on first, the pitcher will probably throw more fastballs early in the count.
- A pitcher usually throws his best control pitch on a 2-2 count.
- A pitcher will be unafraid to throw the same pitch on 3-2 that got him the strike on 3-1.
- When a non-homer hitter leads off an inning, the pitcher will usually challenge him with a fastball on a 3-2 pitch, especially if he is a base stealer.
- If the pitcher is throwing 2-1 breaking balls to a pitcher, it's likely he'll throw breaking balls to everybody.
- If a pitcher doesn't show he can get his breaking ball over, batters should wait for the fastball.

- If a confused-looking pitcher calls the catcher to the mound after his signal for a 3-0 pitch, the batter should look for the slider or change-up instead of the obvious fastball.
- To throw a fastball, a pitcher will usually bring the glove up over his head in the windup to get more power.
- To throw a curveball, a pitcher needs to bring his glove up only to his face or even lower because he doesn't need the same power as on a fastball.
- A batter can often tell when a young pitcher is throwing a change-up because he speeds up his body.
- A batter can often tell a young pitcher is throwing a curve because he slows down his body.
- After a pitcher throws something soft, he usually will come back with something hard.
- Taking a cue from Willie Mays and Roberto Clemente, a batter can entice a pitcher into throwing a second-pitch breaking ball by feigning shock at a first-pitch breaking ball.
- In the American League, batters can look for pitchers to throw breaking balls with two strikes instead of inside fastballs.
- In the National League, pitchers throw more fastballs on two-strike counts.
- A pitcher who is behind in the count will usually be reluctant to mix pitches.

None of these is an absolute. We're talking about odds, what is most likely to be productive. That's how the house in Las Vegas makes millions of dollars. In baseball, the pitcher and the defense represent the house and the odds are always against the hitter.

LOOKING FOR LOCATION

A batter who strikes out a lot, like Sammy Sosa, Jay Buhner, or Henry Rodriguez, may guess the type of pitch that is coming, but he'll swing at it no matter where it is. A batter has to pay equal attention to location.

On our FOX telecasts, we have a three-row, nine-box graphic we call "The Hit Zone," in which we show, through two shades of red, the hitter's best areas of the plate for hitting the ball. Blue boxes represent the locations where the hitter is weakest. The boxes cover outside, middle, and inside and high, middle, and low. The dark red areas are where a batter should look for pitches on 2-0, 3-0, and 3-1 or not swing. That's his hot-hot zone. You will see that Mike Piazza is an inside hitter and Eric Karros likes the ball up; Jeff Bagwell can hit the inside pitch but he can hit the ball away, too; Tino Martinez can hit the low fastball, but he has the ideal Yankee Stadium swing on the high fastball; Mark McGwire can blast a high fastball, but he'll do it with more consistency on a low fastball; Barry Bonds can turn on the inside pitch, but he also hits the outside pitch with power; and so on. The one explosive area for all batters is down-and-in. Incidentally, The Hit Zone is only a general chart. What must be taken into account is what kind of pitch is in each particular area and what kind of action it has going through that spot.

For a pitcher to throw in some zones, he can throw only one type of pitch. So if a batter is "sitting on an inside pitch," he is expecting something hard because pitchers aren't going to throw anything inside that's soft unless it's a mistake. When an announcer calls a guy a "mistake hitter," he's denigrating him, wrongly implying that he doesn't get hits off good pitches, too.

If you're a ground-ball hitter—which is what fast guys without power should be—you look for a pitch you can get on top of. You won't miss or pop up low pitches—you will hit them on the ground. A fly-ball hitter will look for pitches that are up. He may swing through balls that are from the waist up, but he won't hit them on the ground. A batter with fast hands will, generally, hope for the high fastball. (A batter with slower hands will be quicker on pitches that are low.) It's hard to lift a sinkerball. Think about trying to lift a projectile that is going down. A high-ball hitter tries to get the sinkerballer to bring the ball up before he swings. He hopes the umpire won't give the pitcher low strikes so he'll have to throw a bit higher when he falls behind in the count.

The opposite-field hitter will look for pitches from the middle of the plate out. A pull hitter will look for pitches from the middle of the plate in. If he homers on an inside pitch, he shouldn't expect that pitch on the first couple of pitches his next time up. He should look away.

In a key game late in the 1978 season, the Phillies were playing the Pirates in Pittsburgh. In the second game of a doubleheader, Steve Carlton was pitching for us and we were leading 1–0 in the fifth inning. Then Bruce Kison, the Pirates' pitcher who would sport a lifetime batting average of .163, came up to hit. On this at-bat, he moved on top of the plate so that if Carlton tried to throw a slider on the inside corner it would hit him. Instead, Steve threw a down-and-in fastball and Kison hit a rare home run.

Until recently, I never knew Kison's mind-set. He told me that he was forcing Carlton to throw him a ball he could hit if he wanted to go inside. As a pitcher, he understood that would be an effective ploy.

HITTING APPROACHES
IN PRESSURE SITUATIONS

Obviously, the greatest pressure situation for a batter is when the game is on the line, when his next swing can determine the outcome. Let's say the score is tied in the bottom of the ninth inning and there is a runner on third base with less than two outs. Since the infield must play in to cut off the winning run, even "out men" become major threats, especially if they are ahead in the count. All they need to do is make contact because the odds are that the run will come in. With the infield in, anybody who puts the ball in play is dangerous. That goes double for a good hitter. However, the batter knows that unless he is a weak singles hitter or is a strike-out-prone batter facing a strikeout pitcher, he will get *nothing* decent to hit. In fact, he and a comparable on-deck batter will likely be intentionally walked to set up a force play at home. Even if the pitcher doesn't opt for

ODDITIES

Some things fall into the "Who-do-you-congratulate?" category. Last year, I saw the Pirates get three straight singles to load the bases. The fourth batter hit a weak grounder to third, which forced a runner there but scored the man from third. He was the only batter to make an out, yet he was the only batter to get credit for an RBI. That's a case where the three guys who got hits were each more deserving. They were the reason for the run, not the guy who got the RBI.

Similarly, I've always thought it silly that when a batter hits into a fielder's choice, erasing a teammate, and then scores the winning run, everyone congratulates him rather than the deserving guy who was on before him. The other guy got on base; all this guy did was make an out. It's so odd, but I can't imagine seeing everyone making a beeline to congratulate the guy on the bench who had been forced out at second. But from an astute standpoint, that's exactly what they should do instead of running out to mob the other guy.

the intentional walk, he has eight balls to work with, so the batter knows not to expect hittable pitches, although he'll be ready in case one is better than the pitcher intended. The batter must be patiently aggressive because the pitcher wants to pick up a couple of swinging strikes on balls out of the strike zone. Only if the pitcher gets ahead 0-2 or 1-2 might he go after a batter, although probably with more balls. If the batter doesn't swing at the bad pitches and gets ahead in the count 2-0, the pitcher will probably go ahead with the intentional walk or continue to pitch around him. A batter will expect to be challenged by a pitcher with the winning run on third only if the bases become loaded or there are two outs.

In such a game-on-the-line situation, a single over the infield is just as productive as the ball that is driven. He needs only a single, but he doesn't say, "I only want a single." Instead, he should tell himself, "Just make contact." It's almost like on a hit-and-run when he has to make contact, so he keeps his eyes down on the ball. He shouldn't shorten his swing.

With less than two strikes in a pressure situation, a batter shouldn't be thinking of "protecting the plate." If he's not behind in the count, he should be offense-minded. Ahead in the count 2-0 or 3-1, he should look for a pitch in his zone to drive.

I'm not sure that sluggers cut down on their swings or choke up on their bats once they get two strikes on them in clutch situations. But a lot of guys say this is the case. The area of the plate that they must protect with two strikes is larger, and I don't think choking up on the bat makes it easier. Batters shouldn't literally choke up on the bat, although I do like the choke-up-on-the-bat mentality. I think batters should "choke up in their thinking," which means to protect away. It's only their mental approach that should change because if you hold the bat at the end you can still have good bat control. Hitters who don't choke up in their thinking will hit the occasional home run, but they'll also strike out a lot more because they're taking the wrong approach.

Batters rarely look for a ball to hit out of the ballpark. They're not necessarily thinking homer when they try to drive the ball. They just want to put the fat part of the bat on the ball and to hit it hard. In 1997, National League homer champion Larry Walker admitted he was trying for a homer when he struck out in a late-inning situation; the next day he tried to drive the ball instead and hit the game-winning homer. When Todd Hundley has his bad streaks, he swings so hard going for 650-foot homers that he corkscrews himself into the ground. That's the problem with a lot of young players with power. It's important for them to understand: You don't necessarily swing harder to hit the ball harder.

PART V

In the Field

22

SOLID DEFENSE

In the last few years, so many teams have put together potent offenses in order to exploit the small dimensions of their parks that fans have the mistaken impression that defense isn't a part of the game that needs to be stressed. But you'll find few winning teams that don't have strong defense at key positions. Gene Mauch said that if you want to put together a good defensive team, you start with your catcher, then your shortstop, then your center fielder, and then your second baseman, and then you fill in the rest of your lineup with offensive players. If you're an expansion team like the Arizona Diamondbacks or the Tampa Bay Devil Rays, you have to take this approach in starting a franchise. Revealingly, some major-league teams protected their middle defense in the first and second rounds of the 1997 expansion draft. Teams build around defense up the middle because most pitches are hit to the meat, or the middle, of the field. Certainly more ground balls are hit up the middle than are pulled or sliced.

Most teams prefer catchers who are better defensively than offensively—Mike Piazza and Sandy Alomar are exceptions. In fact, a catcher who has exceptional defensive skills and can call a good game can play in the majors even if he is only a mild threat with the bat. Teams also will carry a shortstop solely for his defensive skills. Bob Gibson heckled Cubs shortstop Don Kessinger, "You'd better catch everything," implying that's what it would take to compensate for his weak hitting. (To Donnie's credit, he became a solid offensive player, too.) But the center fielder and second baseman are expected to provide some offense. That's why the Reds demoted Bret Boone in 1997, although he is a skilled defensive second baseman. He has to hit better than the catcher or shortstop.

If a team has a lack of run production, its players had better play good defense to be in the lineup. Managers will put it bluntly: "You've got to catch the ball." At least a defensive specialist can contribute in one way. A team's makeup and whether it is winning or losing will determine if a manager will have an excellent defensive player replace a slumping hitter who lacks defensive skills.

It's smart when teams such as Atlanta strategically stock their benches with just one or two good hitters and have good defensive players in the rest of the slots. That's because the closer to the end of the game you are, the more important defense becomes. If you have the lead, you go for defense; if you trail, you go for offense to mount a comeback. If you're ahead, the offense has put you in position to nail down a win with defense, so now you bring in the good glove men. You rarely take out a good defensive player if you're ahead. With a lead in the National League, a manager should not do a double switch–replacing both the pitcher and a fielder and switching their positions in the batting order–if he is going to bring in a worse fielder. Some managers are guilty of double-switching anytime there is an opportunity and, trying to save their bullpens, they neglect defense. If your team is ahead by one run in the fifth inning and you have the chance to put a team away because the bases are loaded and no one is out, you might remove a good fielder for a strong pinch hitter. But with a lead, I wouldn't hit for the shortstop or catcher until later in the game, if at all, unless I have someone even better defensively on the bench. The odds really have to favor your putting a team away for you to pinch-hit for those guys.

I think the most difficult job in baseball is late-inning defense. It's like handing in your homework in high school. You don't get any credit for just handing it in because you're expected to do it, but if you don't do it you get docked. That always seemed unfair to me. If you do it well, you were supposed to; if you're guilty of a misplay, you're a goat.

Some managers make the mistake of thinking offense is more important than defense in late innings. Reporters were correct to question Phillies manager Danny Ozark after we lost the pivotal third game of the National League Championship Series in 1977, when Los Angeles rallied for three runs with two outs and nobody on in the top of the ninth inning.

All year long, Danny had used Jerry Martin as a late-inning defensive replacement for Greg Luzinski, who was a great hitter but had big problems in left field. But in the ninth inning of this key game, Ozark suddenly decided to leave in Luzinski, and his fielding deficiencies cost us that game, leading to our elimination in Game 4. What was Ozark's explanation? He said that he kept Luzinski in because he was due up fourth in the bottom of the ninth! In other words, with a two-run lead at home in the ninth, Ozark was playing for a tie! That's apparently what John McNamara was playing for when he left Bill Buckner in at first base in the bottom of the ninth inning of Game 6 of the 1986 World Series against the Mets. If he'd replaced Buckner with Dave Stapleton, as he'd done during the season when the Red Sox had the lead in late innings, then Buckner wouldn't have made the infamous between-the-wickets error that gave the Mets the victory and led to their championship. Ahead by two runs in the ninth, a manager has to pick the better fielder over the better hitter.

If managers make such questionable decisions, there's little wonder why fans take fielding for granted. And they do. Have you ever met anyone who bothers to keep fielding statistics of their favorite players? If your name isn't Ozzie Smith, you can win a Gold Glove year after year and still not be voted into Cooperstown unless your offensive production is equal to your fielding prowess. You would think that a player's repeatedly winning an award that signifies he is the best fielder at his position in his league would at least sway writers to vote him in if his offensive stats are almost of Hall of Fame caliber. But fielding is rarely a factor in the voting.

On television, it is sometimes difficult to put fielding plays into their proper perspective. For instance, if nobody is on base, it's common to hail a good defensive play that ends an inning and forget about the better play that began the inning, although that out was more important because it prevented a rally from getting started. Similarly, it's understandable that we get excited when a double play ends a game, although, perhaps, we had barely acknowledged a more important, rally-killing twin killing that occurred early in the game. In the postgame highlights, you may see the shortstop make one or two great plays, but you won't see replays of the four or five routine plays he made in the same game that may have been

Joe Torre had a great line about Gold Gloves: "I won a Gold Glove in 1965 and used it in 1966."

more important to the victory. The point is that in baseball, the *routine,* over a long period of time, is *great.* The Gold Glovers are the guys who make both the routine and the spectacular plays.

It's not easy for announcers to give proper attention to fielders because every play begins with the center-field camera directed at the pitcher and batter. But I think it's important for us to try to inform fans what the fielders are doing off screen, in preparation for the next pitch. From the booth we can see changes in fielders' positions from one play to the next. We can see if there is an infield or outfield shift, if the third and first basemen are creeping down their respective lines in anticipation of a bunt or are hugging the lines to prevent an extra-base hit, if the entire infield has moved in for a play at the plate, if one or all of the outfielders have moved shallower or deeper, if the shortstop and second baseman are cheating toward the bag in hopes of a double play. All this maneuvering could determine what happens to a hit ball, so it's important to alert viewers to it and give the director time to support what we're talking about with a visual.

Rather than wait until the pitcher is ready to deliver the ball, the good announcer must mention fielder positioning directly after a pitch so the director can cut to a relating visual *before* the next delivery. If the timing is a bit off it's usually because the announcer mentions a particular fielder too late for the director to focus on him before the pitch. Or the pitcher might be working so fast that the director won't chance breaking away from the pitcher-batter matchup for shots of fielders. When there is no visual supplied to back up the audio, the *informed* viewer will be at an advantage over the casual fan because he can visualize the positioning of particular fielders when various situations arise.

What the savvy fan also knows is that on every play, even those players who never show up on the monitor are in motion. Almost no one is standing still. As the play takes shape, everyone goes to a specific spot, intending to make a fielding play, back up another fielder, cover a base, or serve as a cutoff man. The director is limited in what he can pick up and what he can replay. For instance, on a simple ground ball to the second baseman, the high-home camera may zoom in only to show him pick up the grounder and then pan to first, following the ball into the first baseman's glove. What doesn't show up on your television is the first baseman running over to the bag from his position, the shortstop moving to cover second, the catcher running down the first-base line in foul territory to back up the play, and the right fielder moving in slightly. On a more complicated play, such as a screaming liner off the center-field wall with a couple of runners on base, nine defensive players will be in motion. The director will be following the three offensive players on the bases, so he'll limit the number of defensive players he shows, probably settling on the outfielders retrieving the ball and whoever handles the ball in the infield.

The fan in the park can see where every defensive player is for the duration of a play, but the fan at home sees only the fielders on his screen. Because the director hasn't time to show the viewer all nine defensive players during a play or even on replays, the viewer should try to visualize what is going on off the screen. For example, when a throw from an outfielder gets by the catcher, the fan knows that the conscientious pitcher is probably backing up the play. Although a camera will eventually find the pitcher, it is more satisfying to the viewer to know from the outset that he is back there doing his job.

Fans who know players' assignments on various fielding plays can get an entire picture of a particular play, but I think for a fuller appreciation they should understand that *everything that happens on the field is the result of choices being made on how to achieve certain results*. While fans can see the results, they might not grasp how they came about. They may not realize that some fielding plays look easy only because of the preparation involved. As Hall of Fame football receiver Don Hutson once said, "For every catch I make in a game, I've made a thousand catches in practice." Similarly, by the time the defensive players in baseball take their positions, they have spent countless hours preparing themselves for every possible situation so that they can just react, letting their reflexes and athletic ability take over. Once a play is under way, it is too late to deduce what to do. The "smart," educated player automatically takes the best options, even on the most complicated plays.

23

GENERAL INFIELD PLAY

Earl Weaver postulated, "You can have good defense without good pitching, but you can't have good pitching without good defense." (I'm reminded of A. A. Milne's "A bird can fly, but a fly can't bird.") Weaver probably was thinking about his great center fielder Paul Blair to a degree, but he was really talking about the guys who make the plays in the infield. Although outfield *positioning* is more important than infield positioning because there's so much more ground to cover in the outfield, infield defense is more important than outfield defense. The only way you can have good pitching without good defense in the infield is if you have an unbalanced staff with a bunch of fly-ball pitchers. Obviously, a sinkerball, ground-ball pitcher needs good infield defense more than a fly-ball pitcher. When the sinkerballer finds himself in a bases-loaded jam, a double play turned by the infield is much more than "the pitcher's best friend"—it's beyond platonic.

Pitchers and infielders are pretty much joined at the hip. There's a rhythm and flow in the way infielders play that is similar to the way guys pitch. In fact, the speed with which a pitcher works—the quicker the better—directly affects the infielders' rhythm and flow. Infielders' positioning is affected by the pitcher's count on the batter, what he is throwing, and the pitch's location. Playing the count is very important because if a good hitter is looking for that one pitch to pull, particularly against a young pitcher, he obviously has a better chance to succeed on a 2-0 or 3-1 pitch than on an 0-2 or 1-2 pitch.

With no one on base, of course, an infielder positions himself where he will have the best chance of throwing out a batter at first. However, the number of outs and base runners, and where they are, also determines an infielder's positioning. Very significantly, with a man on second and two outs, infielders will play deeper. If they can't prevent a hit, they at least want to knock down the ball so the runner will have to stop at third. Especially if the batter is slow going to first, they will have the luxury of dropping back—middle infielders can play at the edge of the outfield grass. Playing deeper with two outs and a man on second is such an important part of fundamentally sound infield play that the good announcer will call viewers' attention to it and the director should show the new positioning.

With a pull hitter at the plate, some managers like to overshift their infielders. You'll see the shift used more against left-handed hitters because they are more inclined, for some strange reason, to hit the ball directly up the middle. By playing the shortstop there, the defense will take away some singles. On this shift, the first baseman plays on the line, the second baseman moves into the hole, the shortstop is behind second, and the third baseman moves over toward second and comes in because he can't make plays on choppers to his side if he shifts over and back—the farther over he plays, the shallower he must be to cut down the angle. I've never believed in an overshift in the infield unless there is a dramatic difference between the number of balls a batter pulls and the number he hits the other way. When the left-handed Barry Bonds hits hard grounders, they almost always go to the right side, so he's one of the rare batters you might shift on. (When he hits the ball to the left side, it's usually in the air.)

Anticipation is what makes major-league infielders extraordinary. You can preach it, but you can't teach it. Teaching anticipation would be like teaching somebody to have heart. The really good infielders, particularly on the left side, get fewer bad hops than the poor infielders who play on the same field. Is that luck? It happens too often for it to be luck. Good infielders have an innate sense for reading the ball off the bat and reading the type of hop they are going to get. A right-side infielder doesn't have to be as adept as the left-side infielder because with more time and a shorter throw, he can afford to bobble a ball and have it drop in front of him. A smart fielder on the left side who goes far to his left to field a grounder will take his time *if* he knows the runner is slow, but it's imperative that he catch the ball in good position to make the throw. So he doesn't want to be going back toward the outfield when he grabs the grounder. Some balls have topspin, and he'll occasionally be unable to avoid the in-between hop. It's important to read the hops and to charge in and get the sure hop or short hop. When I played third base for Montreal, an experiment drawn up in hell, Gene Mauch refused to hit fungoes to his infielders because he realized that the spin of the ball off the fungo bat is different from the spin that results when it goes off a game bat on a pitched ball. It doesn't have as much topspin. The coach you see hitting fungoes before a game can't make it seem as if he's hitting balls off a pitcher because he can't duplicate the dramatic spin.

You've all heard the expression "Don't let the ball play you." Defensive backs in football can back up but not infielders. When an infielder backpedals, he gets eaten alive. When the ball gets to him, the upper part of his body goes back and his hands go up, often over the ball. Former manager Bob Kennedy used to say, "If you're an infielder, you play under the hop." When you play under the hop, you have your glove on or near the ground and devour balls by bringing the hands up. When the hands are above the grounder, you will stab at the ball. Playing from the ground up is right; going down to the ground is wrong. The only infielder who won Gold Gloves while stabbing at balls was Cubs second baseman Ryne Sandberg, who got away with it because of his extraordinary timing and hand-eye coordination. But most people can't do it like that.

At times the exceptional Phillies shortstop Larry Bowa would have his glove drag the ground to keep it under the hop and to push his hands out. When you see replays, you'll notice that almost all errors in which the ball stays down and goes through the infielder's legs occur when his hands are back between his legs instead of out in front of him where he can see them. If the hands are back, that means the rear end is up. A fielder has to lower his rear to push the hands out into proper position. As I've said on the air, you can teach your child the proper fielding technique in your living room. Just drop your hands toward the floor between your spread legs; then lower your rear end. As your rear goes down, your hands are pushed forward.

Infielders get into trouble by gliding toward the ball instead of getting in front of it. The good infielder gets behind everything, while the error-prone infielder stabs at too many grounders. Balls are hit with so many different spins and into so many spots on the infield that infielders often don't have the time to make a play and then position themselves to make an easy throw. You'll often see their athletic skills when they go one way and make the throw back the other way. If they are racing in, they have momentum and have to throw the ball across their bodies, with their arms low, to get it back toward the first-base target. That's not their natural inclination, so it's very difficult.

On a topped ball, the rushed infielder will make a bare-handed play. Some fielders get the entire hand on the ball and have no time to get it down to the two fingers and thumb to make the strongest and straightest throw. When you see the ball squirting from one side to another or popping into the air, that's usually an indication that the ring finger was involved. A player will train himself to use only the thumb, forefinger, and middle finger on a throw. The great Pirates second baseman Bill Mazeroski used to throw the ball into his tiny glove and take it out two hundred times a day minimum, so he wouldn't use the ring finger. My picture of Maz to this day is of him doing that over and over in the dugout between innings. His muscle-memory became such that he automatically made the correct two-fingered throw on topped balls and balls that went into his glove—he was so quick with the transfer that it didn't appear that the ball went into the pocket.

It's harder to play on the left side of the infield because even after you negotiate the tricky hops, you still have a long throw to make. So it's important for the shortstop and third baseman to read the ball off the bat, so they won't be in an awkward position to make the throw.

The footwork you'll see on the left side of the infield is one of the blue ribbons of the game. But even baseball people tend to take it for granted. What's assumed by baseball insiders should be explained on the air. I remember my first, futile attempt to explain it. What I said was that a fielder "rearranged his feet," when what I really should have said was that he "rearranged *the position* of his feet." I haven't yet seen a shortstop athletic enough to put his right foot on his left ankle.

On a hard-hit ball to the left side, the fielder will look at the ball as he puts his fingers across the seams and then he'll take his "crow hop." That's a very familiar term in baseball. The left foot is extended, the right foot comes to it, and the fielder pushes off his back foot. If he didn't crow hop, he'd be throwing flat-footed. The crow hop helps with balance, leverage, and momentum toward first base.

Everybody but pitchers who throw something other than the riding fastball is taught to throw the ball the same way: cross-seamed. If you throw a four-seamer, you get a true rotation and the ball stays on an even plane. Everybody, including the pitcher, wants to throw the ball straight when he makes a fielding play. You don't want to throw a sinker or sailer; you don't want the dreaded ring finger to be involved and throw a change-up.

* * *

Balls that roll between fielders can cause them to collide or hesitate because they fear a collision. In baseball, too, "he who hesitates is lost." The worst approach to anything in baseball is to be caught in between. If there's confusion over who should pick up the ball, nobody will and everybody will be safe. But the more experience the fielders have playing together, the less chance there is for a misplay. After a while, the accomplished third baseman and shortstop have a silent language or feel between them that allows them to make plays without hesitation.

If more than one fielder has a play on an infield pop-up, the pitcher is expected to prevent collisions by calling out the player who should make the catch. If the pitcher doesn't make the call, it's up to the players themselves. The ball goes to whoever calls for it, usually with a hand up. These are big-league players, and no more than one guy should call for it. You don't usually see confusion between infielders who have played together for any length of time. If there's a problem on pop-ups, it's more likely to be between an infielder going out and an outfielder coming in. The outfielder has an easier play if there is hang time, so it's his ball if he calls off the infielder. But the infielder can't give up on it until he is called off. Cleveland fans have been treated to the unorthodox approach of the monumentally talented shortstop Omar Vizquel, who actually practices, and has almost perfected, catching pop flies with his back to home plate. He started doing this so he could shield his eyes from the sun, which is particularly glaring at Jacobs Field. I've said he probably drives home with his car in reverse.

THE INFIELD FLY RULE

The infield fly rule stipulates that with less than two outs and runners on either first and second, or first, second, and third, the batter is automatically out if he hits a fair pop-up that the umpire thinks can be caught by an infielder with ordinary effort. This rule came about because infielders intentionally dropped the ball at the last second in order to get easy force plays on runners who had gone back to their bases so they wouldn't be doubled up. The runners were put at too much of a disadvantage, so baseball got its infield fly rule to protect the offense.

I still think infielders should purposely drop the ball every now and then. The rule says that despite the mandatory out on the batter, base runners can still try to advance at their own peril. If a young base runner has forgotten the rule, since nobody ever drops the ball intentionally, the crafty infielder who drops the ball may trick him into taking off for the next base. The runner might have heard somewhere that he can run at his own peril but not know that he doesn't have to run if the ball drops to the ground.

Even when the infield fly rule doesn't apply because there's only a runner on first, I wish more infielders would consider dropping pop-ups and getting a force at second if they can replace a fast runner on first with a slow-footed batter. If the batter assumes the pop-up will be caught and doesn't bother running, the fielder can even pull off a double play by dropping the ball. Such batters need to be taught a good lesson.

FIELDING ON ARTIFICIAL SURFACE

They no longer play on artificial grass in Kansas City and St. Louis, but this nongrowing grass still exists in the Skydome in Toronto, the Metrodome in Minneapolis, the Kingdome in Seattle, Olympic Stadium in Montreal, Veterans Stadium in Philadelphia, the Astrodome in Houston, Cinergy Field in Cincinnati, Three Rivers Stadium in Pittsburgh, and the new Tropicana Field in Tampa.

When I was a major-league catcher, I was always asked what I thought of the artificial surface. I'd say, "I love it. Except when I'm fielding a bunt or foul pop, I don't play on it. And I can hit on it." I could raise my average on the turf without suffering the damage to knees and ankles that the position players endured. The carpet has no give, no resiliency, and there's no question it is much harder on the legs than grass.

Pitchers work off the mound so they don't have to play on the turf either, but they hate the surface. While balls get to the infielders quicker, they also go past them quicker. Pitchers see that more hard-hit but routine ground balls go through the infield than are turned into double plays.

The carpet changes the game. Infielders must be more agile because it's tougher for them to stop and reposition themselves in order to make throws. Middle infielders must be acrobatic turning double plays because the good traction lets base runners reach second and first quicker. And, because the ball picks up speed as it spins off the hard carpet, infielders must play deeper and have stronger arms to make longer throws. This is especially true on the left side, where if your arm isn't strong you'd better be as innovative as shortstops Dave Concepcion and Ozzie Smith, who gave their accommodating first basemen one-hoppers late in their careers. I'd say the quintessential artificial-surface shortstop was the steady, strong-armed Greg Gagne when he played for Minnesota and Kansas City. Jose Lind, who dazzled on defense with the Pirates and Royals, was an ideal artificial-surface second baseman. Even second basemen must have good arms when they play on the carpet because they often make plays in the outfield. Mickey Morandini, who has the strongest arm among National League second basemen, excelled playing on the turf for several years in Philadelphia.

A lot of infielders don't like the turf, but Phillies third baseman Scott Rolen, 1997 National League Rookie of the Year, has a unique reason. He says that he has trouble on the turf because only on grass are the hops "true." Maybe he's talking as a baseball purist and is just feeling nostalgic for the familiar, often-imperfect-but-unaltered hops that he had been fielding on grass infields since he was a boy. Because, except for where there are seams near the bases and home, you won't see any errant hops on the smooth turf. However, I must say that when three or four balls in a row come skidding off the turf, infielders must feel like they're fielding on a trampoline.

THE CORNERS

The First Baseman

It used to be that major-league managers put the guy who couldn't field at first base. It was like right field when we were kids. Keith Hernandez wasn't the first great first baseman, but in his standout seasons with the Cardinals and Mets in the seventies and eighties, he opened a lot of eyes about the position. He showed that if a first baseman has both baseball intelligence and fielding skills (taking away hits, saving throwing errors), he can turn first into a pivotal position, the anchor of the infield. Hernandez was always in the game, often choreographing the action, it seemed, and played defense in such an aggressive, offensive manner that he caused batters to rethink what they wanted to do.

Hernandez confirmed that first base is a left-hander's position. It's true that a right-handed first baseman has the advantage on balls hit right down the line because his glove is on his left hand. In fact, the hardest play for a first baseman, a slicing ball hit toward the line by a right-handed batter, which has English and an unpredictable hop, is harder for the left-handed first baseman because he must backhand it. However, balls hit to the first baseman's right outnumber those to his left by about five to one, and on all those the left-handed first baseman has an advantage because he goes to his glove side.

Where the right-handed first baseman runs into trouble is making throws to second or third on sacrifice bunts and grounders and initiating the 3–6–3 double play. These are fairly easy plays for a first baseman who is in proper position, but it's much easier for the left-handed first baseman to get ready quickly to throw the ball. Starting the 3–6–3 double play is tough for the right-handed first baseman who is holding the runner on because of the angle of the throw he must make to second base to the shortstop coming across second base. If he throws from where he picks up the grounder, his throw may strike the runner who is on the inside of the baseline, but if he takes an extra step to his left, the delay will likely end the possibility of a double play.

Whatever hand the glove is on, soft hands are a prerequisite of good first basemen. They are needed to absorb wild throws and to take away hits on hard-hit balls. Keith Hernandez and Don Mattingly had very soft hands; Rico Brogna, J. T. Snow, and Mark Grace are three first basemen who have them today. You can tell this when you shake their hands. It's like shaking hands with pie dough. First basemen with soft hands save errors because they caress the ball, from the bottom up. When they scoop the ball their fingers soften. Remember—if you go from the top down, whether you're trying to field the ball or pick it out of the dirt, you stab at it, which hardens the hands and fingers.

Footwork is very important at first. Watch how first basemen shift their feet from the inside of the bag to the foul side to catch some throws. This is a difficult play because they have to reach into the runner to snare the ball. It requires quick feet. You will see a converted outfielder trying to play first, and he'll have trouble with his footwork and timing. Unlike an experienced first baseman, he will not be properly balanced when he puts his foot down on the base to wait for the throw. He might put the wrong foot down, which will make his stretch awkward. Sometimes on a ball hit between first and second, the inexperienced first baseman will go a step too far to his right, and by the time he gets back to the bag to receive the throw from the second baseman, he'll be searching for it with his foot when the runner goes past safely. If he puts his foot in the wrong place, the runner may spike his heel.

While good footwork is essential at first, foot speed is not. Of all the best-fielding first basemen, past and present, about the only ones with good speed have been Bill White, Vic Power, Cecil Cooper, and Jeff Bag-

well. Speed is always an asset, but first is not a position that's going to utilize it to its maximum. What the exceptional first baseman has instead is
quickness and *controlled* speed toward home, which is vital in a bunt situation. First base isn't the reaction position third base is, but quick reactions
and sharp reflexes are fundamental to playing it well.

The only first baseman I can remember having the best arm on his
team was the Cardinals' John Mabry, who played some first before returning to the outfield. Having a good arm is less important to the first
baseman than any other fielder. Not many people know that former Gold
Glove first baseman Steve Garvey couldn't throw well and that was the
reason he had been moved from third to first. Keith Hernandez was one
of the few first basemen to have a strong, accurate arm. Many first basemen don't trust their arms enough to gamble on a throw to third. And
many rarely make the good throw home. They short-hop the catcher or
throw the ball so high that he can't block the plate.

The one throw that all first basemen must make is to the pitcher covering first on a ground ball. The first baseman repeats this play over and
over in spring training, giving the pitcher a soft, underhand toss that leads
him to the base. He wants the ball to reach the pitcher as soon as possible,
so he'll be able to make the catch and have time to find the bag. He
doesn't want the pitcher to be making the catch and looking for the bag simultaneously because he might look down and have the ball hit off the
side or heel of the glove. But if it is a slowly hit ball or the runner is Kenny
Lofton or Brian Hunter, there might not be any time between the catch
and the tag. If the ball is grounded to the first baseman's right, the left-
handed-throwing first baseman has a clear advantage. A right-handed-
throwing first baseman would have to backhand the ball, stop, come all
the way around, and then make the throw to the pitcher covering—a much
more awkward play than for a left-handed first baseman, whose glove is
on his right hand.

Usually, it's the first baseman who makes the putout. On a grounder
to an infielder, he wants to move quickly to the bag to provide a stationary target. He places his foot on the edge of the base so that he'll be closer
to the fielder and not be spiked by the runner. Of course, if he stretches,
the ball will get to him sooner, which is important on a close play, but he
should be flexible enough to catch a wide variety of throws. When he
can't pick up a throw in the dirt, the infielder is almost always given the
error, but a good first baseman should suck up short hops. That's what his
large mitt is designed to do. It's also important that he come off the base
to prevent the ball being thrown away. A poor first baseman will hold his

foot on the base even when the ball can't be reached from there, and the result will be a two-base throwing error. Good first basemen are supposed to prevent errors.

Normally, a first baseman takes everything he can get to on his right. But if he hears a particular designated word from the second baseman coming across, he will know that he should let the ball go to him and cover first or keep going so the pitcher can cover. If the ball isn't hit hard, the first baseman must cut it off because it may bounce all the way to the second baseman, and he won't have time to throw out the runner. A lot of times you'll see that when the first baseman goes after the ball to his right, it hits the end of his glove and bounces to the position the second baseman had been in and away from where he is now. That's often an indication that the second baseman and first baseman need to communicate better.

The first basemen who anticipate the most take *necessary* risks, in my opinion. I saw Hernandez go against the book and play the fat part of the field so many times, and rarely did the ball in the hole between first and second beat him. He was risking getting burned on a ball down the line, but it didn't happen often. He realized that many more balls are hit between first and second for singles than down the line for doubles. He proved that in most cases it's smart for the first baseman to play way off the line. (It's up to the pitcher and catcher to worry about the line when they select pitches.)

Depending on the runner and the situation, the first baseman might play deep instead of holding the runner on at first. He has to hold on legitimate base stealers because they take a big lead and the pitcher has a chance to pick them off. But if he plays directly behind runners who aren't legitimate base-stealing threats, he isn't really increasing their chances of getting a better jump and taking off. When there is a slow runner on first, a good left-handed batter up, and no chance of a bunt, why hold the runner? A first baseman should play in position. By playing close *behind* a lot of runners at first, you may not pick off that many but you will be in better position to field the grounder in the hole because you've cut down the distance from the hole.

Even with a big lead in the early innings, first basemen will be inclined to hold runners on because the other team has time to mount a comeback. If, however, his team is up by more than a run in the late innings and there is no one else on base, he'd be more inclined to play behind him. That's because if you can give your team a better chance to get an important out, it's worth the risk of the runner taking an extra base. Dodgers manager Charlie Dressen didn't think of this concept in the ninth inning of the third playoff game against the Giants in 1951, which means he shares the blame for losing the pennant. The Dodgers led 4–1 in the bottom of the ninth, but when the Giants got their leadoff man on at first, Dressen had first baseman Gil Hodges hold him on despite the three-run lead and the left-handed Don Mueller at the plate. If Hodges had been playing back as he should have been, he would have fielded Mueller's grounder and turned it into a double play, or at least gotten one out. But, instead, Mueller got a single to the right of Hodges's outstretched glove and the Giants rallied to win on Bobby Thomson's world-famous homer off Ralph Branca.

The Third Baseman

In general, third base is where organizations put strong-armed players who hit with power but don't necessarily have speed. These guys are in the lineup because of their bats, but the hope is that they will become decent glove men in time. With some guys, like Wade Boggs, becoming proficient can take many years. The hot corner is a reaction position where you need great reflexes, the nerve to charge the plate when a batter may be swinging away, a strong arm (particularly on Astroturf), and, for some guys more than others, a strong chest. The poor-fielding third basemen are of the knock-'em-down-throw-'em-out school. The good ones, like Edgardo Alfonzo, Matt Williams, Robin Ventura, Charlie Hayes, Scott Rolen, Chipper Jones, and Ken Caminiti, know how to play the position. Caminiti, in fact, is the rare muscularly built third baseman who needn't take too many balls off his chest because he has the soft, sure hands to be an excellent fielder.

While the shortstop, the other left-side infielder, moves primarily from side to side, the third baseman moves either up or back. It's almost like the third baseman is on a drawstring. There are situations where he will move to his left or right, but, for the most part, he should be way off the line in anticipation of the ball in the hole between third and the shortstop position. Many more balls are hit for singles between the two infielders than are hit for doubles down the line. As does the first baseman, the third baseman plays the percentages and pinches the middle of the diamond. Of course, being right-handed, he goes better to his left because his glove is on his left hand. Balls hit to his right are more difficult to play because he must backhand them. He has the most trouble trying to backhand slicing balls hit by left-handed batters.

A third baseman is told that he is supposed to take anything he can get to, in most cases. If he can reach a ball to his left, he shouldn't let the shortstop have it. The shortstop will have a harder time making a timely throw because he is farther from first base and it will take longer for him to get to the ball, plant the right foot, and throw. So unless the batter is very slow, the shortstop wouldn't be able to throw him out. One time the third baseman should let the shortstop take the ball is when he has to dive for it. His diving to his left to catch a line drive is one thing; his diving for a ground ball is another. If he snags it, can he make the play? If not, it's useless to dive and prevent the ball from going to the shortstop, who at least has a

Of my 1,937 appearances in regular and postseason games during my major-league career, only six were made at third base. And that was way too many. I had been only a catcher from the time I debuted with the Cardinals in 1959 until I was traded during the 1972 season to Montreal. Gene Mauch, the Expos' manager, decided to experiment with me in the outfield, where I played fourteen times, and at third. Third was such a difficult position for me to adjust to because I was used to initiating every play, not reacting. Still, I understood the fundamentals of the position, although Mauch probably misinterpreted my look of discomfort for one of confusion. I'm sure that happened in one game we were playing in St. Louis, in front of my father. In the bottom of the fifth inning, the Cards had men on first and second with nobody out, and from the dugout Mauch began giving me finger motions, pointing to where I should go in case the ball was bunted. I understood, but Gene looked at my expression and halted the game so he could send in Bobby Wine to replace me. It was so embarrassing walking off the field—my father, who had seen me play in the World Series only five years before at Busch Stadium, was sitting behind our dugout and I could see him shake his head and lower it into his hand. When I reached the top step, I told Mauch, "Gene, I understood what you wanted me to do." Then I took my seat on the bench, while all the other players looked away as if I had the Ebola virus. At least my career as a third baseman came to an abrupt end that day.

chance to make a throw. As good right and left fielders check the center fielder, a good third baseman checks his shortstop.

The third baseman must position himself at a depth where hard smashes won't get by him yet he can make plays to first or second on bunts and topped grounders. The depth he plays is in direct proportion to the strength of his throwing arm. He must have either the strongest arm in the infield or be able to get to the ball very quickly. That's because he must make the long throw to first from deep along the baseline, while sometimes falling into foul territory, and must initiate long around-the-horn double plays. On the throw to second, he will use a three-quarters delivery to fire a chest-high four-seamer to the second baseman on the bag or slightly behind it if the runner is bearing down on him. To throw out runners at first on grounders he must charge, he will have to be able to throw without planting his feet. If he has to field the ball while coming in from the deep position to where he is even with the bag, he can still get the runner occasionally because of that strong arm or quick release.

The two great third basemen of our time, Mike Schmidt and Brooks Robinson, were totally different. Schmidt was perfect for the artificial turf in Philadelphia's Veterans Stadium because he had the speed and extraordinary arm to play deep. Robinson didn't have a strong arm and compensated by playing shallow, which was possible in Baltimore because they kept the grass high to slow down grounders for him and shortstop Mark Belanger. Quickness is essential at third base, especially if you play shallow, and Robinson was quick as a cat, cutting off scorching grounders to his left and taking away sure doubles with diving backhanded stabs over the bag. But, playing back and having more range, Schmidt could get a lot of balls to the left that Robinson wouldn't have been able to reach. If they got by Brooks they were base hits, but Schmidt had a chance to get them. I'm a huge admirer of Robinson, but I wonder if he could have adapted to playing on the artificial surface on a regular basis. He had those remarkable reflexes, but were they fast enough for him to snatch ground balls skidding off the carpet?

I don't think any young third baseman who comes along will have Robinson's combination of instincts, great hands, hand-eye coordination, and smarts, but he couldn't do any better than to use Brooks as his model, especially if he doesn't have Schmidt's rare athletic skills. Robinson said that in order for him to be able to catch hard grounders while playing shallow, he had to learn to put his hands down as soon as the ball was hit, instead of waiting until just before it reached him. To get a good jump on the ball not hit directly at him, he needed to stay mobile, so he would walk into the play, taking a half step, and when the batter swung Brooks's feet would be parallel with each other and be in motion. He compensated for his arm by quickly getting his feet into position to throw and getting rid of the ball quicker than anyone else to first or second. I don't think I ever saw Robinson spin around to make his throw after stopping the ball to his far left, although I did see Schmidt do it. I usually don't like that spin maneuver, where they pivot off their right foot, but sometimes the third baseman is forced to do it because of the momentum he has when he flags down the ball that is behind him. It's a real balletic play for which you need quick feet as well as the strong arm to make up for lost time, but the obvious problem is that you lose sight of your target.

Robinson's signature play was picking up a bunt or slow ground ball and throwing the runner out at first. Nobody did it better. He established a few of the tricks of the trade: If the ball is stopped or coming to a stop, you bare-hand the ball; if it's a slow roller, you try to pick it up with the gloved hand and bare hand together so you can throw on your next step; on all balls you charge it's imperative to come in with controlled speed so you don't overrun the ball and your angle to throw isn't such that you have to come all the way across your body. At third, you want to bring the ball and glove up to your throwing hand, but the speed of the runner often dictates how quickly you have to get rid of the ball. You may have to lower your release point. A third baseman will usually make throwing errors when he must hurry his throw or has time enough to think instead of just react.

While we praise third basemen when they make terrific stops or throws to a base or home plate, we never seem to commend them for being "creative." Maybe it's because we compare them to the players they are positioned next to, acrobatic and innovative shortstops. But creativity does surface at third every once in a while when the player is willing to go against the book. I'm reminded of Joe Morgan, the former Red Sox manager, back when he was a third baseman and we played together in the minors. He told me what he planned to do someday if he was hit a slow grounder by a fast right-handed batter with two outs and a man on second. If it was obvious that he couldn't throw out the speedy batter, he intended to fake a throw to first and then just turn and tag the runner who was rounding third too far. It was an original idea then, and, finally, one day, he got to put it into action. It worked! Too often fielding strategy, like a lot of stodgy baseball strategy, is based on what has always been done rather than on what will work. In many cases, the book is outdated. In this case, the book would have had him throw to first, where the runner would have been safe.

Guarding the Lines

When a manager wants to prevent an extra-base hit, he may move his third baseman and first baseman to the lines. (The first baseman may be holding a runner on anyway.) When they *guard* the lines, they position themselves so that they can reach hard balls that are hit between them and the lines. They are like guys trying to cut down on their drinking—no doubles. They know their own ranges, so usually the manager or coach who positions the players will allow them to determine the exact spots where they stand. If a third baseman has good range to his right, then he will stand farther off the line, though still closer than he would be normally; if he has much better range to his left, then he will be more inclined to stand closer to the line. Occasionally, a ball will hook over the bag, but third basemen will stop 95 percent of the balls hit down the line if they're set to guard it.

The most common time managers guard the line is in late innings in a close game. But managers may do it earlier in two-out situations, when they don't want the batter to either get into scoring position or drive in a runner on first. Twenty years ago, more managers were inclined to guard the line because that's the way it had always been done. It's like in football when teams with leads go to the old prevent defense and get burned. The manager's approach can be conservative, but every so often he should be willing to add a mad dose of common sense. As a broadcaster, I've railed against managers who guard the line without considering who's batting, who's pitching, and how he is pitching. Too often a manager will set his defense to prevent a double when it's the single he should be worried about. However, to their credit, more and more managers today don't guard the lines unless it makes absolute sense.

Guarding the lines depends on the pitcher and hitter. How a pitcher is working a hitter will dictate whether the hitter will be more inclined to pull. If Edgardo Alfonzo, a right-handed right-field hitter, is batting against right-hander Robb Nen, who is throwing ninety-five mph, why would you put someone on the third-base line in late innings? Alfonzo is not going to pull the ball unless it's a hanging breaking ball or change-up or it's a down-and-in fastball, which Nen doesn't throw. If there is a hard thrower against a right-handed batter, especially one who hits to right, the third baseman should be off the line and it's the first baseman who might guard *his* line. Only if the right-handed batter is a notorious pull hitter like Ron Gant, who can pull anybody's fastball, should the third baseman guard the line no matter who is pitching.

There are times to guard the line and give batters the middle of the field. When a pull hitter with power is up in a tie game in the ninth inning, of course it makes sense. But it's nice to know that most managers are playing the rule—more balls are hit to the middle of the field—than the exception (balls hit down the lines).

THE MIDDLE INFIELDERS

When people praise second basemen, they tend to use the word "steady," but when they praise shortstops they're more inclined to use words like "sensational" and "spectacular." I think the difference in the adjectives has to do with the nature of their jobs. Other than being quick and unflinching on the pivot, his most important function, the second baseman is expected to make the routine play and anything better is a plus. The shortstop is expected to make both the routine plays and the impossible plays that take away runs and kill rallies. Positioning is key to both players. Range and a strong arm, a combination that lends itself to exciting plays, are more characteristic of the shortstop. When a second baseman makes a difficult play, it's usually not too far to his right or left and, unless he throws home or to third on a relay from the outfield, his throw is short. Meanwhile, his partner covers considerable ground and makes longer throws, including the one from the hole, constantly revealing his athleticism and strong arm. In fact, second basemen must resist the temptation to emulate their fancy-fielding partners or they'll blow the routine plays and wind up in too many blooper films.

The Second Baseman

Second basemen aren't expected to have better than adequate arms. Their arms are tested on double plays and when they serve as cutoff men and must throw to third or home, but they're not tested as consistently as the arms of shortstops because most of their throws go only a short distance, to first or second base. If they do have strong arms, like Mickey Morandini and Craig Biggio, it is a bonus that makes them extremely valuable when their teams play on artificial surfaces. (Interestingly, both Morandini and Biggio were signed as catchers, as was the strong-armed Manny Trillo, who played a marvelous second base for several teams in the seventies and eighties.)

It always has been standard policy to sign young second basemen because of how well they make the pivot on the double play, not because they have the potential to cover as much territory as a shortstop. In fact, the small-webbed, small-pocketed glove the second baseman wears to make quick transfers on double-play attempts seems designed to discourage attempts to go far to the left or right to cut off grounders. Range wasn't really a consideration at second until Roberto Alomar came along and showed what an asset it can be at the position. Having tremendous range means Alomar can move toward or into the hole between first and second against a left-handed pull hitter without undermining the double-play possibility. A second baseman with no range must cheat toward second when a double play is in order, and that makes the hole even wider. Alomar can run to the base just as fast as the other guy from farther away because of his foot speed and anticipation. Typically, a second baseman's position is determined by whether or not a runner is on first with less than two outs, but Alomar's range allows him to play in almost the same spot in these opposite situations.

What also amazes me about Alomar is that when the ball is hit to him he is able to wait until the last possible moment to decide whether to try for a force play at second or go to first. Unlike the average second baseman, he doesn't have to commit himself to a base before he gets the ball. In fact, as he proved in the 1997 All-Star Game, he can virtually commit to second for a force, then pull back when he sees the runner will beat the ball there, and still go to first to get out the runner. Because he's one of the few second basemen with a strong arm, he can beat the batter despite the delay.

The second baseman is often taken for granted except on double plays, but he has all kinds of responsibilities, including covering second on most steal attempts with right-handed batters at the plate—except if they are opposite-field hitters—and covering first when the first baseman charges on a bunt attempt. He also ventures into the outfield to serve as a cutoff man or, in some stadiums, to play strange caroms. For instance, at Veterans Stadium, if a ball shoots over first in fair territory, it may bounce off the wall that juts out into foul territory along the right-field line. In 1997, I saw Mickey Morandini run out to mid-right field and field a carom in front of the right fielder. The batter got a double, but Morandini hit the cutoff man and stopped the runner from first at third base.

Easy grounders to the second baseman are quickly forgotten, but I think it's a good idea to watch his form on the basic play. You will see that he moves behind the ball rather than fielding it from the side because if it takes a tricky hop over his glove, he'll be able knock it down with his body and keep it in front of him. Because of the short distance to first, he should have time to pick up the ball and throw out all but the fastest runners. If he fields the ball smoothly with hands low and in front of his spread legs, he knows there is no need to hurry his throw because he is close to either second for a force or first base. Much tougher plays for a second baseman who is playing up or slightly toward first against a left-handed batter are the hard grounders or choppers up the middle behind second base or between him and the bag. If there is a bouncer to his right and there is no force play at second, he must get to the ball as quickly as possible, put on the brakes, and make a strong throw to first. Only if it's not hit hard will he have a chance to cut it off at an angle and not have to turn around completely to throw to first. (It helps to be able to accurately gauge the ball's speed. For example, when Jeff Kent was learning to play second base for the Mets he would mistime such grounders and dive over them, when all he had to do was put down his glove.) The farther out the ball travels, the longer his throw must be and the chances of throwing out the batter at first are diminished. Cutting off the ball on an angle is less common on artificial surfaces because of its escalating speed, which is why Chuck Knoblauch, Craig Biggio, and other turf second basemen must play deeper and have stronger arms.

The Shortstop

A good shortstop needn't be exceptionally fast, but he must have a ton of physical attributes, including great hands, impeccable footwork, and, except in rare cases, a *very* strong arm. He can cover a lot of ground to both sides and in front of him, making accurate throws to first from behind second base; back-handing grounders in the hole, planting, and making the long, hard throw to first; and charging slow grounders and throwing on the run. On double plays, he is equally effective making the first throw to second and the relay to first while avoiding hard-sliding base runners. But talent isn't enough to get batters out and excite the crowd, so he also must have anticipation, daring, and flair.

The shortstop is the most mobile infielder. He's like a fan, going left and going right. Occasionally, he'll also shorten up if a speedster is at bat.

He'll go into the hole to make the hardest infield throw; with two outs and a man on second, he'll play deep enough to dive and knock down balls so they don't go into the outfield; and he'll charge most balls hit in front of him so that if he momentarily bobbles them he will have a shorter throw to first. Because he moves around so much *during* plays, it's important that he move around *before* plays, positioning himself properly. Where he plays is extremely important because he's the string that pulls along the other in-fielders and the center fielder often keys on him. So he watches the catcher's signs to determine where he should stand. If, for instance, a right-handed pitcher is throwing fastballs away to a left-handed batter, he won't move out of position. But if the pitcher goes to off-speed pitches, he might shade the batter to his left.

A young shortstop must learn hitters' tendencies so he can position himself. Without the benefit of experience, he should rely on pitchers or catchers or perhaps an older, more experienced backup to tell him where to play. I think what a young shortstop must learn more than anything else is that what applies to him as a hitter often applies to the batter at the plate. This sounds simple, but some players just don't make the connection. They should know, for example, that if they can pull the ball more often when the count is 2-0 or 3-1, then it makes sense that the batter they are defending against will be able to pull the ball more often on those counts. If they have the tendency to go the other way on the 0-2 count, taking what the pitcher might give them, doesn't it make sense that the batter will do the same thing? As they gain experience, they will learn the many guys who do and the few guys who don't. By combining that knowledge with an awareness of the pitcher's stuff, the intended locations of his pitches, the shortstop will have a good idea of where to play all hitters. But when in doubt, play straightaway.

The current crop of shortstops is extraordinary. Omar Vizquel, Rey Ordoñez, Edgar Renteria, Barry Larkin, Walt Weiss, Mike Bordick, Nomar Garciaparra, Alex Gonzalez, Alex Rodriguez, Deivi Cruz, and Derek Jeter, to name a few, all have singular talents and unique styles. Watching some of these guys, you don't think just of baseball. Vizquel, for instance, has the hands of a violinist, he and Ordoñez are like Nureyev around the bag, and Larkin is poetry in motion going to his right. Some of the new guys do things that can't be done or, more precisely, that I've never seen before. Vizquel hurdles over sliding runners from a flat-footed position, lands on the other side, and then completes the throw to first for the double play. Ordoñez slides to his right on one knee to cut off low grounders. Rey learned that move from his father in Cuba, but I don't see how he could teach it to anybody else.

The Second Baseman–Shortstop Tandem

Depending on what type of pitch is going to be thrown, the middle infielders determine who's going to cover second in case of a steal attempt or hit-and-run. This may change with each pitch. For instance, if there is a breaking ball to a left-handed batter, the ball is likely to be pulled, so with the second baseman shaded toward first, the shortstop will probably cover. (In this situation, the second baseman may alert the first baseman to the expected pitch.) If it's a fastball away, the shortstop will probably play him to hit the opposite way, or more straightaway, so he will give the second baseman the open-mouth sign, meaning "you cover." Similarly, the second baseman will probably cover if a breaking ball is thrown to a right-handed hitter, and the shortstop will probably cover if it is hard stuff away because the right-handed batter will probably not be able to get around on it and the ball will be hit to the right side. I keep saying "probably" because fielders adapt to certain hitters. They learn that some hitters can pull the hardest fastballs and some hitters with good bat control like to go the other way on breaking balls, and if the pitcher places the fastball on the outside corner, some batters can hit it through the middle. With a right-handed pull hitter like Mark McGwire, the second baseman always will cover because the shortstop must play deep in the hole between second and third. If the left-handed Barry Bonds is batting with a man on first, you'll often see a semishift with the shortstop covering second from almost behind the base while the second baseman plays way over in the hole. On a ground ball to third, you can have a very rare third-to-short-to-first double play.

Obviously, there is no guarantee as to where a batter will hit the ball. So the middle infielders play the percentages, hoping the right guy covers and the grounder doesn't go through a vacated position. You can't be everywhere. I think back to when former Red Sox manager Joe Morgan told me that Wade Boggs said matter-of-factly, "If the shortstop is more in the hole toward third, I'll just hit it to the shortstop's left. If the shortstop's playing up the middle, I'll hit it to the hole." Joe said, "You might think that's crazy, but I've seen him do it." Rod Carew also tormented fielders in this way. Some major-league hitters have extraordinary bat control, which can frustrate defensive schemes.

With a man on first with less than two outs, the second baseman and shortstop cheat toward the bag in anticipation of a double play. So when an announcer tells you that the middle infielders are playing in "double-play depth," don't be misled into thinking they are moving back and playing deeper.

If the ball is grounded to the second baseman, he has three different throws to second, all of which should be right around the shortstop's left shoulder as he comes across the bag. That's to protect his double-play partner because if he has to reach back into the baseline on throws to his right or directly at him, the base runner will have a real shot at taking him out of the play. Nothing is thrown from above the shoulder. If the ball is hit right at the second baseman, you'll see the quarter turn and a little sidearm toss. It is soft because there isn't much distance to the shortstop. When he's cheating for a double play and moves to the right to catch the grounder, the second baseman wants to use the softest of his tosses because he is closest to the shortstop. It's a backhanded feed, with the hand going in the other direction and facing the shortstop, who may even take it out of the air bare-handed. If the second baseman has to go to his left, it's the most difficult double play for him to begin because he has to pivot on his right foot and give the shortstop a strong throw. You'll see this double play turned on a slow runner if there's a quick, strong-armed shortstop, but usually there will be only a force at second. If there also had been a runner on second, the innovative shortstop might try an interesting play after getting the force at second. Instead of throwing to first, where there is no play, he will hold the ball and look toward third to see if the runner has rounded the base too far and a play can be made on him. First, look to first; second, look to third.

If the ball is grounded to the shortstop, he wants to give the second baseman a quick, chest-high throw that leads him over the bag. He won't wait for him to reach second before throwing because he wants his second baseman to have time to get out of the way of the sliding base runner. What dictates how the shortstop will throw the ball to second? *Where* he catches the ball. If he must go to his right and backhand the ball, he will throw it overhand and strong; if it's right at him, he'll sidearm his throw; and if it's to his left, which is toward the base, he'll give the second baseman a soft, underhand throw. A good second baseman will know what to expect because he and the shortstop practice this play all the time.

You have to have a lot of courage turning the double play as a second baseman. The shortstop can see what the runner from first is doing, but the second baseman will only be able to glance at first before making his throw. That's why second basemen cheat toward the base. It's very, very important for a second baseman to be able to judge the speed of a ground ball to the left side of the infield. If it's hit sharply, then he knows he has plenty of time to make the turn, so he's more pronounced in making it. But the slower it's hit, the longer it will take to get the ball from the shortstop (or third baseman) and the less time he'll have to get rid of it. He's got to be quicker because the runner has more time to bear down on him. If the runner is doing his job, he's going to try to take him out. At times the second baseman will use the bag for protection, keeping it between him and the runner. Then to get to him, the runner will have to go through the base. Often, the base runner will anticipate a second baseman ending up on the third-base side of second and will slide in that direction to take him out. (The base runner is supposed to be able to touch the bag with his hand while sliding at a fielder.)

I think Roberto Alomar and Mark Lemke are the best second basemen today at making the pivot. When I played, the two players who stood out were the Cardinals' Julian Javier and the Pirates' Bill Mazeroski. They turned the double play in completely different fashions. Javier was the best second baseman I ever saw on the double play because he could not be taken out. He had perfect timing and such quick feet that he was called "The Phantom." He'd come across the bag so it was tough for an umpire to determine whether he was on it when he had the ball. Umpires are going to allow second basemen to cheat a little anyway so they don't get injured on takeouts, and Javier took advantage of their leniency to cheat even more. For every one hundred times he was off the bag, they'd call the runner safe one or two times.

Mazeroski had slow feet but quick hands. When he saw you were sliding into him to break up the double play, instead of going airborne he would defiantly stick out his huge left leg and dare you to slide into it. Second basemen aren't supposed to plant their leg because they risk injury, but sliding into Mazeroski's leg was like sliding into a tree trunk. The reason I thought Javier had a slight edge over Mazeroski was that occasionally big guys could take Maz out with a hard slide. But we paid the price.

Turned correctly, like Mike Bordick and Roberto Alomar do it for Baltimore, the double play is a thing of beauty. That's why I'm glad that my Mets director, Jeff Mitchell, realizes there is no need to try to jazz up double plays with any tricky camerawork. He sticks with his high-home camera, Camera-Two, throughout the play, starting on the fielder who picks up the grounder, panning to second for the relay throw, and following the ball to first. What he wants viewers at home to experience is how the fans in the stands watch the play, with their eyes moving with the ball. So during the play, he won't cut to several shots from different camera angles for this would be jarring to the viewer. But when he follows up with a replay, he will use shots from different cameras. Then the different camera angles enhance rather than confuse.

THE BATTERY

The Pitcher

As soon as the pitcher throws the ball home, he becomes another infielder. A good follow-through is important, but Bob Gibson, one of the great-fielding pitchers ever, had a horrible follow-through. Gold Glovers Greg Maddux and Mike Mussina are always balanced after a pitch, with their bodies squared toward home. If a pitcher is off balance, he won't have time to react to balls hit through the middle—he risks being hit on comebackers—or to make quick plays on bunts and tapped balls. If he's falling off the mound toward one line, it will be hard for him to go after the ball the other way. He will be easy to bunt on.

All pitchers, including the poor fielders, can help themselves by just doing the fundamentals. This means the pitcher must back up plays at third and home in case of wild throws, cover home plate in case a pitch gets by the catcher, and beat the batter to first on a grounder to the right side. On the play at first, he will be getting a leading, underhand toss from the first baseman, and if he is quick off the mound he will be able to catch the ball and then look for the base, which is the way he is supposed to do it. But if he does this play enough times, he will know where the bag is instinctively.

If he throws one of those fifty-six-foot fastballs (often caused by sticky fingers from having put too much resin on the ball) or another type of wild pitch, or if there is a passed ball, the pitcher must rush toward the plate and help the catcher find the ball by yelling and pointing. On a play at home, he'll position himself in front of home plate in fair territory. He catches the catcher's throw and drops his glove, hoping the runner will slide into it. Pitchers never intentionally block the plate unless they are planning to retire after the play.

On an infield pop-up between second and short, the pitcher has got to be the guy to make the call. The catcher's too far away. Ideally, the pitcher calls for one guy to take it and calls the other guy off. He's a traffic cop. The Dodgers used to teach that. If the second guy can't hear you, go over and wrap your arms around him. Even in the major leagues, the pitcher botches this play far too often. The pitcher also makes the call when the catcher converges with either the first or third baseman between the base and home, in either fair or foul territory. And it's up to the pitcher to choose between the first baseman and third baseman on a pop-up in front of the mound.

Unfortunately, too many of today's pitchers are lax about making the call on pop-ups. In 1997, Atlanta reliever Paul Byrd turned around and took off without calling who was supposed to catch the pop-up near the mound. He acted like he shouldn't be involved, and, as a consequence, star third baseman Chipper Jones collided with first baseman Mike Mordecai and Jones just escaped being seriously hurt. Nobody wants to be responsible on pop-ups, especially pitchers. Most pitchers don't bother with the other elements of the game. That's why they generally don't make good managers. They play an isolated position, and usually their thinking is limited only to pitching.

The Catcher

The catcher is usually regarded as a separate entity when people start talking about fielding. In fact, they typically feel uncomfortable grouping him with the infielders and outfielders; he doesn't field, he *catches*. Of course, the estrangement of the catcher is due partly to his facing his teammates during the game, crouching while they stand, spending the game in foul territory, and wearing a mask and gear. But it also has to do with the fact that it's hard to tell where a catcher's receiving duties leave off and his fielding takes over, as the two seem to blend into each other. Perhaps a catcher doesn't technically become a fielder until the batter makes contact with the ball.

Other than when making a throw on a steal attempt or chasing a ball to the screen, the catcher is rarely at the center of attention. Exceptions are when he pounces on a bunt or topped ball in front of the plate and, of course, when he is involved in a play at the plate. Another fielding play that puts the catcher in the spotlight is when he must field a high foul ball behind home plate. He has been taught to turn around completely and face the backstop for the best angle on a pop-up behind the plate. He'll want to whip off his mask to get a better view of the ball in the sky, but he shouldn't throw it down until he spots the ball. Then he'll toss the mask behind him so he won't trip over it and he'll have both hands free to make the catch. There are a couple of dangers: If the ball keeps drifting back, he won't be able to hear the pitcher's warnings, so it's up to him to determine where the railing is so he can protect himself. He also must resist the temptation to run too far under the ball. The ball's spin will send it back toward home plate, and he doesn't want to have to backpedal after it. Every catcher has tripped over his mask or a bat or the umpire's foot going back for a pop-up behind home, or collided with a fielder, or lost the ball in the clear sky, or misjudged it, or just dropped it because he wasn't wearing sunglasses. A catcher has to maintain his concentration and make the catch without incident.

With runners on base, blocking pitches in the dirt is a real fielding skill. As San Francisco manager Dusty Baker told me, it's at least as important as throwing a runner out because all base runners will advance a base. A catcher uses the chest protector to deaden the ball in the dirt rather than stab at it with his mitt and have it glance off the hard edge and bounce away. That's the textbook way to do it. In blocking the ball, the catcher tries to square his body to the infield and takes his right hand and curls it behind the mitt on the ground. The shoulders are hunched over because if they are back and the torso is rigid, the carom can travel farther. Although fewer fastballs are thrown in the dirt than breaking balls, they make up a higher percentage of wild pitches. That's because a catcher is trained to anticipate that a breaking ball or splitter will go in the dirt and he will go down with it and smother it. It might squirt by him because his technique is wrong, but it will never surprise him.

A ball that's hard to catch is one that takes off on the pitcher and sails to the catcher's right or tails to his left. You're down in a crouch giving a low target, so you have a long way to go to catch that pitch. Most passed balls come on pitches that are shoulder high, to the glove-side. Moving from the target, you don't have the chance to square the glove up and the ball hits the heel or goes into the web and plops out.

Announcers and fans will rave when an outfielder holds the batter to a single by cutting off a ball on the line and making a quick throw to second, yet they will think nothing of a catcher keeping the runner on first from advancing the same ninety feet by diving a yard off the plate to block a ball with his chest protector. I think it's because they think the outfielder did something above and beyond his job description, while anything a catcher does is expected. Maybe viewers have to be told when a catcher makes a great play because even if they played baseball at some level, it's unlikely they caught, so they don't really know how difficult the position is. They don't even understand that the catcher's mitt, unlike fielders' gloves, is not made for scooping, swooping, or making slap tags.

It was the Cubs' Randy Hundley who revolutionized one-handed catching by using a mitt with a large break. It was much like a first baseman's mitt and allowed catchers to short-hop balls out of the dirt, in front of us and to each side. Plus, we could keep our throwing hands behind our backs where they couldn't be hurt so easily. Johnny Bench and Jerry Grote

There's no graceful way to go after a passed ball or wild pitch. The catcher flings his mask away as he turns around and starts looking for the ball. The pitcher runs toward the plate, trying to alert his catcher to where the ball has rolled, as if someone has run off with his wallet.

If the ball ends up only a few feet from the plate, there might be a play on a runner going to second or third. But since the throw will be hurried, the shortstop and center fielder should back up the second baseman at second and the left fielder should come in to back up third base. (If the catcher can't find the ball, the second baseman may decoy a runner coming from first by pretending a throw is on the way. If the runner slides, he won't have time to get back up and run all the way to third.)

If a third strike eludes the catcher, the key is not to panic but to find the ball. If there are no base runners and the ball hasn't rolled too far from the plate, he has time to throw out the batter, who must run ninety feet from home to first. The throw will go much faster than the runner, and the right fielder will back up the play. If there is a runner on first and less than two outs, the batter is automatically out, so the catcher mustn't risk an error with a needless throw to first. (Last year I saw a third strike get away from the catcher with a man on first and less than two outs; the batter ran, the first baseman ran over to cover first, and the catcher threw to first. Here were three major leaguers who didn't know the rules.)

As Dodgers catcher Mickey Owen learned the hard way in the pivotal fourth game of the 1941 World Series, there's nothing worse than letting the third strike get by you in a key situation. If there is a man on third, a wild pitch or passed ball is always upsetting, on any count. The only hope for the catcher is to retrieve the ball quickly and throw it toward the plate, hoping the pitcher is covering.

became the best, trendsetting one-handed catchers of my era. I marveled at how quick their releases were. Currently, I'm impressed by the quick releases of such outstanding receivers as Charles Johnson, Ivan Rodriguez, and Jason Kendall.

When I started catching, the chest protector had a seam down the middle so that the ball would carom to the right or left off it. It took the manufacturers a while to figure out how to change the protector's configuration so that the ball would stay in front of us. They also improved the padding, but not before I had my share of deep bruising. Initially, I wore the old one-bar mask that was light and didn't offer as much protection as the one to which I graduated, the birdcage mask that is safer but moves when you throw. The hockey mask that is coming into prominence doesn't move when the catcher throws, which is why it would become popular. The throat protector that dangles from the bottom of the mask was first used by Steve Yeager after that terrifying episode in 1976 in which a sharp piece of a broken bat got lodged in his neck while he was in the on-deck circle. I wish I had been wearing something like that in 1979 when I was struck in the Adam's apple by a spinning breaking ball thrown by Steve Carlton. After spending two days in the hospital with a blood clot on my vocal cords, I had a steel attachment welded onto my mask for protection.

If you combine being beaten up with pitches, the wear and tear on your legs, and taking on speeding base runners on plays at the plate—the one time that fans recognize the catcher's *fielding* skills—you can see that no athlete has it tougher than the catcher. It's necessary to be tough, combative, and macho. That describes Thurman Munson, Johnny Bench, Johnny Roseboro, Tony Peña, Mike Scioscia, Gary Carter, Carlton Fisk, and Randy Hundley. Guys like these are hard to get out of the lineup despite fatigue and numerous bumps and bruises. But you have to give them a breather every now and then. A catcher doesn't get any meaningful rest when he comes out of a game after five innings, so I'd say a manager should convince his catcher to sit out the second game of a doubleheader or a day game after a night game. Sometimes doing this early in the season prevents fatigue later in the year. This very valuable player plays this very vulnerable position, and all care must be taken with him to ensure his availability throughout the season.

24

GENERAL OUTFIELD PLAY

POSITIONING

It is worth repeating: Outfield positioning is more important than infield positioning because outfielders have much more room to cover. This is such a simple statement of fact that one might underestimate its significance.

The positioning of outfielders is about the only thing accomplished of value at pregame meetings. And it is the reason that pitchers keep charts during a game. When you see the next day's pitcher in the dugout with a notebook, you might assume he's making notes on what will benefit him when he faces the opposing hitters. But actually what he's marking down is where on the field the batters tend to hit the ball with the most frequency so that the outfielders (and perhaps the shortstop) can position themselves correctly.

Until recently, most managers were negligent with regard to opposite-field depth. Now, it seems that most opposite fielders are aware of who the hitter is. Still, there are many times I don't agree with the positioning of outfielders. In my opinion, the opposite fielder should play reasonably shallow, the center fielder less shallow, and the pull fielder as deep as the hitter's power warrants. There will be some adjustment made according to the specific hitter and to parks that have large outfield areas or artificial grass, but for the most part this is the alignment I like. When he is defending against light-hitting right-handed batters, I think it's very important that the right fielder play shallow. Defending against light-hitting left-handed batters, the left fielder should play shallow. Too often outfielders play deep and watch little flares fall a few feet in front of them.

For reasons other than a juiced ball, fly balls have been going somewhat deeper to the opposite field in the last couple of years, but playing shallow is still smart. Just because a right-handed batter hits the ball over a right fielder's head doesn't mean that he was playing in too much. The opposite fielder and, though not quite as much, the center fielder should plant themselves only deep enough to make it extremely difficult—not impossible—for a batter to *drive* the ball over their heads. Remember that hitting a drive is not the same as hitting a fly ball. A drive is on a fairly even plane not far off the ground, while a fly ball has the loft that allows an outfielder the time to get back and make the play. If you are playing the opposite field, you can play shallow enough to take away flares and still prevent a lot of drives from going over your head and still be able to go back and catch those balls with loft.

Managers often have their outfielders play deeper on the turf to prevent the extra-base hit. I don't think they should. You have to keep in mind that if the outfielder is deeper, the batter, who has better traction on turf, is going to have his extra-base hit anyway by running hard to second. The outfielder is going to cut off the ball deeper, and his angle is going to require that he make a longer throw and, unless he has an exceptional arm, most good base runners are going to be able to reach second. On the rug, the outfielders shouldn't play deeper, but they should be bunched up more to prevent balls from going into the gaps. They should move toward the gaps and give most batters the lines.

If you see an outfielder play deep for no reason, then he's probably a very cautious, safety-first outfielder. He's losing good positioning because he knows it's easier to come in on a ball than go back. Just because it's easier to come in on balls, you should not play so far back that a ridiculous number of balls will fall in front of you. Some players don't have enough confidence to go back on a ball, so they don't cheat toward the infield. Maybe some outfielders are gun-shy about the ball going over their heads for extra bases, while they feel no shame if the ball drops in front of them.

There are some guys who start their careers playing deep and have never been talked to about it. Maybe it has become their way and it's now impossible to change them. Many managers probably would prefer outfielders to play shallow but figure they can't change their style. When

Davey Johnson managed Darryl Strawberry on the Mets, he would say that when Darryl played a deep right field he was in his comfort zone, and that's why he didn't insist on moving him. I asked, "Can't a comfort zone be closer to the plate?" I added, "The way you make it closer is to have the fielder practice standing closer and going back on balls." Not one time did I see Darryl do that. Rusty Staub used to call where Darryl stood the "Strawberry Patch." It was a brown patch of grass about four feet in diameter. When we'd practice back in the old days, we'd kid each other by saying, "Move around, you're killing the grass." Well, Darryl actually did kill the grass.

I have long been so outspoken about why outfielders should play shallow that it may surprise you that Curt Flood, who was the great Cardinals center fielder during my first tenure with the team, played a deep center field. And Curt was comparable to Willie Mays at catching the ball. That's how good he was. Bob Gibson told me recently that Curt had been influenced to play deep by Billy Bruton, the center fielder on the Braves' championship teams of the late fifties. That Curt played deep successfully doesn't change my mind about where I think center fielders should play because I haven't seen anyone else who played as deep who could race in to catch flares just beyond the infield. He was special, not someone another outfielder should pattern his game on.

Incidentally, Gibson was one of many pitchers who liked his outfielders to play deep. He would say, "I'll give up singles, I don't want to give up doubles." If the pitcher is that way, then you bow to his wishes. You play deep.

Check the outfielders' depths in late innings of one-run or tied games. With two outs and nobody on, I think outfielders should be playing a little deeper to prevent the extra-base hit, even though they may allow singles to drop in front of them. With a man on second, however, they will play in to prevent the run-scoring single. If there is no one on base or a base runner on first, outfielders will want to play back a step or two to cut down the angle. Coaches tell the outfielders, "No doubles." That means outfielders will play a step or two deeper to make sure the ball doesn't get past them. But it's not for the same reason infielders move back with a man on second and two outs to make sure the ball doesn't go through. The infielders want to prevent a run from scoring; the outfielders want to prevent an extra-base hit.

Also important to outfield positioning is lateral movement prior to the pitch. If the infield shifts left or right, it doesn't mean the outfield shifts. Usually when there is a dramatic shift in the infield, there should be, at most, a modest shift in the outfield. I'm not fond of dramatic overshifts in the outfield. Too much of it is done today despite the fact that it has the terrible result of robbing a pitcher of a pitch. When there is a dramatic overshift the other way, the pitcher has no choice but to pitch the batter with the defense in mind. If a good right-handed hitter is up, for instance, he might have to pitch him hard stuff away because of the outfield alignment. He may be a curveball pitcher, but now he has to abandon that pitch and throw hard stuff. He becomes afraid to throw his curve because it's a slower pitch and the batter might pull it. If it goes into left field, a left fielder who is in left-center because of the overshift wouldn't be able to catch this routine fly. As Curt Simmons would say of outfielders, "Play 'em straightaway. Doubleday put them there for a reason." When you look at a major-league outfield, think, "Straightaway is best."

FIELDING

Correct positioning will help an outfielder considerably, but he still has to field the ball, often under difficult circumstances. If a left-handed thrower must run to his left or a right-handed thrower must run to his right, he may have a hard time making the play because he'll have to reach across his body with his glove while he is running. If there is a pop-up just beyond the infield, it's the outfielder's ball if he can reach it, but while charging in he might have to call off and dodge infielders who are backing onto the outfield grass to make the catch. The loft of the ball doesn't always give you the opportunity to camp under it.

Teammates are the least of the obstacles that outfielders must put up with as they try to run down fly balls. There are the swirling winds at Shea Stadium and Wrigley Field. The wind and sun are extremely troublesome at 3Com Stadium in San Francisco. At four o'clock in Coors Field it is hard for fielders on the right side to see. At Yankee Stadium it is the left fielder who loses the ball on hot, humid days. High flies that disappear as they approach the ceilings of domes often drop right next to frightened outfielders. High skies cause outfielders to lose the little white ball in numerous parks. Another day-game nightmare for the outfielder is when a ball that is hit right at him gets lost in the white shirts of the crowd. If all this weren't enough, fans throw objects at opposing outfielders and little kids named Jeffrey lean over railings and grab balls that are headed for outfielders' gloves. The raised mounds in foul territory in those parks that don't have actual bullpens are perhaps the worst obstacle of all. The Players Association should get those things banned because some outfielder (or infielder) is going to be seriously injured tripping over a mound while going after a foul ball.

An outfielder can be his own worst enemy if he has trouble judging fly balls. When a batter takes a full swing, the outfielder can be deceived into thinking it will go farther than it actually will because he doesn't realize that it went off the end of the bat. Other fly balls may die in mid-flight and not have enough hang time for him to adjust. On a short fly, he may worry that if he risks trying to catch it on the dead run, it will fall under his glove and he'll overrun it, allowing the runner and batter to streak for an extra base. He may give up on the ball and then realize he could have caught it if he kept running hard. A misplay by an outfielder can be as damaging as an error because it usually means at least an extra base for all runners. Fortunately, an outfielder with speed can often rescue himself from misjudged balls and other gaffes.

Speed is a tremendous asset in the outfield because only three players cover an area as big as a landing strip. Some teams can get away with slow or moderate-speed players in right and left field, but not if they play on an artificial surface. When he was with Kansas City in the seventies and St. Louis in the eighties, Whitey Herzog was the first manager to realize that

Prior to a game in Wrigley Field, an announcer would be remiss if he didn't tell fans about the havoc the wind can play on a fly ball, either carrying it onto Waveland Avenue or pushing it back toward the infield. Early in 1997, Gary Thorne and I were broadcasting a Mets-Cubs game in Chicago and talking about how shortstop Shawon Dunston wasn't in the lineup. That prompted our director, Jeff Mitchell, to cut to a shot of Dunston in the Cubs' dugout. Shawon just happened to be spending that moment moving a towel up and down in front of his face. It was so obvious from the visual that someone in the dugout had passed gas that there was nothing else I could say but "Well, we've talked about the wind here at Wrigley Field . . ." Everybody in the booth and the truck lost it. I couldn't say anything and had to press the "cough" button on my microphone so people wouldn't hear me laughing. Announcers shouldn't use too much toilet humor and it isn't *my* forte, but I knew we had a picture that was begging for commentary.

three fleet outfielders are needed on the carpet because balls zoom through the gaps to the fences. With its good traction, the turf lets outfielders like Devon White (when he was with the Blue Jays) and Ken Griffey, Jr., utilize their speed to flag down balls, but it really causes problems for slow, plodding fielders.

Fast outfielders always go full blast when they are coming in on a ball or going left or right, but too many don't utilize their speed on fly balls hit over their heads. You'll see an outfielder drift back as if he wants to reach a spot at the same time as the ball. The correct approach is to race back to where you think the ball will be coming down rather than to try to time it. Ideally, the outfielder will have an extra moment to decide whether to climb the wall to try to rob the batter of a homer or to put on the brakes and either play the ball off the wall or catch it on the warning track.

There are times when an outfielder should leap into a wall even though the ball may ricochet far away from the wall if he misses, or he may dive into the hard surface to prevent a single even if missing the ball means the batter will get a double or triple. Two such times are when your team can't afford to fall further behind and when the game is on the line. However, if his team is up by three or four runs, an outfielder should play it safe. With his team up by that margin, a base runner should be very aggressive, but it's the exact opposite with a fielder, who should be passive and willing to give up a single or double rather than risk the possibility of a big inning. His team can afford to give up one or two runs but not a bunch. If there is a blooper that falls into center with a man on second, he won't throw home unless he's positive he can beat the runner there. Instead, he will toss the ball into second, conceding the run, to keep the batter out of scoring position. It's understandable that an outfielder wants to be aggressive, but if he sees a runner stop at a base, he should play more cautiously. Too many times an outfielder will run past the ball while trying to pick it up quickly off the ground, and the runner takes the extra base on the misplay.

Whether the outfielder is aggressive or passive in a tight game may also depend on how effective his team's bullpen is. If your team doesn't have bullpen depth, you have a tendency to play a renegade type of defense because you don't want your team to fall behind. You take more chances to neutralize the poor relief pitching. If you have a few strong relievers, like the Dodgers and Orioles do, you're more inclined to play it safe and give guys singles. While your relievers, particularly the closer, are being more aggressive in the strike zone as they try to close out a game, challenging rather than nibbling, you, ironically, play more conservatively in the field because of their effectiveness.

Media scrutiny has become so intense that I think more guys dive for balls today, even when it's unnecessary. They don't want to be accused of not trying. In a playoff game, Yankee left fielder Chad Curtis dove over a ball he might have caught by just bending over. As a former center fielder, he didn't take into account that balls hit to left-center by a left-handed batter will tail toward the left fielder. The outfielder must decide: "If I make the play, can I do something with it?" Some dives are great tries but are misguided. For instance, when a right-handed outfielder dives to his right on balls low to the ground, he has to backhand the ball with his gloved left hand. He's not going to make that catch very often. Also, you'll see an outfielder dive for the ball and flatten his glove on the ground. You appreciate the effort, but nobody can catch a ball with the back of his glove.

To prevent injury, many of today's outfielders will slide under the ball instead of diving. Feet-first instead of head-first. It's less risky. When sliding into foul territory, a slide will protect them from the fence. Another benefit of the slide is that the glove stays off the ground.

Everybody used to talk about how outfielders should catch the ball with two hands. But no more. When gloves were the size of saucers you had to use both hands, but today they're the size of platters and the other hand is almost an encumbrance. In fact, when fielding a ground ball it's improper for an outfielder to use two hands. An outfielder will charge in, making sure that the entire play (the runners, infielders, and catcher) is in front of him, and field the ball with only his gloved hand. He scoops up the ball and shovels the glove and ball up to his throwing hand by his shoulder, so he's immediately in position to make a strong throw, with his weight and momentum taking him forward. If you want to see a very quick, technically flawless pickup and throw, check out such outfielders as Barry Bonds, Larry Walker, Paul O'Neill, Bernard Gilkey, and Sammy Sosa.

When an outfielder aggressively charges a ground ball, he will usually stop the runner from going to the next base. Often it's not the strength of his arm that stops the runner but how quickly he gets to the ball and gets rid of it. Most runners are conditioned to see where they are and where the ball is when they round the bag. If the ball is in the air on the way back to the infield, that will stop them regardless of the strength of the throw. A hasty throw is more important than a strong throw. He will try to grab the ball across the seams so he can get a true, or straight, throw. Because left-handed outfielders have a natural tail on their throws, they have to condition themselves to throw a four-seamer to the infield. The four-seamer reduces movement.

Thwarting the runner from attempting to take the extra base can be more valuable than having a lot of assists. An outfielder may take away twice as many bases from the opposition as the outfielder who records twice as many assists. If you have the reputation for throwing out runners, your assist total may be low because no one will run on you. If you keep twenty runners from taking an extra base, you are perhaps more effective than an outfielder who has ten assists but hasn't stopped anybody from running.

I think assists are only a valid statistic early in a player's career when he is trying to establish a reputation. I remember that in the early sixties, the Phillies' Johnny Callison accumulated sixty-six assists in his first three seasons as a full-time outfielder because nobody could believe his arm was that good and kept testing it. Once players were convinced his arm was great, they stopped running and his assists went down. Runners challenge guys with weak arms, so those are the guys who will come up with a number of assists. They don't run on Larry Walker anymore, but they did in his early days. They'd say, "So he threw me out the last time; let me see him do it again." So he'd do it again. Then they became less inclined to run. Now his stat totals don't mean as much.

If an outfielder has a low number of errors, that may be as meaningless as the low assist total. It could mean that the fielder isn't aggressive enough to attempt difficult fielding plays or throws. His lack of errors isn't necessarily an indication of talent. Ralph Kiner tried to sneak one past me in 1997, when he inferred that the Phillies' Gregg Jefferies was a good outfielder because he'd made only one error in about fifty games. That was an obvious case where statistics didn't tell anywhere near the truth. Jefferies is a good hitter, but he's not a good fielder, as all our New York viewers knew from having watched him when he was with the Mets. Of course, right after I reminded Ralph about Jefferies's fielding deficiencies, Gregg threw out the potential tying run in the eighth inning, making the best play of his career.

THE THREE POSITIONS

The Center Fielder

Assuming he can get a good jump on the ball and can catch, the center fielder is usually the outfielder with the most speed because he must cover the most territory. It's not necessary that he have a great arm, but he's the guy the team counts on to catch the ball before it hits the ground.

His position is the only one on the defense that *absolutely* requires speed, and the slower the left and right fielders are, the faster the center fielder has to be. If Marquis Grissom is in center, a manager can afford to play a right or left fielder without much range. The center fielder is expected to take anything he can get to, as well as trail balls hit to the other outfielders. On balls hit toward the wall in right or left, if the fielder slams into the wall, the center fielder must be there to pick up the carom or the batter can run all day.

The most difficult play for the center fielder is the ball hit right at him. The fielder may have trouble breaking on it properly because he can't tell how far or fast it is going. When Curt Flood played center field, he judged the distance by the bill of his cap. If the ball was above the bill, he broke back; if it was below the bill, he broke in. The lower the ball is hit, the quicker the fielder's reactions while going forward must be. Then it's very important for him to gauge how hard it was hit. Lofts give the fielder depth perception and time, but if the ball is hit directly over his head, he had better turn the right way or he'll lose two or three steps at the outset. On the other hand, if he breaks back, he may have trouble reversing himself and catching a ball hit off the end of the bat. If the pitcher or weak-hitting eighth-place hitter is the batter, the good center fielder's instincts will tell him to charge in spite of a big swing.

The center fielder is the only fielder who can never play straightaway because if he stood directly behind second base, the pitcher would block his view of the plate. So he moves over a couple of steps to look over the left or right shoulder of the pitcher, and that's his version of straightaway.

In 1971 and '72, sore-armed Chicago White Sox right fielder Pat Kelly occasionally was joined in the outfield by Carlos May in left and Walt Williams in center. May had continued his career despite having had part of his right thumb blown off in 1969 when a mortar had misfired while he was serving in the marine reserves. The popular Williams would have been taller than 5′6″ if he didn't seem to be missing a neck, hence his unique nickname, "No-Neck." As the three players took their positions to begin one game, White Sox announcer Harry Caray delicately said, "Playing outfield defense for the White Sox today are No-Thumb in left, No-Neck in center, and No-Arm in right." Only Harry could have gotten away with that.

I think that's where all center fielders should stand for almost everybody. I can't tell you how many games have been lost because center fielders have shaded hitters one way or another. Curt Flood tracked down everything—once he ran to the wall in Wrigley Field and literally climbed the vines to pick the ball out as if it were a bunch of grapes—despite shading only one player in the National League in the sixties. That player was Henry Aaron, and because he could pull the ball Flood moved exactly three feet to his right.

Flood, like Willie Mays, could catch up to fly balls all over the outfield because he had extraordinary anticipation. Pitchers would think they gave up gappers based on the straightaway alignment, but when they turned around expecting the worst they saw Flood standing in the gap waiting for the ball. How did he know? His anticipation was based on the count and his understanding of who was pitching, what he was throwing, and how hard he was throwing.

I don't think most fans understand how important it is for the center fielder to "play the count." The center fielder, as well as the other two outfielders who are keying off him, play the batter to pull on 3-1 and 2-0. On those counts, a good hitter is looking for that one pitch to drive, particularly against a predictable young pitcher. The center fielder will play the batter to go weakly the other way when the count is 0-1, 1-2, or 0-2 because the batter will be in a defensive mode.

As part of playing the count, the center fielder moves on every pitch according to whether it will be a fastball or a breaking ball. He might key off the shortstop, who has a closer view of the catcher's signs. If he is familiar with the pitcher, he won't need to be told the signs because he'll be able to figure them out simply from watching where the catcher sets up. Flood was awesome at knowing what location meant in terms of pitch selection if a particular pitcher was on the mound and there was a certain count. So he'd watch me like a hawk. When I'd move, I'd see Curt lean. By leaning, that would put him two steps in motion.

When you watch games on television you won't see every center fielder playing every batter straightaway. You can look for some center fielders to cheat into the gaps against some power hitters. If you're Ken Griffey, Jr., and the dominating left-hander Randy Johnson is on the mound, you figure that nobody is going to get around on his fastball, so you might play in left-center when a left-handed batter is up and in right-center when a right-handed batter is up. When a breaking-ball pitcher comes to the mound, you may play more batters to pull. The center fielder has the advantage over the other outfielders in that he sees where the catcher sets up for pitch location and can tell if it will be the slow breaking ball or something harder.

Although I haven't seen a center fielder who is the equal of Mays, Flood, the shallow-playing Paul Blair, and Vada Pinson, Ken Griffey, Jr., and several other current center fielders are exceptional. Devon White, Rondell White, and the much-traveled Otis Nixon can flat-out track down the ball, and they have tremendous range. Nixon has never had a great arm, so he has made sure to limit the number of strong throws he has to make by catching the ball before it drops to the ground to prevent a lot of base running. Ray Lankford is the typical Cardinals center fielder in that he has great gap speed. Jim Edmonds, whose remarkable over-the-head catch in 1997 was only one of his many that have made highlight films, Bernie Williams, and Chuck Finley are fine center fielders. Edmonds and Williams were AL Gold Glove winners in 1997, along with Griffey. The guy I love is Marquis Grissom, who shows that you can play a shallow center and still run down balls hit over your head and cut balls off in the gap. I think Grissom is the best all-around center fielder in the game. Young Andruw Jones of Atlanta may someday establish himself as the best. He plays shallow, and it's impossible to hit the ball over his head. The Braves, more than any other team, perhaps, need a great center fielder because starters Greg Maddux, Tommy Glavine, and Denny Neagle all pitch away, inducing batters to use the fat part of the field. I know they appreciate what Jones can do for them.

The Right and Left Fielders

Speed doesn't determine which of the other two starting outfielders will play left and which will play right. It's the arm. The guy with the stronger throwing arm goes to right field because he has to make two long, equidistant throws while the left fielder's single long throw is to home. If neither guy has a strong arm, then it makes no difference who goes to left or right. You just hope they hit enough to compensate for their arms. How do you play left and right field? In this case, swing the bat. And hope the center fielder has a lot of range.

You may see Bernard Gilkey throw out a lot of runners and make many other on-the-mark throws and wonder why he isn't switched from left to right field. The reason is that his arm is strong enough for a left fielder but not strong enough for him to play right. Those good throws he makes to home come as a result of charging the ball quickly so that his throws aren't so long. His assists come from technique, hustle, and accuracy rather than the strength of his arm.

What also makes Gilkey an ideal left fielder is that he is excellent at going to the line quickly, planting his right foot, and throwing out batters trying for second. Even when he holds the batter at first, he has done something that is fundamentally sound. Keeping the batter out of scoring position means the other team may have to give up an out to move the runner to second.

Barry Bonds is another superb left fielder who compensates for just an average arm by getting to the ball quickly and having a quick release. He has won several Gold Gloves by playing a very intelligently conceived defense. He has an extraordinary sense of how left-handed batters hit to the opposite field because he himself is a left-handed batter. Because fly balls to the opposite field curl toward the line, he plays close to the left-field line. He always seems to be in the right spot.

Of course, it is equally important for the right fielders to get to balls quickly near the line and fair balls that rattle around in the corner or in foul territory, but they are out in right more because of their arms, weapons that not only eliminate overly aggressive runners but also deter countless runners from trying for a seemingly reachable extra base. I can still see Roberto Clemente, who had the strongest and most accurate arm I ever saw, throwing one-hoppers from the fence to home plate. Some right fielders have rifles for arms, but he had a howitzer.

Among the current right fielders with strong and accurate arms are Sammy Sosa, Jose Guillen, Raul Mondesi (who also plays center), Alex Ochoa, Larry Walker, and Paul O'Neill. I love that Walker and O'Neill not only have great arms but also are always in position to throw after

I've always been partial to right field because that's where I started with the Oliver Finnie Candy Company when I was an eight-year-old in Memphis, Tennessee. When you're a kid, right field is where they exile you if they don't know what to do with you. My father was umpiring a game with some older kids and they had only eight players, so he convinced them to let me fill in. Naturally, they sent me to right field. After the game, I got a uniform and was so excited I slept in it.

making the catch or charging a grounder. They never take anything for granted. Walker will even try to gun down batters at first, like Carl Furillo used to do when he played right for the Brooklyn Dodgers in tiny Ebbets Field. He's just a hair below Clemente. O'Neill's an exceptional defensive outfielder despite not having much speed. So many balls he runs down are because of anticipation. Think back to his game-saving catch of Luis Polonia's long drive in the gap in Game 5 of the 1996 World Series.

Usually a coach who was a former outfielder will move the center fielder left or right, and the other two outfielders will follow suit. However, on the ball O'Neill caught off the left-handed-hitting Polonia, he was the only outfielder who was moved. Yankee coach Jose Cardenal moved O'Neill two steps to his right prior to the play, and those were the two steps that rescued John Wetteland from a blown save. Polonia had been fouling off balls to the left side against Wetteland, and it became apparent that if he hit the ball fair it wouldn't be pulled down the right-field line but hit to the fatter part of the field.

It was no big deal that a right fielder moved independently of the center fielder. Left fielders do that as well. When I say that the right and left fielders play off the center fielder, I don't mean that they key on him every play. In fact, what distinguishes all the good outfielders is that they'll position themselves according to experience, knowledge, and feel. Intelligence and independence work hand-in-hand.

PART VI

Around the Bases

25

SMART BASE RUNNING

When people talk about a good offensive player, they usually go on and on about his hitting. Then they might add, "Oh yeah, he's also a good base runner." It's a throwaway line. It shouldn't be. If I had to pick the best left fielder in his prime I would take Barry Bonds over Ted Williams because of defense, sure, but mainly because of his superior base-running ability. And even when Wade Boggs was at his best, I thought Tony Gwynn was the better player because he ran the bases faster and better. The ability to run the bases well and take the extra base makes a player a much bigger offensive threat. Also, good, aggressive base running is vital to a team's success. Stealing bases, an important part of Bonds's game, is a tremendous weapon, but when I speak of good base running, I am also talking about running hard to first, running through bases instead of just to them, and taking the extra base, anything to manufacture runs.

I contend that going from first to third on a single with less than two outs is a much bigger play than many astute baseball observers concede. Yes, even bigger than some home runs, because they are more likely to result in multirun rallies. My broadcast partner Ralph Kiner, speaking as a seven-time homer champion would, wholeheartedly disagrees with that statement and chooses power over speed or good base running. I'll even cite to him many championship teams that won because of speed and intelligent base running and point to the Chicago Cubs and Boston Red Sox, nonwinning teams that have historically been plodding on the basepaths, passive rather than aggressive. It's no accident that the teams with the greatest base runners of all time—stolen-base record breakers like Ty Cobb, Maury Wills, Lou Brock, Bert Campaneris, Rickey Henderson, and even Vince Coleman, as well as Jackie Robinson, Willie Mays (who did more than swing a big bat), Willie Davis, Pete Rose, and Joe Morgan—won championships and the Cubs and Red Sox have failed to win because they rely on power that suits their ballparks.

In 1996, Joe Torre brought to the world champion Yankees the animated running style of the National League, and the other American League teams were as ill equipped to cope with that type of offense as the French were when the Germans under General Guderian smashed through the Ardennes. Over the years, there have been American League pennant winners that have emphasized running—the White Sox of 1959 and A's of the early and mid-seventies, for example—but too many current teams play the base-to-base game rather than the more exciting and smarter through-the-base game of the National League. The small parks and the designated hitter have something to do with that, but the style probably dates back to the twenties, when the Yankees featured the "Murderers' Row" and lived by the long ball. On the other hand, the running National League style probably came from the Cardinals' "Gas House Gang" of the thirties and the influx of players from the Negro Leagues in the late forties and early fifties. Baseball is more fun to watch when that style of play is employed. The game is the same, but when you watch a National League game, you'll see that there's more motion. As I'll tell FOX viewers, the aggressively played National League game is usually a faster game, with more pace and style.

On offense, there are times when you want to let reckless abandon take over. That's where the running game comes in. Just as there is clutch hitting, there is clutch movement on the bases, be it stolen bases, hit-and-run plays, bunts, productive infield and outfield outs that bring home runners or move them into scoring position, or taking the extra base.

A runner has carte blanche to be his own coach 90 percent of the time. So if he thinks he can make the extra base or put pressure on the defense, he should go for it. If it will take an extraordinary throw from an outfielder to cut him down, he should go all the time. The average fan might not understand that the "bad" base runners aren't necessarily the players who are thrown out trying for an extra base but the ones who are too timid to take chances. Of course, the risk you take on the bases should be commensurate with the score. The opposite of fielders, base runners should be more aggressive when their team has a lead. If you're ahead, you can afford to take more risks; if you're tied, you will take fewer risks than when you lead and more risks than when you trail, except perhaps when you trail by only one run. A lot depends on whether you're in early, middle, or late innings and whether or not the pitcher you're facing gives opponents a lot of base runners or runs.

Unless you're playing a passive game and can't afford to be thrown out taking an extra base, your mentality is to think second base with no-body out or two outs and third base with one out. This isn't to say that you can't try for second with one out or third with nobody out or two outs, or even home with no outs, but temper your aggressiveness with intelligent forethought. Take smart chances.

When I came to New York to broadcast Mets games in 1983, I began to talk on the air about how it is fundamental not to make the first or third out at third base. I explained: With one out, it's worth the risk of being thrown out trying to get to third base because you can then score a cheap run on a sacrifice fly, squeeze bunt, grounder, or ball that gets past the catcher. But with no outs, you should stop at second if there is any doubt you can reach third because you can then score on a single or be moved to third with a sacrifice bunt, long fly, or ground-out to the right side. On second base with no outs, you use the hitter to get you to third and not your legs. With two outs, getting to third isn't much better than staying at second because, unless the ball gets by the catcher or there is an error or infield hit, you still pretty much have to score on a base hit to the outfield.

Pitchers don't get to run the bases much, so some managers tell them to go one base at a time rather than risk injury going for an extra base. It depends on the score and on the athlete. You can tell a pitcher isn't an expert base runner when he gets to first and puts on one of those heavy pitching jackets in the middle of a heat wave. He wouldn't wear one of those cumbersome things while pitching, would he?

One way the opposition curtails a runner's aggressiveness is to distract him with conversation. Suddenly, you're the fielder's best friend. Believe me, it's artifice, not sincerity. Almost all smiles are false during a game, especially those worn by infielders talking to base runners. A runner should pick up his coach and not engage in wasted chatter. The fielder doesn't really care about your hitting, your wife, your kids, your grandmother, your dog, your hometown or homeland, your new car, or how you were able to reach base.

The runner must pay attention to the game. Whether he's on first, second, or third, his primary responsibility is to check the positioning of the outfielders. Determining this is as important as knowing the number of outs. If the runner knows where they are playing, then after picking up the ball off the bat and gauging its speed and loft, he'll be able to determine whether it's going to fall in or not. This is more significant to the runner on first or second because base running is easier for the man on third with less than two outs—unless the infield is playing halfway or in and he has to try to score on contact.

Anticipation is central to good base running. In fact, my Cardinals teammate Dick Groat, who was slow afoot, proved you could be a great base runner if you can accurately guess whether a ball will fall in or be caught. Groat always took the extra base if he judged the ball would fall in instead of waiting to make sure that the outfielder couldn't make the play. Willie Mays, the best all-around player of my day, was the best base runner *ever*. You couldn't get any better. Willie had remarkable instincts. When he was on first, he'd see a pop fly and know instantly if it would fall in, so he'd end up on third while a wait-and-see runner would have stopped at second. I have always believed that the greatest players know when to take that extra base, without halting for even a second to make sure the ball will drop in.

Proper sliding is essential to good base running. On a tag play at second, the best way to go into a base is with the straight-in pop-up slide, as was the case a hundred years ago. When the foot hits the bag, that brings the body up. Depending on the runner, the slide itself can be on either leg. A straight-in pop-up slide has good extension, and the tucked-under back foot doesn't drag. On a throw from the catcher, a good way to elude a tag is to do a straight slide to the right of the bag and to touch it with your left hand. On throws from outfielders, you should slide to the left of the bag and tag it with your right hand.

On the outdated hook slide, the runner slides past the base with the front foot and tries to hook it with the trailing foot. I think this slide is rarely the smartest option for a runner because it takes more time to use the back foot. My least favorite sliding method, however, is the injury-risking hands-first slide. Rickey Henderson has gone into second on steals and stretches singles into doubles using both the feet-first and hands-first methods over his career. I'd say he used the hands-first style 35 percent of the time. But you must understand that when you teach sliding to young players you want to teach them the norm, not the aberration. Henderson is an aberration. He can do what he does better than anybody who might copy him. But young players look at his extraordinary numbers as a base stealer and run scorer and try to be like Rickey. Even major leaguers are starstruck.

Base running is so important, yet in 1997 I watched the worst base running I'd seen in my thirty-seven years in baseball, even by the elite teams in the postseason. Some of today's players have the tendency to think they start from home plate and end up at home plate and anything in between is superfluous. If they're on first, second, or third, they think it's up to the next guy to bring them around instead of running the bases. They think they should be aggressive when they're hitting, not running. Maybe it's because base running, other than stolen bases and being caught stolen, doesn't show up in the box score. They reason: If it's not a stat, why work on it? Thinking about what they should do on the basepaths from the moment they leave the batting box would solve a lot of problems. If they were prepared in each situation, they could just allow their instincts to take over.

THE BATTER

I have a problem with batters who don't run hard out of the box four times a game. The importance of running out of the box was preached to me when I was coming through the Cardinals' system. By doing so, you can stretch a single into a double or a double into a triple, and that can make a huge difference. By not doing so, you can wind up at second on what should have been a sure triple or at first when you could have coasted into second. One stat really reveals the sluggishness of many batters: Triples, which result from the batter's first two steps out of the box, have gone down in number decade by decade for the last fifty years.

One problem is that power hitters like to admire their long drives, as if they were artists admiring their handiwork. The difference is that artists don't have to throw down their brushes and run to first. How many times does a batter break into his home run trot only to have the ball hit the top of the wall and stay in play? He ends up at first or second instead of third, or he may be gunned down trying for second. You can't Cadillac it down to first, you must motor down the line.

As bad as the guy who doesn't run because he overestimates the distance of his drive is the batter who doesn't run hard to first because he assumes his fly or pop-up will be caught. If the wind takes hold of that ball or the fielder loses it in the sun or closes his glove too soon, there is no excuse, if the ball has average loft, for the batter who winds up at first instead of second. Too many batters take it for granted the ball will be caught. Like the first rule of good journalism, never assume.

It has gotten to the point where we announcers single out batters for praise if they "hustle" down the line on a ground ball. Why would we take what a batter is supposed to do as part of his job and compliment him for it? Trying to beat out a base hit can even be construed as self-serving because it raises the batting average. Believe me, batters smell base hits. It's much more virtuous to run hard to first to prevent a double play because once the batter has forced out the runner at second, his average is going down regardless of whether he is safe at first. If he runs hard to beat the throw to first for the team, then he has "hustled."

Also, when a batter runs down the baseline on an easy grounder, he should make sure to touch first base. You may be thinking that all major leaguers touch the bag automatically, but just in 1997 on FOX games two batters, the Reds' Bret Boone and the Yankees' Jorge Posada, put their lead foot down beyond the bag. They were almost acts of defiance, like them saying, "Why should I put my foot on the base if I'm going to be out anyway?" They were angry at themselves, but they have to touch first so that the first baseman can't just tag them out if the throw pulls him off the base. On FOX we had replays of Boone and Posada going over the base just to show fans that this happens even in the majors. Then, because we had miked Joe Torre, we were able to hear him tell Posada to never miss first again.

I'm sure you've seen batters dive headfirst into first base trying to beat out grounders—it's an exciting visual when captured by the low and high right-field cameras. In this case, there's an admirable competitive instinct at work, but while it's understandable, it's also wrong. You don't get there any quicker, and you may end up on the disabled list. It's like Yehudi Menuhin diving into the orchestra pit if he's late. Like great violinists, ballplayers make their living with their hands. You've got to break this habit by telling yourself that your business partners, your hands and your fingers, are too important to risk such a reckless act.

On a hit to the outfield, the batter shouldn't assume the outfielder will make a quick or clean play. He runs hard down the line and rounds the base in full stride so that he won't have to switch gears for an attempt at second base if there's a misplay or a throw to third or home to get a runner. Eddie Stanky said it best: *You run through the base, not to the base, to give yourself a chance to take an extra base.* The batter should always take a wider turn on balls hit to the left of second base, when the left fielder must go to his left or right. No left fielder is going to throw behind the batter at first.

He'll throw to second. If the ball is hit to right, the runner can't always chance that wide turn. He's less inclined to look for that extra-base hit on balls to the right side because he has to respect the arms of most right fielders, who will throw behind the batter on a wide turn at first.

If the batter singles with a man on second, he may round first to force a cutoff of the throw home so that the run can score. But not always. It depends on the speed of the runner at second, how hard the ball was hit, the strength of the outfielder's arm, and the score of the game. If you're trailing 9–2, the runner isn't going to be sent around third if there's even a slight chance he'll be thrown out. If it's a tight game in the seventh inning and an average-speed runner is rounding third, and strong-armed Sammy Sosa is throwing home, you absolutely want to make the cutoff man cut off the ball and go after you. Because Sosa might very well throw out the runner at the plate. You are taught that if you don't trail by more than one run, you trade an out for a run.

You can't be foolishly aggressive, especially if your team is behind. It's a terrible play when a team is trailing by several runs and the batter makes the first out by trying to stretch a single into a double or a double into a triple. When your team trails by two or more runs in the middle or toward the end of the game, you are forced to play it one base at a time.

With two outs in a tie or one-run game, it's a good time to stretch a single into a double. Unless it's the sixth inning or later, the only batter whose aggressiveness should be held in check is the eighth-place hitter on a National League team. If he is thrown out trying to stretch a single into a double, that means the pitcher will lead off the next inning rather than the leadoff man. He should risk it only if there is a pinch hitter in the wings for the pitcher.

With one out, the eighth-place hitter also should refrain from trying for second base if there is a chance of being thrown out. It's not worth the risk because the pitcher will be asked to bunt him to second anyway. It might, however, be worth the risk with no outs. Then a sacrifice bunt by the pitcher would put him on third with one out, an ideal scoring situation.

THE RUNNER ON FIRST

Even if the manager doesn't send the runner on first on a straight steal, bunt, or hit-and-run, the runner has responsibilities. If there is a short wild pitch or passed ball, he should consider going to second. You will see how few runners, including good base stealers, are willing to do this. When Eddie Stanky became a manager, he tried to remedy this on his team in spring training by dressing his top base runners in catching gear, putting them behind the plate, and then short-hopping balls to them. After they experienced firsthand how difficult it is for a catcher to retrieve a ball that got away and throw out a base runner, they became more aggressive when pitches bounced in the dirt.

On a line drive to the left side, the runner can't be doubled off first. There's no need to get a quicker break off first because if the ball is hit over the third baseman's or shortstop's head, the average-speed runner will make it only to second anyway in most instances. It's more understandable for a guy to get doubled off first on a line drive to the right side of the infield because had the ball gone through, he would have had a good shot at reaching third.

On a ground ball, the runner must run at full steam toward second base. On a force play, the best way to go in is as fast as he can, straight ahead. If the runner realizes he's got little chance of being safe at second but there are less than two outs, he'll still complete his slide in order to break up the possible double play. Without running out of the baseline, he'll want to slide hard and knock the legs out from under the pivotman so he'll have difficulty making a strong throw to first. As mentioned, sometimes to reach the pivotman, he has to go through the base. If a runner decides to block the pivotman's throw by going into second standing up, as the Yankees' Chad Curtis did against the Indians in 1997's divisional playoffs, he takes the chance the fielder won't drop down and throw sidearmed directly at his face. He must be willing to pay the price. I thought Curtis's tactics around second were unorthodox and dangerous, but I can't deny he shook up the Yankees' offense in a positive way by breaking up a double play. But I wouldn't recommend that he go into second standing up on a regular basis unless he wants to end up looking like Anne Boleyn after she upset Henry VIII.

The rule is that the slider must be able to touch the base. A lot of times you see that there's no way he can reach it. On those plays, the runner anticipates where the shortstop is going to be when he comes off the bag, and often that's two or three feet to the outfield side of the base. Technically, a runner should be called out for being out of the baseline, but umpires rarely make that call unless it's really an extreme case. In turn, pivotmen are given out calls on "neighborhood" plays, when they never actually touch the base or touch it before they catch the ball.

Eddie Stanky used to say that if a slow grounder is hit to the second baseman's left, the runner from first should go into second standing up on the outside part of the line because by sliding he clears a path for the second baseman to throw to the shortstop for the force at second. It's perfectly legal, and the worst that can happen is that he'll get hit in the back and be safe. The second baseman may even go to first to avoid attempting that throw. It's an interesting play to think about.

Depending on where a fly is hit in the outfield, the runner advances a half to two thirds of the way toward second and waits to see if the catch is made. If there is a catch, he will have time to scamper back to first without being doubled up. If the ball drops in front of an outfielder, he'll have time to reach second before the throw comes in from the outfield. If there is a lead runner on second, the man on first may be able to run to third if there is a play at the plate. On long flies, he may tag up and run to second if there is a throw to get the lead runner at third or home. On some long flies, a lone runner on first may quickly tag up instead of taking the usual route if he thinks he can beat the throw to second.

I would compare a runner on first, who bases his decision on whether to race toward third on where the outfielder is playing and the speed, loft, and distance of the ball that is hit to him, to a driver whose decision to cross into an intersection is based on the distance and speed of approaching cars. With nobody out, he can't chance being doubled off and killing an opportunity to score. He should be more cautious than if there were one out on a fly that might drop in. With one out, if the runner sees the ball off the bat and he sees that it's going to be a sinking liner in front of an outfielder who is playing deep, then he should take off for third. If he delays, he'll have to stop at second. It is worth the risk of being doubled up if the outfielder makes a great catch, especially in a tie game. But if you're down by two runs, you can't take that chance, and you settle for second base.

Say a runner is on first when the batter singles to left. If the left fielder has to move to his left to get the ball, the runner should be able to go to third (especially on a hit-and-run) because the fielder's momentum into left-center field makes a throw to third difficult. The play's in front of the runner, so if he winds up at second he probably was too cautious. There is, however, a possible excuse for caution: If the runner thinks a grounder may be snagged by the shortstop, he stops thinking of going to third and instead tries to take out the second baseman at second to prevent the double play. In this situation, you try to take out the second baseman by running straight along the basepaths and you have no intention of making a turn toward third. If the grounder gets by the shortstop, your turn around second base would be very wide and increase your chances of being thrown out at third.

Let's say there are runners on first and second. If the outfielder is play-ing deep and there is a grounder through the infield, both runners should be aggressive and make the outfielder throw them out going for the extra base, especially if there is one out. If there is a slow lead runner on second who tries to score on a ball hit to right, the runner on first will go to third in hopes of forcing a cutoff of the outfielder's throw by an infielder. He wants the defense to make a play on him so the slow runner can score without there being a play at home. A run scores on the decoy. If the man on first is also slow and the team is behind by two runs in the ninth inning, the manager should replace *him,* rather than the man on second, with a fast pinch runner. The trail runner is the one who counts, so you've got to get him around the bases to tie the game.

Poor base runners take one step, see the outfielder, and stop at second base. Utilizing speed means going from first to third on a single and, often, first to home on a double, although coaches will usually stop the runner at third with no outs. Lou Brock, who led off for the Cardinals, used to say that going from first to third is more important than a stolen base. Dick Groat, who batted second, agreed: "When there is the opportunity to go from first to third, make them throw you out." It's a huge play.

When you run from first to third, your reliance on the third-base coach depends on where the ball is. On anything from right-center around to the left-field corner, you have to be your own judge. You know what kind of jump you had off first and whether your legs are fresh. Too many young players are obsessed with picking up the third-base coach when the ball's in right-center. All you have to do is give one look and the play's in front of you, so there's no need to look again. Only if the ball is in the right-field corner does the runner have to pick up the coach because he may have determined where the ball was heading but he can't see what is happening out there. The ball may rattle around in the corner and elude the right fielder, or there may be a late bobble that the runner misses. The runner relies on the third-base coach because he has a view of the corner.

The third-base coach will signal the runner if he can come into the base standing up or if he must hit the dirt. Runners who slide hands-first into third base don't get there any quicker. Pete Rose did it because he was competitively, wonderfully arrogant. All of us who saw Pete play can still see him flying through the air and sliding on his stomach into third, cov-ering the front of his uniform with an inch of dirt. He did it from a psy-chological standpoint. But along the way he convinced so many young players to try to do it like he did it, and other than Rickey Henderson they haven't been able to do it like he did it without risking injury. Pete never hurt himself going headfirst into a bag. But there are so many things that can go wrong. It's okay to bruise the palm of your hand, but if you just slightly bruise a finger you can't hit or throw.

THE RUNNER ON SECOND

The runner on second is already in scoring position. Whether the manager wants to move him to third where he can score in many more ways or be content with him at second depends on the type of batter at the plate, the pitcher, and the speed of the runner, as well as the number of outs, the count, the score, and the inning. But under most circumstances with no one out, the lone runner on second can be moved to third with a bunt by a nonpower hitter or a grounder or long fly to the right side. Most times, with one out, but not when you want hitters to bat without distraction on a 2-0 or 3-1 count, stealers should think about swiping third. But even they may be content to stay on second with a good RBI man at the plate. Generally, all types of runners on second should stay put with two outs because the benefits of being on third aren't worth the risks of getting there. Anyway, a fast runner can score from second on most hits.

In a one-run game, you can't get picked off second with no outs. You don't lean toward third. You must take a passive approach because a bunt or productive out can move you to third with only one out. If there is a right-handed batter who often goes the other way, you have to heed the third-base coach's warnings of the shortstop edging toward second because he can catch you napping and pull off a pickoff play with the pitcher. With one out, you can be more aggressive and take a bigger lead, and lean more. You might want to steal or at least be ready to move up on a short passed ball or wild pitch. With two outs, you take your biggest lead because you want to score on a single. You can do this safely because the infielders are less concerned with you and are playing deeper to prevent grounders from going through. If the runner doesn't have the legs to score on a single with two outs, he should cheat more toward third, especially on artificial turf, where balls get to outfielders quicker. With two strikes on the batter and two outs, he should take off if he sees the pitch in the hitting area.

If you see the runner on second making strange gestures, that likely means he's stealing signs from the catcher and then signaling the batter about upcoming pitches. He's the one base runner who can do it. If Bob Gibson thought a runner at second was stealing signs from me, he would step off the mound and say to him, "You're going to get somebody hurt." He would mean it. That would stop that stuff.

I think sign stealing is overrated because it's too difficult for most runners to determine the types of upcoming pitches unless they've stood out there for a while. Many batters don't know whether they can trust the runners. What most runners will try to do is determine pitch location from where the catcher sets up. To give location to the batter is easy. For instance, he can just hold his left hand out to the side, and that means a pitch away to a right-handed batter. Maybe he'll clap or move one leg or take his hands on or off his legs. Anything that the batter can pick up quickly. Of course, the man on second mustn't get so preoccupied with the batter that he forgets his main responsibility is as a base runner. (If he is thinking of stealing third, stealing signs or locations can be beneficial to him as well as to the batter.)

On a routine grounder to the left side, the lone runner on second doesn't run to third if the ball is hit at him or to his right because an easy tag play can be made on him at third. But with nobody out, he should run to the vacated third base if the third baseman has to move in to field a tapped ball. The throw will have to go to first, so he'll be on third with one out. If the infield is in, meaning there is also a runner on third, the runner on second will go to third on any ground ball when the lead runner tries to go home because no one will be covering third. If an infielder snares the grounder, he will throw to either home or first. A third-base coach usually has a sign for the runner at second if the runner on third is going home on a grounder. A hitch of the belt will suffice.

Runners on second are told not to run to third on balls hit to the left side. Harry "The Hat" Walker, however, had a play for when the lone runner is on second and the ball is grounded to short. On a ball grounded to the shortstop's right, Harry said the runner should edge off second while the shortstop makes the play. The runner knows that if the shortstop goes into the hole or has another difficult play, he'll be thinking about planting his foot and the long throw to first, not about the runner. Having moved away from second, the runner can scoot the shorter distance to third *after* the shortstop releases the ball toward first, especially if he has good speed. The distinction is that the runner doesn't go until after the throw is made. It's not routine, but it's good, aggressive base running that can get you a runner to third with one out.

On a grounder to the right side, the runner on second runs immediately to third. But if the ball is lined, he can't proceed until he can pick up that neither the first baseman nor the second baseman will catch the ball in the air.

On a long fly ball to an outfielder, the runner stands a third of the way between second and third and watches the play. He wants to be close enough to the base to be able to go back and tag up and still run to third if the ball is caught, and he wants to be far enough from the base to be able to attempt to score if the ball drops in.

As is the case with all base runners, the man on second must know the position of the outfielders *before* the ball is hit. You'll see that many bad base runners on second will look around just as a ball bloops into center. They think the blooper may be caught, and by the time they see that the center fielder is playing too deep to field the ball, it's too late to score. If now, with one out, there's a double play, the inning will be over with no run scoring. This doesn't show up in the box score but it's yet another time when poor base running can cost the team a run.

On a base hit, the runner on second must look at the third-base coach because he can't turn around to watch the play and run at the same time. The only guy I ever saw who could both run and watch the play was Willie Mays. He was uncanny. He would run just fast enough home to draw the throw in order to give the batter a chance to reach second. He'd slow down. Cardinals manager Johnny Keane would tell our outfielders that unless Mays was the tying or winning run in the late innings they shouldn't throw home if he was on second regardless of how hard the ball was hit or how shallow they were playing. We knew he'd be safe, and we didn't want them to get another base runner on second.

When the runner comes around third on a base hit and there is a play at the plate, it makes for great television. On Mets games, Jeff Mitchell will have the low-first camera on the runner coming home, trying to capture the emotion. Then he will cut to the high-home camera so he can see the convergence of the two lines: the runner from third coming in and the ball coming in. He sets it up as a race between the runner and the ball.

The best way to go into a catcher is to go in with your pop-up slide, although you won't pop up because you'll run into his shin guard rather than the strapped-down bag. You try to force the catcher's left shin off the plate. The best guy at doing this was Tommie Agee, who weighed over two hundred pounds, had thick thighs, and could run. On two occasions, he hit me with such force that he went through my shin guard. He actually stuck in my shin guard—I had to unstrap and remove it from his spike.

(That's why it's understandable when most catchers' cruciate ligaments are damaged, even severed, at a very early age.) Those were perfectly clean plays, and all I could do was tip my cap to Agee and go back to my job, saying, "Damn, that hurt." Four years ago, Tommie told me that Johnny Roseboro, the onetime Dodgers catcher, taught him that the best way to get into home is straight in with that right spike going right into the shin guard, full force ahead and straight-legged for leverage and power. If you bend your leg, you curl up like a tissue that's on fire.

Don't even talk to me about a runner trying a hook slide into a catcher. Catchers eat those guys alive. And when guys come in hand-first, catchers chew them up. All catchers are big, they have their weight on their left foot, they've got protection—you think a runner coming in hand-first intimidates them? They are cake.

Shoulder-first into the catcher is accepted by catchers as a clean play, unlike when the runner leaves his feet. That's one of the more grueling aspects of that position—especially when it's a big guy who is bearing down on you. Of course, the runner hopes the catcher will drop the ball in the collision.

Pete Rose's infamous game-winning "slide" into Ray Fosse on Jim Hickman's hit in the 1970 All-Star Game was a legitimate play. Anybody who thinks otherwise just doesn't know the catching position. You've just got to take your knocks. That blow to Fosse's left shoulder cost him a lot of years in the big leagues, but it is part of the deal.

The ugliest home-plate collision on a clean play I ever saw was on Opening Day in 1976, when Dave Parker crushed the much smaller Phillies catcher Johnny Oates. Johnny received a weak throw from Greg Luzinski and had to stay down to field it like a grounder. He looked up just as Parker arrived at the plate. A catcher is trained to meet the resistance flexibly so he can give with the punch, but Parker drove Oates into the ground and separated his left shoulder. It was like having a piano dropped from the second story onto him. Johnny went on the disabled list, and that's when I became Steve Carlton's exclusive catcher. A bad break for Johnny, but more playing time for me. The unfortunate laws of the catching jungle.

THE RUNNER ON THIRD

Managers emphasize getting runners to third base with one out because the chances of scoring go up dramatically. The runner doesn't have to wait for a base hit to score him but can come in on a sacrifice fly, squeeze bunt, ground-out, infield error, wild pitch, or passed ball. He can even occasionally coax the pitcher into a balk with a fake break toward home. There is no need to be quiet at third. Give the pitcher something to think about.

Arguably, the lead off third is the most important one (especially when the runner is trying to score on contact). After all, the next base is home plate. Because the runner moves uncomfortably close to the batter as he comes down the line, his lead is in foul territory, so he won't be automatically out—or be knocked out—if he is unable to dodge a hot smash off the bat. (The only exception is on a double-steal play with a runner on first, when the man on third stands in the baseline so the catcher can't see how far away he is from the base.) Where a runner on third begins his lead is relatively unimportant because, unlike the other runners, he will always take a walking lead. If there are less than two outs and he is going on contact, he is trained to put his right foot down when the pitch goes into the hitting area. The reason for this is twofold: The runner can use the right foot for momentum to go toward home if there is a grounder or wild pitch, or use it as a brake if there is a fly ball so he can go back to third and tag up. Seventy percent of major-league runners at third don't approach the contact play properly, which is why it is among the most botched plays in baseball. When you're at the ballpark and the infield is in and anticipating the runner going on contact, check to see how few base runners take the walking lead.

On a fly, the runner on third puts one foot (usually his left foot) on the edge of third base and lines up with home plate. He's like a sprinter waiting for the starter's gun to fire, only he's waiting for the fly to land in the outfielder's glove before taking off. Sometimes the third-base coach will say, "Don't go, don't go, don't go!" and you don't go because he's got at least three reasons to keep you there. But the vast majority of times the runner is on his own and doesn't wait for instructions. He knows his own speed and should know the fielder's throwing ability. He can see for himself if the outfielder is coming in or backing up to catch the ball. If he intends to run, he waits for the catch and then pushes off with his foot. He may just try to draw a throw, hoping for an error.

The smart runner also will tag up on foul balls because often the outfielder is impeded while making the catch and can't get off a good throw. Similarly, infielders may catch balls with their backs toward the plate or become entangled in fences or with photographers, fans, or TV cameras and be unable to make a strong throw to the plate.

If the third baseman moves in to guard against a bunt, the runner on third should follow him down the line, staying even with him, keeping his balance, and never going back. If he is running on contact, he'll run on ground balls hit to the right or left side of the infield. In a tie game or with any lead, if there are men on second and third with one out, it makes sense to run on contact and risk an out at home to score a run. The worst that can happen is that with two outs there will be men on first and third instead of second and third. If the ball is hit to the third baseman, the runner on third runs inside the line to obstruct the catcher's view of the ball thrown home. If he realizes he will be out by several strides, he should stop and initiate a rundown, which he will try to stay in long enough for other base runners to advance or for the batter to reach second.

On a grounder to the right side, the runner on third will anticipate a throw from the second baseman or first baseman, so he'll slide to the outside of home plate and make the catcher come all the way around to make a tag. If the catcher blocks his path home, he may have to kick the catcher's shin guard to dislodge him from the plate. If the catcher puts his weight on his right foot, the runner can hit his left leg and spin him like a

Conventional wisdom is often wrong, and that is the case in one instance involving a lone runner on second or third. Here's the setup: The only runner is on second or third in the ninth inning—it can't be any other inning—with no outs or one out, and his team must be trailing by *more* than one run. Everybody has always said that he has to let the ball go through before advancing, but I think he should break if the ball is hit to the third baseman (who is playing in), the shortstop, or, best of all, the pitcher. A pitcher will instinctively look at the base runner, who hopes he will take the bait and try to throw him out instead of taking the sure out at first. He might be dead and the announcer will probably be telling fans that he made a bonehead play, but with his team trailing by more than one run his being thrown out is no worse than the runner at first being thrown out. His objective isn't to give the batter enough time to reach second base. He wouldn't bother leaving the base for that. He intentionally gets himself into a rundown because he wants the pitcher, usually the poorest fielder in the infield, to get involved in a play that's much more likely to be screwed up than the simple throw from the pitcher to first base. That throw is only thirty feet. The runner wants the pitcher or infielder to make the top. You'll see some guys slide around the catcher and swipe the plate with the left hand. The runner doesn't want to make a hook slide or come in hands-first—he wants to make a straight, forceful feet-first slide.

Although runners who come home from third don't have the same momentum as those who are tearing in from second base, collisions can be pretty frightening. In fact, in 1963 with the Cards, I was the runner on third against the Dodgers in the worst collision Leo Durocher said he'd seen in his fifty years in baseball. Vern Benson, our third-base coach, said to make sure the ball went through before running home. There was a grounder to Tommy Davis at third base. I made a mistake and went anyway and saw that I would be out by ten feet. The Dodgers' catcher was Johnny Roseboro, who was like a mobile brick wall. He'd catch the ball and come down the line to meet you. You may have seen the *Mister Ed* episode where Johnny climbs up a screen rather than block the plate with the horse galloping down the line. Don't believe it. He absolutely loved contact. Even before I made my mad dash for home, I remembered that

wrong choice by making him forget that he is of no importance even if he scores. Getting the batter out at first is important. The good defensive manager will say, "I don't care if you can reach out and touch the runner, throw to first base," but the runner must try to entice the pitcher to do otherwise.

I guarantee that a pitcher who is worried about his ERA will more often than not take the bait. He's going to try to keep you from scoring. You think that's wonderful because you're going to get the pitcher and catcher in a rundown and there will be a lot of throws. The proper throw is to first: one throw, one out. All the defensive players want is that one out, so if you make them resort to throws that are unconventional and risky, you've done your job.

The only exception to this play involves the lone runner on second. If the ball is hit to short, the runner is going to try to go to third to entice a throw over there, which, if it's not thrown away, will initiate a rundown. However, if the ball is hit to the right of the shortstop and he doesn't have a play at first, the man on second shouldn't break and give the shortstop a chance to make an out of any kind. In this case, the runner leaving second for third would be the easier out. Why help the defense?

Daryl Spencer, who was a huge guy, had once intentionally jumped into Roseboro's left thigh trying to take him out, and Johnny took Spencer's left foot and flipped him like a rag doll toward the on-deck circle—and then picked up the ball and tagged him out. He had splintered Spencer's ankle and knocked him out for the rest of the year. So now when I saw Johnny coming toward me, I said this is self-preservation and lowered my head and hit him on the left side of his neck. He had planted his left leg, and it twisted around. Even his glasses under his mask turned. Although John stayed in the game, he would miss about two weeks with a wrenched knee.

Later in the game, Roseboro was back behind the plate, and I go up to bat. My neck is killing me, and I looked like the Phantom of the Opera. I had left the left side of my face on Roseboro and his equipment; the skin from below the eye to my lip was gone. You hear of strawberries on the rear end, but I had one on my face. And Rosey says through his mask, "Are you all right?" "Yeah, I'm fine, are you?" "Oh, fine." There was a beat, and he said, "That's the way you've got to do it, you know." My respect for this man went up a hundredfold.

THE FIELD COACHES

Naturally, you can't talk about the running game without mentioning the two field coaches.

The first-base coach's function? Maybe he'll try to make the umpire aware that the pitcher is balking on his pickoff move. Also, if he was a good base stealer himself in his playing days, he might say something to the runner about the pitcher's move. Otherwise, he's there to remind the runner of his responsibilities. Nowadays, you'll see that while base hits are still in play batters will make a quick turn so they can come back to the base and shake hands with the first-base coach. This drives me crazy. When Pete Rose went around first, he'd take that wide turn and watch what was transpiring, not do any glad-handing. There would be very little bantering with the first-base coach. But today there's a little ritual involving a handshake and the transfer of gloves, helmets, and shin guards. It's as if the runner thinks the first-base coach is a bellhop.

First-base coaches, usually popular ex-players, are often super presences in the clubhouse, but it's the third-base coaches who really earn their money during the game. The third-base coach is the manager on the field: the relayer of signs, the stealer of signs, the stop-and-go guy who relies on experience and instincts. He is important to any team but especially to teams that work to get a lot of base runners, hit-and-run, sacrifice bunt, and score runs in many different fashions. The importance of a third-base coach goes up dramatically if a team lacks power.

The third-base coaches of today are well schooled in *situational baseball*. They understand that things change according to the score and inning and with every out and pitch count. They pay attention to where the fielders position themselves (particularly the center fielder) and know the speed and arm strengths of outfielders and how well they come in or go back. They also are aware of the tendencies of opposing pitchers and managers. So they know when to send runners. All of these things are very, very important.

A third-base coach has different responsibilities when balls are hit into the opposite corners of the outfield and there is a runner on first. If the ball goes into the right-field corner, a good third-base coach will come way down the line toward the plate. He always will bring the runner around third because no relay man on the right side will ever chance a throw across the diamond in hopes of getting behind the runner. If there is a throw, it will go home. The coach can bring the runner more than a third of the way down the line from third before he must determine whether to let him come all the way or send him back to the base. He waves him around the bag and down the line, but if he sees the right fielder has made the play quickly and has hit the cutoff man, he stops the runner. Some third-base coaches will come almost to home plate and run up the line toward the runner signaling and yelling, "Hold it!" and "Get back, get back!" That's the proper way to do it.

On the ball hit down the left-field line with a runner on first, the third-base coach will usually remain in his box. He can't bring the runner around the bag because the shortstop or third baseman is right there and if the runner takes too big a turn, there will be a relay throw behind him and he'll be out. The one time the coach brings around the runner is when there is a bobble by the left fielder.

The good coach gives runners tremendous latitude on the bases. But he'll put the brakes on runners who want to take too big a gamble trying for home with no outs. He'll also give runners signals when they can't see the play developing behind them: the runner on first on balls hit to the right-field corner and batters trying for triples on balls hit to that corner or over the right fielder's head. You'll see coaches motion with palms down for the oncoming runner to slide or with palms out for him to come in standing up. If men are on first and second and a ball is rifled into the gap, the third-base coach will immediately start concentrating on the trail runner because the guy on second is going to score easily.

One of the most interesting split-screen shots is the third-base coach giving signs with a runner on first. The left side of the screen has the third-base coach giving signs. The top right has the runner on first watching him. The bottom right has the guy at home watching him. What I like is when the coach turns his back to the hitter and runner, denoting he is through giving signs, and in unison the runner and batter go back to their responsibilities. It's an interesting shot.

Third-base coaches are integral to teams' offenses, yet they are rarely noticed. That's why I like to call attention to them on the air, which sometimes means replaying significant base-running plays to show their roles in each.

Back in 1986, we Mets broadcasters put the spotlight on a coach in an unusual way. The coach was Ozzie Virgil, the onetime utility player—the first Dominican to play in the majors—who had become the third-base coach for Dick Williams. Williams was fired as the San Diego Padres' manager in spring training of 1986 but he was hired a month later to manage Seattle, and took Virgil with him. Because they had switched leagues, that meant they wouldn't be visiting Shea Stadium that year. Yet when the Padres came into Shea in early June, there was a note on the bulletin board in San Diego's clubhouse that read: "Ozzie Virgil, call your sister!" She lived in the Bronx, where Ozzie was from, and had probably called so that they could see each other, but for some reason she had no idea that Ozzie had left the Padres two and a half months before. So I got on the air that day and asked, "How close is this family?"

Everybody was laughing about this, particularly the Padres. The fans also thought it was funny, and we got a ton of humorous mail. About a week later, we were on the road when Bill Webb, who then directed Mets telecasts, came up with the idea to call Ozzie Virgil in Texas, where Seattle was playing. So I interviewed Ozzie on the air, and Ozzie asked, "Oh, my sister wanted me to call her?" I asked, "How often are you in contact with your sister?" It was hilarious. We came off a ten-day road trip, and when we got to Shea we saw a banner and ten or fifteen T-shirts in the stands that read, OZZIE VIRGIL, CALL YOUR SISTER! For another two weeks, the fans in the parking lot were yelling, "Ozzie Virgil, call your sister." So that's how a third-base coach became a *cause célèbre*. It wouldn't have been so much fun if Ozzie Virgil had been a superstar player getting notoriety or didn't take it with good humor. Baseball, as we try not to forget in our booth, is more than just the guys who put up the big numbers. In some cases, it's the guys who don't put up any numbers at all.

26

STEALING BASES

I often talk on the air about the *psychology of the stolen base,* about how when great base stealers threaten to steal that does as much damage as when they do steal. For one thing, speed on first may cause a pitcher to anticipate a stolen-base attempt early in the count and, perhaps against his better judgment, throw fastballs to give the catcher a better chance of throwing out the runner. The runner may not go, but the batter can take advantage of a fast pitch down the middle of the plate. If a pitcher becomes so preoccupied with a potential base stealer, he'll lose his rhythm and concentration by throwing over to first repeatedly—that's how speed slows down the game. His pitching will suffer, and there may be a rally in the offing that doesn't even include a stolen base. So the runner's delaying a stolen-base attempt or bluffing a stolen base can be a very strong weapon. Of course, for a runner to be able to disrupt a pitcher's routine, he must first prove that he is adept at stealing bases.

Great base stealers are given the green light at all times because there is little risk they will be thrown out. While unpredictable, they usually run early in the count. A manager is likely to put on the steal sign at this time because he doesn't want the batter distracted throughout the count. That's because the batter, who will have the option to swing, can choose to take a pitch or two without falling deep in the hole. Counts of 1-0 and 2-1 are particularly good early counts on which to run because a pitcher won't pitch out—which would give the catcher his best opportunity to throw out a speedy runner—because he doesn't want the batter to then have a 2-0 or 3-1 count.

If the count does go to 2-0 or, better, 3-1, the runner should usually stay put. You will see traditionalist managers giving the runner a steal sign with the count 2-0, but this is a hitter's count, not a runner's count. The batter will have a free swing, probably on a fastball strike, so why distract him? At 3-1, it makes no sense to risk stealing second base or, if there are men on first and second, third base—the batter is one ball away from being walked. Getting thrown out on a 3-1 (or 3-0) count is as careless as being picked off at a crucial point in the game. Make the pitcher prove he can throw strikes before attempting a steal.

The pitcher can afford to pitch out on 0-0, 0-1, 0-2, and 1-2 because another ball won't get him into trouble with the batter. However, 1-2, providing there is no pitchout, along with the other two-strike counts, 2-2 and 3-2, are excellent times to run. One reason is that the catcher's first responsibility is to stay back and make sure the strike is called, so he won't be as aggressive in charging out from his crouch to make a good throw. Another reason is that pitchers throw their most effective pitches to get the final strike, and those are the hardest to catch. You are right in thinking 1-2 and 0-2 are good times for a pitchout, but with two outs the pitcher will probably be trying to get the batter to swing at a ball just off the plate to get out of the inning. A breaking ball in the dirt is ideal for a steal attempt. If the batter takes on a ball and the runner is thrown out, at least the batter will have a clean slate when he bats the next inning.

It is easy to run off a tall pitcher with a high kick. These guys always have bad moves to first because they have so much to do. This is also true of pitchers like Hideo Nomo, who have unusual, head-and-body-twisting deliveries. Even if some of those pitchers have high-velocity fastballs, it's during their slow deliveries that runners take off, knowing the ball will take longer to reach home than a slower fastball thrown by a pitcher with a low kick. The type of pitcher a base stealer prefers is a sinkerballer or a pitcher who throws a splitter or forkball. The catcher, especially if he's tall, will have trouble getting a ball out of the dirt and making the transfer from his glove to his hand for the throw, giving the stealer a big advantage. A catcher will catch maybe one out of three balls in the dirt; most of the time the ball hits his body and rolls out a couple of feet. If the runner takes off when the ball hits the dirt, he almost always makes the next base.

For the catcher, the toughest of the pitches in the dirt to handle is the toppling splitter. Trying to come up with the short hop and making the quick transfer is very difficult, so if the stealer correctly guesses splitter he will probably be safe. The runner can't be positive when to expect a tumbling splitter or forkball in the dirt, but a pretty good guess is a 1-2 or 2-2 count, when the pitcher is trying to polish off the batter. It helps to know the pitcher. Tommy Glavine and Greg Maddux almost never throw the ball in the dirt, so base stealers can't wait for such pitches from them. But they know their staff mate John Smoltz and other star pitchers like Hideo Nomo and Rod Beck throw nasty splitters that are hard for the catcher to handle with two strikes. As mentioned, Nomo has two split-finger fastballs, one that is low and a better one that goes into the dirt. His better splitter is the one on which to run. The runner knows that Nomo will be more concerned with a dangerous left-handed batter than with him, which means that with two strikes he will not be challenging with fastballs but with his strikeout splitter in the dirt. The runner should be ready to go.

STEALING SECOND

When a potential base stealer gets on first, listen to the broadcaster. Good announcers tell the viewer what to look for because it's different with every pitcher and every base runner. For a guy with a good move, we try to use the low-first camera, but keep in mind that the cam-

Batters aren't expected to protect base runners who get bad jumps on attempted steals. It happens too quickly for them to do anything. There is, however, a good, rarely used ploy for batters who want to protect speedy runners without actually swinging the bat. It was done expertly by onetime Mets shortstop Buddy Harrelson. He'd upset me because it was a legitimate play and I couldn't do anything about it. Buddy would square around to bunt without having the intention of bunting, and before pulling the bat back he would put the barrel of the bat right in line with the pitch, blocking my vision. That bat kept me back when I wanted to explode out of my haunches toward second base. My timing and footwork were messed up, and I couldn't make a decent throw. I would meekly ask the umpire to call interference, and Buddy would kind of laugh because he knew I had no grounds for argument. What Buddy did is kind of a lost art. It's a very, very effective play.

era is usually located in the well next to the dugout rather than down the line, where there would be a straight line from it through first base to the mound. The camera is where it is because there are more shots to worry about than just the pitcher's move. It can pick up most of the action but can't pick up the throw to first with the best angle, so some directors try to get that with a high camera. Because he doesn't want to forget the batter, who is very much on the minds of the runner and pitcher, the director may use a three-box split screen to show all three players. I might add that because of costs, most local telecasts have too few cameras to cover this situation from all angles. In postseason play, John Filippelli, our FOX producer, makes sure he has an ample number of cameras, including one down the right-field line.

The runner wants to take a good lead off first, hinting that he will steal or take off on a bunt or hit-and-run. He'll dare the pitcher to throw over because he wants to see how good his move is in order to figure out how big a lead he can take. I don't think that the first time on base is the best time to get a jump. Someone may counter this statement by saying that a player's first time on may turn out to be his only time on in the game, so he shouldn't let an opportunity go by. That could be true, but the more he sees the pitcher throw and the more he sees of his pickoff move, the better idea he will have on when to run. If he wants to run his first time on base, he should know something about the pitcher from previous games.

When my Cardinals teammate Lou Brock, who held the season and career stolen-base records before Rickey Henderson, was unfamiliar with a pitcher, he would take a one-way lead. He'd take a bigger lead as if he were stealing, but it was a lead where he intended only to return to first

Dick Sisler, whose homer won the 1950 pennant for the Phillies, was the batting instructor and first-base coach for the Cardinals in the sixties. One of life's great people, Dick had trouble saying the letter "G" without stuttering, which, having a great sense of humor, he'd joke about. He and Lou Brock would laugh about the time Lou was taking one of his one-way leads off first while the pitcher attempted to pick him off. Each time Dick told him, "G-g-get back," Lou would be back before he got it out. On the fourth throw, it was "G-G-Goddammit, he got you." Lou was a tough competitor and hated being picked off, but that time he was almost laughing.

safely. He used a two-way lead if he was geared to go either back to first or to second. He was executing an intelligent Maury Wills concept, which was to take a big enough lead to entice the pitcher to throw to first so he could see and time his move.

Even when Brock was planning to steal second, he would slide back into first or go in standing up if the pitcher threw over. Wills went back hand-first, arguing that if you don't have to dive back into the bag, you don't have the proper lead. Diving back definitely takes you back faster, but going back spikes-first also has its benefits. In either case, the runner should go to the outside part of the base so the first baseman has to make a longer tag.

For base stealers, it's important to know a pitcher's pickoff stats. They aren't concerned about the stolen-base success/failure ratio, but they want to know if a pitcher has a good move. Some base stealers care if the catcher has a good arm, but the good ones don't care who's behind the plate as long as they get a good jump. They steal on pitchers. Some pitchers like Andy Pettitte and Terry Mulholland have such great pickoff moves that runners should play softball rules and stand on the base until the batter makes contact. If the pitcher has a great move to first, you don't abandon your running game, you just change it, maybe opting for the hit-and-run or bunt, or even waiting until you're on second to steal.

When a runner is caught in no-man's-land on a pickoff or pitchout, often it's best to motor down to second with his head down, hoping to either beat the throw or elude the tag. There's always the chance of a dropped ball or throwing error. When the runner sees a pickoff throw bounce far enough away, he will reverse his direction and head for second. You'll see him look over his right shoulder to find the ball and determine whether to slide into second or continue running to third. If the runner loses sight of the ball, he should try to pick up a signal from his third-base coach. He doesn't want to slide into second and then discover that he had enough time to reach third. As long as the ball is on the playing field after an overthrow, the base runner can run forever, but at his own peril.

* * *

To be a good base stealer it isn't enough to be fast. For instance, the Yankees' Bernie Williams has speed and is good at taking the extra base, but he hasn't developed into a proficient base stealer. When stealing bases, technique and savvy are as important as speed. Maury Wills wasn't as fast as all the base-running specialists he paved the way for, like Lou Brock,

Rickey Henderson, and Vince Coleman, but he was very smart and made a science of base stealing.

There are many good times to steal second:

- A base stealer will watch a left-handed pitcher. If he sees his right foot go behind his left leg, he goes because if the pitcher throws over to first it should be called a balk.
- When the first baseman suspects a bunt and breaks in prematurely. The pitcher can't throw over to first, so the runner can just take off.
- Some right-handers get into the habit of throwing to first only after they look to third, so if they don't look to third, take off. Others break their front leg noticeably and you can take off immediately. Some lean toward home before they throw. When they lean, you go.
- If there's good speed on first in a one-run or tie game and singles hitters are at the plate and on deck, it's often a good time to run.
- If the middle infielders aren't paying attention, the average-speed runner may try a delayed steal.
- If a manager holds a base stealer while a batter tries to bunt him over, he may send the runner if the batter picks up two strikes. If the batter strikes out and the runner makes a successful steal, the result is the same as if the sacrifice had worked. It rescues a negative—the batter not doing his job—by turning it into a positive, which is good psychologically.
- If there are two outs and a good batter is behind in the count, being caught stealing is sometimes acceptable. Then the batter will lead off the next inning with an 0-0 count.
- You often hear it said, "You never send the runner on first with the pitcher up and two outs," because if he's thrown out, you've got the pitcher leading off the next inning. But change "never" to "*almost* never" if the manager has a good pinch hitter available to lead off the next inning. If it's the late innings, the manager might be content having his pitcher go another half inning and then pinch-hit for him. So he can send the runner, and it's a positive if he's safe and not a negative if he's out.

* * *

Of course, a good stealer knows *how* to run as well as when to run. He has to be careful not to try to look too casual because experienced catchers will pick up on that and know he's going. His stance shouldn't be too wide. His knees are bent, and his hands hang low to the ground—think of Rickey Henderson's classic pose—and he's on the balls of his feet, ready to pivot in either direction. He shouldn't put his hands on his knees because he'll have to take them off to run and that's a wasted movement that can be the difference between being out and safe.

The runner who intends to steal second should take his lead on the baseline and not behind it since the shortest distance between two points is a straight line. The pivot is very important. There are players who make the double mistake of picking up their right foot and bringing it back as they start to run. What the stealer should do is pivot on his right foot—if he picks it up he will only have to put it down again. He then crosses over with his left foot and is in full stride on his first step. He accelerates with two or three short, choppy steps, running like a sprinter. Tall base stealers take a little longer to get into full stride.

Earlier I said that all slides should be executed with the feet first, no matter the success that Rickey Henderson and some of his hands-first imitators have enjoyed. The technically correct base stealer starts his slide a good distance from second base so that he won't jam his leg on the bag. He bends his arms for balance and slides on his bent left leg—most runners slide on their left legs—and on the left side of his rear, toward the base, touching it with the bottom of the foot of his stretched right leg, the lead leg. His momentum is such that he will be able to pop up when he reaches the base.

You may see that the runner is safe and the replay will back you up, showing that the fielder got the ball on the short hop and the runner went under the tag. However, it's often the case that the stealer is still called out. Unlike the neighborhood play, where the umpire gives the benefit of the doubt to the fielder, on an attempted steal and other tag plays it's often the case that if the ball beats you, you're out.

Unless you're Maury Wills. Then you're never out . . . or so it seemed. Perhaps Wills's greatest skill was sliding. No one has ever been better at sliding into a base. He was a little guy who slid late and very, very hard. If he knew it would be a close play, he'd slide hard and kick the ball out of the glove or he'd avoid the tag and reach the corner of the base with his hand. He had a sixth sense that told him how to be safe.

STEALING THIRD

A third-base coach may alert a runner on second that he can get a good jump and should "be alive," but he will *never* give him a sign to steal unless there is a 3-2 count on the hitter and there also is a runner on first.

The runner is the only guy who knows whether he can get a good jump or not. With no one holding him on second, he can get different types of leads, perhaps basing his distance from the base on whether the pitcher is throwing hard stuff or breaking balls or pitching inside or outside. If the runner on second is conservative, he'll never make it to third. Calculated risks must be taken to steal third. A good jump is also essential when the stealer doesn't have exceptional speed. Once, when I was tagged out trying to steal third, Cardinals coach George Kissell said some words that stuck with me: "You weren't tagged out at third, you threw yourself out at second," meaning my jump wasn't good enough. Perhaps I was worried about being picked off. The runner is given freedom by the manager and third-base coach, but he must be vigilant about pickoff plays and pay attention to the second baseman. It's up to the third-base coach to pay particular attention to the shortstop, who might work a pickoff play with the pitcher, especially if he is already cheating toward second because the batter tends to hit to right field.

Only the man on second takes his lead behind the baseline, walking into it so he can stay on the balls of his feet and be mobile. In this way, he gets momentum toward third without venturing too far away from the base. To steal third, momentum is more important than the size of the lead. As a runner, you have to know how fast you can accelerate. You try to pick up patterns from the pitcher. For instance, if he repeatedly looks back to second twice and then throws home, you might chance running as soon as he's looking back the second time and can't stop himself from throwing to the plate. If his movements are too consistent, it means he's not worried about you and his guard is down. Remember, almost all pitchers are rightly more concerned with the batter.

When you attempt to steal third, you want to make sure it is worth the risk because you are already in position to score on a base hit. You have less to lose if your team is ahead. Also, there should be one out because, as I've said, a runner isn't supposed to make the first or last out in an inning at third base on a gamble. With no outs, you can be bunted or pushed (with a ground ball to the right side) to third; with two outs, you stay put because you won't be able to score on a fly ball or a ground-out from third anyway. With one out, it's even better to steal third if the bottom part of the order is coming up, as the weaker hitters will have to do less to drive in a runner from third than from second. If once he takes off and sees that the third baseman has taken the catcher's throw on the inside of the bag, he will slide to the back side of the bag, to make the tag longer. He slides straight ahead—which is much better than a hook slide—

with his body a full arm's length from the base and touches it only with his left hand.

As is the case when there is a runner on first, the runner on second should stay put on hitter's counts, particularly 3-1, when he will probably get a ball to drive. In 1997, the Mets' Carl Everett committed a double sin when he got thrown out trying to steal third with two outs and a 3-1 count on the batter. He was thrown out on ball four. How many times does a walk end an inning? It was a bad, bad play. If you attempt to steal third with two outs, you may cost your team a run for no good reason because with two outs a base runner on third will pretty much score only on the same hits that would score him from second. Managers hate that with two outs.

THE DOUBLE STEAL

With men on first and second and one out, the manager might send his runners on a hit-and-run or on a double steal, with the batter taking. He'd prefer having a right-handed batter at the plate to block the catcher's view of third.

The ideal double-steal situation is when the faster runner is the lead runner. If the lead runner increases his lead, he'll do it slowly, moving into the line and timing his jump. The trail runner has to make sure the man on second runs toward third before taking off. If the trail runner delays too much, he may be thrown out by the catcher, who will go to second instead of third. If the lead runner bluffs going to third, he runs the risk of leaving the trail runner hung out to dry. The Big Red Machine used to pull off this double steal in the 1970s with guys like Joe Morgan, Dave Concepcion, and Pete Rose as the lead runner and Johnny Bench as the trailer. The Reds worked the double steal better than any team I ever played against.

* * *

With runners on first and third, there can be a double steal in which the runner on third runs home when the catcher tries to throw out the other runner going to second. One version is this: With two outs and any count but 3-2, the slow runner on first takes off for second and stops halfway. If the catcher throws through to second base, he risks the runner on third racing home during a rundown. This play succeeds more than it should. Johnny Keane used to call it a semipro play that works. I don't believe a stolen base should be credited to the runner coming in from third because it isn't his speed that is responsible for his reaching home but the length of time it takes the infielder to return the ball to the catcher to make the tag.

The runner on third always leads off in foul territory except when the double steal is on with men on first and third. In this case, he wants to block a catcher's depth perception so he doesn't know how big his lead is. When a catcher sees you in foul territory, he can tell how far off the bag you are, but if he can't see the bag, he can't tell. The runner doesn't move into the line until the man on first runs. The catcher will throw to the third baseman if he sees the runner is way off the bag, but he'll go to second if he can't tell—only to have the man on third scamper home because he had a bigger lead than the catcher thought. The runner on third should be prepared to have the throw to second cut off by the pitcher or shortstop so there can be a quick throw back home. If he senses this play is on, he may bluff running home and be content with his teammate's successful steal of second.

STEALING HOME

To me the only legitimate steal of home is when the runner takes off and beats the pitch home. Like Ty Cobb, Pete Reiser, and Jackie Robinson used to do, although nobody ever mentions that Robinson's famous steal of home in Game 1 of the 1955 World Series was a truly foolish play with his team behind by two runs. Besides, as Yogi Berra still contends, he should have been called out.

Why do most ballplayers go through their entire careers without stealing home? The pitcher's mound is only sixty feet six inches from home while a runner on third is ninety feet away, and a pitcher can throw a ball over ninety mph to the plate—how many people do you know who can run that fast? The only reason runners ever get away with a straight theft of home is that they surprise the pitcher and catcher, who don't expect a runner would do anything so risky. It's even less likely when a left-handed batter is up and the catcher has a clear view of the runner.

On a straight steal of home, unlike on a squeeze play, the runner *must* break soon because in order to succeed he has to outrun the pitch to the plate. If he breaks at the right time, the pitcher will be in his windup and have difficulty altering his pitch selection, a trouble most pitchers have. The pitcher will continue with his pitch and hope it beats the runner to the plate. The catcher can do nothing but catch the pitch and then try to quickly tag the runner. He won't have time to block the plate. At least he doesn't have to worry about the batter swinging because he's taken by surprise, too, and just gives way to the daring runner.

27

TO BUNT OR
NOT TO BUNT

When a batter tries to bunt for a base hit, he does it on his own. A drag bunt may surprise his own manager, but the key is to catch the defense unawares. A good time is when the third or first baseman is playing back. Obviously, power hitters who bunt once a decade or slow and moderate-speed batters have the best chances of pulling off a surprise, but the fast runners are usually the guys who drag bunt.

The manager calls all other bunt plays. When he wants to put on a play to move up a runner or runners, he has the option of signaling for a straight steal (or double steal), a hit-and-run, or a sacrifice bunt, the play with the least risk. Early in games, stolen-base attempts and the hit-and-run are viable options—in fact I prefer them if the pitcher isn't up—but the later it is in the game, the greater the chance the conservative manager will select the sacrifice bunt or play it straight up and let the batter hit away.

What would your choice be? You should consider that if the batter does hit away, even if he's very adept at going to right field, more things can go wrong than if he bunts. He could hit a fly ball to an outfielder and the runner would have to return to first. He could ground into a double play. Or he could line into a double play. That's why when there is a runner, even a base stealer on first with no outs late in a tie game, the conservative manager probably will sacrifice him to second. In most late-inning situations, I see the hit-and-run as a better second option than the steal attempt. That's because there are fewer base runners who can steal than batters who can execute the hit-and-run.

If the runner does have exceptional speed, however, I would not necessarily go along with the conservative manager. Against some pitchers and catchers in the eighth or ninth innings, I would choose the least conventional route and have the skilled base stealer attempt to swipe second. I think the more aggressive choice is the right one in this situation, but only if the runner has far better than average speed. If the batter is left-handed, that would give me another reason to try the steal because the catcher would have a much tougher throw with the batter in his way.

It is an entirely different situation if the base stealer is on second with no outs in a tie game in the eighth or ninth inning. His attempting to steal third is a low-percentage play. If you sacrifice him to third, it's a well-spent out because with one out the opponent will have to bring in its infield and many crazy things can happen to score him. There are times to be imaginative, but in this case it's best to be conventional and sacrifice the runner to third.

In some situations, doing anything other than sacrificing makes no sense. Yet some managers claim they don't like to sacrifice under almost any circumstances. Earl Weaver said he didn't like to do it because he didn't want to give up an out for any reason. As the manager of many powerful Orioles teams, he said it was much smarter to play for a big inning that featured three-run homers. Davey Johnson, who played for Weaver, is also a proponent of the big inning. In homer-friendly parks like Camden Yards and Coors Field, it is easy to think that the sacrifice bunt sabotages big innings. When managing Baltimore, Johnson did call for a sacrifice bunt in the final game of the 1997 ALCS with men on first and second and nobody out. Roberto Alomar's bunt resulted in a force at third and the next batter, Geronimo Berroa, bounced into an inning-ending double play. The next day in the Baltimore *Sun,* Johnson mused, "I normally don't bunt on that situation, but Alomar is such a good bunter." Since the Orioles lost 1–0 in eleven innings, I'm sure Johnson's view of the sacrifice bunt didn't improve.

There are too many variables to make it clear-cut whether an offense should go for big innings or bunt and sacrifice an out to increase the possibility of scoring one run. But going for three runs or one run depends mostly on the inning and the pitcher—my pitcher, not the opposing pitcher. If Greg Maddux, Randy Johnson, Roger Clemens, or Kevin Brown is on the mound, I'm going to bunt early. With such pitchers, one run *is* a big inning. They can protect a 1–0 lead. I love three-run homers; who doesn't? In the perfect world, I'd wait for them every time. But the odds of getting one aren't always that good, so I believe you have to blend that three-run-homer mentality with a willingness to sacrifice bunt in certain situations. Davey Johnson says he doesn't want his players to think he has no confidence in their hitting ability if he tells them to bunt. That's reasonable enough, but keep in mind that the closer to the end of the game you are, the more one run looks like a three-run homer. Give a 1–0 lead to a closer like Randy Myers, who blew just one save opportunity in 1997, and the game is over.

Interestingly, while Earl Weaver employed his no-bunt approach when Frank Robinson, Boog Powell, and Brooks Robinson went up to bat, with the weaker hitters like Mark Belanger and Paul Blair, he would bunt all the time. He just wouldn't call attention to it when he talked about his philosophy. People fail to realize that managers who espouse certain theories don't always follow them. That would make them too predictable.

There are definitely times when the sacrifice bunt is not the way to go. Certainly when there is a man on first and no one out early in the game, the straight steal, the hit-and-run, or no movement at all can be better choices. At Coors Field I'd be reluctant to bunt under almost any circumstances considering how the ball travels there and the big bats in the Rockies' lineup. As manager Don Baylor says, anybody with a bat in his hands is in scoring position, so only pitchers should be ordered to bunt.

Other than the pitcher in the National League and ninth-place hitter in the American League, the leadoff man, second-place hitter, and, if there is a pinch hitter on deck, eighth-place hitter are the guys who would most likely be called on to sacrifice with men on first and second and nobody out. If the lead runner on second is slow, the bunt must be better to get him to third. With a fast runner on second and a slow runner on first, some fielders may go to second for the trail runner.

The artificial surface also makes sacrificing more difficult. It's harder to deaden balls on the carpet, so infielders can play deeper and still get to the ball quickly. A bad, hard bunt could lead to a double play.

When a left-handed pitcher is on the mound, that could make bunting the ball to third more difficult. Watch how a lefty comes off the mound. He comes off toward the third-base line, which is where most bunts are placed. A right-hander is usually easier to bunt against because he has the tendency to go toward first base.

If a batter has two strikes against him, should he attempt a sacrifice bunt? Unless he's a pitcher, no. Two-strike sacrifices are strikeouts if the ball goes foul and usually aren't effective even if they go fair. The best bunts are down the lines, but with two strikes a batter—except perhaps the pitcher—can't chance bunting down the line. There seems to be a growing trend in which position players who don't get the bunt down on the first or second strike take it upon themselves to bunt with two strikes. More often than not, they don't get it down then, either. (Also, how many times have you seen a batter lay down a bunt when there is a runner on at second base and there is at least one out? Rey Sanchez did it during the 1997 divisional series for the Yankees. In this situation, even if you are trying to bunt for a base hit, you've picked the wrong time to do it because you are leaving it up to the next guy to do what you should do. It makes managers scratch their heads.)

There is one time that I really hate to see a sacrifice bunt, even when it works. Don't you think it's foolish for a .280 hitter to bunt to move up a runner when there's a .220 hitter on deck? It's bad baseball. Yet when he goes to the dugout, everybody will pat him on the back! It drives me crazy: You're a run down, you're in the middle innings, and you elect to bunt the runner to second for the bottom part of the order to drive in. You do this although a double will drive in the run and you would become the potential go-ahead run. It's self-serving. If the hitter is trying to beat out the bunt, he'll either wind up with a single—fielders will be surprised he's sacrificing in this situation—or a sacrifice bunt, an unofficial at-bat. That's a good deal for *him*. He forgets the score, he forgets his team. This is a play that's usually done by "light" .300 hitters who think of their average first and producing runs for the team second.

There are better times to sacrifice bunt:

- An early sacrifice bunt is a proven way to get an early run, and, as Gene Mauch said, every run counts the same. Mauch always sacrificed early in the game because teams that score first usually win. A team with strong pitching that plays many close games probably will want to bunt early in the game to grab an early lead.
- The leadoff man doubles in the first inning. A sacrifice bunt down the third-base line is tough for a third baseman, especially an inexperienced one, because he is caught between going back to third and charging.

- There is a man on second with no outs. A right-handed batter wants to move up a runner. If his natural stroke isn't to right field, it is better for him to bunt than to try to hit to the right side.
- If a batter has trouble against a particular pitcher—maybe they're both right- or left-handed—a bunt may be the one way he can move a runner to second.
- If the batter is not a good bunter, the manager might try a *bunt-and-run*. If the runner on first is going, then the bunt doesn't have to be perfect. On the bunt-and-run, he will take off with the pitch and it's up to the batter to bunt the ball on the ground. The runner, however, must look back after two steps to pick up what happens when the bat hits the ball to make sure there is no pop-up.
- If there is a man on first with one out and the pitcher fouls off two bunt attempts, the sacrifice bunt shouldn't necessarily be abandoned. Unless the runner is an excellent base stealer, usually the best scenario is to have the pitcher bunt again. With two strikes, he is going to have to bunt to the fat part of the infield because a foul is a strikeout. He wants to bunt toward the pitcher, so for the runner not to be forced at second he should take off with the pitch. This bunt-and-run play isn't used enough, especially on the artificial surface. The pitcher may be a better bunter with two strikes because he can relax now that he doesn't have to lay down a perfect bunt.

* * *

If the visiting team is down by a run in the top of the ninth, should the manager have a batter sacrifice bunt to move the tying run into scoring position? The book says you shouldn't play for a tie on the road. The reason is that even if you tie the game in the top of the ninth and hope to win it in the tenth, the home team has the advantage of six outs in that inning-and-a-half period to your three outs. So even if you tie the game, the odds are two to one against you. That's why you're supposed to play for a win on the road and play for the tie at home.

But there are different schools of thought. I'm inclined to believe that the batter should swing away. But if the visiting team's bullpen is stronger than the home team's, the visitors might want to play for the tie. If its bullpen is weaker, it will have no choice but to play for the win, and that means it can't give up an out to move up runners. Its bullpen might not be weaker for long, however, because if the visiting team ties the game against the home team's stopper, it's likely that a less stellar reliever will be pitching against the visitors in the tenth inning. So your thinking changes as the situation changes.

SQUEEZE BUNTS

The squeeze, on which the batter tries to bring the runner home from third base, is the riskiest bunt. But, as Don Zimmer asks rhetorically, "If there's a man on first and third with one out, and you've got a guy at the plate who can bunt real well, it's one run for sure, so why not do it?" If you want to squeeze, you won't be deterred if the infield is playing in to cut off the run at the plate. As a matter of fact, the depth of the infield has nothing to do with it, but because of the increased risk, it is imperative that you get the pitcher into a situation where he must throw a strike.

The third-base coach should signal to the hitter that the squeeze is on as soon as the batter enters the box, before everybody is watching. (This is a good practice to follow on all signs.) If you see a batter back out of the box and ask the third-base coach to repeat his signals, keep in mind that he hasn't only caught your attention but is also alerting the defense that something unusual may be on.

Atlanta manager Bobby Cox says that the best time to squeeze is when the defense is at its most unsettled, for instance, when runners have been flying around the bases and there have been throws all over the field. That's why Cox and other managers may attempt the squeeze after a run has just scored. Everybody always talks about ex-managers Tommy Lasorda and Don Zimmer in regard to the squeeze, but I think Cox is the manager with the most uncanny knack for knowing when to squeeze. In the 1995 World Series against Cleveland, Rafael Belliard was able to pull off a successful squeeze because Cox reasoned the timing was ideal for a surprise maneuver. Cox had just futilely argued with second-base umpire Bruce Froemming that Indians shortstop Omar Vizquel hadn't had full control of the ball when he got an out call at second. When he returned to the dugout, I'm sure Indians manager Mike Hargrove thought he was still too consumed with that play to think of anything else. He was fuming, but he had the presence of mind to put on the squeeze on the next play. It was a great move because of its timing.

Zimmer has a great line about squeezing: "What you should do is get the other team to think you're going to squeeze and then don't. And then when they think you're not going to do it, you do it." He asserts that once you get the reputation of a manager who likes to squeeze, opposing pitchers might fall behind in the count by pitching out or throwing balls that are tough to bunt. You get your batter a favorable count. If you have the reputation for not squeezing, like Davey Johnson, then it's detrimental when you have a player on third with less than two outs. The defense has one less thing to worry about. If a manager doesn't like to squeeze, I think he should do it a couple of times early in the season just so other managers and advance scouts will think he could do it again.

The two types of squeeze bunts are the *safety squeeze,* which is not one of my favorite plays, and the *suicide squeeze,* which is more daring and more effective.

When the third baseman is playing in with a man on third and less than two outs, the runner can follow the third baseman in. In fact, he can come all the way down the line until he is parallel with the third baseman.

There is a rare bunt play that is impossible to defend that manager Chuck Tanner used when he had men on first and third with less than two outs. A batter pushes a bunt down the third-base line. (A left-handed batter would have the easier time because of the angle of his bat.) He should bunt fairly hard because he wants the third baseman to field the ball as if it were first and second and nobody out. The runner follows the third baseman down the line, perhaps as far as halfway to home plate. Then, if the third baseman throws to first, he'll be able to lope home before a second throw can be made from first to the plate. The worst thing that can happen is that the third baseman will look the guy back to third and the batter could be safe at first. No manager has executed that play to my knowledge since Tanner retired, although Jim Leyland told me that he thought about it in spring training but never worked on it. He says that the way to foil the play is to have the first baseman charge in and cut off the throw to first and then make the shorter throw home. I pointed out that if the runner on third goes back to the vacated third base, the batter has a base hit. The shortstop can't cover third because he's responsible for second base. So the play guarantees a run or a single that will load the bases or put runners on first and third. Why doesn't anybody do it anymore? It's the baseball equivalent of a perfect crime.

On the safety squeeze, he doesn't commit himself to run home until he sees the ball hit the ground. So he will not be out if the batter misses the bunt. If the bunt goes down, the runner has an advantage in that the fielders may be too surprised to react quickly and go after the ball. Even if there is no surprise, a good bunter can place the ball where he wants and make it difficult for the fielder to pick it up in time to throw the runner out at home. The one major disadvantage of the safety squeeze is that not too many major leaguers are good bunters because they have trouble placing the ball where they want. So there may be a wasted out while the runner stays put at third.

On a suicide squeeze, the runner on third doesn't have the choice of running or staying put. When the pitcher is ready to release the ball, he breaks. The batter must get a piece of the ball. The runner can't break too soon or the pitcher will pitch out on his own or throw at the hitter. He must be fearless because there is no turning back, even if the batter misses the bunt or the pitcher pitches out. If the ball is popped up, he may be doubled up; if the batter can't get wood on the ball, he may get caught in a rundown. Remember, while most runners leading off bases try to get a good jump, the runner on third on a squeeze play intentionally doesn't get a good jump because he does not want to give the play away. He must *delay* breaking until the pitch is released. As a matter of fact, he should take a step *back* toward third when the pitcher starts his delivery—it's a great reminder.

Also, the batter knows that when he squares around too early, some pitchers, rather than pitch out, might throw a fastball at him so that he can't bunt. So he intentionally squares around late, when the pitch is on its way. At this point, his job is simple: Make contact and put the ball on the ground.

Expect a batter to squeeze only if there is one out because with no outs there are many easier ways to score a runner from third. The hitter wants to be ahead in the count so there is less chance of a pitchout, a pitch being thrown at him, or a waste pitch that is so far out of the strike zone that he can't bunt it. The worst counts for squeezing are 0-1, 0-2, and 1-2 because the pitcher can pitch out. (Even if the pitcher guesses wrong, he won't have hurt himself much.) A count of 1-0 is a good squeeze count, 2-1 is better, and 3-2 can be good because the pitcher must come in with a strike, unless he doesn't mind walking the batter with first base open. (However, the players who are called on to squeeze aren't the guys the pitcher would want to put on.) On the 3-2 count, few managers will be gutsy enough to have their pitcher pitch out or throw at the batter because that will be ball four. Counts of 2-0, 3-0, and 3-1 are good counts on which to hit away, not squeeze.

The major advantage of the suicide bunt over the safety bunt is that the bunter needn't be as skilled. Even if the runner has moderate speed, all the batter needs to do is put the ball on the ground because even if the fielder is right there, there's almost no chance of his throw beating the runner to the plate.

Sometimes the squeeze is the right play to call to score a runner. But when it fails it's like earning a lot of money by working hard and then blowing it in Vegas on one roll of the dice. It's a shame when you get a guy to third with less than two outs and then have one pitchout do him in. On the other hand, if you fail to score the tying or winning run from third by using other means, you'll look back and agonize that a simple bunt could have been the solution.

28

PRODUCTIVE OUTS: AS GOOD AS A BUNT

I maintain that it's the combination of little things that usually wins base-ball games rather than what makes newspaper headlines. The batter whose single drives in the winning run from second with two outs in the ninth will be surrounded by reporters after the game, but what about the previous batter who moved the runner into scoring position? A slug-ger may lift his team to victory with a long blast in the ninth inning, but what about all that happened during the course of the game that put him in position to win it? It is always the seemingly minor things, well done, that keep teams in ball games or provide the margin of victory. Beating out ground balls to prevent the double play, fighting your way on base to make sure a big hitter will get an extra time at bat, stretching a single into a double or going from first to third on a single with one out, and bunting runners over so they'll have a better chance to score are some of the little things. Probably the least recognized of all the little things a good offensive player contributes is the "productive out."

A bunt isn't the only means for a batter to move up a base runner by intentionally making an infield out. With no outs, a batter can have pro-ductive outs. Move a runner on a failed hit-and-run to second and he can score on a single; move a runner from second to third and he can score on a wild pitch, passed ball, sacrifice fly, squeeze bunt, many ground-outs and infield hits. If the infield is playing deep with the intention of making the play at first, just put the ball on the ground and it's usually enough to score the runner from third. These are very productive outs that score cheap runs.

I usually think of productive outs as being part of a series of things that produce a cheap run. I love this scenario: A batter walks, steals second, moves to third with no outs on a bunt or productive out to the right side, and scores on a ground ball to an infielder, a productive out. No hits, one run. Don't laugh—this was the Dodgers' offense in the sixties, and they won world championships in 1963 and 1965. Sure they had Koufax and Drysdale, but they had to score to win.

When a right-handed batter moves up a runner to third with a grounder to the right side, it is more of a *sacrifice* than a sacrifice bunt because he is charged with an official at-bat and his batting average goes down. It would be selective scoring, but I think a right-handed batter should get credit for a sacrifice when he intentionally grounds out to the right side to move a runner to third. He shouldn't be charged with an at-bat if, in the official scorer's judgment, he was deliberately trying to move the runner to third.

Unless there is an RBI, productive outs don't show up as a positive in the box score, but they are essential to winning baseball, especially on teams that play a lot of close, low-scoring games. The smart fan knows the value of the guy who gives himself up and gets no statistical credit. He provides fiber to the offense, just like the good middle reliever who records "holds" does to the pitching game.

But let me say that all intentional outs that move runners from second to third aren't productive. In fact, when you trail in late innings by more than a run, you can't afford to give up an out under any circumstances. If the game is tied, the offense has the lead, or the defense leads by only one run, some right-handed batters will want to go the other way with no outs to advance the runner to third. But it shouldn't be an RBI man. The batters in the middle of the lineup shouldn't give themselves up and leave it to the weaker hitters to drive in runs. When an RBI man takes it on himself to go the other way and moves along the runner with an out, you'll see him being congratulated by his teammates when he returns to the dugout. But most of the time it was inadvertent or not a smart move on his part. Do you think Mark McGwire should ever try to get a runner over for the next guy to drive in? His long flies to left-center can get the runner over as well as a grounder to the other side can, and there's a good chance they will go for extra bases or out of the park.

29

THE HIT-AND-RUN

The hit-and-run is a valuable play with no outs or one out for managers who see the merit in a potent running game. For instance, if the manager doesn't want to give up an out by bunting with a good hitter at the plate, the hit-and-run is a good alternative. Or, if he sees that a good hitter has been trying to do too much to get out of a slump, he might have him hit-and-run because all he has to do is put the bat on the ball. Or, if he wants to send a runner but worries he will be thrown out stealing, he can have the batter protect him by executing the hit-and-run.

I'd usually pick the straight steal by a fast runner or sacrifice bunt over the hit-and-run in crucial late-inning situations, but I think the hit-and-run can be the best choice earlier in the game because it can jump-start the offense and disrupt the defense. I love plays that combat what the defense is trying to do, and that's why I'm a proponent of the hit-and-run. For instance, if a fouled-off bunt attempt causes the defense to start scurrying around in anticipation of a second attempt, a smart manager will try to take advantage of the disarray by taking off the bunt and going to the hit-and-run. What I also like about the hit-and-run is that with a man on first, it is the most aggressive way for a manager to produce a coveted first-and-third situation. Because the runner on first can move up *two* bases, the well-executed hit-and-run is more productive than the sacrifice or steal. This is especially true if there is one out and a weak hitter on deck because the weak hitter won't have to do much to bring a runner in from third.

Here's the blueprint for the hit-and-run: The runner makes sure the pitcher throws the ball home and takes off from first with the pitch; the second baseman or, for most left-handed batters, the shortstop, leaves his position to cover second on what he thinks is a stolen-base attempt; the batter shoots the ball through the spot he just vacated; and the runner races past second into third.

The hit-and-run should really be called the run-and-hit because the runner takes off before the batter swings. Before taking off, the runner must make sure the pitcher throws home and not to first because there's no way he can allow himself to be picked off when the hit-and-run is on. When the runner leaves first at top speed, he should look back after two steps into the hitting area to determine if the ball has been hit in the air or on the ground—or missed. If the batter doesn't make contact, the runner will slide into second and try to beat the throw from the catcher. If the ball is bounced to an infielder or the pitcher, chances are there won't be a play at second because of the early break. If there is, the runner will be near the base and in a better position to break up the double play with a hard slide into the base and fielder. If the ball goes through the hole, he won't stop at second but will head full steam into third. The only time he will need the

This is hard to believe, but in the small confines of Parc Jarry, the unlamented first home of the Montreal Expos, my manager, Gene Mauch, was able to detect who was covering second by looking at the veins in the necks of the middle infielders as they mouthed who'd cover second while hiding their faces behind their gloves. Open mouth—"you cover"; closed mouth—"I cover." When I was at bat, if Mauch yelled my uniform number, "Come on, Six," it meant the second baseman was covering, and if he didn't yell anything it meant the shortstop was covering. Against pitchers without exceptional speed, I had good enough bat control to quickly adjust where I'd hit the ball. I picked up about five hits in half a season because of Mauch's vein reading. It made me money and Mauch justifiably proud of himself.

third-base coach is if the ball is hit behind him to the first baseman or down the right-field line. He doesn't want to depend on a fielder to let him know whether the ball is on the ground or in the air.

On a hit-and-run, the batter simply wants to meet the ball and hit it sharply on the ground. Managers prefer to hit-and-run with a right-handed batter who can go the other way through the vacated second baseman's position because the runner has a better chance to reach third on a ball hit to right. Pitchers may try to come inside, but some batters like Edgardo Alfonzo, whose natural stroke is to right, and Derek Jeter, who has a great inside-out swing, have no trouble going to right with the inside pitch. If a batter can easily go to right, fine, but I don't think it's necessary for all right-handed batters. On the hit-and-run, I think the batter shouldn't worry about hitting the ball to one side or the other. He should just hit it on the ground and take his chances that it will go through a vacated position or elude a fielder who has stayed put because you never know for sure which middle infielder will cover second.

I'm sure that you've often heard broadcasters say, "This would be a good time for the manager to hit-and-run, but the man on first isn't a fast runner." That has nothing to do with it, if everything works properly. A fast runner may assure the manager that an infielder will leave his position to cover second, but he would still be as inclined to hit-and-run with a slow runner on first. You will hear announcers say that the manager's reason for sending the slow runner is "to stay out of the double play." While that may be true, it's not why he should put it on. The manager should have a more positive approach, which is to send the runner in order to get men on first and third with one out. If he sends a runner to avoid the double play, it's a defensive approach. He's saying that he has to protect himself because the hitter is incapable of getting a base hit. That's hardly showing confidence in his batter.

What continues to befuddle me about major-league managers is that so few of them take into account the type of hitter and the type of pitcher that are preferable for a successful hit-and-run play. In deciding whether to hit-and-run, a manager should consider whether the batter is a contact hitter because the runner is counting on him to put the bat on the ball. The manager also must consider whether the pitcher is a contact pitcher or a high-ball flamethrower who piles up strikeouts or is wild. The batter wants to get on top of the ball to hit a grounder on the hit-and-run, and what makes the contact pitcher who throws strikes ideal is that he almost surely throws the low pitches that result in ground balls. If the manager sees a matchup of a contact hitter and a sinkerballer, and the count is right, he should send the runner. (Even if the batter misses a low pitch, the catcher may have difficulty with it and the runner will reach second safely.)

As on a squeeze bunt, the best counts for a hit-and-run are those when there is little chance of a pitchout. Pitchouts, as well as bad pitches that will get you out if you swing, are most common when the pitcher is ahead in the count 0-1, 0-2, and 1-2. If a sinkerball pitcher is behind in the count 1-0 or 2-1, the chances for a pitchout are minimal, so it's a good time to send the runner. The best count is 2-1. Many managers will send their runners on a 2-2 count with two outs, but I don't think it's a good time because if the batter takes and the runner holds and the pitch is a ball, the runner doesn't lose anything because he'll be running anyway on 3-2. Of course, the batter will be swinging at 2-2 strikes and borderline pitches, and if he occasionally hits one into the gap, a runner who took off with the pitch will score. But if the count goes to 3-2, a ball in the gap will score the runner from first easier.

As I said, the hit-and-run is employed only with no outs or one out. With two outs, you're more likely to send the runner. A distinction should be made between the terms "send the runner" and "hit-and-run." Some people wrongly think that "hit-and-run" is implied whenever they say it's a good time to send the runner. Actually, they are two different things. Unless there are three balls on the batter and less than two outs, anytime you send a runner who is not a base stealer, it is a hit-and-run. On a hit-and-run, the batter must swing. But if all the manager signaled for was for the runner to go, the batter will not swing at a definite ball on a 3-1 or 3-2 pitch. He will take the walk. When Ken Boyer was at the plate, he would want to know if the man on first was running on a 3-1 count because if the pitch was a borderline strike, he couldn't depend on the umpire to call it a ball and would swing to protect the runner. He wouldn't feel obligated to swing if the runner had been given a steal sign.

If you're going to send a runner on a 3-1 count, it should only be if there is a contact hitter at the plate, like Alfonzo or Craig Counsell. You don't do it with a Todd Hundley, Andres Galarraga, or any other power hitter. A count of 3-1 is not a good time to rob a power hitter of the ability to choose the pitch he can hit. As a catcher, I loved it when guys ran on that count because often the batter swung at what would have been ball four and fouled it back. So now, instead of having men on first and second, the runner is still on first and the count is 3-2 on someone who strikes out a lot.

Jim Fregosi was the only manager whom I've ever heard say he doesn't ever like to send runners on 2-0 and 3-1 counts.

* * *

Let's say you're in the early or middle innings and there are men on first and third with no outs. Is this a good time to send the runner on first? No. The manager may want to stay out of the double play, but this double play will score a run he might not get after the runner is thrown out stealing. So the sure run on the double play looks good in comparison to a possible run. There's a big difference: With one out, your sending the runner prevents a double play that would end the inning, but with no outs you're sending the runner to prevent a double play that would score a run. In this rare case, making two outs is preferable to making one out.

* * *

The hit-and-run I'd like to see managers employ far more often is one with men on first and second and nobody out. It's often talked about in spring training but not used during the season. Generally speaking, the more people who are moving on the infield, the better time it is to move the runners. The runners should be as animated as the infielders. In this situation, it's likely that the infielders will be moving around in anticipation of a bunt. Perhaps the defense will be working the rotation play, which means both the second baseman and shortstop will be out of position. In this case, the batter definitely doesn't need to worry about hitting the ball to one side or the other.

On this hit-and-run, the lead runner is off with the pitch. The ball is in front of him, and he needs no help from the third-base coach if the ball goes through. The trail runner takes off with the pitch so he can get all the way to third on most singles. On a line drive or any ball in the air, he retreats to first. In the final game of the 1997 divisional championship series against Cleveland, the Yankees tried a hit-and-run involving two slow runners, Mike Stanley, who was on second, and Charlie Hayes, who was on first. Stanley took off with the pitch, but apparently Hayes missed the sign and didn't run until he saw Stanley go. Tardy going to second on what turned out to be a grounder, Hayes was unable to break up the double play, which proved significant in a one-run loss. The trail runner must take off with the pitch. This was proof positive that the inability of players to do a little thing can cost a team not only games but pennants.

30

COMBATING THE RUNNING GAME

Any manager wants to relax while his starting pitcher mows down the opposition. But he relishes the challenge of devising strategies to foil plays that involve base runners, like steals, bunts, and squeezes. It's great fun for the fan to think along with him.

FOILING THE STOLEN BASE

With a Man on First

With a man on first, a pitcher working from the stretch has to keep an eye on the runner while not losing focus on the batter. Therein lies his dilemma. It can be a difficult balancing act. He may throw over to first once, twice, or more times to keep the runner close or to try to pick him off, but he can't let the runner break his concentration because his task at hand is to get the batter out. He doesn't want to fall behind in the count or throw a lollipop because he's thinking about the runner. On each pitch, a catcher can tell if the pitcher's mind is on the guy on first. Gene Mauch professed: "When throwing to first, concentrate one hundred percent on the runner, and when throwing to the plate, concentrate one hundred percent on the batter. It's the eighty to twenty percent formula that will get you in trouble." I agree with Mauch's theory, but I think the quality of the batter and runner can change the percentages a bit. If a hot batter is at the plate, then the concentration should be more on him and less on the runner. If the eighth-place hitter is at the plate, then the concentration may be more on the runner. Then the pitcher figures he can get the batter out with less than his best pitch and will throw an alternate pitch that the catcher can handle easily in case he must make a throw to second.

If a pitcher has trouble holding a runner on, the catcher tries to encourage him to pitch without worrying about the runner. It's important for him to make the pitcher understand that often a steal of second is not as bad as what the batter can do and that if a great base stealer gets a good jump, he's going to steal anyway. Speed on first will cause a catcher and pitcher to anticipate a steal early in the count and tempt them to throw fastballs so the catcher can make a quick throw to second. However, though he wants his best chance to throw out the runner, the catcher must resist calling only fastballs because that puts the hitter at too much of an advantage.

With a fast runner on first, the best deterrent is to wait. Like great thoroughbreds, fast runners have a rhythm all their own, and that is disrupted if the pitcher just holds the ball. Also, if a pitcher repeatedly bluffs a throw to first, it may throw off the concentration of both the runner and batter. For an aggressive approach to dealing with the potential base stealer, the pitcher has four choices: (1) throwing to first, which is designed to pick off the runner or at least keep him close (as it will do with all runners anticipating a bunt or hit-and-run); (2) slide-stepping toward home; (3) pitching out; or (4) having the catcher try to throw out the runner at second.

1. Throwing to First (the Pickoff Attempt)

If a pitcher repeatedly throws to first, it may upset a batter's concentration. If he varies the timing of his throws it may also confuse the runner. If it looks like he's ignoring the runner to concentrate solely on the batter—the smart thing to do when a pitcher really wants to focus on the batter—it may be a ruse to lure him into taking too big a lead. He and his catcher might be setting up the runner for a pickoff attempt or the pitcher might really be focusing on the batter.

On a pickoff attempt, the pitcher wants his delivery to look the same as if he were throwing home—only he will throw to first. That's how Andy Pettitte freezes so many runners. The pitcher wants to throw the ball low and inside the bag so the base runner sliding back actually tags himself out. In this bang-bang play, it's likely that a high throw will let the runner return safely to first.

* * *

A good first baseman will have a feel for when the runner is going to take off. He must hold him on, but he might try varying his routine. For instance, sometimes he can slide over with the runner as he takes his lead and sometimes he can stay close to the bag in case there's a pickoff attempt. Usually, he will move into the baseline when he is holding a runner on, but last year I saw Mark Grace move behind a runner. Sometimes it's just style or guys trying new things. I remember that Don Mattingly would move to his right directly in front of the runner, blocking his view of the pitcher and the plate. He'd go as far as the runner would go. If you're playing off the bag, the runner will usually not venture farther off than you because he's dead if the pitcher has quick moves like Andy Pettitte, Terry Mulholland, or Armando Reynoso.

The first baseman catches the pickoff throw in a low position and tries to make a quick sweep tag. It helps if he's left-handed because he doesn't have to lean clear over his body to apply the tag. If the runner is coming back hand first, the first baseman blocks the bag with his glove. He won't try to block it with his foot or knee more than once. He'll get over that on the next pickoff attempt when the runner changes his style and goes in feet first. It's a legitimate play to go right into the knee with your spikes. That prevents an infielder from blocking any base. The only guy who blocks a base is the one guy who has the protection to do it—the catcher.

On a pickoff throw from the catcher to first base, there is no need for a signal if the first baseman is holding the runner on. He can throw over there any time and the first baseman will be ready. But if the first baseman is playing behind the runner, there will be a signal. The first baseman can show the catcher the open glove or the catcher can give a fist sign or rub his right thigh.

Sometimes, if the runner is dead in the water, he may try to go hard to second base. The first baseman must step toward home and throw inside the line to the shortstop to avoid hitting the runner.

Avoiding Balks

When a pitcher is matching wits with the base runner, nothing frustrates him more than when an umpire calls him for a balk, awarding all runners one free base. The runner has freedom to do anything over at first; all penalties go to the pitcher. According to the rule book, there are thirteen ways an unlucky pitcher can "balk," and trying to explain any of them to a new baseball fan in the stands is futile, unless it's a rare obvious balk: The ball slips out of the pitcher's hand while he's on the rubber, or the pitcher goes toward home with his arm but doesn't release the ball. Most of the time, the thirty thousand fans will have no idea why any of the other balks were called because even if they understand the rule they would have needed binoculars focused on the pitcher to have detected what he did wrong. On television, even with replays from the center-field and low-first cameras, the viewer and announcers often have a difficult time seeing the balk.

The most common balk is called when the pitcher does not come to a dead stop for the count of *one thousand and one* after bringing his hands down from the stretch. The first-base umpire will call this balk on the left-handed pitcher and the third-base umpire will call it on the right-hander because they are looking right at them. This is a balk that could be called many times each game because most pitchers cheat on the time. These two umpires also will call a balk if the pitcher momentarily breaks his hands. Another commonly called balk is when the pitcher throws to first instead of completing his delivery home once his foot has made contact with the rubber and he's taken the ball out of the glove. Both the right-hander who pivots and the left-hander can be called for a "step-over" balk by the first-base umpire. There is an imaginary line that runs from the end of the rubber toward an area on the first-base line that is about sixty feet from home, two thirds of the way to first. Technically, if a pitcher's front leg goes to the home-plate side of the imaginary line and he throws to first, it is a balk. You've got to step toward first in order to throw to first. In addition to this, a left-hander can be called for a balk if he throws to first base once his right foot has gone behind his left leg and he has committed himself to going home. National League umpires are more likely to call it; American League umpires are liberal with the pickoff move of left-handers like Andy Pettitte.

The pitcher knows the runner is a threat to steal, but he shouldn't alter his motion by trying to get the ball to his catcher quicker. A pitcher is not allowed to depart from his regular delivery and use a motion that is meant to *deceive* a base runner and inhibit his ability to steal a base.

In fact, a balk is the act of deceiving the runner with an illegal move. If you commit to going home with your feet and go to first instead, it's technically a balk. So the pitcher will try to pick off a runner without balking, right? Without deceiving the runner, right? Well, no. If you don't deceive the runner, you don't pick him off. It's that simple. Good moves are balk moves that pitchers get away with. Smart pitchers work on these disputable balks for the express purpose of deceiving the runner. It's not cheating like putting a foreign substance on the ball because the umpire sees what you're doing and can call the balk if he wants. Umpires don't call good balk moves because they're borderline balks. Until they do, pitchers just take advantage of their leniency. (I think the time umpires really should be more liberal is when the pitcher does something inadvertently while concentrating on the batter and not because he is trying to deceive the runner. For instance, why should a pitcher be called for a balk for not coming to a complete stop if there are two outs and the only base runner is the pitcher, who is wearing his jacket and isn't going anywhere?)

Every pitcher in the big leagues has a specific place where he brings his hands when he comes set. He has to bring his hands together in the same place every time or it's a balk. Luis Tiant was very cagey in that he had *three* stopping points before delivering the ball. He'd stop at his chest, stomach, and waist regularly, so the umpires didn't call a balk for varying his stopping point. However, if a pitcher comes set with his hands at his chest on his first pitch to a batter with a man on first and comes set at his waist on the second pitch, the umpire will call a balk. You probably didn't realize that umpires know the moves and stopping places for every pitcher in their league. They make it a point to become familiar with young pitchers' moves so they will know if there is deception involved.

It's not necessarily true that the pitcher has a good pickoff move just because the base runner is almost out. It could be that the base runner has maximized his lead against a poor pickoff move and that's what's making it close. It's the lead, not the move. Few power pitchers have a good move to first. They need the high front leg kick to drive the ball, and it is tough for them to unravel. Sinkerballers have better moves because they don't need as high a leg kick to get the pitch over.

Generally, a left-hander being quick to first has nothing to do with the effectiveness of his move. If the runner knows the throw is coming, he can get back to first before any quick throw. But if the pitcher is deceptive enough to freeze the runner, he can be slower to first and still catch the runner. Left-handers with deceptive moves and quickness, like Andy Pettitte, Terry Mulholland, and Mark Langston, are lethal to base runners. Pettitte, who challenges runners to go with the arrogance Clint Eastwood displays when he challenges street punks to make their move—"Make my day"—even throws out guys who have no intention of going. Joe Torre calls this Pettitte's "power pickoff move." Because he keeps all runners close to first, he led the American League in 1997 in getting ground-ball double plays.

If a base stealer sees the right foot of a left-handed pitcher going behind his left leg, he takes off for second because if the pitcher throws over to first it's technically a balk, but pitchers can kick the leg up high and maybe get away with it. Jerry Koosman tried to teach Steve Carlton his high-kick move. When he'd take his right-leg kick, he'd have the sole of his right foot facing the base runner. A runner usually freezes when he sees the sole of the right foot from a lefty, and that gave Koosman time to choose between going home and throwing to first. That was part of his move. It was easier for Koosman than Carlton because he had great flexibility in his groin and back and could kick his leg up like a Rockette.

Terry Mulholland has a super pickoff move. No one runs on him because he is so uncannily quick at backing his left leg off the rubber and throwing to first. It's unusual in that he doesn't bring his right leg up. He throws almost flat-footed. He just gets the sign from the catcher and steps off and fires to first. That move must have taken him years to perfect because he's by far the best I've ever seen doing that. He's really hard to get a good jump on because he goes to first in the blink of an eye and is as fast to home because his leg kick is only about four inches off the ground.

Of course, left-handers have an advantage holding on runners because they are facing first base. The right-hander has to be faster to first because he has to spin. The one thing that makes right-hander Armando Reynoso so good is that when he spins, his feet and arm are in sync. Most pitchers spin and then throw: It's a spin-then-throw. Reynoso has a spin-throw. Don Drysdale also did that. It was interesting watching Drysdale with a man on first because the moment he leaned on his left leg, the good base runner would lean toward second. When a pitcher leans forward it is supposed to mean he is committed to going home, so the runner figured that if Drysdale threw to first the umpire would call a balk. But Drysdale would do that spin-throw move and nail runners and get away with it. He was balking, but in all the years I saw only one umpire call it on him.

One pickoff move that works as often as the sun rises in the west is when men are on first and third and the pitcher fakes going to third and then turns and goes to first in hope of catching that runner leaning (usually with two outs). In 1997, Gary Thorne got so excited when his lifelong dream of seeing that pickoff move work *almost* came true that he shouted into the microphone, "WHOA, I THINK HE'S GOT HIM—THROW IT!" and almost gave me a heart attack. My pencil flew over my shoulder. It's a good thing I wasn't driving. Later in the year, we watched the Mets actually pick a runner off first—the Reds' Joe Nunnally—by using the fake throw to third. It seemed anticlimactic.

2. The Slide-Step

Generally speaking, power pitchers don't hold runners on very well because they have to lift their legs high on the delivery to generate power and it takes longer for the ball to get home. So, the harder the thrower, the easier it is to run on him. That was the case with Bob Gibson, Nolan Ryan, the young Dwight Gooden, and Roger Clemens. Ryan would get into the most trouble with potential stealers because he put so many on with bases on balls. You might think that a pitcher who has a great fastball will get it to the plate faster, but that's usually not the case. It should be pointed out that the base runner is not trying to only beat the ball to the plate. He's running to beat the combined time of the delivery and pitch. He gets his jump on the long delivery.

Some pitchers who have trouble holding runners on have gone away from the high kick to the low slide-step. The slide-step has come into vogue as there are more drawn-out pitcher–base runner confrontations that add to the length of games. This low-energy delivery is done with the front foot, so, obviously, a right-handed pitcher slides toward the plate with his left foot and the lefty slides with his right foot. This results in the ball getting to home quicker.

But if you give up the kick, you lose power on the pitch. That's a good reason a lot of managers and pitching coaches don't like it. It can be effective for the pitcher against a base runner but may detract from his effectiveness against the batter. That's not a good solution because the batter is more important. Fortunately, all pitchers who have terrible moves don't go to the slide-step. It can be effective for certain guys, but some should just forget about it. The slide-step fits more into the way a guy like Jimmy Key normally delivers the ball. Because Key is a control pitcher, a slide-step approach is more suited to his natural delivery. It is not going to take as much off his fastball as it would Roger Clemens's four-seamer. You wouldn't want Clemens to change his style to use the slide-step because it would take too much away from his overpowering stuff.

3. The Pitchout

It used to be that when the pitcher threw over to first, that would eliminate the possibility of a pitchout. Nobody threw to first, then threw a pitchout. That has changed for the better because the pitchout can be an effective weapon when pickoff attempts only fuel the runner's determination to run. In addition to thwarting steals, the pitchout prevents both the bunt and the hit-and-run because the batter can't put the bat on the ball. If the runner hasn't gotten a good jump, he is a dead duck because the catcher will be standing when he catches the ball and can make a clear throw to second base. A pitchout will cost the pitcher a ball on the count, but it can give a catcher his best chance to throw out a base stealer.

If the defensive manager smells a steal on a particular pitch, he can signal the catcher to call for a pitchout. As I stated before, unless there is a man on second who may be stealing signs, the fist is the catcher's sign for a pitchout. A runner on third or the third-base coach can't see the sign because the catcher drapes his mitt over his left knee to conceal his right hand. A pitchout with a runner on first is best called for when it won't put the pitcher behind in the count. So 0-1, 0-2, and 1-2 are good counts for a pitchout. However, if the catcher thinks the runner is going on other counts, he might still call for the pitchout. But he doesn't want to guess wrong and risk the batter getting too favorable a count.

The catcher wants the runner to think it's safe to take off for second, so only at the last moment does he rise from his haunches and jump outside to catch the pitchout. The pitcher counts on the element of surprise, so his motion on the pitchout is deceptively similar to that on other pitches. He throws the ball—he doesn't aim it or slow down his delivery. He wants the pitchout to be a fastball a few feet off the plate and letter high so that the catcher can take it in position to make a quick transfer from glove to hand and then be in the right position to throw. Then the pitcher should duck, just in case he has come off the mound into the path of the catcher's throw to second.

The catcher moves forward and away from the hitter to get the ball quicker and get momentum toward second base. He wants to make a strong throw that whoever's covering can take right over the bag and low so that the runner slides into the glove and puts himself out. "Smooth" isn't a word that's often used to describe catchers, but a catcher can be as smooth as silk on that play. He'll rise from the crouch, move to his right or left, catch the ball in a throwing position, and gun down the speedy base runner all in one continuous motion!

On the pitchout, the second baseman can leave his position and go toward second because he doesn't have to worry about the bunt or hit-and-run. When he sees the catcher rise, he races toward second to receive the throw and tag the runner who is attempting to steal. If the throw is on line, there is no need to catch the ball in front of the bag and bring it back for the slap tag, as you will see many middle infielders do. The proper way to receive the ball is by straddling the bag. Only if the throw is fading into the runner should the second baseman come off the bag to catch it and apply the tag. If the throw reaches the base at the same time as the second baseman and sliding base runner, the ball can end up in center field, so the shortstop and the center fielder must back up the play to prevent the runner from continuing to third base.

4. The Catcher Throws to Second

Of every ten guys I threw out at second, eight were on fastballs. How many of those fastballs were around the letters? Eight. If all things are equal, a fastball around the letters gives the catcher his best chance of throwing out the runner, other than on a pitchout. (Things aren't equal if the runner gets an extraordinary jump or the pitcher takes too long getting the ball to the plate.) The catcher's priority is not to have a good pitch for throwing out the runner but a good pitch to get out the batter. If the catcher's only concern is throwing out a base stealer, he'll want a pitch that is high in the strike zone, but because there's a guy with a bat standing between him and the pitcher, that pitch may never reach him. So there is a dilemma as to what to throw. You can't let the speed of the runner on first dictate the pitch you call, but at the same time you don't want the runner to steal. Again, the best approach is to come to grips with the fact that the runners with great speed will steal their bases. You don't want your pitcher to disregard the runner, but you encourage him to pay more attention to the hitter. That's easier said than done because speed on the bases can be more intimidating than power at the plate.

A pitcher can have a good move yet be easy to run on because the types of pitches he throws are hard for the catcher to handle. More often than not, the pitch he has to handle determines whether a catcher can throw out a runner. Of course, there are catchers who don't have exceptional arms, but when people criticize a catcher for having a weak arm because a stealer easily beat his throw, they may not have a clue. If the receiver is making the catch near or on the ground and must make the transfer all the way up by his shoulder, it's tough to throw out the runner even with a strong arm.

For catchers, the toughest pitches on which to make throws are sinkers, splitters, or breaking balls in the dirt because they can have tremendous action as they go down. But if that's what your pitcher throws best, then that's what you have to call for, even with a fast runner on first. A splitter pitcher like Hideo Nomo must throw balls in the dirt to be effective, so he can't abandon his splitter even if it makes him easy to run on. Mike Piazza,

Nomo's catcher on the Dodgers, knows he must call for the splitter, although his mitt isn't designed to scoop balls out of the dirt in order for him to make quick throws to second. Even though a catcher knows a pitch is coming, the action of the pitch could take him out of the flow of throwing. He'll open up and push the ball to second base instead of keeping the shoulder closed and throwing the ball.

I had the problem of not realizing how quick my transfer was from the mitt to my hand. So I'd try to speed it up by reaching into the glove and taking the ball out instead of bringing the mitt up to my right shoulder and making the transfer. When you bring the mitt up to the right shoulder, you properly close your left shoulder, but if you instead just take the ball out of the glove, you open up and lead with the elbow. Particularly on a ball thrown to second base, this causes the ball to tail into the runner.

If the catcher rushes, the upper part of his body will speed up and his feet won't be able to keep up. They lag behind. Footwork is very important behind the plate. In fact, if a catcher has a strong arm, you can bet he has good footwork. A couple of years ago, Todd Hundley's arm was criticized, but his arm was fine. He was a little sluggish with his feet, and that resulted in his trying to get to his throw quickly by taking the ball out of his mitt instead of bringing the mitt to the hand, the same problem I had. Good footwork behind the plate isn't dissimilar to the footwork of a second baseman as he turns a double play. The steps are quick and short, and everything is a fluid unit. Arms and legs move together. Watch Ivan Rodriguez and you'll see the most compact catcher in baseball. Everything works in unison so well, and that's why his throws are on the money. The Marlins' Charles Johnson is also extremely compact and quick for a big man. His feet and hands always work together—and I do mean *always* or he wouldn't have set the all-time record for consecutive errorless games. All his throws are accurate.

Where footwork really comes in handy is when a left-handed batter is at the plate. It's at least twice as hard for a catcher to look at the guy on first and to set up and throw when a left-handed batter is blocking his view. He must position his feet in a certain way to make a clear throw. Because of the batter, he has to go away from his normal movement.

Often strong-armed catchers, even Rodriguez, throw from their knees on stolen-base attempts, but I think some of them are showing off their arms rather than saving time. A catcher can get the ball to second just as fast and just as accurately if he stands up and gets his entire body behind his throw. Just watch Charles Johnson, the Pirates' Jason Kendall, or the

Astros' Brad Ausmus, who all get up quickly and display great arms on the throw to second.

With a stealer on the move toward second, the catcher does what he is trained to do. He picks out an imaginary spot beyond second base and throws the ball as hard as he can so when the ball reaches second it has pop on it. He's throwing through the bag, not to it. Does that sound familiar? That's what I said the pitcher must do when coming home, so his pitches don't lose power before hitting the catcher's mitt. Technically, a throw to second base should be from the knees to the ankles on the glove side of the shortstop or second baseman, on the first-base side.

If there are men on first and second and there is a double steal, a catcher has the option of throwing to second or third or not throwing. The throw to second is longer than the throw to third, but it might be less of a risk if the trail runner is slower. The catcher has a harder throw to third when a right-handed batter is at the plate.

As I've stated, on an attempted steal, it's often the case that if the ball beats the runner, he's out. The replay shows that the runner went under the tag, but when the fielder brings his glove down quickly and then up—to show that the ball is firmly in the glove—it often results in an out call by the second-base umpire. To get the call at second on a close play, the fielder must make his tags quickly and authoritatively. One-two and the umpire's out call is three.

With a Man on Second

Obviously, pitchers don't use a full windup with a man on second because they don't want to chance his taking off for third. There is, however, one time when it's not necessary to pitch from the stretch. If the team in the field has a two-run lead in the ninth inning and a good hitter like Edgar Martinez is at bat, it's a good idea to go to the windup. The man on second doesn't matter because he represents an inconsequential run, so the pitcher should go full out against the hitter who does count and let the runner take third. In other words, pitch as though no one is on. The windup will give the pitcher more drive on hard stuff and let him throw a better breaking ball. I'm surprised more pitchers don't wind up in this situation.

With a potential stealer on second, a manager or pitching coach may remind or instruct the pitcher to look twice at him before coming home. If there is an experienced runner, the pitcher should exhibit variety between pitches. For instance, the pitcher mustn't look home and then to the runner and then back home before three straight pitches. If he's that predictable, the runner may take off before the fourth pitch as soon as the pitcher looks away from second because he knows he won't look back. He has to break up the pattern and vary his looks to second.

When does the pitcher attempt to pick off the runner at second? An obvious time is when the runner is taking an extremely big lead. Even if he doesn't pick him off, the pitcher might make him stay closer to the bag for the rest of the count. A catcher also might call for the pickoff if the runner seems to be leaning toward third–"leaning the wrong way."

Often the best time to pick off the runner on second is with two outs because he's trying to take the extra step in order to score, especially if he doesn't have good speed. If, however, you want to catch a base stealer who is set to swipe third, the best time to attempt a pickoff is with one out.

You will see that during the pitcher's stretch, the shortstop moves from his position onto the basepath between the runner and second base only to return to his position as the ball is thrown. He may just be decoying the runner, unnerving him so he'll move closer to the base to avoid being picked off. Or he may want the runner to get used to him in the baseline so that he stops paying attention to him. That is the best time for the pickoff attempt. The pitcher and the shortstop have worked out a "daylight play" to pick off runners. (The hardest players to pick off are other shortstops because they are familiar with the play.) With an eye on the activity around second, the pitcher will whip around and throw to the base the moment he notices daylight between the runner and the shortstop. The daylight means that the shortstop has quickly left his position and run to second, getting a jump on the runner. If timed properly, the ball and shortstop will arrive at second at the same time, a moment before the runner's return. The pitcher wants to make a low throw so that the shortstop can just catch the ball and watch the runner slide into his glove for the out. You'll sometimes see the Mets' Rey Ordoñez blocking the runner's hand with his knee. He's clever with that, but he risks injury if the runner slides in with his spikes.

The daylight play is a "feel play," where the shortstop senses he can get behind the runner and then beat him to the bag. Teams don't have a sign for the play because they fear it would restrict the shortstop with structure.

If the runner on second is picked off on the daylight play, it could be the third-base coach's fault because it's his responsibility to watch the shortstop. The runner is responsible for the second baseman. It's also likely that the pitcher and second baseman have worked out a "timing play," which is a pickoff attempt orchestrated by the catcher. The pitcher goes into his stretch, the second baseman breaks for the base, the catcher drops his mitt, and the pitcher turns and throws. Again the pitcher will try to make a low throw so that the runner will slide into the glove.

If the pitcher throws home and the runner takes off for third, the catcher hopes that the batter doesn't hinder his throw. The closer the pitch is to the right-handed hitter, the tougher it is to throw to third base. The same pitch will be on the outside corner to the left-handed batter and easier to throw and the catcher can make a good throw to third because he is already moving that way, he can see the runner, and there are no distractions from the batter. He's in great position to make the throw, which should be low and on the inside of the bag so the third baseman can make an easy tag.

With a Man on Third

Don Drysdale didn't understand why every pitcher didn't use the full windup with a lone runner on third because a steal of home is such a long shot. But only about 30 percent of the pitchers do that nowadays. Relievers almost always pitch from the stretch because they usually come in when there are base runners, but I don't know why most starters stop throwing from the windup with a runner on third.

If there is just a man on third and you think he is going to give you problems, then you should go into the stretch, and eliminate the thought from your mind that he is going to steal home. It rarely happens. The stretch might not be as effective, but you've eliminated the psychological advantage the runner had over you. However, if by going to the stretch you take too much away from your pitches, definitely stick with the windup.

FOILING THE BUNT

The Drag Bunt

Infielders will creep in if they expect a bunt from a speedy leadoff hitter or other player known for bunting. But if that player also has power, they will stay back a bit for obvious reasons, giving the batter a little better edge if he should lay one down. The third baseman is the fielder who must be the most aggressive, but also the most cautious. Since more balls are bunted toward third for base hits, the third baseman will have to play up. At the same time, however, he must work out the odds of the hitter hitting the ball past him. He doesn't want to charge in and see a hard smash coming his way. In order not to commit himself too early, he won't charge the plate until he sees the batter's top hand slide up the barrel of the bat. It's usually both hands with the left-handed batter bunting toward third.

The type of bunt and the speed of the runner should determine whether the third sacker will bare-hand the ball, use two hands to scoop it up and throw, or not throw at all. As stated before, the word "bare-handed" doesn't mean that he picks up the ball with the entire hand. If he gripped the ball with all five fingers, his throw to first would act like a change-up. What he really does is grip the ball with only his thumb, forefinger, and middle finger, leaving his ring finger and pinkie off it. The ball that lands in the bare hand must be maneuvered into the three digits without the benefit of a glove.

If the ball is drag-bunted to the right side, there is no problem if it goes to the pitcher or first baseman. However, if the second baseman makes the play, he will almost always have to bare-hand it and throw on the run to first.

The Sacrifice Bunt

In a sacrifice-bunt situation, the first order of business is to keep the runner close to the base. The obvious way to do that is for the pitcher to throw over a few times. He isn't necessarily trying to pick off the runner, but he wants to keep him close so as not to allow him to break for second when the first baseman breaks for home. When the runner has to dive back to the base a couple of times, his concentration level also takes a dive. Regardless of the runner's speed, he is held on if there is the possibility of a bunt. The first baseman will cheat some so that he's three steps toward home by the time of the delivery, but he mustn't break in prematurely because a good base runner will take off for second. Keith Hernandez used to fool runners into taking too big a lead by going in two steps and then he returned to first for the throw. Now there is a sign for this play because it is done commonly by John Olerud (who learned it from Hernandez) and other first basemen. Even if the throw over doesn't get the runner, it will stop him from taking any kind of lead on the next pitch, although the first baseman might not return to the base.

If the defense is unsure that a sacrifice-bunt play is on, it would be a smart move by the pitcher to step off the rubber once or twice because the batter might square around prematurely. The pitcher and his fielders would love to get a glimpse of that to know what to expect. If the pitcher has a high fastball in his arsenal, he should throw it because pitches above the hands are the toughest to bunt. Even on artificial turf, where infielders can play a little deeper because it's hard to deaden bunts, they don't want to go in motion and move out of position if the bunt isn't on. Of course, a fielder must always beware of batters who square around to entice him to charge in and then swing away.

If pitchers understood the fear a hitter has when he squares around to bunt against hard stuff, they would be more effective in combating the bunt. The innate fear of facing a pitch head-on when normally you'd ward it off by swinging is a strong reason why the letter-high fastball or slider in the strike zone is intimidating. Even if umpires aren't calling the high strike anymore, these pitches are ideal because they're still too close to take and are difficult to get on top of to bunt on the ground. There's a good chance batters will pop them up. Pitchers who throw curves or sinkers are giving the bunter exactly what he wants, pitches that will be below the barrel of the bat, making them easier to hit downward.

* * *

Good bunters can lay down even tough pitches, so the pitcher must be prepared to spring off the mound and field the ball. If the first and third basemen are playing deeper than normal, he knows that he may be the one who makes the play. But he should be aware of possible collisions with them or the catcher and should get out of the way if one of them picks up the bunt, diving to the turf if necessary to facilitate the throw (particularly by the third baseman).

Everybody has an assignment on a bunt play. The first baseman will inch down the line in anticipation of a bunt, but he has to be wary of the batter swinging away, especially if he is left-handed with power or a good right-handed opposite-field hitter. He should charge before the batter squares around. If he waits, he won't be close enough to go to second in time. If the pitcher is quick off the mound, the firmness of the bunt and its direction will determine whether the first baseman should pick it up or back off and let the pitcher make the play. If he's a right-handed first baseman, a right-handed pitcher might have a better angle on a throw to second.

As soon as the batter squares around, the second baseman must race over to cover first because he knows the first baseman will be charging home. You can't leave a base unprotected, so the shortstop is expected to cover second on a throw there to cut down the base runner. Think of the first baseman with an invisible string hitched to his belt. When he moves in, he pulls the second baseman to first, who in turn pulls the shortstop to second.

The third baseman will inch down the other line in anticipation of a bunt. He is wary of the right-handed hitter with power or the left-hander who is a good opposite-field hitter and might swing away. Remember—he will charge the plate only when he sees the batter's top hand slide up the barrel. By the time the batter is fully squared around, the third baseman wants to be breathing down his neck. He will determine if he, the pitcher, or the catcher has the better play. If he picks up the ball and throws to first, the catcher is responsible for covering third base. Otherwise, the runner on first can go to second and continue running to the empty base.

If there is a lone runner on second, the third baseman will take a step toward home, but if he sees that someone else can pick up the bunt, he will go back to the bag in case the throw goes there on a tag play. He knows the slide will be to the outside of the base, so he will make a swipe tag.

On sacrifice bunts, the pitcher and the two corner men will be coming toward the plate and the catcher will be coming out from behind the plate. To avoid confusion, the catcher becomes the instant captain because he's the only one who has the play in front of him. No one else can see the bases or the runners. If he backs off and lets one of the other three players field the bunt, his job isn't done. Because the fielder can't see the base runner going to second, the catcher must let him know which base to throw to by yelling and pointing.

If the bunt rolls dead anywhere near the plate, the catcher is the one expected to pounce on it and make the throw to first or second. When he fields a good sacrifice bunt down the third-base line, he will be facing away from first base, so the pivot to his left on his right foot is the proper play. In this way he can angle himself properly and get more on his throw. If he should turn to his right, he won't be able to get his feet set. So on this play a catcher should plant his right foot, turn around, and throw.

With runners on first and second and nobody out and the bunt in order, the third baseman would prefer that the pitcher handle a bunt down the line so he can go to the base on the chance of a force play there. He will be able to hang back only if the pitcher is quick to the line. A left-handed pitcher should have less trouble going toward the third-base line after he throws the ball because it's the more natural follow-through for him, but a right-hander has the tendency to go forward a couple of steps after releasing the pitch and then go toward the third-base line. There is a delay, and the third baseman usually has to commit himself to charging the bunt and vacating third. It was Dodgers right-hander Don Drysdale who told me that it is imperative that the right-hander break directly to the line after he releases the pitch so that the third baseman will know immediately that there's no need for him to charge the ball and that he should be ready for a throw from the pitcher to the base. The right-handed pitcher will have the confidence to go straight toward the third-base line because the first baseman will be covering the mound, coming forward and across if necessary to field the ball.

If the bunter tries to cross up a pitcher who is taking a beeline toward the third-base line by pushing the bunt toward first, the defense has made him do what it wanted. It's got him. The first baseman will be there because he has no one to hold on. Now it's just a matter of whether the ball was hit hard enough for there to be a play at third. Keith Hernandez cheated so much toward the mound that the best bunt would have been down the first-base line. But he knew few bunters would think to do that against him.

At any time in the game with men on first and second and nobody out, the defense often uses the "rotation play" to counter a sacrifice bunt. The intent is to get a force-out at third base. You will see that when the defense rotates, the first and third basemen charge the plate, the second baseman covers first, and—this is the unique part—the shortstop covers third. This leaves the middle open, so the manager must be sure that the batter is bunting or all he needs to do is hit the ball anywhere but down the lines to have an easy base hit. That's because the only defender of the middle is the pitcher, which is like leaving the cook to defend the castle. As mentioned before, the Indians used the "wheel play" to foil strong-hitting Roberto Alomar's surprising bunt in the final game of 1997's ALCS—third baseman Matt Williams threw to shortstop Omar Vizquel for the force—but this play is usually put on with weak hitters at the plate, particularly pitchers. When a weak hitter squares around, you start the play because even most decent-hitting pitchers (or .200 hitters) don't have the bat control to fake the bunt to initiate the rotation of the infielders and then to swing away. Few pitchers who square around have the confidence to do anything else but bunt in this situation. So you can put on the rotation play without much worry as long as you haven't given away the play too early. If the third baseman commits too early, the batter won't necessarily square around at all, but may swing away. You want him to bunt.

Overall, the rotation play has made it more difficult for the bunter to routinely lay one down because he has that much more to think about. Usually, the hitter wants to bunt to the third baseman, but that changes if the rotation play is on. The infielders are, in effect, ganging up against the one hitter, and that in itself may throw off his concentration.

I want to tell you about an obscure but fascinating play that I think the defense can employ against the bunt with men on first and second and nobody out. It's obscure because it can take place only in the ninth inning and only if the team in the field is up by exactly two runs. In theory, it can be done with the visiting team at the plate, but let's say the home team is at bat because they are more likely to be playing for a tie and will be more likely to bunt in this situation. A good bunter will be at the plate, and he will want to bunt the ball to the third baseman. The defense will start with the premise that the runner on second doesn't matter. Without the need for a throw to third, there will be no need for the rotation play. The only runner who counts is the trail runner on first, who represents the tying run, so you want to keep him out of scoring position. What the manager does is bring in the third baseman, who will play the bunt as if his team were up by only one run and there were a lone runner on at first. He charges in, plays the ball, and throws immediately to *second* base. When the trail runner sees the third baseman charge in, he assumes the rotation play is on and that his throw will go either to third base to force the lead runner or to first base. The trail runner has *never* seen a third baseman throw to second in this situation, although that is the smartest play. He doesn't even think the shortstop will be covering second, so he may relax while running there. If he slows down, he may be forced at second if the third baseman goes there to the shortstop covering. That's what the defense wants. It would love to get the 5–6–3 double play, but, realistically, it will end up with runners on first and third with one out—which is still *much* better than second and third because the important trail runner would be in scoring position.

On May 1, 1970, the Phillies had this exact situation. (I remember the date because the next day I broke my hand on a foul tip and one out later Mike Ryan, who had come in for me, broke his hand.) We were at Candlestick Park in San Francisco with a two-run lead, and the Giants got men on first and second with no outs in the ninth inning. Phillies manager Frank Lucchesi came to the mound, and Don Money, the third baseman, joined the conversation. I said, "Frank, what we want is for Don to charge the bunt and go to second base." Don asked about the runner going to third, and I explained that he didn't mean anything. We had talked about this in spring training. Frank listened to us both and said, "You really want to do that?" I said, "Yeah." Frank said, "Okay." So the bunt goes to Money, and he throws to second as we had planned, and, naturally, he throws it away and we end up losing the game. Don was a very good fielder, but perhaps the strangeness of the play made him think it was more difficult than it actually is. He only needed the confidence he would have had making the throw to second with a runner on first, a play he made successfully all the time. In fact, if he saw that the runner on first had a good jump, he had the option of going to first. Fielders know that they can go into any play with an intention of doing one thing but can change their minds and make the more conservative play.

You may wonder why I say that you can't do this defensive ploy earlier in the game with a two-run lead. The simple reason is that the runner on second is important in earlier innings and you would rather throw him out than the trail runner. If he scores in the eighth inning, for instance, the team that is behind will trail by only one run going into the ninth inning. So you save the play for the ninth inning. It really should be more of a routine play because it can win you a ball game or two.

The Squeeze

How many times have you seen a third baseman or first baseman make a play at the plate to nail a runner on a squeeze play? Almost never. Occasionally, a pitcher will get an assist, but for the most part, if the runner breaks and the batter gets the bunt down in fair territory, the run almost always scores. For the defense to prevent a successful squeeze, it relies almost entirely on the pitcher and catcher working together before the ball is bunted. They try to get some sign of a squeeze. A catcher looks for something unusual when a hitter is returning a sign to a first-base coach. If the batter is acting as suspiciously as Bonnie and Clyde outside a bank, the squeeze may be on.

If nothing is evident from the interchange between coach and batter, the pitcher can still get the batter or the runner to give something away by waiting and stepping off the rubber. An anxious batter might start to square around or an antsy runner might start his break too early. The more radical approach is the pitchout, which may catch a runner on a suicide squeeze. You don't do it with nobody out because teams don't squeeze then. Of course, a pitcher can afford to pitch out on 0-2 and 1-2, but those are such obvious pitchout counts that few runners will dare come home. A count of 1-1 is both a good one on which to squeeze and a good one for a pitchout for the same reason: The runner doesn't think the pitcher will be willing to give up another ball. When an offensive manager sees a pitchout when he had no squeeze planned, he often gets the idea of putting it on now that the count is the more favorable 2-1. See if this happens when you are watching a game.

If the runner on third breaks at the right time, the pitcher will continue with his pitch. If he breaks too soon, the pitcher will simply throw a pitchout. The catcher will just stand, move outside, and receive the ball. Then he can tag the runner or get him in a rundown. This is an easier play with a left-handed batter at the plate.

When pitchers in some organizations see the runner on third breaking for home, instead of pitching out they throw at the batter to make sure he doesn't bunt. The catcher can do nothing but catch the pitch and then try to quickly tag the runner. He won't have time to block the plate. At least he doesn't have to worry about the batter swinging away.

FOILING THE HIT-AND-RUN

Anytime in a close game when there's a runner on first with less than two outs and a contact hitter is facing a contact pitcher on pretty much a neutral count, the defense shouldn't be surprised if there is a hit-

The most unusual suicide squeeze play I ever saw occurred in the bottom of the twelfth inning of the third game of the ALCS in 1997. With the Indians' Marquis Grissom on third representing the winning run, the count was 2-1 on Omar Vizquel. Because Vizquel was perhaps the best bunter in the American League, we talked on the air about the possibility of the squeeze. Sure enough, Grissom took off with the pitch. Surprisingly, Vizquel bunted through the ball, although it had been right down the middle of the plate. Catchers assume 90 percent of balls over the plate will be hit or fouled back and the percentage on bunts is much higher. When the bunter misses a ball on a suicide squeeze, the runner usually has no chance of being safe at the plate because of his delayed break toward home, and Grissom should have been out by five feet. But the ball squirted by Orioles catcher Lenny Webster and Grissom crossed the plate to give the Indians the victory. Perhaps Webster's vision was blocked by Vizquel's bat or he closed his mitt prematurely. Grissom was credited with a steal of home. It's important to point out that if the safety squeeze had been on, rather than the suicide squeeze, Grissom would have gone back to third because Vizquel didn't make contact.

and-run. So the middle infielders will be primed on a grounder to make a quicker throw to second against even the fastest runner. But there wouldn't be any drastic positioning changes. The middle infielders will cheat toward second the same as they would in all double-play situations; and, as happens any time a running threat is on first, one of them will be ready to cover second if the runner should break with the pitch. The only possible variation is that if the hit-and-run is a strong possibility, the second baseman might hold his position or first take two steps in, instead of going immediately to second base. By coming in, he doesn't give up his position yet cuts down the distance between himself and second base. If the batter swings through the ball, he is able to take the throw from the catcher.

A lot of pitchers try to crowd right-handed batters so they won't go the other way on a hit-and-run. But there are batters who can go the other way with the inside pitch better than they can with the outside pitch. As I've pointed out, Derek Jeter and Edgardo Alfonzo can take inside pitches the other way. What the defense hopes for on a hit-and-run is for the batter to swing through the pitch or hit it in the air. If he does hit it on the ground, the defense hopes it is to a middle infielder so it can still get the lead runner.

A liner to an outfielder playing shallow also can result in runners being doubled up. The outfielder has everything unfolding in front of him and should have no problem determining where to throw the ball.

There will, of course, be base hits on hit-and-run plays, doubles as well as singles. That doesn't mean the runner on first will automatically reach third or come in to score just because he was off with the pitch. As on all base hits to the outfield, strong team defense, with outfielders and infielders working together, often can negate aggressive running.

THROWING PLAYS ON HITS TO THE OUTFIELD

If an outfielder has a play at second or third, he will fire the ball on a line, as low as he can. If the throw is low, it is harder and will get to the target quicker. It may be on one hop, especially to third from the right fielder, but the one-hopper won't necessarily reach the fielder faster than a ball he catches in the air. The point is that in throwing to the target, he hits the cutoff man.

The catcher wants the one-bounce throw from an outfielder all the time. A ball thrown home on one hop gets there quicker than one thrown on the fly. That's because very few outfielders have arms strong enough to throw a ball that is low enough to be caught by the cutoff man, yet, if he lets it go through, it will remain on the same low plane all the way to the catcher's mitt. If the throw reaches the catcher in the air, you can bet its trajectory had a hump that both slowed it down and made it impossible for the relay man to cut it off. So the best that one can hope for is that the outfielder will throw it on the line to the cutoff man and, if he lets it go through, get it to the catcher on only one hop. Outfielders, like hitters, need to have drive off their legs to make good, low throws.

On a hit to the outfield with a man on first, this is what to watch for on a perfect relay to the plate: The outfielder recovers the ball quickly and makes a throw on the money to an infielder serving as a cutoff man, whose relay throw home is strong and accurate. The weaker the throw, the more dangerous it is for the catcher with a runner bearing down on him. Ron Fairly, the former L.A. Dodger and current Seattle announcer, made the point: "Once the outfielder gets to the ball and gets rid of it, he's done his job. Now it's up to the player who receives the throw."

* * *

On plays involving throws from the outfield, the television director will employ various cameras so that the viewer will be able to follow the ball no matter where it goes. Thus, you can see that at specific times all four infielders serve as cutoff men, with the pitcher backing up plays at third and home. The purpose of the cutoff man is to minimize the damage done by a base hit. By making strong relay throws or just by being in the proper position to make throws, he prevents batters from stretching singles into doubles and doubles into triples. On singles, he tries to stop base runners from advancing more than ninety feet; on sure doubles with a man on first, he wants to hold the batter and runner to two bases.

If an infielder realizes that a throw from the outfield won't be in time to get a runner, he can cut off the ball to make an easier play on another runner or the batter who is trying to take an extra base. He positions himself according to the strength of the outfielder's arm, knowing that the stronger the arm the less of a hump there will be on the throw and the closer to him he can stand. The closer to the outfielder he can stand, the quicker he can cut off the ball and the quicker he can get off his relay throw.

On a hit to left or right with a man on second, the first and third basemen are the primary cutoff men on throws toward the plate. They position themselves in line between the outfielder making the throw and home, between the mound and their base. When the first baseman cuts off a throw, he hopes his relay throw to the second baseman covering first or shortstop covering second will trap the batter between those bases. A relay from the third baseman could go to either second or third base.

On balls hit to the right side when there's a runner on first, the second baseman will instinctively go into shallow right to serve as a cutoff man. He'll go down the right-field line on balls hit into the corner. He'll take the right fielder's throw back to the infield or relay the ball to the base where either the batter or a runner is heading. With no runner on, if a throw to second to get the batter is strong and on line, he will let it go past to the shortstop covering.

When a runner attempts to score on a ball hit far down the right-field line, both the second baseman and first baseman serve as cutoff men, aligning themselves with the right fielder and home plate. Unless it's the rare instance when the first baseman has the stronger arm and quicker release, the second baseman will serve as the point man and make the relay throw home. The first baseman can cut off his throw to make a play elsewhere. Of course, if the winning run is attempting to score, all throws home go through and all balls thrown elsewhere are cut off and relayed home.

When a runner tries to score from first on a ball down the left-field line, the shortstop and third baseman form a similar cutoff tandem. However, the shortstop's better angle toward the line always makes it easier for him to be closer to the left fielder. If the left fielder overthrows him, the third baseman will be there.

One of my most embarrassing moments occurred in 1973 when I was making a rare appearance as a first baseman during my second tour of duty with the Cardinals. We were leading the Phillies 8–1 in the ninth inning, so the runner on second was of no importance. If a ball went through the infield, an outfielder was supposed to forget about the runner scoring and throw the ball in to second to keep the force play in order for the next batter. Del Unser hit a ball to my right for a base hit. I'm thinking about how I should have made the play when all of a sudden Jose Cruz's throw from right field whacks me right in the back. I screamed, "Jose, that's the first time you've *hit* the cutoff man all year!"

On singles to the right side, when a runner on first attempts to go to third base, the shortstop is the lone cutoff man, positioning himself on the infield grass between the right fielder and third base. On a single to center, he will stand on the outfield grass between the center fielder and third. He will either let the ball go through or cut it off to stop the batter at first. If the batter attempts to reach second on the throw to third, the shortstop can make a relay throw to the second baseman on the bag.

If there is a base hit to fairly deep center field with a man on first, the shortstop races deeper into the outfield to be a relay man, ready to make a throw or to run the ball back to the infield. If the shortstop takes a relay throw from deep center just as the runner from first rounds third and the batter rounds second, he'll listen for instructions from the second baseman, who has drifted over. Judging the speed of the runner going home, the second baseman will yell to the shortstop, "Third!" or "Home!" Everyone will get down to clear the way for the throw.

THE RUNDOWN

A runner can find himself trapped between bases as the result of pitchouts, pickoffs, falling down, rounding a base too far, balls being hit to the pitcher, throws from the outfield being cut off by infielders, and a number of other reasons. Ideally, whoever catches the ball will be able to tag the runner without a throw. But often there will be a standard, back-and-forth rundown play. In all rundowns, the defense tries to push the runner back to the previous base without letting him reach it and to make as few throws as possible before tagging him out. If the infielders have trapped a trail runner, possibly the batter, in a rundown between first and second, they must keep their eyes on the lead runner. If he makes a dash for third or home, a fielder has the option of forgetting about the trail runner and going after the lead runner, perhaps getting him in a second rundown. The rundown between third and home, which can be covered by several cameras, is the most exciting for the obvious reason that the runner will score if the play is botched. It is vital to force the runner back toward third. You don't want the runner breaking toward home while a fielder near third has the ball. Get the ball to the catcher and he will charge the runner, forcing him back to third and getting him to commit. The catcher is like a stock car going from zero to sixty mph. It's important to know that your back is covered—someone must protect the plate.

When a runner is stranded between second and third, here's what the defense will do: A throw to the third baseman stops the runner from going toward third. The third baseman holds the ball in his right hand and runs hard at the runner. As soon as the runner commits to going back toward second, the third baseman throws to a middle infielder at the base. If a right-handed batter was up, the second baseman probably will cover and the shortstop will back up the third baseman. Ideally, the second baseman will take one step and make the tag. But if the runner stops, the second baseman will advance on him and force him toward third, tightening the trap. He doesn't want the runner to race for third, so he'll quickly throw the ball to the third baseman or shortstop covering that base. In a prolonged rundown, the third baseman, second baseman, and shortstop will continually change positions in a figure-8 maneuver similar to the classic three-man weave in basketball. For instance, after the third baseman throws to the second baseman at second, he will run behind him and his backup, the shortstop, will take over; the second baseman will then throw to the shortstop covering third and, as the third baseman takes his position, run behind the shortstop; the shortstop will then throw to the third baseman covering second and, as the second baseman takes his position, run behind the third baseman and so on until the tag is made. All three fielders are right-handed, so throws from third to second must be on the inside of the line and throws from second to third must be outside it or the runner can reach the base safely without leaving the basepath. Always they try to turn the runner toward second, so if the play is botched, at least he won't have gained the extra ninety feet.

In case the runner escapes the rundown because of an errant throw, the catcher covers third base and the pitcher covers home. The manager doesn't want the pitcher involved in a rundown because he's probably the poorest fielder and, worse, he might be injured, but the defense mustn't let the runner see a vacant base in front of him.

PREVENTING A RUN ON A FLY BALL

When the runner is tagging up at third base on a fly ball with less than two outs, watch the third baseman. He might be trying to get in a line between the runner and the outfielder catching the ball to block the runner's line of vision. The runner will have to look around him, so his timing on when to leave is thrown off. This could make him leave prematurely or late.

On a possible sacrifice fly in which there are one, two, or three base runners and the man on third does not represent the winning run, the outfielder catches the fly while running in so he can get his full body behind his throw to the plate. To save time, the catch and throw must be made in one continuous motion, so he must get a firm grip on the ball as soon as it goes in his glove. His four-seamer throw should be low enough for it to either be cut off by an infielder or reach the catcher's mitt on only one hop. If the runner will clearly be safe at home or if he has stayed on third, the cutoff man on the infield grass will catch the ball and see if there are any relay possibilities. Meanwhile, the pitcher will back up the catcher because he doesn't want the ball getting away, especially if the runner on third is intending to stay put. He can't take anything for granted.

If there is a fly out to right with the winning run on third, the only cutoff man will be the first baseman. If it is skied to left, the only cutoff man will be the third baseman. They are there strictly for alignment, to get the outfielder to make a low and accurate throw to the plate. If they cut off the ball, their relay throw home would normally be too late.

ODDITIES

There is a time when an undeserving player receives congratulations, and it makes you wonder. The home team trails by two runs, say, 8–6, in the bottom of the ninth, and there is a man on third with less than two outs. The defensive team is playing back because it is looking for outs and doesn't care about the meaningless run on third. The batter hits a sacrifice fly. He doesn't deserve congratulations, right? In 1997, I told my director Jeff Mitchell to have the camera follow the Mets' John Olerud back to the dugout after he hit a sacrifice fly in this exact situation because I told the viewers that I was positive that Olerud would be congratulated by his teammates. Sure enough, when he reached the dugout, the home crowd was cheering his RBI and every teammate came over and shook his hand. Why? They wouldn't shake his hand if he'd flied out with nobody on third, and in effect that's exactly what happened. That run didn't matter. The batter's potential run mattered to the offense. The out mattered to the defense. The defense got what it wanted. Everyone should look into the other dugout and see how jubilant the opposing team is before they shake hands with the guy who hit the sacrifice fly. The pitcher is going, "All right!" The defensive manager is saying, "Okay!" How can both teams be congratulating their players? Somebody's wrong. In baseball, both teams can't be happy!

There is no more difficult a situation for outfielders than when the winning run is on third with less than two outs in the bottom of the ninth. The defensive manager has no choice but to bring in all his outfielders, along with his infielders. My complaint is that outfielders often don't come in far enough. An outfielder can't allow a ball to go fifty feet or so past the infield grass and drop in front of him because the game will be over. And because a sacrifice fly wins the game for the other team, he must be able to make the catch and throw out the runner at home while standing almost flat-footed. Where he stands is exactly how close to the infield he must be to make a quick, accurate throw home. So what if the ball goes over his head if he is playing shallow—if he had stood out there where the ball landed and had made the catch he wouldn't have been able to throw out the runner at home from that distance. That longer fly wins the game no matter what, so he positions himself where he can prevent shallow singles that the drawn-in infielders can't reach and can throw out the runner at home if he should test his arm. I guarantee you that quite a few of the outfielders in the majors play where they can catch the longer fly rather than from where they can make a successful throw. Most don't understand the concept. The finer points of the game often elude them. Because they stand so far from most of the action, outfielders are less inclined to understand the finer points of defense, including their own responsibilities.

BRINGING THE INFIELD IN

If there is a man on third with less than two outs in a close game or the team in the field is far behind, check out the defensive manager when there is a shot of the dugout. He or a coach may be motioning his infield to come in for a play at the plate. He does this although he knows that a drawn-in infield greatly increases the likelihood of a hit. A power hitter can shoot it past the immobile infielders before they can reach out their gloves, a batter with good bat control can place seeing-eye singles through the large seams or up the middle, and even weak hitters can become dangerous RBI men by hitting bouncers that would normally be ground-outs or looping balls to the edge of the infield that would normally be pop-outs. If the manager puts his defense in such a vulnerable position, you know that he thinks stopping the run from scoring is crucial to the outcome of the game. For instance, in a tied game in the bottom of the ninth, he has no other choice.

If the run on third isn't important, managers will have their infielders play deep. If the run matters but there is also a runner on first, the manager may cross his arms, which means they will play halfway. This gives the infielder the option of going for two if the ball is hit hard, or coming home if the ball is hit weakly.

With no outs and a man on third, it's usually not a good idea to bring in the infield for a play at the plate unless you can't afford to fall any further behind or the runner represents the winning run. If you play in with no outs, you also will stay in with one out, so that means you're going to give the opposition two chances for easy hits that will not only bring in the run but also could start a rally. You have to be twice as fortunate because it's unlikely there will be two consecutive ground balls that are hit right at stationary drawn-in infielders. The only batters you'd feel at all comfortable pitching to with no outs and a man on third are the pitcher, the eighth-place hitter with the pitcher on deck, and the ninth-place batter in the American League. You can't play in with nobody out against a first- or second-place hitter because the risks of a multirun inning become too great. However, with one out you can make a better case to play in because it's not unlikely that one batter will hit a grounder directly at an infielder. Get that second out and you can then play deep.

Until the last few years, few managers would bring their infields in with one out unless it was late in the game. Now most managers will play in with one out and a man on third in the early innings against most batters. This makes sense if his team leads by a run, is tied, or trails. However, he may play his infield deep and concede the run on a grounder to try to shut down the multirun inning. An infield also will play deep if there are men on second and third in the early innings because a single through the drawn-in infield might score two runs. Giving up the one run on a grounder makes sense unless you are trailing by several runs and simply can't afford to give up any more runs.

Another time I think playing in is the wrong strategy with less than two outs is when you're playing on artificial turf and there is only average speed on third. Managers should encourage their infielders to play halfway because the ball will get to them faster and they can still get the guy at home.

With a man on third, some managers will try to cause confusion by having their middle infielders move all the way in from a deep position *during* the windup. The Montreal Expos were the first team to do this, but I saw the Mets' Bobby Valentine and the Cardinals' Tony La Russa employ it several times last year. At first, I didn't like this play because I thought everybody in the park knew what the infield was up to. But I've

When your team gets men on first and third with nobody out and the defense plays back, you think the scorekeeper should go ahead and put a "1" on the scoreboard on your team's line and get some of the crooked numbers ready. But good defense can shut you down, often in unexpected ways. I think back to May 30, 1967, when the Cards went into Cincinnati leading the Reds by half a game in the standings. Despite two rain delays, Dick Hughes pitched 7⅔ perfect innings against the Reds before Vada Pinson had a checked-swing double that led to two runs. We trailed 2–1 going into the bottom of the ninth, but Orlando Cepeda had a lead-off single against their ace right-hander Jim Maloney, and, es-chewing the bunt, I followed with a single to right, moving Cepeda, the potential tying run, to third. At this point, Reds manager Dave Bristol brought in Don Nottebart, a sinkerballer, to deal with the first-and-third, no-out situation. The batter he faced was pinch hit-ter Phil Gagliano. Bristol played his defense in double-play depth, but on a slow grounder to the left side, the infielders had the op-tion of coming home. Gagliano hit a hard grounder, a two-hopper that shortstop Leo Cardenas grabbed two steps to his right. Cepeda made the mistake of not breaking for the plate on contact and Cardenas's look froze him at third. That look was the key to what happened. Assuming Cepeda wasn't going anywhere, Carde-nas went for the 6–4–3 double play, throwing to Tommy Helms at second. Because Cardenas had delayed to look Cepeda back to third, I was right on top of Helms when he made his pivot and knocked him clear out into left field. But his throw to first baseman Deron Johnson still had enough on it to beat Gagliano to first. Meanwhile, Cepeda decided to risk a delayed run home. Johnson, who didn't have a great arm, threw a strike to catcher Johnny Ed-wards, and Cepeda also was out. On a very difficult play, the Reds defense had worked everything perfectly and the result was one of thirty-three times in major-league history that a game has ended with a triple play.

(A side note: I hit Helms so hard on that play that I was con-cerned enough to call him after the game. In my entire career, that was the only time I called an opposing player to find out if he was okay. No opponent ever called me. So when I retired I was ahead 1–0 on empathy calls.)

changed my mind because this late maneuver does confuse two people in the park: the runner on third and the third-base coach. With the infield back, the third-base coach may tell the runner, "You're going in on a ground ball hit to short or second," but when the infield moves in with the pitch, the runner's not sure what to do if the ball is hit to short or second because these fielders now have a shorter throw home. Moreover, since he may have been watching the hitter in anticipation of his making contact, he might not have noticed that the infield has come in for a play at the plate. So this tactic has added an extra burden to the runner and third-base coach.

Let's say the score is tied, the bases are loaded, and there is one out in the bottom of the ninth. On a ground ball, the runner on third has no choice but to run home. Where should the infield play in this tense situation? In. Because the play at the plate is its one and only priority. (The outfielders are shallow, too.) If the manager plays his infielders in, he commits them to come home and it doesn't matter that they won't be able to attempt a second-to-first double play because the second baseman hasn't the good angle going to second he gets when he plays at double-play depth. The double-play possibility you have on a grounder is a force at home and a throw-out at first. Only on Astroturf would you even consider setting up for the second-to-first double play with the winning run on third. On the rug, a team can afford to play halfway for some batters because balls get to infielders quicker and the second baseman has a good angle toward the base. If the batter is slow and hits into a lot of ground-ball double plays, then obviously you would be more influenced to play for the double play.

When it's the bottom of the ninth and men are on at first and third in a tied game with no outs, the man on third doesn't have to run home on a ground ball, but the infield still must play in to dissuade him from running (or, if they can't, to cut him down at the plate). There is no thinking of a double play unless you first can freeze the runner on third. With one out and a slow runner or average-speed batter, the infield might play halfway and consider the double play. The speed of the grounder determines whether the infielder goes home or attempts a double play. Remember—if he's in, he can only go home. If the runner is going on contact, which he will do with one out, any infielder who catches the ball throws home immediately. On a hard grounder, the fielder can take his time. If a runner on third freezes when the ball is hit hard to a fielder or does not go on contact on a ball hit to the left side, the fielder should make sure he's not going and then throw out the batter at first. If the ball is grounded to the second baseman, he is correct to assume that the man on third took off with the crack of the bat. So as soon as he grabs the bouncer, he needs to make a strong, straight throw to the catcher, low and to his glove side.

THE PLAY AT THE PLATE

On a tag play at home plate, the catcher will ideally receive a one-hop, knee-to-waist-high throw from an outfielder and a hard, low throw from an infielder. He gets low, wanting to be in position to tag the sliding runner as soon as he takes the throw. The catcher may make a quick tag after a perfect throw and still let the runner score. If he doesn't do a good job of blocking the plate with his weight on his left leg, the runner's foot may have room to go under the mitt and reach the plate.

I firmly believe in denying the runner the plate in very close, bang-bang plays, which is why it really vexes me that few catchers block the plate anymore. Blocking the plate is not only becoming a lost art, it's be-

In the final game of the 1997 divisional championship series between New York and Cleveland, the Indians scored their fourth and, it turned out, winning run on a tag play at home plate. Sandy Alomar came around third on a hit to right. Right fielder Paul O'Neill made a beautiful throw to the plate. It was a little late arriving, so Joe Girardi slid out his left leg to prevent Alomar from having free access to the plate. In fact, Alomar had to fly over Girardi's leg knees-first, as if over a low hurdle, and try to catch the back of the plate with a foot. Girardi thought Alomar flew over the plate and didn't touch it, so he tagged him. But the umpire called Alomar safe, saying his foot had grazed the plate. The replay from the low-third camera showed that Girardi's smart maneuver with his leg had worked and that Alomar hadn't been able to get his foot down until just beyond the plate. We showed where the skid mark began! After the Yankees' 4–3 loss, I informed the dejected Girardi of what our camera had shown. Apparently, Joe thought Alomar had missed the base, but there was no one to support him. Andy Pettitte, who as the pitcher backing up the play had the best view, should have been the one to shout "Out!" before the umpire had the chance to signal. He's the one who could have argued with the umpire.

coming a lost part of fundamental defensive baseball. The second and third basemen straddle their bags rather than guard them, but the catcher is protected, and it is his job to guard the plate. He should literally block the plate so that the runner won't have a clear path to it.

What makes the tag at home the most problematic call for umpires is that most catchers are taught to block the plate a moment before they get the ball. If they're good at it, they plant their left leg so the runner slides into it rather than the plate and then catch the throw and make the tag. That's technically illegal, but it's rarely called because it's so quick.

The catcher faces third and, illegal or not, plants himself on the third-base line in front of home, putting his weight on his left foot and pointing his shin guard at the runner for protection. If he puts his weight on his right foot, the runner can hit his left leg and spin him like a top. The catcher's left leg blocks all access to the plate, and for the runner to score, he will have to go around him or through him to reach the plate. The runner is running full speed, so the catcher should brace himself for a collision and not make a swipe tag to avoid one. As I've pointed out, the catcher's mitt isn't designed for a swipe tag.

The best way for a catcher to make the tag is to get the ball in his bare hand inside the mitt and make the tag with the back of the mitt. Sometimes he won't have time to do this, although the speed of throws on artificial surface may help, but if he can get the ball in his bare hand, he can be knocked unconscious in a collision and still hold on to the ball for the out call. It happened to me twice, once in high school and once professionally. It's a dead man's grip. There's almost no way the runner can knock the ball out of the hand.

I've noticed that more catchers now are keeping their masks on when making the tag. I'm not a proponent of this. I've talked to Mets catcher Todd Hundley about this, and we disagree. He thinks he's protected more. I think it's a greater cause for injury because your peripheral vision is obstructed. You don't need peripheral vision when you're focusing on the pitch, but you do when you're receiving a throw, particularly from right field when the runner is coming around third and blindsiding you. If you receive the throw and turn around, you stand the chance of greater injury to yourself and the runner when direct contact is made with the mask. If the runner elects to bowl you over and he rams his helmet into your mask, he can really do damage to your face. A lot of fans assume that the padded mask prevents injuries, but on foul tips and contact with runners, the iron around the mask has the tendency to twist into your jowls. (I don't know how it is with the new hockey mask catchers are using.) You might say that if a 240-pound runner hurts you when you're wearing the mask, he'd really hurt you if you didn't have it on. But I think your neck is much more flexible when you don't wear the cumbersome mask. The mask cuts down on the flexibility and maneuverability of the body. I'd throw it away, as we were taught at St. Louis.

With or without the mask, you will take shots from runners' elbows and shoulders. They have every right to do this if you're blocking the plate. I found that out early when I was smoked in the forehead, face, and nose when I was a junior at Christian Brothers High School in Memphis by a player at Central High. He also split my left front tooth. It was cracked and turned dark, and I had to have it capped about ten years ago. I had to have a root canal. I have joked about that on the air, saying that one of the nice things about life is that you can only have a maximum of thirty-two root canals.

Catchers who block the plate won't get through their careers unscathed. But they have to do it. It's part of the job. I guess I should have taken it as a compliment when my doctor told me during a recent physical, "You look okay . . . for the lifestyle you have chosen." Some compliment.

IN THE FUTURE

I think baseball is on the verge of a popularity explosion that it has never experienced before. I don't know if it will regain its status as the most popular American sport, but it certainly will have its place in the hearts and pocketbooks of America. And Canada. And elsewhere, because I foresee expansion into Mexico City or Monterrey; Vancouver; and, depending on air travel, Tokyo and a European city like London. If you think interleague play was a boon to attendance, wait until international play. New television technology also will play a big part in the growth of all sports, including baseball. WWOR's Rick Miner tells me that he must soon make decisions involving the advent of digital television. Whether he and other producers choose true high-definition television or a standard-definition digital television in a wide-screen format, baseball viewers will feel much more like they are at the game. That's very exciting for fans and broadcasters. However, what I think is needed is a conscientious effort on the part of the players to improve the product.

* * *

A lot of old-timers are stingy with their praise of today's players, and I don't think that's fair. These players are bigger and stronger and more talented than players of the past, and in the future they will only improve—records will be obliterated. But players being bigger and stronger should translate into the game being played better, and so far that hasn't necessarily been the case. In the forties, fifties, and sixties, teams were better from top to bottom. More players had better all-around skills, and all players were fundamentally sound because they received the necessary schooling in the minors that today's high-priced youngsters don't get. Mediocrity was the worst you got. Today, it's often below that because young players are rushed to the majors (especially when there is expansion) and many players become complacent once they sign enormous long-term contracts.

It's alarming that agents have become so influential that they can dictate how their players are used on certain teams. What do agents know about how the game should be played? I wonder if any agent tells his client that he must learn to hit the cutoff man. No agent will state the obvious, which is that organizations should put more money and time into instruction. Agents worry this could delay their clients' arrival into the major leagues, but it could prolong their stay there.

Fundamentals have to be learned through restatement by managers, coaches, and instructors. On their own, some superstars don't pay much attention to the basics. They think it is more important to have flair and style. What they do is less important than how they look doing it. I think players should have a responsibility to learn to play the game more thoroughly, including fielding and base running. They should no longer take things for granted. For the sport to capture the imagination of the public as it once did, I think that it's up to the players to raise the caliber of play in the major leagues to the level of their amazing talents. They owe it to the fans, they owe it to themselves, and they owe it to baseball.

INDEX

ABOUT THE AUTHORS

TIM MCCARVER is a baseball analyst for the FOX Network. In a twenty-one-year playing career, he was a star catcher for the Cardinals, Phillies, Expos, and Red Sox. His previous books are *Oh, Baby, I Love It!* and *Baseball for Brain Surgeons and Other Fans,* also written with Danny Peary. He lives in Pennsylvania.

DANNY PEARY has written extensively on film and television, including the books *Cult Movies; Cult Movie Stars;* and *Alternate Oscars.* He is also the author of *Cult Baseball Players; We Played the Game: 65 Players Remember Baseball's Greatest Era, 1947–1964;* and *Super Bowl: The Game of Their Lives.* Danny Peary is the collaborating writer on Tim McCarver's radio show. He lives in New York City.